teach yourself...
Quattro Pro 5.0
for Windows

CHRISTOPHER VAN BUREN

MIS:
PRESS

A Subsidiary of
Henry Holt and Co., Inc.

First Edition—1993

ISBN Book 1-55828-325-0
Printed in the United States of America.

10 9 8 7 6 5 4 3 2 1

MIS:Press books are available at special discounts for bulk purchases for sales promotions, premiums, fund-raising, or educational use. Special editions or book excerpts can also be created to specification.

For details contact: Special Sales Director
MIS:Press
a subsidiary of Henry Holt and Company, Inc.
115 West 18th Street
New York, New York 10011

DEDICATION

For the leaders: Joe Lucchesi, Breck Stephenson, Tom Sherwood, Joey Galon, and Bob Tench. You're all awesome.

ACKNOWLEDGEMENTS

Thank you's are due to several people for helping me with this project: Debra Williams Cauley at MIS:Press for managing the project and my schedule. Nan Borreson at Borland for providing software and author support. Len Feldman and Carolyn Kraus for their work on the previous edition. Tom Sherwood and Joe Lucchesi for generously providing work and personal space while I was in transit. Also to Joe for letting me use his computer and equipment. Alexander Van Buren for helping me stick with it and appreciate my tools. Matt Wagner at Waterside for guiding my career and being the middle-man on so many things. Carol Underwood at Waterside for understanding.

Contents

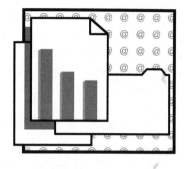

Introduction

Welcome to Quattro Pro for Windows 5.0! I think you'll find this program easy to learn and use—and a powerful addition to your computer tools. I've used just about all spreadsheet products for Windows and I believe that Quattro Pro has the best overall user interface and design. This means that it's the easiest spreadsheet to understand and use.

Quattro Pro's classic features remain the backbone of the program. Property inspectors group commands and options together so you can access them when you need them. They let you avoid searching through menus and dialog boxes for commands that apply to your current action. Instead, they group commands by task, so that all your options are available at once. A simple right-click on an object or screen element produces a property inspector. SpeedBars give you point-and-click access to commands and options. Just locate the desired SpeedBar tool and click to accomplish the action. Quattro Pro comes with two general-use SpeedBars and several specialty SpeedBars. Quattro Pro uses SpeedBars to provide the commands and options for several special operations, such as checking your spelling, analyzing data, and building graphs. Each of these tasks has its own SpeedBar of tools that presents convenient shortcuts to commands and options. Plus, you can create your own SpeedBars using Quattro Pro's new SpeedBar Designer—grouping tools from various built-in "Tool palettes" lists into your own SpeedBar designs.

Quattro Pro still has some of the most powerful graphing and graph annotation features available, including the ability to draw pictures to accompany your graphs and import graphics and backgrounds from outside the program. You can combine your graphs and drawings into on-screen slide shows.

These are only a few of the classic features in Quattro Pro. If you have upgraded from the previous version, you'll probably be familiar with these features. Now let's highlight a few of the new features. A spelling checker lets you correct spelling errors in your notebooks; the new Data Modeling Desktop lets you perform cross tabulation models from your database data. Scenario management lets you store sets of values for specific input cells in your worksheets—so you can view different scenarios side by side. And Quattro Pro 5.0 comes with advanced help and training features, including Object Help, Complete On-Line Help screens, and Interactive Tutors. The new Experts go even further...they actually perform complex operations for you, such as creating a graph, consolidating worksheets, and using analysis tools.

This book will get you started with all the classic and new features in Quattro Pro for Windows 5.0. It provides general information about Windows and moves through Quattro Pro's commands and options at a comfortable, yet brisk, pace. Many procedures are given in step-by-step lists, while options are presented in easy-to-read summaries. Plus, you'll find numerous shortcuts and notes spread throughout the book, providing expert advise on using these features.

If you have updated this book from the previous edition, you'll find that all new features in Quattro Pro 5.0 are highlighted with a special icon for your convenience. A summary of these features appears in Chapter 2. You'll also find that this edition contains more intermediate and advanced information. If you have any questions or comments about the topics in this book or would like information about the companion diskette, you may contact the author at

Christopher Van Buren
Teach Yourself Quattro Pro
PO Box 117144
Burlingame, CA 94010

Who Should Read This Book?

This book provides an introduction to Quattro Pro for anyone who is new to the program. Even if you've used a spreadsheet before, this book provides valuable instructions for the most commonly used Quattro Pro features. If you have upgraded from Quattro Pro for DOS, this book provides valuable comparisons and background information to get you started quickly. In short, this is a "first book" on Quattro Pro for Windows for both new and experienced spreadsheet users.

How To Use This Book

This book is organized to give you the most basic information first. It begins with an introduction to Windows and DOS conventions and proceeds with information about building spreadsheet applications. Later, you progress to creating graphs, using drawing tools, and performing database tasks. Afterward, you can read about customizing Quattro Pro through macros and user-interface elements. If you decide to read the book from front to back, you'll find this organization most helpful since you'll be able to use Quattro Pro as you read the book.

However, feel free to skip around. If you are more experienced with spreadsheets, you might want to turn to specific instructions and examples. Skipping around won't disrupt your progress, because the book is designed with many cross references. Each task can be used individually and does not rely on tasks previously learned. So go ahead and turn to the sections you want help with right away—then return to the previous sections to cover any points you've missed.

Here is an overview of the book's chapters.

Chapter 1, "Getting Started," provides basic information you need to know about Windows and DOS. If you are already familiar with DOS directories and windowing procedures in Windows, you can skim through this chapter for special tips, and then get right into Chapter 2.

Chapter 2, "A Quick Tour of Quattro Pro for Windows," is useful for beginners and experienced users alike. It will give you a quick tour of Quattro Pro's most important features. Experienced users might find this all they need to get comfortable with Quattro Pro. Beginners will come away with a valuable overview of the program.

Chapter 3, "Starting a Spreadsheet," details the various types of information you can enter into a Quattro Pro notebook file and how to navigate through your work. You'll learn how to enter and edit data, select cells and blocks, and move to various parts of your notebook.

Chapter 4, "Notebooks and the Quattro Pro Environment," explains the Quattro Pro notebook metaphor. You'll learn about notebook pages, page tabs, ways to modify the basic notebook appearance, and how to customize your workspace through windowing techniques. (This chapter also describes Quattro Pro's SpeedBars.)

Chapter 5, "Formatting Data and Worksheets," describes Quattro Pro's numerous formatting commands and options. Formatting options are available primarily through the Active Block property inspector. You'll learn how to change fonts and type styles, add borders and shades to the worksheet, and much more.

Chapter 6, "Formulas and Functions," explains how to use cell and block references in your formulas and functions so that you can create more powerful and flexible applications. You'll learn about Quattro Pro's @functions and get an introduction to the most commonly used functions.

Chapter 7, "The Data Modeling Desktop," provides full details about using the new Data Modeling Desktop to turn your database information in to cross tabulation models. This chapter explains how and why you would use this feature for analyzing your sales and marketing data.

Chapter 8, "Special Spreadsheet Features," gives information about several specialized features in Quattro Pro, including scenario management and worksheet consolidation. These tend to be more advanced features, so it's best if you are familiar with the basics before hitting this chapter.

Chapter 9, "Printing," provides all the details about printing from Quattro Pro. You'll learn how to set up your reports and print using various printers.

Chapter 10, "Creating Graphs," gives you instructions on turning your numbers and values into attractive graphs. You'll learn the two main ways to create graphs in Quattro Pro: through the **Graph>New** command and the **Graph** tool on the SpeedBar. You'll also find out about the various graph types available in Quattro Pro.

Chapter 11, "Customizing Graphs," explains the numerous graph customization options and properties available for your graph elements. You'll find that you can modify every element in your graphs, including the titles, values, axes, and more. Graph customization uses property inspectors to make your job easy.

Chapter 12, "Annotating Graphs," explains Quattro Pro's handy drawing tools that can be used to annotate graphs. You can also use these tools to illustrate your notebooks or to create slides for a slide show. There's also plenty of design advice here to help make your graphs more effective.

Chapter 13, "Creating Slide Shows," explains how to combine your graphs into slide shows that you can present from your computer screen. Slide shows can employ special effects and macro controls that will turn your show into a self-running demonstration.

Chapter 14, "Using Database Features," shows how you can use Quattro Pro's database features to store and retrieve records, as well as to prepare summary reports and extract information from a database.

Chapter 15, "Creating Macros," dispels the myth that macros are complicated. You'll learn how to create macros quickly and easily for your worksheets and how to attach those macros to buttons and other worksheet objects. This chapter also tells you how to use the macro recorder.

Chapter 16, "Building a Custom User Interface," introduces you to Quattro Pro's powerful user-interface builder. You'll learn how to build your own SpeedBars and dialog boxes so that you can control Quattro Pro's commands and data on your notebook pages. Although this is only an introduction, you'll get enough information to begin creating your own SpeedBars and dialog boxes.

Appendix A, "SpeedBar Tools and Commands," gives you an at-a-glance view of Quattro Pro's command structure and the various tools in Quattro Pro's many built-in SpeedBars. This is a handy reference when you have forgotten a command or the location of a tool.

Appendix B, "Additional Topics," introduces topics that you may want to explore after reading this book. These topics are more advanced and can be found in the Quattro Pro User's Guide or a more advanced book about Quattro Pro for Windows.

Conventions Used in This Book

Below are illustrations and descriptions of the three standard MIS:Press icons. These icons are provided to call your attention to important data as well as tips and techniques that will help you work effectively in Quattro Pro for Windows.

Note

The Note icon indicates that the reader should give special attention to a particular piece of information. This icon may also denote helpful features, hints, or special conditions.

Shortcut

The Shortcut icon indicates that an action can be performed more quickly by using a keyboard shortcut or by following the suggestion in the text.

Warning

The Warning icon indicates cautionary information or serious warnings, such as the possibility of losing data or that missing a particular function could jeopardize your data, disk, or system operation.

New Feature

The New in 5.0 icon indicates a new feature in this version of Quattro Pro.

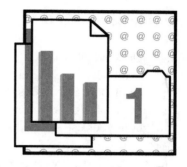

Getting Started

Before getting into all the details about Quattro Pro 5.0 for Windows, it's important that we cover a few basic concepts. You need to learn about Windows before you can begin with Quattro Pro for Windows. And, since Windows programs rely on a few DOS basics, it's appropriate to cover those basics here. Moreover, if you are new to spreadsheets, you'll find this chapter especially important for key concepts about spreadsheet software in general. If you are familiar with Quattro Pro, or have upgraded from a previous version, you'll find the overview of new features and key concepts sections helpful. At least skim over this chapter for any basics you might want to review. In this chapter, you'll learn about:

- Naming files under DOS/Windows
- Using the mouse in Windows
- Installing printers in Windows
- Why to use a spreadsheet program
- Installing Quattro Pro for Windows

Getting Started with DOS

Although Windows lets you avoid using most DOS file management commands, DOS is still very much a part of Windows, so it will help to know some concepts about DOS and the restrictions it applies to your Windows programs. Your knowledge of DOS directories and file names will be particularly helpful throughout your use of Windows.

Understanding DOS Directories

DOS is your computer's operating system—the fundamental piece of software that gets your computer up and running. DOS lets you communicate with your computer's hardware, such as the central processing unit (*CPU*) and the random access memory (*RAM*). Because DOS is so fundamental to the operation of the computer, it automatically takes control of the computer as soon as you turn the computer on.

There are several versions of DOS, including MS-DOS, PC-DOS, and DR-DOS. The version you have will make little difference as far as this book is concerned. However, if you want more information about DOS, refer to a basic book on DOS.

Since DOS communicates with the hardware in your computer, it's through DOS that you can store and retrieve files from your internal hard disk or any other disk. You can store *system files* (files that are part of DOS itself), *program files* (files that come with your programs), or *data files* (files created by your programs that contain personal data) onto your hard disk to make them available for future use.

To help you keep track of the various files on your hard disk—you can accumulate a lot of them—DOS lets you segment the hard disk into individual areas, called *directories*. Inside these directories, you can stores files or other directories, called *subdirectories*. By including subdirectories inside other subdirectories, you can create a treelike structure of individual storage areas. This structure is illustrated in Figure 1.1

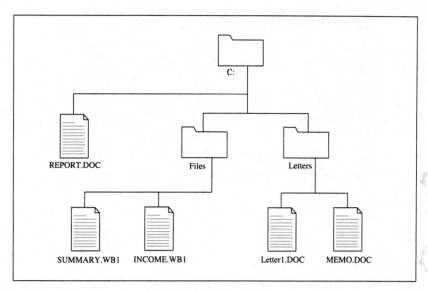

Figure 1.1 A directory tree.

Remember that directories can contain files and/or other directories. If you start with the main directory (also called the *root directory* or *drive C*) and follow the *branches* of the tree from subdirectory to subdirectory, you can eventually locate any file in any directory. You can describe the path you take to a file by listing the names of the directories in order from the root—separated by the backslash character (\):

C:\FILES\INCOME.WB1

This is called the file's *path name,* which is simply the name of each directory in the file's path as well as the file name itself.

Whenever you store files onto the hard disk or retrieve files already stored, you'll probably have to follow the path to the file. In Quattro Pro, you can save a file into a specific path using the **File>Save** command and open a file located in any subdirectory by using the **File>Open** command. Both of these commands (along with a few others) present the Directory List dialog box shown in Figure 1.2.

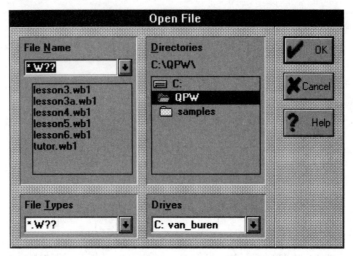

Figure 1.2 The Directory List dialog box for selecting files and directories.

You can use this dialog box to navigate through your disk's directory tree. The dialog box shows the current directory path under the word *Directories* on the right half of the box. You can specify a different directory path by double-clicking on the root directory (for example, **C:**) at the top of the Directories list box. Then, double-click on each directory in the path—in the order it appears. When you double-click on a folder (that is, a directory name), all directories inside it will appear beneath its name. In this way, you "navigate" your way through the disk's directories by clicking on the various folders in this dialog box. When saving a file, you can choose the directory or subdirectory into which you want to store it; then type the file name into the File Name entry box and press **OK**. This stores the file into the directory path you chose. When opening a file, you can search through directories and subdirectories to locate the file. Each time you click on a directory name in the Directories list, all Quattro Pro files appear by name in the Files list on the left side of the dialog box. Double-click on the file name to open the file.

Your current location in the tree and all branches available to you are displayed in the Directories list in this dialog box. By double-clicking on folders (or directories) you can go further down a branch or back to other branches. The directory path describing your current location is shown at the top of the list.

A selection of files available in the current directory—that is, in the directory currently displayed in the Directories list—is displayed in the File Name list to the left of the Directories list. You can display all files in the directory by entering *.* into the File Name entry box. Or you can use other entries to narrow the list down to specific groups of files. There will be more discussion on file names and specifications in the following section.

Enter the file and path into the File Name box

When opening or saving a file, you can avoid navigating through directories and file names (that is, you can avoid using the two list boxes) by typing the complete path name, including the file name, into the File Name entry box. For example, if you want to open the file named **BUDGET**, which is located in the path **C:\FILES\WORK**, you can simply type the entire path: **C:\FILES\WORK\BUDGET.WB1** into the File Name entry box. Quattro Pro will locate the file in the path you specified.

Understanding DOS File Names

When you create subdirectories or store files on your disk, you must adhere to the naming rules imposed by DOS. These are simple, but somewhat limiting. First, you are limited to eight characters in a file or directory name plus a three-character extension. You must separate the name and the extension by using a period. An example is **NAME.EXT** or **MYFILE.XLS**. Second, you should not include spaces or the characters \ " / ; : [or] in your file or directory names.

When you save files in Quattro Pro or any other Windows program, you'll be required to adhere to these conventions. Windows, because it runs along with DOS, is limited by the DOS naming rules.

In the Directories dialog box shown in Figure 1.2, you can locate or save a file by typing the file's entire path name into the File Name entry box—including its extension. Or you can use the Directories list to specify a particular path and use the File Name list or entry box to specify the file itself. When saving files in Quattro Pro, you need not apply the extension—Quattro Pro automatically adds the WB1 extension to its notebook files. Unless you have a reason for changing this extension, go ahead and let Quattro Pro add it for you.

When locating files in the File Names list, you can use wildcards to specify groups of files. Wildcards are discussed in Chapter 14.

Getting Started with Windows

A few basic Windows concepts will help you get around in Quattro Pro for Windows and all your other Windows programs. If you are already familiar with Windows programs, using the mouse, and selecting menus and dialog box options, you can skip this section. For more information on Windows, look for an introductory book on the subject. The following pages will provide a general overview.

Using a Mouse in Windows

Windows doesn't require that you have a mouse, but you'll find that it's designed to be used with one. If you have a mouse, you'll be able to perform many actions with simple mouse movements—actions that might otherwise take several keystrokes. There are three basic mouse movements you should know: *click, double-click,* and *click and drag.*

- **Click** One of the most common mouse actions is the simple click of the left or right mouse button. Throughout Windows and in most Windows applications, the left mouse button is used for the majority of actions. But in Quattro Pro, clicking the right mouse button is also common. It displays one of the *property inspectors,* which are dialog boxes that contain information about the object on which you clicked.

  Mouse clicks are used to select, or *highlight,* items. You can click on a cell to highlight that cell. You can click on a file name inside a list box to highlight the file. Click on a tool in the Quattro Pro SpeedBar to invoke its function.

- **Double-click** If you click twice in rapid succession, you have performed the double-click. This is used to open documents or to make selections. Often, a double-click can be used instead of clicking once on an item then clicking on an **OK** button. For example, to open a document you can click once to highlight its name in a list, then click the **OK** button. Or you can double-click on the name.

- **Click and drag** The click and drag motion is accomplished by clicking the left mouse button on an element and holding down the button while you drag the mouse to another location on the screen. When you reach the destination, release the button. The click-and-drag motion is used to move items from one place to another or to select several items. For example, if you click on a cell in Quattro Pro and drag the mouse, you can highlight many cells. If you click on a graph in the notebook and drag, you can move the graph. Dragging is also a common activity when you use Quattro Pro's drawing tools.

These mouse activities are used throughout Quattro Pro and will be referred to often in this book. Make sure you are familiar with these actions before continuing.

Change the mouse setup from the Control Panel

You can switch the right and left mouse buttons if you are left-handed or if you simply prefer using the right button for most mouse activities. You can also alter the double-click speed—the speed at which you must click for Windows to consider the two clicks to be a double-click. If your clicks are too slow, Windows will not perform the double-click action. To make these changes, use the Desktop settings in the Windows Control Panel.

Windows and Windows

Quattro Pro appears on the screen in a program window—known as the *program workspace*. Inside the workspace window are your individual documents or files, called *notebook windows*. All windows that appear on the screen in Windows can be manipulated in similar ways. Manipulating a window—such as changing its size and shape, moving it, and closing it—is called *windowing*. Most windowing commands are available from each window's Control menu— the menu that is displayed when you click in the upper-left corner of the window. Figure 1.3 shows the Control menu for a notebook window.

Here is a summary of these window manipulation commands and tips on using shortcuts to accomplish these windowing tasks.

- **Restore** Returns a window to its previous state after maximizing or minimizing. In essence, this command "opens" the window. You can restore a minimized window by double-clicking on the minimized icon. You can restore a maximized window by double-clicking on the title bar (this applies to program windows only) or by clicking on its **Restore** button in the top-right corner of the screen.

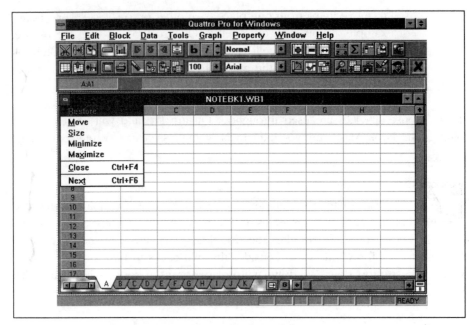

Figure 1.3 A typical Control menu.

- **Move** Moves a window to another location. Program windows can be moved anywhere on the screen (provided they are not maximized), and worksheet windows can be moved anywhere inside the program workspace. You can also move a window by clicking and dragging on its title bar.

- **Size** Changes the size and shape of a window. The easiest way to change a window's size and shape is to click and drag on one of its edges—that is, on one of the small borders that surrounds the window.

- **Minimize** Reduces a window to its minimized form. Worksheet windows are displayed as icons within the program workspace, and program windows are displayed as icons on the Windows desktop. You can also minimize a program window by clicking on its **Minimize** button.

- **Maximize** Expands the window to its maximum size. Program windows will fill the entire screen, and worksheet windows will fill the entire program workspace. You can also maximize a window by double-clicking on its title bar or by clicking once on its **Maximize** button.

- **Close** Removes the window. If a worksheet window is closed, the worksheet is "put away." If a program window is closed, the program is exited, and you'll return to the Windows Program Manager or another open application. You can also close a window by double-clicking on the Control menu.

- **Next** Moves to the next window. This command is displayed only for worksheet windows and is useful only when you have two or more windows active at the same time. You can also press **Ctrl-F6** to move between windows or use the Window menu in Quattro Pro.

Menus and Dialog Boxes

Most Windows programs use menus and dialog boxes in the same basic ways. Many menu commands invoke immediate actions. The **Edit>Copy** command, for example, immediately copies your selected data. But some menu commands offer you additional options through *dialog boxes*, boxes or windows on the screen that prompt you for additional information or offer you additional choices.

Selecting Menu Commands

There are three main ways to choose commands from menus. You can use whichever method seems best at the time. If you have a mouse, you might find the mouse method easiest. Here is a summary of these techniques:

- Using the mouse, click on the menu name within the Menu bar at the top of the screen. This "pulls down" the menu commands inside the menu. Now click on the desired command inside the menu.

- Press the **Alt** key; then type the letter associated with the desired menu name. Each menu name contains an underlined letter, called the *Action key*. Now press the **Action key** for the command you want inside the menu. For example, press **Alt**, **F**, **X** to select the **File>Exit** command. Notice that the action key is not always the first character in the menu name or command name.

- Press the **Alt** key; then press the **Right Arrow** and **Left Arrow** keys to highlight the menu name you want to view. Press **Enter** to reveal (or pull down) the highlighted menu. Now use the **Up Arrow** and **Down Arrow** keys to highlight any command within the menu. Press **Enter** to invoke the highlighted command.

In each of the keyboard methods, you can press the **F10** key instead of the **Alt** key to activate the menus. Plus, you can combine different parts of these three methods. For example, you can click on the menu name with the mouse; then use the arrow keys to highlight the desired command in the menu. Experiment for best results.

Many of Quattro Pro's menu commands have keyboard shortcut alternatives. You can bypass the menu itself and activate the command through a series of keystrokes. For example, you can press **F5** to invoke the **Edit>Goto** command. Many keystroke commands combine the **Ctrl** key with another key, as in **Ctrl-X** to invoke the **Edit>Cut** command.

Selecting Dialog Box Options

Some commands do not perform actions right away. Instead, they bring up dialog boxes that present additional options. Dialog boxes may be filled with options and selections, whereas others may be simple messages or Yes/No questions.

Using the mouse, you can usually click on a dialog box element to select it. Click on a button to select the button; click on an item in a list to select that item; click on a check-box to select it or again to remove the check mark from it. You might be asked to enter information into a dialog box. To place an entry into an entry box inside a dialog box, simply click on the entry box and then type the entry. You might, however, have to erase an existing entry by using the **Backspace** key or the **Delete** key.

If you don't have a mouse, you can move through the options in a dialog box by pressing **Alt** with the **Action key** associated with the desired option.

Your Windows Setup

Settings that you choose in Windows using the Control Panel affect all your Windows programs. For example, when you install a printer in Windows using the Control Panel's Printers tool, that printer is available to all your Windows programs automatically. Similarly, the fonts you use with Windows will be available to all your Windows programs that use fonts.

Fonts and printers are two important aspects of Quattro Pro that are controlled entirely by Windows itself. The following sections briefly discuss these settings.

Fonts

The term *font* describes a particular typeface in a particular size and style. A *typeface* is a unique graphical design of letters and numbers. Windows 3.1 comes with several typefaces, including Arial, Courier, and Symbol (see Figure 1.4).

Figure 1.4 Basic Windows 3.1 fonts.

Sizes, also known as *point sizes,* measure the height of the characters. *Type styles* describe versions of a typeface, such as bold, italic, or underlined type.

Windows 3.1 comes with a special font-display technology, called *TrueType.* TrueType is a method of displaying fonts on the screen and printing them. TrueType makes it easy to use fonts with different types of printers, including PostScript, dot matrix, and LaserJet. The only drawback is that you must have TrueType-compatible fonts. Windows 3.1 comes with several TrueType fonts; many others are available through Microsoft and other commercial sources.

Besides TrueType, other font-display technologies available for Windows include Adobe Type Manager (ATM) and FaceLift from Bitstream. If you are using one of these alternative font management programs, the Adobe or Bitstream fonts will be available along with the TrueType fonts (Windows 3.1 only) in Quattro Pro. For more information on selecting fonts in Quattro Pro, refer to Chapter 5.

Printers

Your Quattro Pro printouts depend greatly on the capabilities of your printer—its resolution, color capabilities, shades and patterns, and so on. You can control your printer's features through the Windows printer setup options in the Control Panel. First, you must install your printer(s) and then set the specific printer options available for each printer.

To install a printer in Windows 3.1, follow these steps:

1. From the Program Manager in Windows, activate the Control Panel by double-clicking on its icon. The Control Panel icon is located in the Main applications group.

2. Double-click on the **Printers** tool in the Control Panel program window. Figure 1.5 shows the screen at this point.

3. Click on the **Add** button to add a new printer to the list of installed printers.

4. Choose a printer from the list that is displayed by double-clicking on its name in the list.

5. Insert the diskette indicated by Windows. You will need your original Windows diskettes for this. If needed, insert other disks as indicated by Windows. Your printer's name should now be displayed in the list of installed printers.

6. Click on the **Connect** button and choose a connection port for the printer. This should be the actual socket into which the printer is connected. Refer to your computer manual for more information on the ports available on the computer. Click on **OK** when finished.

7. If you want this printer to be the standard, or default, printer for all your programs, click on the **Set As Default Printer** button.

You can now proceed to use the Setup button to access specific printer features. Since each printer is different, you'll have to consult the printer manual if you have questions about the Setup options. Chances are, the options will be self-explanatory. When finished with the Setup options, you can close the Setup windows and return to the Control Panel. Printer setup is discussed more in Chapter 9.

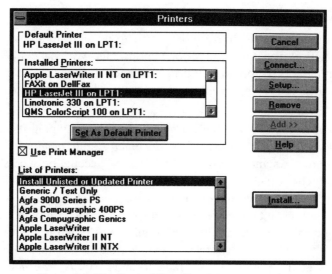

Figure 1.5 The Control Panel's printer setup options.

Why Use Quattro Pro 5.0 for Windows?

Before you actually start using Quattro Pro, take a few moments to get acquainted with the program. If you're new to spreadsheets, you'll benefit from an overview of what Quattro Pro for Windows can do. This section will cover some basic spreadsheet operations and provide some ideas for the types of projects for which you can use a spreadsheet program. Then, turn to Chapter 2 for a more detailed overview of Quattro Pro for Windows.

What Is a Spreadsheet?

You may already have a general idea that spreadsheet programs are used for numerical calculations, financial projects, and other types of number-crunching work. That's true, but it's only half the story. Today, spreadsheet programs provide a host of features to help you process and manipulate data in various ways. And Quattro Pro for Windows offers a wide variety of features, including Number Crunching, Data Formatting, Database Management, Graphing, Graphics and Slides, and Custom Application Development.

Number Crunching

The original task of spreadsheet products was to manipulate and make calculations on numerical data. Quattro Pro for Windows lets you make all types of calculations, using special formulas and mathematical functions. You can use formulas to total columns of values, average statistical data, and create financial models.

When you enter data into Quattro Pro, you will be typing it into a worksheet. Worksheets are also called *files, documents,* and *notebooks*. Notebooks are divided into rows and columns—much like an accounting worksheet or the sheets in your check register. Since each worksheet begins as a blank page, you determine what each row and column means and what data it will contain. Then, you can easily total the columns and rows, produce running totals, or calculate specific values based on the data. It all comes down to the formulas you use in a notebook. Formulas calculate values based on information entered into various parts of the notebook. A single formula can *reference* several other pieces of data in the same notebook. Formulas are described more in Chapters 3 and 6.

After you enter all the data and create all the formulas for a worksheet, you can begin using one of the most valuable features of a spreadsheet—the *what-if* analysis. The what-if analysis lets you substitute different values into the notebook so you can instantly calculate new results from the formulas. "What if I save $150 a month instead of $200?" "What if I increased my income by 5%?" All these what-if tests give you new results for purposes of comparison.

Some worksheets can get rather complex. The formulas and calculations in them can take a lot of time and effort to design, but the result is a valuable tool for your work. In fact, you can design a worksheet that others in your office can use to complete their work, too. These types of worksheets are often called *applications*. The goal is to create your own applications to help you get your work done. You can use the same application over and over again—inserting new data and producing new results.

One common spreadsheet application is a financial statement. Using certain worksheet formulas, you can produce a balance sheet and income statement based on any financial data you enter. Most likely, this type of application requires several notebook pages linked together. On one page, you might enter your financial records, whereas another page produces the balance sheet and income statement.

Since some applications are commonly used, you might find that someone else has already created what you want. There is no telling how many people have created financial statements with Quattro Pro. Many existing applications are available for you to use right away. Just enter you own data and the worksheets take over from there.

Data Formatting

Besides just being able to calculate data, spreadsheet programs—and Quattro Pro specifically—let you format that data for professional reports. Formatting includes the use of type styles, text alignment, and graphic elements, such as lines, borders, and boxes to highlight specific data. You can also use shading and colors to format your reports in Quattro Pro for Windows. And you're not limited to formatting numeric data. You can use the row/column orientation of spreadsheet pages to create many types of reports using text and graphics. Data formatting is covered primarily in Chapter 5. Refer to "Spreadsheet Ideas" below for a list of ways in which you can use formatted spreadsheets.

Database Management

Spreadsheet programs can double as database programs. Because many financial applications require the storage and retrieval of large amounts of data, spreadsheet programs have added database features to their repertoire. In Quattro Pro for Windows, you can create databases to store all types of data—from names and addresses to checking account transactions to historical stock market data. Database management involves a few simple tasks:

- **Storing data** The ability to store large amounts of data. Generally, databases store data in the form of *records*, which are a collection of individual pieces of data relating to a common item. For example, the various pieces of information in an address are collected into a record for a particular individual, say, John Smith. Hence, you can store John Smith's address record. In Quattro Pro for Windows, you can build all kinds of databases for data storage and determine the individual pieces of information that go into the database.

- **Sorting data** The arrangement of data in alphabetical, numerical, or chronological order. Stored records can often be sorted, making it easier to locate information at a glance. When records are sorted, they are more easily searched for specific information. In Quattro Pro, you can sort and re-sort your database records by any piece of data inside the record. For example, you might sort an address list by ZIP Code and later re-sort the list by last name.

- **Retrieving data** Databases store and sort data so that you can easily retrieve specific records. Data retrieval involves "searching" for records in the database. *Searching* is a process of identifying the known characteristics of the record you want to find. For example, in a large address list, you might want to find John Smith's address. By searching for records containing the last name of Smith, you might find the one you want. You can create more specific search criteria by including any other known information about the record. For example, you might search for John Smith in California. Quattro Pro offers a robust set of search criteria rules for locating your database information quickly and easily.

- **Editing data** Database information often changes. You need access to individual records and the ability to edit the information in them. Editing includes inserting new records and deleting old ones from the database—as well as making modifications to existing data.

Graphing

The ability to display numeric information in graphical form is a primary aspect of spreadsheet programs. Graphs can automatically represent numeric information in a number of styles. Line graphs, for example, show the trends in large sets of numerical data. Pie graphs show how parts comprise a whole. Quattro Pro for Windows offers some of the most sophisticated graphing features available for a microcomputer. With over 40 different graph types to choose from, you can present data in an easy-to-understand form. Plus, Quattro Pro offers powerful graph customization options so you can enhance the basic graph.

Since graphs are created as individual objects on the worksheet page, you can move them around at will—displaying them on the same page as the numeric information they represent. Or you can move them into another program, such as a word processor, and include them with your professional reports. Using Object Linking and Embedding (OLE) technology, the inserted graph can retain its link to the data inside Quattro Pro—so that changes you make to the data that affect the graph will automatically appear in all copies of the graph.

Graphics and Slide Presentations

A natural extension of graphing capabilities is the ability to display graphs and other information in a presentation, like a slide show. Quattro Pro is the only spreadsheet that includes this capability. You can add graphs and other "slides" to your custom slide shows for on-screen presentations—or print these images for handouts or transparencies. Using Quattro Pro's graphics features, you can create all sorts of slides for your presentations, such as title slides, pictures, and logos. For more information about these features, refer to Chapters 11 and 12.

Custom Application Development

Large spreadsheet applications are often used by several people in an organization. For example, a financial statement spreadsheet might be used by several members in the accounting office, while using data from the Sales Report spreadsheets. When creating spreadsheets that may be used by several people, you might want to build in some ease-of-use elements, so that users can get right to work on your spreadsheet, without having to be experts in Quattro Pro for Windows. Quattro Pro's macros and interface-building features let you create applications that resemble stand-alone applications. That is, users may not even realize that they are inside Quattro Pro for Windows. You can create custom menus, custom dialog boxes, and custom commands and even change the appearance of the screen.

Customizing Quattro Pro for Windows and your spreadsheets will be more clear as you progress through this book. For complete details about custom spreadsheet applications, see Chapters 15 and 16.

Spreadsheet Ideas

By now you're ready to start creating some worksheets of your own. No doubt, you have some tasks that Quattro Pro can perform. But you might not realize all the things you can do with Quattro Pro. Allow us to suggest some ideas:

Household Tasks

Checkbook register and reconciliation

Credit card register and reconciliation

Home inventory

Simple address book

Financial Tasks

Income/expense log

Bookkeeping system with balance sheet and income statement

Tax preparation

Job-flow reports

Billing system

Purchase orders

Inventory tracking system

Personal net worth statement

Insurance analysis worksheet

Lease vs. buy analysis

Budget worksheet

Loan analysis and amortization schedule

Business Statistics

Trend analysis and projection

Depreciation analysis and calculation

Net present value and internal rate of return calculations

Survey statistics

Population statistics

Employee records

Payroll preparation and analysis

Personal/Business Management

Tickler file and task management with calendar

Sales contact worksheet

Organization charts

Pert and Gantt charts

Slide-shows and presentations

Other

Simple flyers, invitations, and ads

Form masters for photocopying or printing

The list goes on and on. Quattro Pro is limited only by your ability to use it. And that's what this book is all about. By the end of this book, you'll be able to tackle most of these application ideas. And many examples are available for you to scrutinize.

Installing Quattro Pro

The Quattro Pro installation is very simple. Most of the information you need is already on the screen during the installation process. To begin installing Quattro Pro for Windows, first start your computer and run Windows. Now insert the **Quattro Pro Install Disk 1** into your floppy drive (we'll call this Drive A). Finally, select the **File>Run** command from the Windows Program Manager and enter **A:INSTALL** into the space provided. (If the install disk is in Drive B, enter **B:INSTALL**.) Soon, you will see the sign-on and install options screen as shown in Figure 1.6.

Enter your name and other information; then examine the options at the bottom of the dialog box. You have the option of installing all of Quattro Pro's elements or just those that apply to you. Following is a brief description of each element. To install the element, leave the check mark beside its name. To avoid installing the element, click once on the item to remove the check mark.

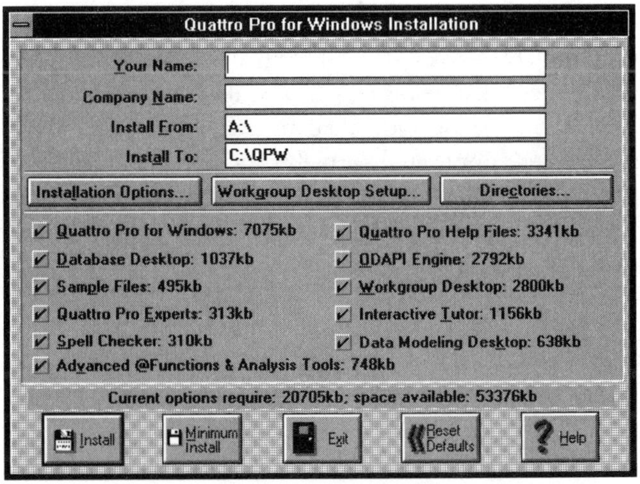

Figure 1.6 The Installation Options screen.

- **Quattro Pro for Windows** This is the main Quattro Pro program. Make sure this item is checked unless you are adding elements after having already installed the program. (You may run the installation program again to install any elements you left out the first time.)

- **Database Desktop** The Database Desktop lets you access and manipulate external database data. You can access database information through the Software Query Language (SQL) or directly from dBASE files or Paradox tables. Pulling database information into Quattro Pro for Windows lets you process and analyze the information with Quattro Pro's powerful features—including the new Data Modeling Desktop, which performs data cross tabulations.

- **ODAPI** The Object Database Application Program Interface (ODAPI) is a proprietary set of instructions that lets Quattro Pro communicate with data on other computers in a network through SQL. The resulting benefit to you is that you can use Quattro Pro to access mainframe computer data or data in any SQL-compliant application.

- **Sample and Clip Art Files** Quattro Pro provides a number of sample files that use various features of the program. A Data Modeling Desktop example provides a complete database with data models to show you how data modeling works. You might find that using these files in conjunction with this book is helpful—or you might create your own samples from the illustrations in this book. Clip art samples can be useful in your slide shows and presentations.

- **Workgroup Desktop** Quattro Pro's workgroup desktop makes it possible to share your spreadsheet files with other computers in your network. You may share individual pages in a spreadsheet notebook, or entire notebook applications—making it possible for other computers to access your Quattro Pro files. If you are not connected to a network or do not plan to share your data with others on a network, you can eliminate this option from the installation.

After you select the installation options that apply to your system, continue the installation process by clicking on the **Install** button. Watch the screen for additional instructions.

Summary

This chapter provided basic information about DOS and Windows so you can comfortably move around in Quattro Pro for Windows. With these basics under your belt, you will be able to get started with Quattro Pro through the next few chapters of this book. However, before going too far, you should get more familiar with DOS and Windows by reading beginning books on these subjects. Remember that Windows, and all Windows programs, are restricted to DOS limitations in file names and path names.

This chapter also introduced the new features in Quattro Pro for Windows 5.0. You'll find most of these features covered in this book and marked with a special icon to call your attention to them. The next chapter gets you started using Quattro Pro for Windows by taking you through a quick tour of the program.

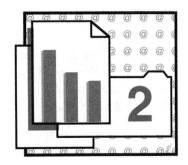

A Quick Tour of Quattro Pro for Windows

If you're ready to get up and running with Quattro Pro for Windows, this chapter is for you. Here you'll get an overview of Quattro Pro's features and important commands—with special attention to the new features in version 5.0. Plus, you'll get a quick tour of the program and create a simple expense worksheet along the way. This chapter is a good introduction to Quattro Pro, providing a solid background to the program before you continue with the more complete descriptions throughout this book. In this chapter you'll learn

- Quattro Pro's essential features
- What's new in Quattro Pro 5.0 for Windows
- Elements of the Quattro Pro screen
- How to build a simple worksheet
- How to format your worksheets
- The basic steps for creating a graph

The Quattro Pro for Windows Screen

Before we get into the details about Quattro Pro for Windows, let's take a moment to examine the basic elements of the Quattro Pro screen, or *program workspace*. When you start Quattro Pro from Windows, your screen will look something like Figure 2.1.

Starting Quattro Pro from Windows

To start Quattro Pro from Windows, double-click on the Quattro Pro for Windows program icon, which looks like this:

Or choose the **File>Run** command from the Program Manager and enter **QPW\QPW.EXE** into the space provided; then click on the **OK** button.

This screen shows the Quattro Pro program workspace and a blank document (or notebook) window within it. The document window, named **NOTEBK1.WB1**, is where you'll enter your data and do most of your work. Each document is called a *notebook* and consists of 256 individual worksheets, or *pages*.

At the top of the screen are Quattro Pro's menus in the Main Menu bar. Below this are two SpeedBars, or rows containing buttons and tools. The first row of buttons is the Standard SpeedBar and the second row of buttons is an Auxiliary SpeedBar. Later, you'll learn how to access other SpeedBars and even create your own custom SpeedBars. Here is a description of the various screen elements in Quattro Pro for Windows—as shown in Figure 2.1.

- **Menu Bar** Contains Quattro Pro's menus, which in turn contain commands for performing tasks. To access a command, click on the menu name; then click on the command name within that menu. For more information, see Chapter 1. Note that the Menu bar changes from time to time, depending on the activity you are performing. For example, when you activate a graph window, the Menu bar changes to include graphing commands.

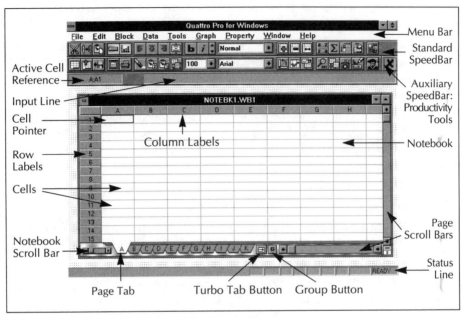

Figure 2.1 The Quattro Pro start-up screen.

- **Standard SpeedBar** Provides a series of buttons, or *tools*, that perform common tasks quickly and easily. For example, you can quickly change the format of a cell using the **Styles List** tool, which displays the word Normal in Figure 2.1. A list of SpeedBar tools and their descriptions appears in Appendix A. In Chapters 4 and 16 you'll learn how to create your own SpeedBars.

- **Auxiliary SpeedBar** Offers additional tools for regular use in Quattro Pro for Windows. There are several Auxiliary SpeedBars available, the one shown in Figure 2.1 (which automatically appears) is called *Productivity Tools*. Tools in this SpeedBar include opening and saving notebooks, printing, copying data, viewing the worksheet (zooming), and accessing different features of Quattro Pro.

- **Input Line** Displays data as you type it into the cells of the notebook. The Input Line is where you actually enter and edit data in the notebook—although the data you enter show up on the page below.

- **Active Cell Reference** Displays the address, or *reference*, of the currently active cell. This is the combination of the column letter and row number of the cell's location in the spreadsheet. You can activate any cell by clicking on it or using the various movement commands discussed in Chapter 3.

- **Notebook** Contains your data. A Quattro Pro document is called a notebook and contains 256 pages, shown by the page tabs at the bottom of the notebook window. Each notebook appears in its own window inside the program workspace, and you can open as many notebooks as you like at the same time. You can also change the size and shape of the notebook window. Refer to Chapter 4 for more information about manipulating notebook windows, including the use of multiple notebooks at the same time.

- **Row Labels** Identify the rows in a notebook. Notebooks are divided into rows and columns. Rows are labeled from 1 to 8192.

- **Column Labels** Identify the columns in a notebook. Columns are labeled from A to Z, then from AA to AZ, then from BA to BZ, and so on—all the way to IV.

- **Cell** Displays data that you enter into the notebook. The intersection of a row and a column is a cell. All data is entered into cells. You can change the format of information in each cell individually. For instance, one cell can display data in a large, bold typeface, whereas another can use a smaller typeface.

- **Cell Pointer** Identifies the active cell. You can move from cell to cell by moving the cell pointer, shown in the highlighted block on cell A1 of Figure 2.1.

- **Page Tabs** Give you access to each page of the notebook. Click on a tab to move to that page. You can see only a few tabs at one time, but the Notebook scroll bar lets you view more.

- **Page Scroll Bars** Allows you to move around the current page. Use the scroll bars to view other areas of the current page.

- **Notebook Scroll Bar** Displays more page tabs. Use this scroll bar to view a page tab; then click on that tab to move to the page.

- **Turbo Tab Button** Allows you to move quickly to the last page of the notebook. The last page is the Graphs page, containing all the graphs you created in this notebook. For more information about the Graphs page, see Chapter 10, "Storing Graphs in the Notebook."

- **Group Button** Establishes a group of pages, which can be manipulated together to save time. Refer to Chapter 4 for more information.

- **Status Line** Displays information regarding the command or option you have selected. As you highlight a command in a menu, a description appears on the Status Line. This line also displays the current *mode*, which helps you determine what activity Quattro Pro is expecting you to perform. For example, Ready mode means that Quattro Pro is ready for your command.

Quattro Pro's Key Features and Concepts

Quattro Pro has numerous features and capabilities. You'll probably not use them all. A few key features are common to most applications, however, and should be explained. The following sections describe some important concepts you'll need to know when working with Quattro Pro for Windows and highlight key features you'll use in all your applications. You'll also get an overview of the new features in Version 5.0.

Object Help and Topical Help

Quattro Pro 5.0 for Windows offers several types of on-line help, starting with simple *Object Help*, which provides brief descriptions about commands and tools inside Quattro Pro. Simply point to the object on the screen for which you want help, then press the **Ctrl key** as you click the right mouse button (**Ctrl-Right Click**). Up pops a simple help window with information about the item you selected. Figure 2.2 shows an example.

If Object Help is not enough information, the next step is *Topical Help*, Quattro Pro's full on-line help text that is available through each Object Help window. For more details about the object you selected with **Ctrl-Right Click**, just click on the **Help** button inside the Object Help window. This takes you directly to the complete on-line help topic as shown in Figure 2.3.

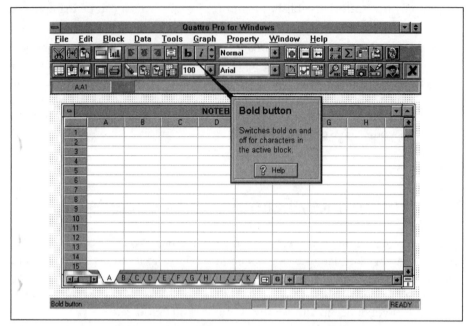

Figure 2.2 Use Ctrl-Right Click to get object help for many objects that appear in Quattro Pro.

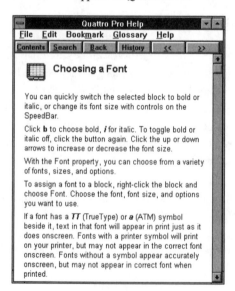

Figure 2.3 You can access help topics through the Object Help windows.

You can also access help topics through the Help menu's Contents and Search commands. Quattro Pro's interactive help system follows the Windows standard for Topical Help—so if you know how to use the Windows help system, you know how to get Topical Help in Quattro Pro for Windows. For more information, refer to a basic book about Windows.

If you need more hands-on instruction about a topic or procedure, try the Interactive Tutors available in Quattro Pro. And if that's not enough, Quattro Pro's Experts can do many complex jobs for you. Refer to the next two sections for more information about Tutors and Experts.

Interactive Tutors

Quattro Pro provides hands-on tutorials for many basic tasks. These tutorials, called *Interactive Tutors*, walk you through each step of a task while you work on your own worksheet data or sample data provided by the Tutor. In other words, you can get your work done while learning how to use Quattro Pro. Interactive Tutors are available for numerous tasks (see Figure 2.4) and are accessible by clicking on the **Interactive Tutor** button on the Productivity Tools SpeedBar. Clicking this button brings up the Interactive Tutor contents page (see Figure 2.4).

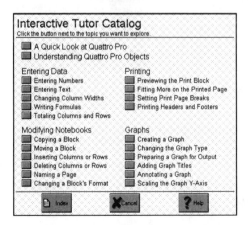

Figure 2.4 View the Interactive Tutor contents page by clicking on the Interactive Tutor button on the Productivity Tools SpeedBar.

Select the topic you want to learn and follow the instructions on the screen. For more information about the Interactive Tutor system, refer to Appendix B.

Experts

Experts are the most advanced level of help in Quattro Pro for Windows. Experts are so helpful that they actually do the job for you. Experts are available for several complex tasks in Quattro Pro, such as consolidating worksheets, creating graphs, and increasing the performance of your system. Experts are covered throughout this book as they apply to topics discussed. In brief, you can access the Experts by clicking the Experts button on the Standard SpeedBar. This brings up the Experts menu shown in Figure 2.5.

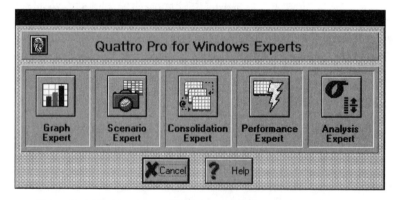

Figure 2.5 The Experts available in Quattro Pro are available when you click on the Experts button.

When you are ready to perform one of these tasks, use an Expert to complete the task using your data.

Drag and Drop

Quattro Pro for Windows lets you use your mouse to the fullest. Its convenient drag-and-drop procedures let you control your data blocks as objects on the screen—copying and moving them with simple mouse movements. Version 5.0 adds the ability to drag a single cell as well as a block of cells. To drag a range of cells, just select the range as described in Chapter 3; then click the left mouse button anywhere in the range and hold the button for a moment. When the "drag hand" appears, you can move the range around the screen. Drag and drop is covered in detail in Chapter 3.

Spelling Checker

Quattro Pro's new spelling checker lets you correct spelling errors throughout your notebooks and graphs. You can correct information in selected ranges or throughout an entire notebook at once. The simple Spelling Checker SpeedBar makes it easy to see your document as you make corrections. Refer to Chapter 3 for complete details about the new spelling checker.

Data Modeling

Many spreadsheet applications require that you collect large amounts of data for analysis, such as statistical data. To help you quickly analyze statistical data, Quattro Pro 5.0 for Windows includes the new Data Modeling Desktop (DMD). By copying your spreadsheet data into the Data Modeling Desktop, you can easily manipulate the data in cross tabulation tables—generating multiple reports based on different models. You can rearrange a data model (your statistical data presented in a cross tabulation table) to view the data in different perspectives. Simple mouse movements let you change the orientation of data elements.

Since the Data Modeling Desktop is part of Quattro Pro for Windows, you can move your finished models back into your notebook pages for integration with the original data. Or you can print reports directly from the DMD. Data models can also be linked to other notebooks or applications using live Dynamic Data Exchange (DDE) links. For details about the Data Modeling Desktop, refer to Chapter 7.

Scenarios

Quattro Pro's new Scenario Manager lets you store multiple sets of inputs for your notebooks, so you can perform what-if tests without having to reenter data repeatedly. Just store different data sets as individual scenarios and switch among them at any time. The Scenario Manager lets you use any input cells in a scenario and then save and name the scenario for future use. Scenarios are useful for cost estimation worksheets and many other applications. Chapter 8 provides details on the Scenario Manager.

Notebooks and Pages

Each time you start a new Quattro Pro document, or application, you get a series of blank pages bound together in a notebook. Each new document you start with the **File>New** command presents 256 blank notebook pages on which you can enter your data. Pages are labeled from A through IV. Chances are that you won't need all 256 pages for your applications, but they are available if you need them.

Combining pages into notebooks serves several purposes. First, it lets you keep important applications together. Each time you open the notebook, all the pages are available at once. Second, you can create links between notebook pages so you can break up a large application into several different pages and link them together. This helps you organize your work and keep core pieces of an application separate from the others. Finally, notebooks let you do what comes naturally: start your work in the top-left corner of each page. Rather than spread your work across a single page, you can now use several pages and begin at the top of each.

Formulas and Functions

The backbone of any spreadsheet is its formulas and functions. Formulas are entered into the cells of your notebook pages and calculate values based on other cells. In this way a formula *links* one cell to another and lets you change the results of your calculations by making changes to a few key cells. By changing an input value in one cell, all cells that depend on that value will also change.

Quattro Pro gives you access to powerful spreadsheet functions as well. *Functions* are special entries that provide special values for you. Using functions, you can determine whether a cell contains a numeric value, a zero, or nothing at all. Functions go hand in hand with formulas to give you more calculations for you notebooks. Quattro Pro 5.0 has over 300 functions to serve your needs. Many of these are explained in Chapter 6.

Formulas and functions usually refer to other cells through *cell references.* A reference is simply the name of the cell, as in C5 or G35. As an example, the formula **+C5+G35** adds the values contained in the two cells C5 and G35. The formula can be entered into any cell other than C5 and G35.

Select Then Do vs. Do Then Select

Many commands and options in Quattro Pro operate on blocks of cells. When you perform a block-oriented command, you can save time by selecting the block before choosing the command. For example, to format text with boldface type, you can first select the cells containing the text and then click on the **Boldface** tool in the SpeedBar. Boldface will be applied to the cells you selected. Many commands and options work on selected blocks, including most commands in the Block menu.

Some commands give you the opportunity to select a block of cells after you've chosen the command—or to change the cells you selected before using the command. These commands display the selected block in a dialog box, as Figure 2.6 shows.

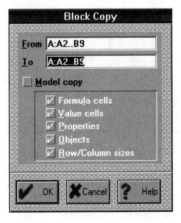

Figure 2.6 Many commands display the currently selected block before executing the procedure.

When the command or option displays the selection, you have the opportunity to change your mind. Just double-click on the current entry and Quattro Pro will return you to the active page where you can change the selection. Press **Enter** when you have finished. In this way, you can make your block selection after starting the command.

Property Inspectors

Quattro Pro version 1.0 introduced a powerful concept in Windows programs, called the *property inspector.* A property inspector shows you the properties of anything on the screen. Depending on the object you are inspecting, a range of properties might be displayed. For example, if you inspect the properties of a cell, you will see settings for its numeric format, font, text color, height, width, and so on. If you inspect the properties of the active notebook page, you'll get settings for the page name, borders, grid lines, and other properties.

To view the properties of a screen element or object, simply click the right mouse button on the item. This produces the Property Inspector dialog box; Figure 2.7 shows the Property Inspector dialog box for a cell or block.

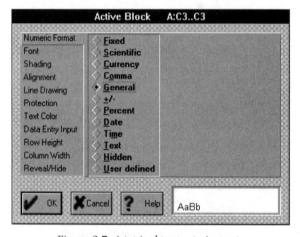

Figure 2.7 A typical property inspector.

Along the left side of a property inspector is a series of items. These are the various categories of properties available for the item. On the right side of the inspector are the actual properties for the item chosen on the left. Click on any of the items on the left side to view the associated properties on the right. In

Figure 2.7, the Alignment properties are showing. Remember that all properties in the inspector apply to the item you've selected.

Property inspectors are a convenient way to view the attributes of the various screen elements in Quattro Pro, as well as your data and graphics. Everything in Quattro Pro has properties that can be inspected. What follows are some items on which you can click on (with the right mouse button) to view properties:

Properties for	Right-click on
Cell or block	The cell or highlighted block, then choose Block Properties
Active page	The page tab
The notebook (all pages)	The title bar
Quattro Pro (overall settings)	The Quattro Pro title bar or program workspace
A floating graph	The graph
Elements of a graph	The element within the graph window

NOTE Normally, right-clicking on an object produces the object's property inspector immediately. However, there is one exception: When you right-click on a cell or block, you will get a shortcut menu. Choose the **Block Properties** command from this menu and then you will see the property inspector.

Shortcuts and SpeedBars

To make your work easier, Quattro Pro offers a series of shortcuts for commonly used commands and procedures. Shortcuts come in several forms. Command-key sequences, for example, are key combinations that perform actions, such as pressing **Shift-Ins** in place of using the **Edit>Paste** command. There is also a shortcut menu that appears when you right-click on a cell or selected block in the notebook. This shortcut menu provides a list of commands that you might want to use while working on a block of cells. It also provides access to the Active Cell Property Inspector. The most common type of shortcut is the

SpeedBar button. SpeedBar buttons perform commands quickly at the touch of the mouse. Click on the **Paste** button to perform the **Edit>Paste** command. A complete list of SpeedBar buttons appears in Appendix A. You can determine the meaning of any SpeedBar button by moving the mouse pointer over the button and then looking in the bottom-left corner of the screen. Quattro Pro displays a brief description of the button on which the mouse pointer is located (you need not click the mouse button at all—just position the pointer on the screen).

Graphing and Graphics

Quattro Pro's graphing capabilities are among the best available. You can quickly turn your numeric data into beautiful graphs and then enhance those graphs through numerous commands and properties. After you create a graph of your data, you can place the graph anywhere on the page—or display it in a separate window. All graph enhancements and customization take place inside the graph window. Figure 2.8 shows a graph window.

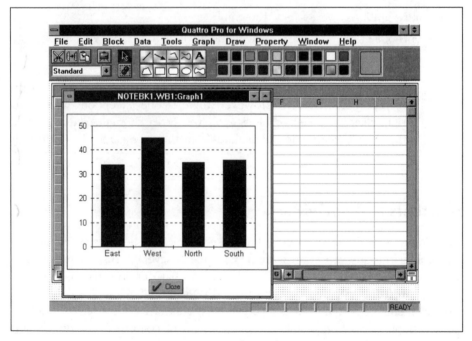

Figure 2.8 A typical graph window.

Quattro Pro 5.0 adds new, powerful analytical graphing features to the basic graphing capabilities. This includes creating moving averages, aggregation, linear fit regression, and exponential fit regression. While the graph window is active, you can also use Quattro Pro's drawing and annotation tools. These tools let you draw simple pictures and annotate your graphs with a variety of graphic objects. For instance, you can use circles, squares, and polygons to draw a logo in the graph window (see Figure 2.9).

Notice that this graph window contains no graph—only the elements of the drawing. Empty graph windows can be used as blank areas for drawing—a common procedure for creating slides.

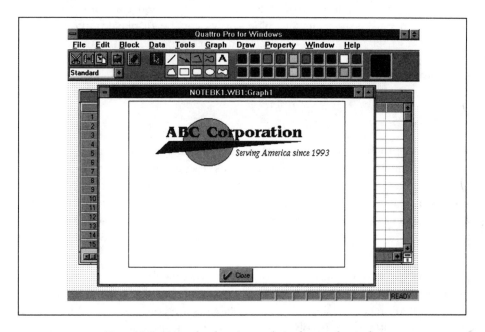

Figure 2.9 Using the drawing tools in the graph window.

Importing and Exporting Graphics

Among Quattro Pro's powerful drawing capabilities is that of importing and exporting graphics. Quattro Pro can read and display a variety of graphic images created by other programs. After these images are displayed in Quattro Pro, they can then be converted to a series of other graphic formats using Quattro Pro's powerful export features.

Graphic importation and exportation takes place in the graph window. You can use imported graphics to fill objects and graph backgrounds. You can even modify some graphic images. You'll see that Quattro Pro comes with a host of clip art that you can import into your graphs, slides, and illustrations.

Slides and Slide Shows

As described previously, a blank graph window can be used to create a slide. Slides can then be combined into slide shows. A *slide show* is a combination of images that can be displayed in sequence on the screen with a variety of transition effects. Using Quattro Pro's slide show features, you can turn your computer screen into a slide viewer. Slide shows can be displayed automatically, requiring no user interaction—or they can be dependent on the user to move through the slides. You can also print your slides to standard EPS or PostScript files for 35mm slide imaging.

Databases

Spreadsheet programs are not just for making calculations. You can use them to store data, much as a database program does. Using rows to store your records, you can enter more than 8000 records into each page of a notebook, and then use Quattro Pro's powerful data-query procedures to locate and manage that data. You can even use Quattro Pro's powerful SQL and Database Desktop features to access the data in external database tables, such as your dBASE and Paradox data.

The new database form lets you enter and edit database records in a convenient on-screen entry/edit form. You can view any record in this form and even locate and edit records using the form. Databases are commonly used in spreadsheet applications that involve business transactions or records. Examples include employee records, payroll, accounts payable, accounts receivable, income and expense logs, and tax records.

Macros

Macros make your work easier by automating complex or repetitious tasks. You can create a macro to perform a task and then run the macro whenever you want to complete the task. The macro runs in seconds—much faster than if you performed the task yourself. Quattro Pro comes with a host of macro commands that are equivalent to menu commands, mouse movements, and keyboard activities. Combine these commands to perform numerous tasks into a single macro. You can also record your own actions and let Quattro Pro translate them into macro commands.

Customizing the User Interface

You might find the need to build applications that will be used by other people. These applications tend to be more complex than your own personal ones. When a notebook will be used by others, you might find it helpful to build in some user-interface elements. These include custom SpeedBars, menus, and dialog boxes. You can use a custom dialog box to control the values and formulas used in the application—or to help the operator switch among different graphs or view different areas of the notebook. In short, custom interface elements make it possible to use your application without having to know much about Quattro Pro. The more extensive your custom interface elements, the less knowledge of Quattro Pro will be needed to use the notebook.

Custom user-interface elements can also be useful in your own applications for making data entry and other tasks easier. The new SpeedBar Designer lets you quickly and easily construct your own, custom SpeedBars using any of the existing tools in Quattro Pro. Or you can create your own, custom tools and add them to the SpeedBar. You'll find a detailed description of Quattro Pro's custom interface elements in Chapter 16.

Data Sharing and Connectivity

Quattro Pro includes some of the most powerful data connectivity features available. You can share your Quattro Pro data as a client or server—using network OLE and DDE. Plus, Quattro Pro lets you mark notebooks and individual notebook pages for network sharing to make your data available to others in your workgroup. Data connectivity and sharing lets you keep your data current with other users. Quattro Pro 5.0 for Windows even includes a network installation option, so you can use Quattro Pro on several machines in a network with only one installation burden. For more information about Quattro Pro's network connectivity features, refer to Appendix C.

A Tour of Quattro Pro

Now that you have an idea of Quattro Pro's main screen elements and key concepts, let's begin our tour of the program. In the next few pages you'll create a simple application and use many of Quattro Pro's fundamental commands and options. Most important, you'll get a feel for how notebook applications are created and how easy they are to build. If possible, follow the steps exactly as they are presented. If you need to stop in the middle of the process, use the **File>Save** command to save your work so you can complete it later. See the following note for details about saving and reopening a notebook in Quattro Pro.

Saving and Opening Notebooks

Following are the procedures for saving and opening notebooks in Quattro Pro. Use these steps if you are unable to complete this tutorial example in one sitting. To save your work:

1. Select the **File>Save** command.
2. Enter a name for the notebook, including any directory path if desired (see Chapter 1 for information about directory paths). If you are unsure about this, type the name **EXPENSE** into the Save entry box.
3. Click on **OK**.

After you save your document the first time, you will not have to enter the name again when using the **File>Save** command. To open an existing notebook after quitting Quattro Pro:

1. Start Quattro Pro.
2. Select the **File>Open** command.
3. Enter the name of your notebook into the space provided (for example, enter **EXPENSE**). If needed, you can enter the entire directory path to the file, as in **C:\QPW\EXPENSE**.
4. Click on **OK**.

Starting Quattro Pro

The first step is to start Quattro Pro from the Windows Program Manager. Windows offers many ways to run a program, including using the **File>Run** command, using the program's **Start-up** icon, and running the program from the File Manager. The following steps give one method:

1. Locate the Quattro Pro Program icon in the Windows Program Manager window. You might have to open the Quattro Pro for Windows Application Group window (see Figure 2.10).

2. Double-click on the **Program** icon labeled Quattro Pro for Windows. Quattro Pro is displayed on the screen with a blank notebook window in view.

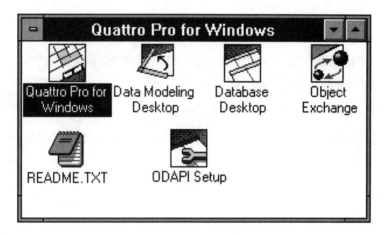

Figure 2.10 Quattro Pro's Program icon.

You will soon be inside the Quattro Pro environment with a blank notebook on the screen. The following sections will show you how to begin your spreadsheet application.

Entering Column Headings

Let's begin by typing our main column headings into the notebook page. In this application, we'll compare three months of expense data, so our column headings will simply be January, February, and March. Here is the easiest way to enter these headings:

1. Use the arrow keys to move the cell pointer to cell C3.

2. Type **Jan** and press **Enter**. Notice that as you type, the word is displayed on the Input Line. When you press **Enter**, it shows up in the cell.

3. Hold the **Shift** key down and press the **Right Arrow** key two times to highlight all three cells. Figure 2.11 shows the screen at this point.

4. Click on the **SpeedFill** button in the SpeedBar. This is the second button from the right edge of the SpeedBar. As soon as you click on the button, Quattro Pro fills the cells with the remaining month abbreviations—starting with your entry of **Jan**.

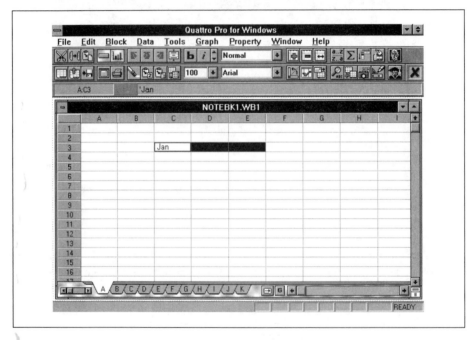

Figure 2.11 Highlighting cells for the column headings.

Entering Labels and Numbers

With the column headings set, we can begin our expense labels along the left edge of the sheet. After this, we can enter the numeric data for each month. You'll find these labels and numbers easy to enter—just move to the desired cell and type the information. Here are the steps.

Correcting errors (a quick fix)

If you make a mistake while entering data in this example spreadsheet, just complete the entry by pressing the **Enter** key. Then just retype the information; the new entry replaces the old one. While you are actually typing the entry (before pressing **Enter** or **Down Arrow** to finish it), you can press the **Backspace** key to erase the previous character typed.

1. Using the arrow keys, move the cell pointer to cell B4 (or just click on cell B4).

2. Type **Auto Fuel** and press the **Down Arrow** key once to move to the next cell. Continue to enter the following labels, pressing **Down Arrow** after each one:

Auto Loan	**Insurance**
Bank Fees	**Medical**
Charity	**Mortgage Interest**
Clothes	**Mortgage Principal**
Entertainment	**Other Expense**
Dues	**Subscriptions**
Food	**Taxes**
Home Maint	**Telephone**
Housing	**Utilities**

3. Use the vertical scroll bar to move back to the top of the notebook; then click on cell C4. Enter values for each of these expense categories in all three columns. Remember to press **Down Arrow** after each entry. If your records are not available to find these values, just enter temporary values into these columns. (The point is to see how Quattro Pro can calculate the values.) Figure 2.12 shows the notebook after some values are entered.

Centering a Title Over the Columns

Now that we have all the columns in the worksheet, we can center a main heading above them. In the next procedure you will enter a main title above the column headings and then center the heading automatically. Automatic centering over columns lets you adjust column widths while keeping the heading centered above them. You'll see how this works in this and the next sections.

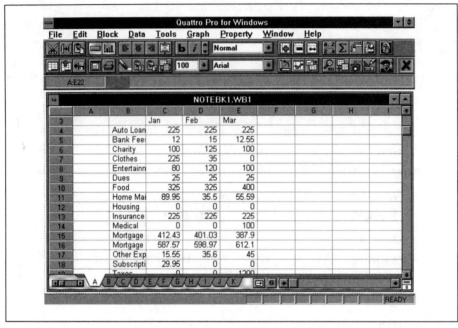

Figure 2.12 The notebook after completing all labels and numbers.

1. Click on cell B2 to select it.

2. Enter the main title **Expenses** into the cell and press **Enter**.

3. Hold the **Shift** key down and press the **Right Arrow key** until you highlight the block B2 through E2 (referred to as the block B2..E2).

4. Click on the **Block Center** button to center the heading within the highlighted block.

Changing Column Widths

Notice that the expense labels do not fit within their column. Before you entered data into column D, the expense labels were able to "spill over" into that column. However, when you filled column D with information, the labels in column C were chopped off. The cure for this is to expand the width of column C to match the data more adequately. Here are the steps for expanding a column's width.

1. Right-click the mouse on any cell in column B, then click on the **Block Properties** option. The Active Block property inspector is displayed on the screen.

2. Choose the **Column Width** option in the left column of the inspector. The Column Width properties appear in the dialog box, as shown in Figure 2.13.

3. Click on the **Auto Width** option within the Options column; then press **OK**. The width of column B should now match the entries in that column. Figure 2.14 shows the result.

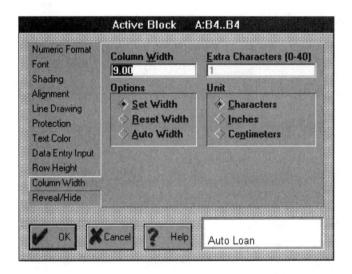

Figure 2.13 The Column Width properties.

Repeat these steps for any column you want to change. You can also change several columns at once by highlighting cells in all columns at the same time (that is, highlight a block of cells spanning the columns). Notice that when you change the column widths in the notebook, the centered title above the columns remains centered. That is, it automatically adjusts to the new column widths. This is a benefit of automatic title centering.

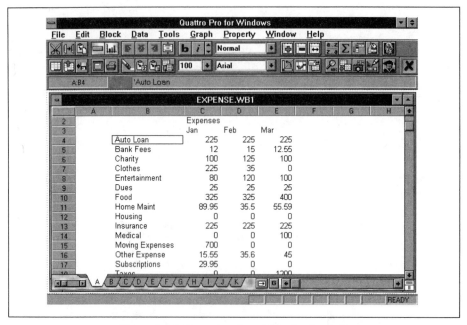

Figure 2.14 Changing the width of column B.

Saving the Notebook

Be sure to save this notebook for future use—or if you plan to stop before you're finished with the example. The **File>Save** command lets you save the notebook to any directory on your system. Quattro Pro automatically enters the file extension WB1, so you need not include an extension. Saving the worksheet with **File>Save** from time to time is a good way to avoid losing data if the system shuts down for some reason.

1. Choose the **File>Save** command.

2. Enter **Expenses** into the space available for the file name; then press **Enter**. If desired, you can change directories and save the file into any directory of your choosing—or enter a directory path along with the file name as explained in Chapter 1. Otherwise, just type **Expenses** and press **Enter**.

This saves the file into the default directory location, which appears under the word *Directories* in the Save File dialog box. (Unless you change it, this should automatically be the **C:\QPW2** directory where the Quattro Pro program files are located.)

Calculating Column Totals

Now you're ready for the exciting part—calculating totals. You'll find that Quattro Pro offers a quick and easy way to produce column totals in your worksheet. The following steps show how you how. (You can enter formulas in many different ways; see Chapter 6 for more information about formulas.)

1. Click the left mouse button on cell C22 and hold the mouse button down.

2. Drag to the right to highlight the block of cells including C22, D22, and E22. This is known as the block C22..E22. Release the mouse button when the block is highlighted.

3. Click on the **SpeedSum** tool in the SpeedBar. This is the fourth tool from the right edge of the bar. Quattro Pro quickly sums all three columns and places the totals in their respective cells. Figure 2.15 shows the result.

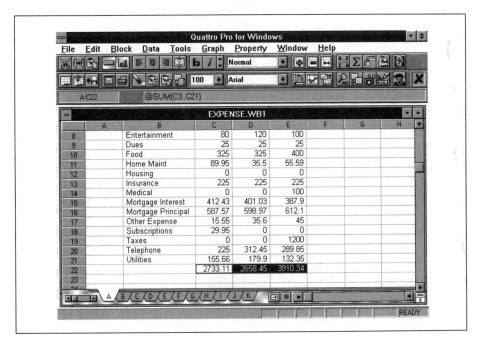

Figure 2.15 Using the SpeedSum tool in the SpeedBar.

Editing the Application

Editing is a big part of developing a spreadsheet application. You often have to insert forgotten information or remove unwanted data. The following steps show you how to use the powerful drag-and-drop procedure to move blocks of data around the page and how to delete blocks of data while keeping the application intact.

1. Move to cell B17.

2. Hold the **Shift** key down while you use the **Right Arrow** and **Down Arrow** keys to highlight the block B17..E22.

3. Click inside the highlighted block and hold down the mouse button. After a moment, the mouse pointer changes into a hand shape.

4. Drag the mouse down one row to move the block exactly one space down. Figure 2.16 shows the result after this step.

5. Move up to the inserted space and add the entry

    Moving Expenses   700   0   0

6. Highlight the block B16..E16.

7. Select the **Block>Delete>Rows** command. Then, click on the **Partial** option in the dialog box that appears. This tells Quattro Pro to delete only the highlighted cells and not the entire rows containing those cells.

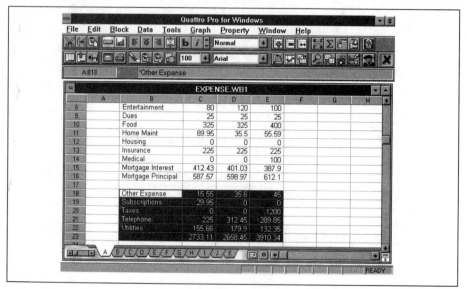

Figure 2.16 Use drag and drop to move the highlighted block down one row.

When you inserted and deleted data from the columns, notice that the column totals adjusted to your edits. This is the nature of automatic totals—provided you insert or delete data within the first and last cell of each column. For more information about editing worksheets, refer to Chapter 3.

Formatting the Notebook

After the data is entered, you can concentrate on formatting the worksheet—making it more readable and attractive. You'll find that formatting is an important part of your notebook applications and should not be taken lightly. Quattro Pro offers some powerful formatting capabilities to make your applications more effective. The following steps use a few basic formatting commands and options in the sample application:

1. Right-click on the page tab for the current page. That is, move the mouse pointer to the "A" page tab and click the right mouse button. The Active Page property inspector appears on the screen.

2. Choose the **Grid Lines** option to display the grid-line properties.

3. Click on **Vertical** and **Horizontal** to remove the check marks from both options.

4. Click on **OK**.

5. If the block C21..E21 is not already selected, select that block now. You can do this by clicking on C21 and dragging to E21. Now click on the arrow beside the Styles List tool on the SpeedBar (the Styles List tool displays the word *Normal* in it—the arrow appears immediately to its right).

6. Click on the **Total** option to format the columns totals.

7. Select the block C4..E21, consisting of the numeric data and totals; then select the **Comma** style from the **Styles List** tool in the SpeedBar. This formats the numbers—giving them two decimal places and placing commas between thousands. Figure 2.17 shows the result.

8. Highlight the block C3..E3.

9. Click on three tools on the SpeedBar: **Bold**, **Italic**, and **Right Justify**. These are in positions 8, 10, and 11 from the left edge of the Standard SpeedBar. Also click on the **Font Size Increase** button twice. This is the top half of the button to the right of the Italic button.

10. Move to cell B2 (the cell containing the title) and repeat the **Bold**, **Italic**, and **Font Size Increase** selection procedures as described in the previous step. By clicking on the **Font Size Increase** button twice, you can increase the font size of the main title so that it's larger than the column headings. Figure 2.18 shows the result.

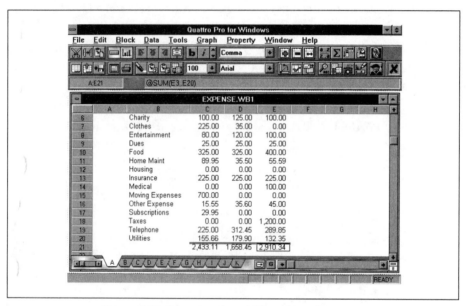

Figure 2.17 Removing the grid lines from the screen.

Changing the Values

By creating formulas in your notebooks, you can change the data used to produce the totals—Quattro Pro will automatically recalculate the totals to reflect the changes. Try this in the sample notebook. Move to any of the values in columns C, D, or E and type a new value. Watch the total at the bottom of that column change.

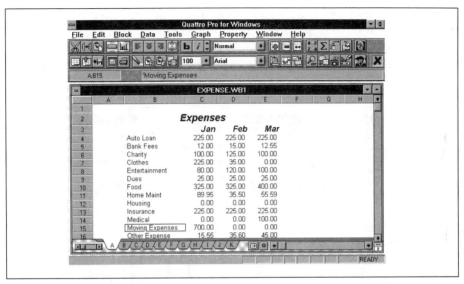

Figure 2.18 Formatting the numeric data with the Comma style.

Creating a Graph

Graphing is a powerful tool for communicating numeric information. Quattro Pro offers numerous graphing capabilities and lets you prepare attractive and informative graphs from your data. Graphing is not difficult, but it provides you with many choices. The following steps give you a quick and simple idea of Quattro Pro's graphing capabilities. See Chapters 8 and 9 for the complete story on graphs.

1. Highlight the block B3..C17.

2. Click on the **Graph** tool in the SpeedBar. This is the fifth tool from the left edge of the SpeedBar.

3. Click and drag on the notebook page to create a box. When you release the mouse, the graph appears in this box. Figure 2.19 shows the screen.

4. Choose the **Graph>Type** command and click on the **Pie Graph** option. Press **Enter** when finished. The graph changes to a pie, as Figure 2.20 shows. If the **Graph>Type** command is not active, click once on the graph to highlight it and then press the **Delete** key to remove the graph. Now repeat this procedure to try again.

As a final task: try moving the graph around the screen by clicking on the graph box and dragging it to a new location. Notice that as you drag past the edge of the screen, Quattro Pro moves the notebook page within the window so you can see where you're going. For more information on graphing and graph options, refer to Chapter 10.

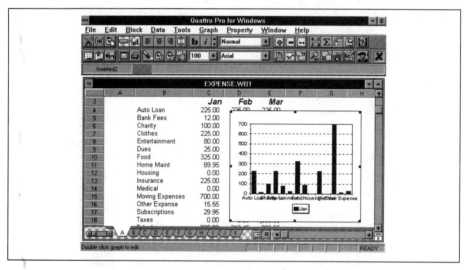

Figure 2.19 The completed formatting.

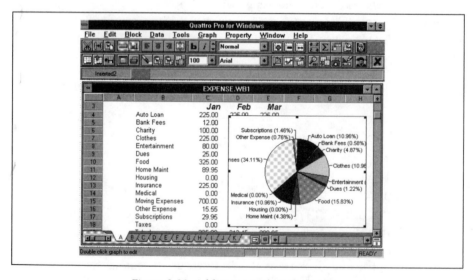

Figure 2.20 Adding a graph to the screen.

Summary

Quattro Pro has dozens of commands and options from which to choose. You'll probably get familiar with a handful that you use most often. You can refer back to this book when you forget any of the others. It's not important that you know all the commands and options in Quattro Pro. What's important is that you have a good general understanding of what you can accomplish in your applications. This chapter provided an overview of Quattro Pro's features and commands and gave you a quick tour of those commands through building a sample application.

The remaining chapters in this book take these concepts further—giving you details about each important option and even alternative ways of accomplishing these options. You'll begin in the next chapter with information about starting your spreadsheet application.

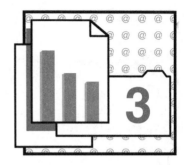

Starting a Spreadsheet

When you create a Quattro Pro spreadsheet application, you need know about three basic tasks: entering data, moving around the notebook pages, and editing data. This chapter covers these three basic tasks and describes

- The four types of data you can enter into Quattro Pro
- How to use formulas to calculate the values in other cells
- What a cell reference is
- The easiest way to enter dates into your notebooks
- Ways to move around the notebook
- Methods for correcting errors and retyping entries
- How to insert and delete data
- How to use the built-in spelling checker

Entering Data

When you're ready to begin entering data into your spreadsheet pages, it's important that you consider how Quattro Pro looks at data. There are four types of data you can enter—numbers, text labels, dates, and formulas—each of which serves a different purpose in your applications and comes with different requirements for data entry.

The following sections discuss Quattro Pro's four types of data and how to enter each type. After you have entered your data, you'll be ready for information on editing.

Entering Numbers

Your worksheets will consist largely of numbers—entries that contain numerals and other numeric symbols. Numeric entries differ from other entries in that they can be used in calculations. They can contain only these characters:

1 2 3 4 5 6 7 8 9 0 - + . % ( ) $

You can begin a numeric entry with any of the numeric values, a decimal point, a dollar sign, a minus sign, or a plus sign. A number may contain only one decimal point. A percent sign, if used, must be placed at the end of the number, and it converts the number to its decimal equivalent. A number can start with **(** (an open parenthesis) and end with **)** (a closed parenthesis)—however, the number will not be negative but positive. (Generally, parentheses are used to group operations in a formula, not to indicate a negative value. To display negative numbers using parentheses rather than minus signs, you must change the numeric format, as described in Chapter 5). If you enter a dollar sign at the beginning of the number, Quattro Pro ignores it. Quattro Pro also allows you to enter a number in scientific notation. Some acceptable numeric entries follow:

567

567.123

.567 (displays 0.567)

567.00 (displays 567)

-567

(567) (displays 567)

9% (displays 0.09)

2.35E+8 (displays 235000000 when the column width =9 and 2.4E+08 when the column width = 8)

Notice that Quattro Pro will normally add leading zeros to a fractional number, so you see 0.123 when you type **.123** into the cell. Percentage values are displayed as decimal values. Hence, the value 9% appears as 0.09 on the Input Line as well as in the cell. The value displayed in the cell can be formatted to 9%, however, by changing the cell's properties.

Exceeding the cell's width

NOTE If you enter or calculate a number that's too large to fit into the cell, Quattro Pro displays * * * in the cell. This tells you that you need to widen the column, a process described in Chapter 5. (Chapter 5 also shows you how to round a number.)

Occasionally, you might need to enter a number as a text label . For example, you might want to enter the number **342342** to indicate a product number; but you want this to appear as a heading for a column or row, too. You can do this by entering the value preceded by one of the label prefixes (^ " or '). Details on label prefixes appear in Chapter 5 under "Changing Data Alignment." Other numbers that should be entered as labels are telephone numbers and ZIP codes.

Entering Descriptive Labels and Text

Notebook pages are usually full of descriptive labels, headings, and other text. Text consists of any information that is not a date, does not consist exclusively of numeric values, or doesn't begin with a numeric value. Virtually anything you type that includes an alphabetical character will be a text label on the notebook page. Some examples of text entries follow:

Product ABC

Product 123

John Smith

Oct 92 (text entry—see also "Entering Dates and Times")

The following are not text entries:

234 First Street (begins with a number)

04 Oct (begins with a number)

+A7 (formula entry)

1234 (numeric entry)

You can type up to 900 characters in a cell. A long text entry may exceed the current width of its cell and appear to "flow" into the next cell (the cell to the right). Actually, the text is contained entirely by the original cell and appears to spill into the next cell only when the next cell is empty. If the text is very long, it might be visible only up to the next filled cell. The entire entry is still in the cell, but only part of it can be seen. Figure 3.1 illustrates this.

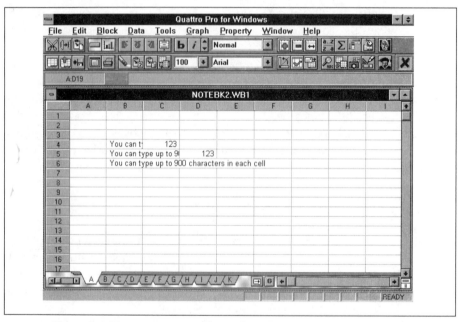

Figure 3.1 Text entries can spill into the cell to the right, providing that cell contains no data of its own.

Each cell in Figure 3.1 contains the same information but displays it only as far as the adjacent cells allow. When you move the cell pointer to a cell, its data appears in the formula bar in its entirety; you can see the entire text label in the formula bar, even when that text is chopped off in the worksheet. In this way, the Input Line shows the actual cell entry even though the notebook page does not.

Quattro Pro's text-formatting powers

Chapter 5 shows how you can format text to get many different effects in your notebook pages. You can align text with different sides of the cell, change fonts and font sizes, select various colors for the text, and put in shadings for the background of a cell or block of cells. Chapter 5 also shows you how to adjust the widths of columns and the heights of rows.

Entering Dates and Times

To enter a date into a Quattro Pro cell, you can format the cell to accept a date and then enter a date in one of the valid date formats. You can also enter the *Julian date* (the date serial number) and then format the cell to display the serial number as a date. A date serial number is a date expressed as the number of days elapsed since January 1, 1900. Hence, the date **January 2, 1900** is expressed as the date serial number 2. In this way, every date is really just a numeric value that represents days elapsed since 1/1/1900. Date Serial numbers allow you to perform date calculations called *date math*.

When you enter a date, it's unlikely that you'll know its serial number. You have to tell Quattro Pro that you are entering a date. Press the key combination **Ctrl-Shift-D**; then enter a date using a valid date format (see list of valid formats below). The cell will display the date you entered and the Input Line will contain the corresponding Julian date. What follows are some ways you can enter valid dates into Quattro Pro after pressing **Ctrl-Shift-D**.

30-Apr-93 (DD-MMM-YY)

30-Apr (DD-MMM)

Apr-93 (MMM-YY)

If the Clock Display is set to **International** in the Property>Application dialog box, these formats are valid:

05/04/92 (MM/DD/YY)

05/04 (MM/DD)

31.01.93 (DD.MM.YY)

31.01 (DD.MM)

31/01/93 (DD/MM/YY)

31/01 (DD/MM)

As you can see, many of these formats are simple variations on a single idea. You can abbreviate the month or use a month number. These are not the only ways to format dates in Quattro Pro just the ways in which dates can be *entered*. Chapter 5 explains how to access a subset of the date formats to change an existing date.

SHORTCUT

Presetting cells to accept only dates

You might find it inconvenient to use **Ctrl-Shift-D** each time you want to enter a date, so Quattro Pro lets you preset cells as date cells. After setting the cells with this option, you can then just type the date—Quattro Pro already knows that you are entering a date into the cell. To use this option, first highlight the desired cells and then right-click on the highlighted block. Now click on the **Data Entry Input** option in the Active Block properties that appear. Finally, choose **Dates Only** from the list of items provided. Press **OK** when finished.

Times are handled by Quattro Pro in much the same way dates are. A time entry is converted to a *time serial number,* which is a decimal fraction of a 24-hour period. Hence, the time 12:00 PM is expressed as the time serial number .5 indicating that one-half of the day is equal to 12:00 PM. The serial number will be a value from 0.000 - 0.99999. Quattro Pro uses military time (or 24-hour time) to determine whether the specified time is AM or PM when not specified. Here are some ways to enter times into Quattro Pro:

18:35 (displays 06:35 PM)

6:35 (displays 06:35 AM)

6:35:25 PM (displays 06:35:25 PM)

18:35:25 (displays 06:35:25 PM)

18.35.00 AM (displays 06.35.25 AM)

Entering dates and times

You can enter the current date and time with the function @NOW. Enter only the date with the @TODAY function. These functions enter the serial number for the date and time or current date, and can be formatted into either a date or a time or both. See Chapter 5 for details about formatting dates and times. Note that the @NOW and @TODAY functions are updated each time you open or calculate the notebook page. Hence, the date/time in the cell containing this function will be continually updated. This may be inappropriate for some applications. If you want the date/time to remain "frozen," use the **Edit>Copy** and **Edit>Paste Special>Values Only** commands to convert the function to its value. These commands are described in more detail later in this chapter.

Entering Formulas and Cell References

Formulas are an essential part of any spreadsheet task. The value of Quattro Pro is that it can perform calculations based on the data you enter. You can add these calculations to a notebook page through formulas that you enter into individual cells. A formula entered into cell D12, for example, might add the numbers in the range D5 through D11. Such a formula might look like this:

+D5+D6+D7+D8+D9+D10+D11

This formula begins with a plus sign and continues to list the cell references and mathematical operations for each cell. In this case, you're adding all the cells. The first plus sign is needed to tell Quattro Pro that you are entering a formula and not a text label. This is necessary in all formulas that do not begin with numeric values. The simplest of formulas might just be a cell reference:

+D5

This copies the value in cell D5 into the cell containing this formula. This formula can now be entered into any cell *except* cell D5. (If you enter it into cell D5, you'll get a "circular reference" error.)

Generally, formulas use cell references in their calculations; this makes the data variable. If you change the value in a referenced cell, the result of the formula changes to incorporate the new value. The cells being referenced can contain numbers or formulas of their own.

NOTE Pointing to cell references using the mouse or keyboard
You can enter a formula by typing the cell references or by pointing to the cell with the mouse or keyboard. This can be useful when you don't know the exact cell address because it's located out of view. Just type the plus sign; then click on the cell you want to reference. You also can type the plus sign and use the arrow keys to move to the cell you want to reference. Type the desired operator—plus or minus, for example—and click the next cell. When you finish, press **Enter**.

You can add *constant* values to your formulas—values that are not based on cell references—by simply typing them into the formula. For example, you can add 100 to the total of cells C3..C7 using a formula like this:

+C3+C4+C5+C6+C7+100

The value 100 is a constant value, whereas the others are variable and based on cell references. You can also calculate constant values, as in the formula (**125+13**), but this defeats some of the benefit of using a notebook page. Instead, enter these values into two cells and enter the formula using references to those cells. This way, you can change the values to recalculate the result. Here are some guidelines for using formulas:

- Start with a numeric value, or use a plus sign. If your formula begins with a number, you can just begin with that number. However, if it begins with a cell reference, you should start by typing a plus sign.

- Use mathematical operators for calculations. Between each pair of values or cell references, you must enter a mathematical operator to specify the operation to perform on the values. (Operators are discussed in the next section.)

- Use cell references (addresses or block names) or constant values. You can enter cell references in your formulas, provided those cells contain numeric values or formulas that produce numeric values. Whenever possible, use cell references rather than constant values; this makes the spreadsheet more flexible.

Operators for Your Formulas

Operators are symbols indicating the mathematical operation to be performed. Formulas in notebook pages can be very simple, containing only one operator, or very complex, containing both mathematical and logical operators. Quattro Pro uses four types of operators—arithmetic, relational, logical, and string.

Arithmetic operators are used to perform common operations such as addition and subtraction:

+	Addition
-	Subtraction
*	Multiplication

/   Division

^   Exponentiation

Relational and logical operators are used to examine the relationships between one or more values in a formula. Relational operators available in Quattro Pro are

<   Less than

>   Greater than

> =   Greater than or equal to

< =   Less than or equal to

< >   Not equal to

=   Equal to

Note that relational operators produce the values 0 or 1 to indicate whether the relationship is true (1) or false (0). For example, the formula **+A1>A2** asserts that cell A1 is greater than cell A2. If the two cells contain the values 5 and 6, respectively, then the result of the formula is false, or 0. In Chapter 6 you'll learn how you can use the @IF function to act on these relationship tests. Figure 3.2 shows an example of a formula using a relational operator.

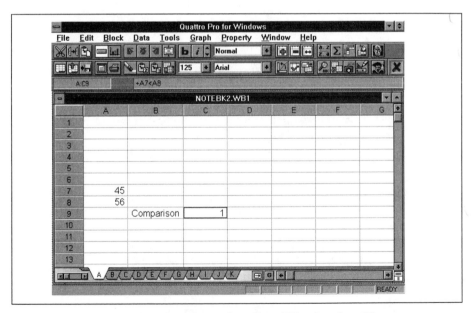

Figure 3.2 The value in the cell A7 (45) is less than 56.

NOTE

Using relational operators to compare text strings

When comparing two text strings, relational operators will compare the strings letter by letter, from left to right, until it finds two that differ. For example, the formula **+"Carolyn" < "Carmen"** is false. The first three letters are the same. The evaluation is made based on the fourth letters, *o* and *m*. The letter *o* does not precede the letter m in the alphabet; therefore, "Carolyn" is not less than "Carmen." Notice that when you use text in formulas, the text is surrounded by quotation marks.

There are three logical operators that add conditions to the relationships tested with relational operators. The logical operators are #NOT#, #AND#, and #OR#. Logical operators, because they work with relational operators, produce values of 1 (true) or 0 (false). The formula **+A7 = B5#AND# 7** will evaluate to true if the values in both A7 and B5 are 7. Should the value in either A7 or B5 be something other than 7, the formula will evaluate to false, and a 0 will be displayed in the cell containing the formula.

#NOT# represents logical negation. #NOT# can be used to determine whether a cell contains a value or is blank. **#NOT#A7** will return a value of 0 (false) when the cell A7 is blank and a 1 (true) when the cell contains a number, character, or other value.

Logical operators are commonly used in conditional statements. These are formulas that use the @IF function. (Refer to Chapter 6 for more information on the @IF function and how you can use the logical and relational operators in conjunction with @IF.)

The string operator is represented by **&** (an ampersand) and is used to concatenate text—to combine two pieces of text into one longer piece. The text can be located in cells or typed directly into the formula. In Figure 3.3 there is a database containing the names of salespersons and other information. The last and first names are in different cells. To combine them in a memo header, use the formula **+B5&" "&C5**. (The " " creates a space between the two parts of the formula. Otherwise, the text would appear as MarySmith.

Cells can be referenced by their addresses or block names. See Chapter 6 for more information on cell references.

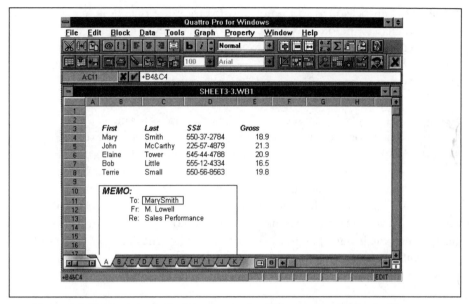

Figure 3.3 Text strings, including spaces, should be surrounded by double quotes.

Controlling the Order of Operation

When a formula contains more than one operator, the operations are performed in a special order that is determined by the precedence assigned to the operators. Operators with a higher precedence are evaluated before operators with a lower precedence. Operators that have the same precedence are evaluated from left to right. These are the Quattro Pro operators and the precedence assigned to them:

^	7
- + (negative, positive)	6
*/	5
+ - (addition, subtraction)	4
< < =	3
> > =	3
< >	3
#NOT#	2
#AND# #OR#	1
&	1

Parentheses can be added to formulas to override the operators' natural precedence and change the order in which the formula is evaluated. For example, the formula **+C5*(5+(12/2))** calculates to a very different answer when the parentheses are not present. When cell C5 contains the value 10, the formula calculates to 110 with the parentheses and 56 without them.

Matching parentheses help decipher complex formulas
When you type a long formula with a complex set of expressions, you might find Quattro Pro's matching parentheses feature useful. As you type parentheses in your formula, Quattro Pro indicates which opening and closing parentheses match each other by displaying them in a special color. Any open (unmatched) left parenthesis appears in a special color until you match it with the right parenthesis. As you complete the formula, you can quickly see which right parentheses are missing by checking the colors of the left parentheses.

Entering a Series of Values

Many spreadsheet applications require a series of cells to be entered with data that follows a pattern of some sort. A common example would be a budget requiring the months of the year to appear across the top row of the spreadsheet. Another might be section numbers running down the left-hand column. To make data entry of this kind less tedious, Quattro Pro provides the Block Fill operation, which lets you easily enter a series of numbers, years, months, dates, and times. Here's how to use Block Fill.

1. Select **Fill** from the Block menu. Figure 3.4 shows the dialog box that is displayed at this point.

2. Type in the coordinates of the cells in which the entries are to be made. If you highlight the cells before selecting **Block>Fill**, the highlighted range will already be referenced in the Block entry box.

3. Indicate a Start value—the first value to be entered in a cell. Type the start value in the space marked Start.

4. Type the Step value into the space marked Step. The Step value represents the interval between each entry in the series. This value can be a positive or negative number—negative numbers make the series extend backward. (Note that the Step value is closely associated with the series type specified in Step 7, below.)

5. Indicate a Stop value. This is the final value you want entered into your spreadsheet. The series will stop when it reaches the last cell in the block indicated, or the Stop value, whichever comes first. If you want the operation to continue for as many cells as possible, enter a Stop value of **999999**.

Stop, Start, and Step values can contain a variety of data
These three parameters need not be restricted to whole numbers. They can also contain dates, times, and formulas.

N O T E

6. Indicate the fill order. When the block to be filled contains several rows and columns, this becomes an important parameter. Selecting columns means the cells will be filled column by column. Selecting rows indicates that the cells are to be filled in row by row.

7. Indicate the type of series you want Quattro Pro to use. **Linear**, **Growth**, and **Power** are arithmetic series. **Year**, **Month**, **Week**, and **Weekday** are date series. The rest are time series.

8. Select **OK**.

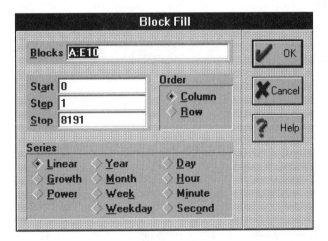

Figure 3.4 The Block>Fill command provides many varieties of sequences based on your input.

The Growth series multiplies each consecutive value by the Step, whereas the Power series creates exponential growth to the power indicated as the Step value. For example, a Growth of 1 would create the series 2, 4, 8, 16, 32 from a Start value of 2 and a Step value of 2. A Power of 2 would create the series 2, 4, 16, 256, 65536.

As a shortcut to entering a series of values, Quattro Pro provides the SpeedFill tool. This tool quickly creates a Linear series from your starting values. Just enter two or more starting values, such as **2** and **4** into adjacent cells. Next, highlight the starting values and any blank cells into which the series will continue. Now click on the **SpeedFill** tool, and the series is automatically continued. You can also use this tool to create a series of dates, month names, and day names.

You can also access the SpeedFill feature through the Active Block shortcut menu. Just highlight the starting values and blank cells, then right-click the selected block and choose the **SpeedFill** command. This is the same as clicking the SpeedFill button.

Cell and Sheet Protection

If your notebook will be used by anyone other than yourself, you might consider protecting your valuable data and formulas. Quattro Pro lets you prevent cells from being changed or edited—and even lets you protect the entire notebook from being accessed by unauthorized individuals. To protect a cell from being changed in any way, follow these steps.

1. Right-click on the cell you want to protect. You can also highlight a block of cells and right-click anywhere in the block to protect all the highlighted cells. Next, choose the **Block Properties** option. (You can also highlight the block and select the **Property>Current Object command**.)

2. Click on the **Protection** option in the left-hand list.

3. Click on **Protect** to mark the cell as protected or **Unprotect** to mark the cell as "changeable." Normally, all cells start out protected. Figure 3.5 shows the protected items in this dialog box.

4. Select **Property>Active Page** to view the page properties.

5. Click on the **Protection** option.

6. Click on **Enable** to activate—that is, to protect—all cells marked as protected. Click on **Disable** to allow protected cells to be changed. Protection starts out in the Disabled state so you can create your worksheet without having to unprotect each cell.

7. Click on **OK**.

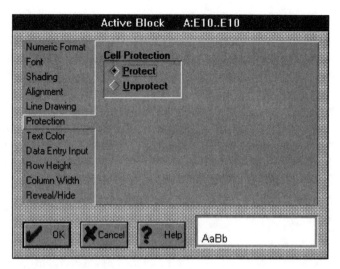

Figure 3.5 The Object Properties dialog box with the Protection options in view.

When you try to enter information into a protected cell while sheet protection is enabled, Quattro Pro will inform you that the cell is locked. You can unprotect all cells that the spreadsheet operator must fill out while leaving all other cells protected for safety.

Remember that all cells are protected by default, but pages are not. Therefore, if you simply turn **Page Protection** on, your entire worksheet will be protected. When you use the cell protection feature, you must unprotect the cells that you don't want locked before you turn **Page Protection** on. To unprotect the entire page, highlight all the cells on the page before you start these steps. (Selecting blocks and the entire page is described later in this chapter.)

Another form of protection is known as *data-entry restriction*, which helps ensure that data is entered properly into the cells of the notebook page. Quattro offers two types of data-entry restriction:

- The **Data>Restrict Input** command prevents the cell pointer from moving outside of a preestablished range. Just select the desired range; then choose **Data>Restrict Input**. The arrow keys will then be able to move the cell pointer only within the specified block. This is ideal for activating data input ranges. To restore normal operation, just press the **Esc** key.

* The **Properties>Current Object** command has an option for restricting input to labels or dates within a specified block. Select **Properties> Current Object** or right-click on the desired block. Now select the **Data Entry Input** option and choose the type of information you want entered into the highlighted range. Select **General** to allow any data to be entered. Selecting blocks is described later in this chapter.

A final type of protection offered by Quattro Pro is *notebook protection*. You can prohibit unauthorized people from opening a notebook in Quattro Pro by protecting the entire file. When you use the **File>Open** command to open the protected notebook file, Quattro Pro asks for the password. To protect a file, select the **File>Save As** command and enter a password into the Save File dialog box as shown in Figure 3.6. Note that only **#** symbols appear as you type the password; others are therefore prevented from viewing the password as you type it. You will be asked to enter the password again to confirm it. When you finally click on **OK**, Quattro Pro saves the notebook with the password protection active.

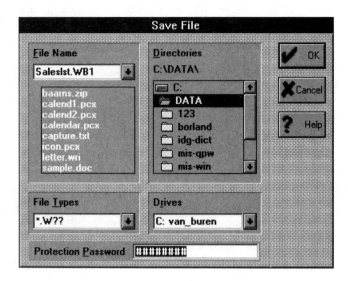

Figure 3.6 Entering a password into the Save File dialog box.

Moving within a Notebook Page

As you create applications in Quattro Pro, you'll find that you need to jump around the notebook page to position the cell pointer as you enter information. There are many tools available for moving around the page: You can use the mouse, a number of keyboard commands, or the **Goto** command. The following sections describe these features.

Moving with the Mouse

The mouse can be used to position the cell pointer in a visible cell or to scroll the page to make a cell visible. To move the cell pointer to any cell in the active page, click on the cell itself; the cell will become the active cell. If the desired cell is not visible, click on the vertical and/or horizontal scroll bars until it becomes available. This is ideal for making small jumps within the active window. For larger jumps, try using the **Edit>Goto** command, which is described later.

Moving with the Keyboard

It is sometimes easier to move from one cell to the next, or just a few cells away, with the keyboard rather than the mouse. For short hops from one cell to the next, the arrow keys are very effective. Pressing one of the arrow keys moves the cell pointer one cell in the direction of the arrow.

Special keys and key combinations make it easy to move quickly around the entire page. When the **Home** key is pressed, for example, the cell pointer moves to cell A1 of the active page. Pressing the **Page Down** key scrolls the display down to the next screen.

The display can also be scrolled from left to right. Both the **Tab** key and the **Ctrl-Right Arrow** key combination will move the display one screen to the right. The column now appearing first on the screen will depend on the active page's column-width settings and the number of columns being displayed. To shift the display one entire screen to the left, use **Shift-Tab** or **Ctrl-Left Arrow**. Table 3.1 summarizes these movement commands.

Table 3.1 The keyboard movement commands.

Key	Moves
Arrow	One cell in the direction of the arrow
Ctrl-Right Arrow (or **Tab**)	One screen to the right
Ctrl-Left Arrow (or **Shift-Tab**)	One screen to the left
PgDn	One screen down
PgUp	One screen up
Ctrl-PgDn	To the next notebook page (see Chapter 4)
Ctrl-PgUp	To the previous notebook page (see Chapter 4)
Home	To cell A1

Moving with Find and Goto

There will be times when you know exactly where you want to position the cell pointer, either by location or by cell content. Rather than using the cursor keys or mouse to scroll around the active page, you can move the cell pointer directly to the new location. The two functions provided for this purpose are Goto and Find.

Using Goto

To move directly to a cell address or block name, use the Goto feature. The Goto feature can be accessed in two ways: by pressing the **F5** key or by selecting the **Edit>Goto** command. Figure 3.7 shows the dialog box that appears regardless of the method used.

When the dialog box appears, either type in a cell address in the reference edit box or select a block name from the Block Names list box. (Block names will appear in the list if you have named any cells or blocks on the worksheet. Refer to Chapter 6 for more information about naming cells and ranges.) Note that you can enter any cell reference or block reference into the Goto dialog box. Any cell on the current page can be specified by typing its address (for example, **G12**); you can also specify a range on the current page by entering the entire range reference (for example, **G12..G15**). To specify a cell or range on a different page, just precede the reference with the page name (for example, **D:G12**). You can quickly jump to cell A1 of any page by double-clicking on the page reference in the Pages list of the Goto dialog box. For more information on cell and range references refer to Chapter 6.

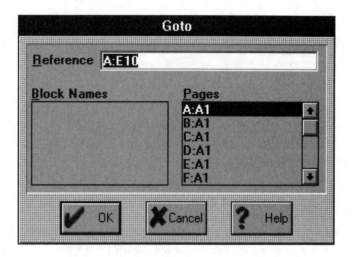

Figure 3.7 The Goto dialog box initially references the current location of the cell pointer.

Using Find

To find a string of characters or numbers on an active page, use the **Search and Replace** function found in the Edit menu. This command lets you locate any data in the worksheet—whether it is part of a formula, the result of a formula, or just a text entry.

1. Highlight any part of the active page to search within the highlighted area. If you want to search the entire page, just highlight one cell.

2. Select the **Edit>Search and Replace** command. Figure 3.8 shows the Search/Replace dialog box that appears. The Search/Replace dialog box shows you the current block(s), the area or areas you highlighted prior to selecting the **Search and Replace** function. If you highlighted only one cell, Quattro Pro leaves this area blank to indicate that the entire worksheet will be searched. You can change the block specification if you're not satisfied

with it; just type a new range reference into the Block(s) entry box or point to the range on the notebook page using the mouse. (You might have to move the Search/Replace dialog box aside to access the worksheet.)

3. Place the cursor in the Find edit box and enter the number, text, or conditional statement you wish to find.

4. Select the appropriate Look In option. Selecting **Formula** tells Quattro Pro to search for your specified data in cells that contain formulas. Selecting **Value** tells Quattro Pro to ignore formulas in cells and examine only the values displayed in the cells. Selecting **Condition** tells Quattro Pro that you have entered a conditional statement as the Find criterion. (A conditional statement is one that begins with a relational operator. For example, the entry **A1>100** searches for all cells containing values greater than 100, beginning at cell A1.)

5. Indicate the search direction. Select **Row** to perform the search row by row, left to right. Select **Column** to perform the search column by column, left to right, top to bottom.

6. Indicate whether the search should locate those parts of character sets that match or only whole character sets. Let's say the Find criterion is "ate." If Match is set to **Part**, the search operation would find occurrences such as "material." If Match is set to **Whole**, only the word "ate" would be found.

Restrictions when setting Match to Whole

If the Find criterion is a text string and Match is set to **Whole**, Quattro Pro will not find the text unless you precede the entry with the appropriate label prefix or set Look In to **Value**. For example, to find the word *Widget*, you should enter '**Widget** when Look In is set to **Formula**.

7. Indicate whether the search should be case sensitive. If the Find criterion entered is **"United States"** and Case is set to **Any**, Quattro Pro will find occurrences of "United States," "UNITED STATES," "united states," or any other combination of upper- and lowercase letters. When Case is set to **Exact**, Quattro will find only the exact match—"United States."

8. Select **Next**. The cell pointer will be located in the first cell that is found to contain the specified criterion. Click on **Next** again to find the next occurrence, or click on **Cancel** to end the operation.

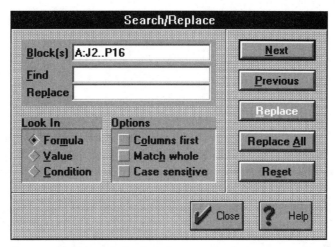

Figure 3.8 The Search/Replace dialog box showing you the active search area, or Block(s).

Selecting Cells and Blocks

Selecting or highlighting cells and blocks is an essential part of using Quattro Pro. Often before you can apply commands to your data, you must first select the data. By selecting the cell or block before choosing the command, Quattro Pro is able to apply the selected feature to the block you've specified. You'll find that selecting cells is critical for operations like formatting and graphing. The following sections describe various ways to select cells and blocks in Quattro Pro.

Selecting with the Mouse

The mouse can be used to highlight an entire column, row, page, or group of cells. You'll find the mouse offers the easiest way to select blocks in your notebooks. Here are several mouse-oriented methods.

Selecting Blocks

To highlight a block of cells, move the mouse pointer to a cell at one of the four corners of the block. Click the left button and move the mouse down, up, left, or right, until the desired cells are highlighted. Now release the button. The cells that have been selected will be in reverse video. An alternative method would be to follow these steps.

1. Select a corner cell with the mouse pointer.

2. Hold down the **Shift** key.

3. Move the mouse pointer to another corner of the block.

4. Click the left mouse button.

Selecting Multiple Blocks

To highlight multiple noncontiguous blocks of cells, start by following the directions for highlighting a single block of cells; then press the **Ctrl** key and repeat the process to highlight a second block. With the **Ctrl** key pressed, your second block selection does not replace the first; it is added to it. Continue this process to highlight as many blocks as you want. Figure 3.9 shows a page with several blocks highlighted.

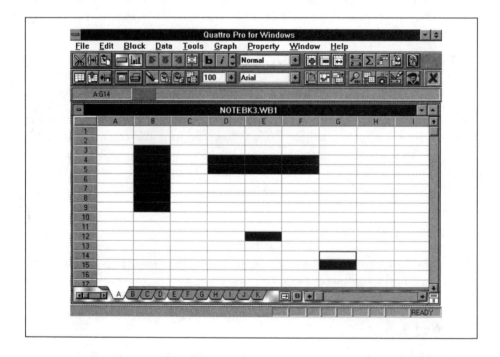

Figure 3.9 Highlight several blocks with the mouse by using the Ctrl key as you drag on the worksheet.

What does a multiple block reference look like?

You can enter a multiple block reference whenever Quattro Pro expects a block reference. Simply type in each block reference and separate them with commas. The reference shown in Figure 3.9 would be entered as **B3..B9,D4..F5,E12..E12,G14..G16**.

Selecting Rows and Columns

Each active page is framed with column and row indicators. Columns are labeled with letters; rows, with numbers. To highlight a column as shown in Figure 3.10, position the mouse pointer so it points to the column letter and click the left mouse button.

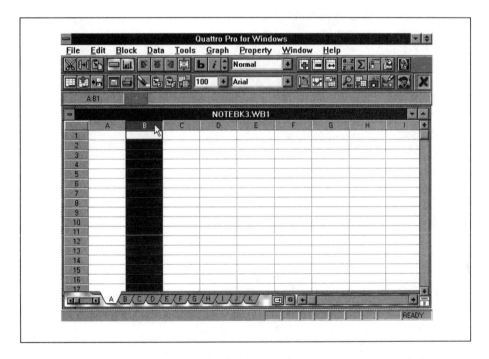

Figure 3.10 The entire column was selected by using the mouse to click on the column's heading.

Selecting an entire row is equally easy. Position the mouse so it points to the number of the row to be highlight. Now click the left mouse button. You can select several rows or columns by dragging the mouse across the row or column headings. Select noncontiguous rows or columns by holding the **Ctrl** key down as you click on each heading. Figure 3.11 shows an example of multiple rows and columns selected.

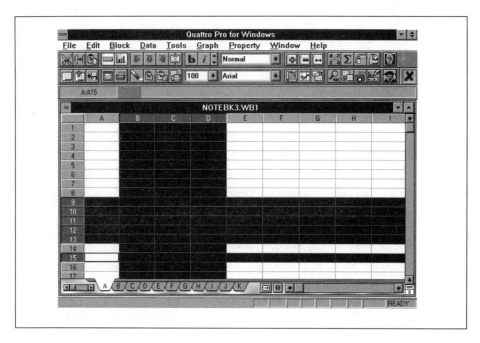

*Figure 3.11 Highlight multiple rows and columns using Ctrl as you click
and drag on the headings.*

Selecting an Entire Page

To highlight an entire page, click on the rectangular button at the intersection of the row and column headings. This falls to the left of column heading A and above row heading 1. To deselect the page, move the mouse pointer to any cell on the active page and press the left mouse button.

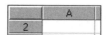

Selecting with the Keyboard

Some keys on the keyboard can be used to highlight areas of the active page. To highlight multiple cells, first place the cell pointer at one end of the block of cells to be highlighted. To highlight the rest of the cells, press the **Shift** key along with the appropriate cursor key. You can also highlight a group of cells using the **Shift** with **PgDn**, **PgUp**, **Ctrl-Arrows**, and **Home**. Adding **Shift** to these pointer movement keystrokes will highlight as you move. Experiment to see how these commands work.

The keyboard can also be used to highlight noncontiguous blocks when it is in Point mode. To do so, highlight the first block using the **Shift**-*cursor key* combination. Now press **Shift-F8** and select another block with the keyboard commands.

Selecting with the Goto Command

Finally, you can select cells and blocks by using the **Goto** command. If you choose **Edit>Goto** and enter a cell or block name into the Goto dialog box, the cell or block will be selected as soon as you click **OK**. You can also use the **Goto** command to select a block of cells when you don't know the exact block reference. Just highlight the first cell in the block (for example, the upper-left corner); then choose **Edit>Goto** and enter the address (reference) of the last cell in the block (the opposite corner). Finally, hold the **Shift** key down as you click on the **OK** button in the Goto dialog box. This moves to the cell you specified while highlighting from the current location.

Editing Data

After you enter data onto the worksheet, you'll probably find several cells that need editing. Perhaps you want to update information or correct a mistake. Quattro Pro offers several editing tools. You can edit your entries by retyping them or by modifying individual portions of the entry using the Input Line.

In addition to changing a particular entry, you can also edit the notebook itself. For example, you can delete data completely or even remove cells from the notebook. Likewise, you can insert new cells into the notebook to make extra space for new data. If you want to rearrange the data, Quattro Pro lets you copy and move the existing data using convenient mouse actions or menu commands. The following sections explain the details.

Retyping Entries

To replace the contents of a cell or group of cells, position your cell pointer on the cell to be replaced; now type in the new contents. The new entry completely replaces the old one. Should you wish to replace a larger group of cells with a smaller group of cells, delete the contents of the cells first. (Deleting entries is discussed later in this chapter.)

You might not always want to replace an entry completely, just edit the existing data. This is much more convenient when you have long entries or complex formulas that require editing. The next section shows you how to edit portions of an entry.

Editing Entries

The ability to edit the contents of a cell allows you to add, delete, or change characters in a cell without retyping the entire entry. To edit a cell, you must first enter Edit mode. Move to the cell you want to edit, then press the F2 key. This places the cursor on the Input Line. You also can click on the Input Line with the mouse, and the cursor will appear as seen in Figure 3.12.

Navigating the Input Line

When you enter Edit mode, your cursor will be at the end of the cell entry. To move the cursor to the beginning of the entry, press **Home**. To move the cursor back to the end of the entry, press **End**. To move the cursor one character at a time, use the right and left cursor keys. Between these two extremes exists the ability to move the cursor five spaces at a time. To move five spaces to the right, use the **Tab** key or **Ctrl-Right Arrow**. To move five spaces to the left, use the **Shift-Tab** key or **Ctrl-Left Arrow**. You can also move the cursor within the Input Line by clicking where you want the cursor to be.

Deleting Data from the Input Line

There are several ways to delete characters while in Edit mode: **Backspace**, **Delete**, and **Ctrl-Backspace**. The Delete and the Backspace will erase one character at a time. To use either key, position the cursor to the right of the character to be deleted. Then press the **Delete** or **Backspace** key. The character will be gone, and the cursor will have moved one space to the left.

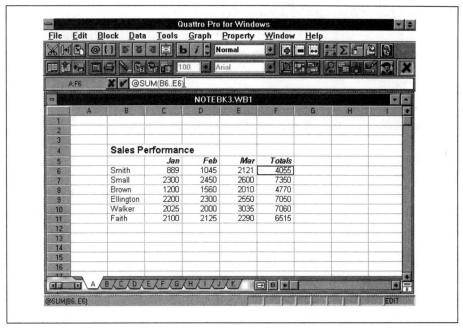

Figure 3.12 Click on the Input Line or press F2 to place the cursor there for editing.

You can also use the mouse to select several characters before using the **Delete** or **Backspace** keys to delete. Here's how.

1. Position the mouse pointer at the beginning of the characters to be deleted.

2. Click the left button and drag to highlight as many characters as you like.

3. Press the **Delete** or **Backspace** key to remove the data.

Double-click to highlight a whole word

If you double-click on any word in the Input Line, Quattro Pro highlights the entire word. This could be a useful shortcut when you edit. You can also remove characters using the keyboard. Instead of highlighting the characters with the mouse, press the **Shift** key while you use any of the navigation keys on the Input Line. For example, **Shift-Right Arrow** highlights characters to the right; **Shift-Ctrl-Left Arrow** highlights one word to the left. The **Ctrl-Backspace** combination is a quick way to delete all the characters on the Input Line at once. The cursor can be positioned anywhere on the Input Line when this key combination is activated.

Adding Characters to the Cell Entry

To insert characters into an existing cell entry, start by placing the cursor where the new character(s) should be inserted. Now all you have to do is type in the additional letters and/or numbers.

Exiting Edit Mode

After you have changed the cell entry, you can exit Edit mode and register your changes in the cell, or you can return to Ready mode leaving the original contents of the cell intact. To exit Edit mode without changing the contents of the cell, press **Esc** or click on the **X Tool** to the left of the Input Line. The simplest way to exit and save your changes is to press **Enter** or click on the **Check Tool** to the left of the Input Line. Besides pressing **Enter**, you can use any of the pointer movement commands to accept the changes and move the pointer. For example, pressing the **Right Arrow** key exits the Edit mode, accepts your changes, and moves the cell pointer up one cell.

Converting Formulas to Values

Quattro Pro provides a special editing tool for dealing with formulas. Pressing the **F9** key calculates the formula currently on the Input Line and displays the results. This is an excellent way to convert a formula into its value. Just press **F2** to enter the Edit mode; then press **F9** and **Enter** to convert the formula.

Another way to convert a formula into its value is to copy the formula using the **Edit>Copy** command and then paste the formula back onto the page using the **Edit>Paste Special** command. Select the **Values Only** option from the Paste Special dialog box that appears.

Editing with Search and Replace

Quattro Pro lets you change a particular piece of data that appears throughout a workbook page. You can change all occurrences of "XYZ" to "ABC" with one simple procedure. The **Search and Replace** procedure was introduced earlier in this chapter when we discussed "Moving with Find and Goto." After choosing the **Edit>Search and Replace** command to get the Search/Replace dialog box, we filled in our search criteria but left the Replace With edit box empty. Now we will fill it in with a set of replacement characters. This way, Quattro Pro will find the information we specify and then replace it with the replacement entry we specify. After we indicate all our Find criteria, we are ready to activate the replacement operation. Refer to "Using Find" earlier in this chapter for more details.

Correcting Spelling Errors

Quattro Pro's new spelling checker lets you edit spelling errors in your notebooks and make corrections to individual entries or the entire notebook at once. You'll find the spelling checker a quick and easy way to double-check your worksheets for mistakes. Here's how to use the spelling checker.

1. Highlight the block of cells containing the information you want to check. If you want to check the entire notebook, then highlight only one cell. The spelling checker will begin at the cell you specify and return to the beginning of the page to complete any other entries. It will then move to the next page.

2. Click on the **Spelling Checker** tool on the SpeedBar. The Spelling Checker SpeedBar appears on the screen as Figure 3.13 shows. (Note that you can remove the SpeedBar and quit the spell checking session at any time by clicking on the **Close SpeedBar** button on the far right of the SpeedBar.)

3. Click on the **Start** button on the far left side of the SpeedBar. This will start the session, and Quattro Pro will locate the first misspelled word and place it into the Misspelled entry box in the SpeedBar as shown by the word "speling" in Figure 3.13.

4. Suggested words will appear in the Suggest drop-down list. You may choose from any of the suggested words by clicking on the word in the list. If you don't find a suitable suggestion to the misspelled word, simply enter the desired word into the Suggest entry box yourself.

5. Click on the **Change** button to replace the misspelled word with the word in the Suggest entry box. The spelling checker now moves to the next misspelled word.

You may not always want to correct or change the located word. Often, perfectly correct words are located by the spelling checker because they do not appear in the dictionary. You can skip these words or add them to the dictionary. Following is a summary of the spelling checker controls and options.

Figure 3.13 The Spelling Checker SpeedBar contains all spell checking commands and options.

Start/Stop   At any time you can press the **Stop** button to end the session. This turns into the **Start** button between sessions.

Suggest   This entry box displays all suggested words for the misspelled word. If no suggestions appear, then Quattro Pro cannot find a suitable replacement. You may type any corrections into this entry box or select from the suggested words. When you click on **Change**, the information in this box replaces the misspelled word

Change   Use the **Change** button to replace the misspelled word with the word inside the Suggest edit box.

Change All   Use the **Change All** button to replace all future occurrences of this word with the word inside the Suggest edit box. Future occurrences apply to this spell checking session only. When you stop this session, your Change All choices are reset to normal.

Skip   Use this button to skip a correctly spelled word that was flagged as misspelled by Quattro Pro. This is useful for names and other words that you don't want to add to the dictionary.

Skip All   Use this button to skip all future occurrences of the word in question—so you will not encounter it again in this session.

Add   This button adds the word to the current user dictionary. If Quattro Pro flags a word that is correct, you can add it to the dictionary so you will not encounter it again in this or any other notebook. When you use this option, you permanently add words to the dictionary, so be sure that you are adding correct words.

This is useful for creating specialized dictionaries, such as legal and medical words. (See Options below for more information.)

Close

This button closes the Spelling Checker SpeedBar to end your session completely.

Options

This button presents a list of spelling checker options that you can select. The options appear in Figure 3.14 and provide a list of items that Quattro Pro can ignore while locating misspelled words. For example, you might find it useful to ignore words in all UPPER-CASE letters, since these might be macro commands. Click to place a check mark beside any option you want to activate in this list. Another option in this dialog box is the ability to choose a different user dictionary. If you have a different dictionary, you can activate it by clicking on the **Choose New Dictionary** button and locating the dictionary on disk. The **Remove Current Dictionary** button clears the current dictionary from this session of the spelling checker, but it does not'delete the dictionary from the disk.

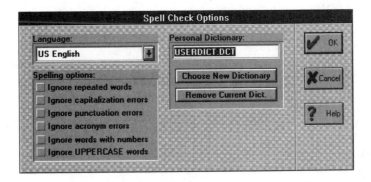

Figure 3.14   The spelling checker options.

Note that you can use the worksheet normally while the Spelling Checker SpeedBar is active—even in the middle of a spell-checking session.

Deleting Entries

Sometimes it is necessary to erase the contents of a cell or group of cells. Quattro Pro allows you to do this by using either the mouse or keyboard or through menu commands. The menu commands are found on the Edit menu and in the block shortcut menu (right-click on the active block). They are **Cut**, **Clear**, and **Clear Contents**.

- **Cut** Erases the contents of the highlighted cells and places a copy on the Clipboard. The shortcut for this command is **Ctrl-X**.

- **Clear** Erases the contents of the highlighted cells and resets the properties of each cell in the block to "Normal Style."

- **Clear Contents** Erases the contents of the highlighted cells, but the properties of the cells remain unchanged. For example, if the alignment is set to **Center**, new entries made to these cells will automatically be centered.

When using these commands, highlight the block to be deleted prior to accessing the command in the Edit menu.

You can also delete the contents of a cell or block of cells by simply highlighting them and pressing the **Delete** key. The contents of the cell(s) will not be placed on the Clipboard.

Finally, you can cut data from the page by using the SpeedBar's **Cut** button. After you highlight a cell or block of cells, use the mouse to click on the **scissors** icon. The contents of the cell(s) will disappear, and a copy will be placed on the Clipboard.

 Use the Shift-Delete key combination to cut blocks to the Clipboard. The **Shift-Delete** key combination is a common way to erase data from the work surface and copy it to the Clipboard. Using this key combination along with **Shift-Ins (Paste)** will make it easier for you to move data from application to application or within a page. In short, **Shift-Delete** works just like **Delete**, but it also copies the data to the Clipboard where you can paste it into another area or application.

Recalling deleted text

If you delete something by mistake, you can retrieve it by using the **Edit Undo** command. If you have used the **Cut** command, you can also retrieve the cell contents with the **Paste** command—but be sure to paste right away!

Inserting and Deleting Cells, Rows, and Columns

It is possible to insert and delete entire or partial rows and columns anywhere on the active page. When deleting cells, you should first highlight the block, row, or column that you want to remove and then use the **Block>Delete** command. When inserting cells, you should first highlight the area into which the new cells are to appear. These are the cells that will be moved to make room for the inserted cells.

To insert cells, highlight the block where you want to place the new cells. This block should indicate exactly how many cells you want to insert. Now click on the **Block Insert** button located on the SpeedBar. Figure 3.15 shows the Insert dialog box that appears. An alternative method would be to use the **Block>Insert** command.

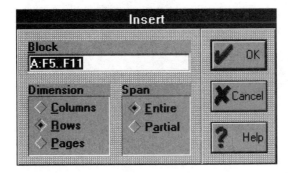

Figure 3.15 Highlight the desired block; then click on the Block Insert tool.

Inserting partial rows or columns really means inserting a groups of cells above a highlighted block or to the left of a highlighted block. Select the **Columns** dimension to insert the new cells and push existing information to the right.

Select the **Rows** dimension to insert the new cells and push the existing information down. The **Entire** option inserts entire rows or columns; the **Partial** option inserts only the number of rows or columns indicated by your highlighted block.

Figure 3.16 shows a page with three cells in row 5 highlighted. The result of a Partial Row Insert operation is shown in Figure 3.17. In this case, the **Entire** option should have been used so that the names in column B moved down with the rest of the columns. If you highlight an entire row or column before using the **Block Insert** tool, Quattro Pro assumes you want to insert the entire row or column and completes the procedure for you. Note that deleting rows and columns presents the same options and is handled in the same way. Just click on the **Block Delete** tool in the SpeedBar (to the right of the **Block Insert** tool) to delete rather than insert. Similarly, you can use the **Block>Delete** command.

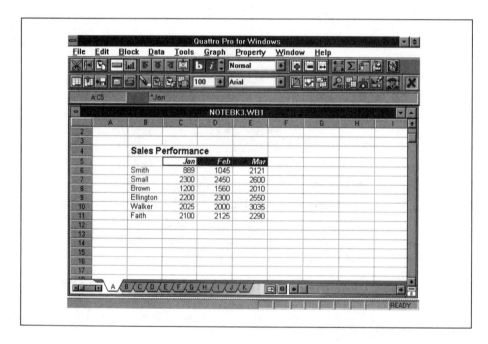

Figure 3.16 The new cells are inserted, and all the data has shifted one row down.

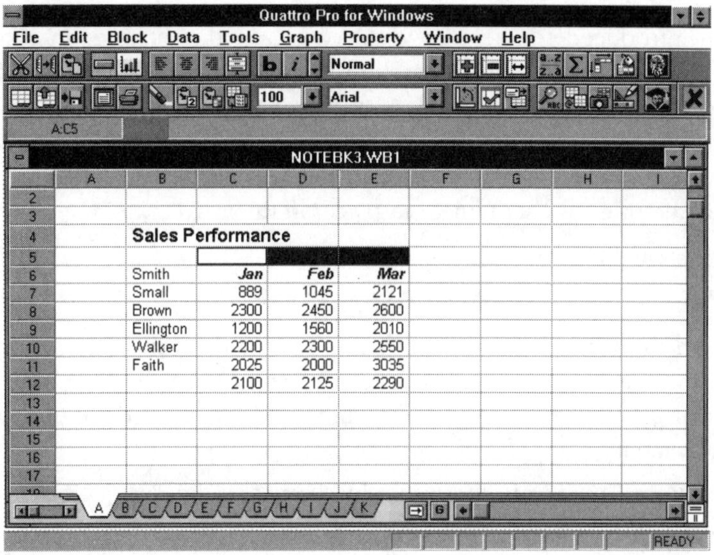

Figure 3.17 *The new cells are inserted, and all the data has shifted one column down.*

Quattro Pro takes care of your cell and range references

When you insert or delete cells from a page, Quattro Pro automatically adjusts any cell or range references affected by the change. You need not worry about your formulas. However, if a formula references a cell that you have deleted, then that formula will produce an error.

Moving and Copying Data

Moving and copying data to new locations are very common operations in electronic spreadsheets. Quattro Pro provides several methods for accomplishing these operations, each suited to different types of data. You can use the **Cut**, **Copy**, and **Paste** commands in the Edit menu, the new drag-and-drop features, or the **Move** and **Copy** commands in the Block menu.

Moving and copying formulas

Special considerations exist about the resulting cell references when you move or copy formulas. For information about these considerations, refer to Chapter 6.

Using the Cut, Copy, and Paste Commands

You were introduced to the Clipboard earlier in this chapter in the section "Deleting Entries." Using the Clipboard to move data means deleting it from the active page and then pasting it back on the active page in a new location. When you delete the data, Quattro Pro automatically places it onto the Clipboard, which is a temporary storage location for the data. Copying data is similar, except that the original data remain in place on the active page.

To move or copy data:

1. Highlight the data to be moved or copied.

2. Click on the **Copy** button to copy the data or the **Cut** button to move the data. These are the first and second buttons in the SpeedBar. Alternatively, you can select the **Copy** or **Cut** commands in the Edit menu or Block Shortcut menu.

3. Move the cell pointer to the upper-left corner of the destination block. This location can be on the active page, a different page, a new notebook, or even a different program. You can also paste data into the Input Line by pressing **F2** then using the **Paste** command.

4. Click on the **Paste** button, which is third from the left. This pastes the data into the location you specified. You can also use the **Edit>Paste** command.

Using Drag and Drop

A quick and easy method for moving and copying data is to use the drag-and-drop technique. This is a mouse-only technique that makes copying and moving data within a page easy. Follow these steps.

1. Select a block to be copied or moved.

2. To move the block, place the mouse pointer anywhere on the highlighted block and hold down the left mouse button. A hand symbol and a block outline should appear. To copy the block, hold down the **Ctrl** key prior to clicking on the block.

3. By moving the mouse, you will be able to drag the block to a new location. Figure 3.18 illustrates this procedure.

4. Release the mouse button. The block will drop in place.

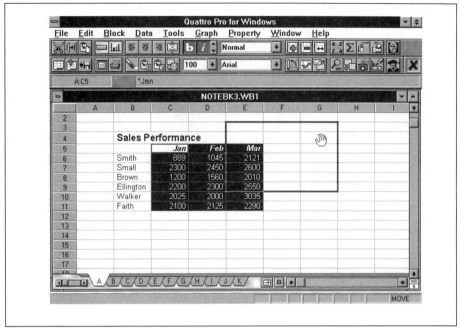

Figure 3.18 A highlighted block with its new location represented by the block outline.

WARNING

Copying and moving noncontiguous blocks

The drag-and-drop method can't be used with noncontiguous blocks. Noncontiguous blocks should be copied or moved using the Clipboard commands.

Using Block Commands

Block>Move and **Block>Copy** are menu commands that let you move and copy blocks of cells. When you select one of these commands, you will see a dialog box. The dialog box requires a From location and a To location; the From location defaults to the currently selected block, but you can change it if desired. Enter any To location on this or any other page of the notebook.

The advantages of the Block commands over the equivalent SpeedBar tools is that you can specify blocks by name, use either contiguous or noncontiguous blocks, and use references to any block on any notebook page. (There is more discussion of cell and range references in Chapter 6, as well as information about naming blocks.) Plus, the **Block>Copy** command includes the flexible

Model Copy options, which let you specify exactly which part of the information you want to copy: You can copy just the formulas, just the formats, just the objects that appear in those cells, or any combination of these items. Following is a description of the Model Copy options:

- **Formula Cells** Copies only cells in the highlighted block that contain formulas—skipping any text entries, dates, or value cells.

- **Value Cells** Copies only cells in the highlighted block that contain values—skipping any formulas. Text and dates are considered values.

- **Properties** Copies all properties applied to the cells. You can see and select properties by right-clicking the cell or block. By copying properties, you can reapply an entire set of cell properties to another cell instantly.

- **Objects** Copies any objects floating above the selected cells.

- **Row/Column Sizes** Copies the sizes of rows and columns to the destination location.

Select or remove any of these options that apply to your selection. Normally, all items are selected, so you might want to remove some items that don't apply—after clicking on the **Model Copy** option.

Summary

This chapter explained how to enter and edit data in Quattro Pro and detailed the fundamentals of starting your own notebooks and setting them up to calculate data. Remember that there are basically four types of data: numbers, text labels, dates, and formulas. Dates can be entered only after you press **Shift-Ctrl-D**. Formulas require that you consider mathematical operators and the use of cell and range references. More information about using formulas appears in Chapter 6.

Quattro Pro gives you several editing commands. You can edit any cell by moving to that cell and pressing **F2**. The easiest way to move or copy data is to use the drag-and-drop technique: Highlight the data; then click and drag on the highlighted block. Finally, you can insert and delete cells on the active page by using the **Block Insert** and **Block Delete** tools on the SpeedBar.

The next chapter tells you how to use and organize several pages in a notebook.

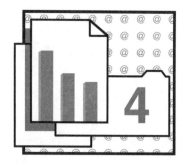

Notebooks and the Quattro Pro Environment

Unlike some spreadsheet programs, Quattro Pro for Windows does not present you with individual worksheets for your applications. Quattro Pro provides notebooks for your applications instead. A notebook is a collection of 256 individual worksheet pages that work together to form a large application. Use as many of these notebook pages as you like.

This chapter explains how to get around in a notebook. You'll learn about

- Moving among notebook pages
- Controlling the overall notebook environment
- Naming pages
- Making changes to several pages at once
- Splitting the Notebook window into two panes
- Adding extra Window views to a notebook
- Locking page titles into place
- Removing grid lines from the page
- Adding extra SpeedBars provided by Quattro Pro
- Protecting data from accidental changes
- Working with SpeedBars

Understanding Notebook Pages

When you first start Quattro Pro, you are given a new, blank notebook into which you can type your data. All new notebooks consist of 256 blank pages. You can enter data onto any or all of these pages—you'll probably find that the first several pages are the most convenient to access. For example, you might enter an employee list on one page and payroll calculations on another page of the same notebook. This way, your employee database is always available when you calculate payroll. However, you would not want to add your bowling statistics to the same notebook since it has no relationship to the employee information. Use a fresh notebook for this application.

The key is to use pages for holding different parts of the same application. Use separate notebooks for separate applications. As you saw in Chapter 2, you can open a new, blank notebook by using the **File>New** command.

The next few sections in this chapter explain how to manipulate notebook pages. When you get familiar with using multiple pages, you'll be able to create some powerful applications in Quattro Pro.

Moving Among Pages

You probably won't need all 256 separate notebook pages that Quattro Pro gives you. You might decide that you need no more than two or three pages to hold your data. If you require several pages, you'll need to know how to move among them easily and efficiently at any time.

Each individual workbook page has a tab at the bottom of the screen. By clicking on a tab, you can quickly bring that page to the top of the notebook. To the left of the tabs is the Tab Scroller, which lets you view page tabs that do not initially fit on the screen:

To the right of the tabs is the Turbo Tab button:

The page tabs, Tab Scroller, and Turbo Tab button are tools that make it easy for you to move from page to page using the mouse. You can also move from page to page using keyboard commands and the Goto feature.

Switching Pages with the Mouse

The fastest way to bring a page into view is to click on its tab. (When a page is placed on top, the tab will be the same color as the page.) Bringing a page to the top does not, however, shift all the pages in the notebook to the left, making the top page the first page. At first, a notebook shows page A as the active page, with the tabs for pages B through K to the right. Now look at Figure 4.1. Page D is now the active page. Even though it has been moved to the top, the page tabs for pages A through C are still visible to the left.

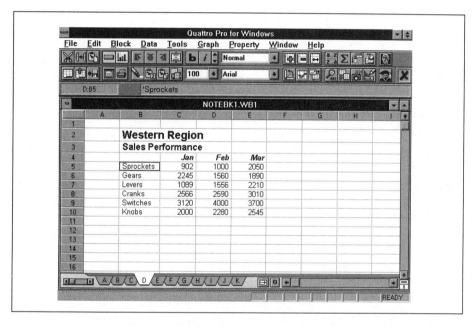

Figure 4.1 The active page (D), with three tabs for pages A, B, and C still visible on the left.

It is obviously not possible to view all 256 page tabs at one time. To bring page tabs into view so they can be selected with the mouse, use the Tab Scroller. The Tab Scroller works like any scroll bar; it contains two directional arrows and an elevator box. Initially the elevator is all the way over to the left of the scroll bar. To scroll the notebook to the right and view additional page tabs, click on the right arrow of the Tab Scroller; this moves the elevator to the right. To move quickly through the tabs, you can click on the scroll bar between the elevator and the arrow or drag the elevator to the right. As you move through the tabs this way, those on the left will scroll out of view to make room for new tabs on the right. After you make a page tab visible, activate the page by clicking on its tab.

Switching Pages with the Turbo Tab Button

The Turbo Tab button allows you to move quickly between the active page and the last page of the notebook, the Graph page. If you click on the **Turbo Tab** button when the arrow points right, Excel takes you to the Graph page. At this point, the arrow on the Turbo Tab button points in the opposite direction, indicating that the button will now take you back to the active page. Note that the active page can be any of the 256 pages that are currently "on top" of the notebook. Scrolling through the tabs does not change the active page until you click on a page tab.

Switching Pages with the Keyboard

Quattro Pro provides two keystroke combinations for moving between pages— **Ctrl-PgDn** and **Ctrl-PgUp**. Pressing **Ctrl-PgDn** activates the next page in the notebook. If page D is the active page, for example, pressing **Ctrl-PgDn** makes E the active page. Pressing **Ctrl-PgUp** activates the previous page.

Using Shift with Ctrl-PgDn or Ctrl-PgUp to select pages

If you hold the **Shift** key down as you press **Ctrl-PgUp** or **Ctrl-PgDn**, you will be selecting those pages over which you are moving. This is a useful method for performing an operation on multiple pages at the same time—an action known as "group mode." You can also select multiple pages by holding the **Shift** key down as you click on a page tab. All pages between the active page and the page you select will be selected as shown by the underline beneath the tabs:

Switching Pages with the Goto Command (F5)

In Chapter 3, you saw how to move around a page quickly by using the **F5** (Goto) function key or the **Edit>Goto** command. The **Goto** command also moves between pages. When you press **F5**, the dialog box in Figure 4.2 is displayed. The highlighted reference is the current page and cell where the cell pointer is located. In the figure, the reference is A:A1. To move to another page, double-click on the page reference in the Pages list of the Goto dialog box. This moves you to cell A1 of that page when you click on **OK**. You can also type the page reference along with a cell reference into the entry box, as in **C:B4**. If you had changed your page name to "January" using the method described below, you might move to that page by typing **January:A1** as the reference for the **Goto** command.

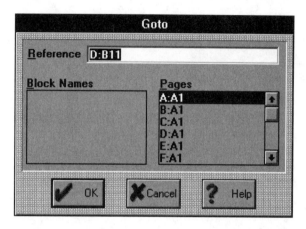

Figure 4.2 The Goto dialog box.

Naming Pages

Quattro Pro begins by using alphabetical names for the page tabs—starting with A through Z, then AA through AZ, then BA through BZ, and so on. With the exception of the Graph page, you are free to change the name of any page. Here's how:

1. Right-click on the page tab to be changed. You might have to use the Tab Scroller to get the desired tab into view. Alternatively, you can activate the desired page; then use the **Property>Active Page** command. Either way, you see the dialog box in Figure 4.3.

2. Type in the name you wish to give the page. Your new name should replace the letter name in the Page Name entry box.

3. Click on **OK**. Quattro Pro will update the page tab with the name you've just entered. Figure 4.4 shows some named pages.

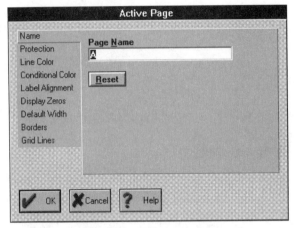

Figure 4.3 The Active Page dialog box.

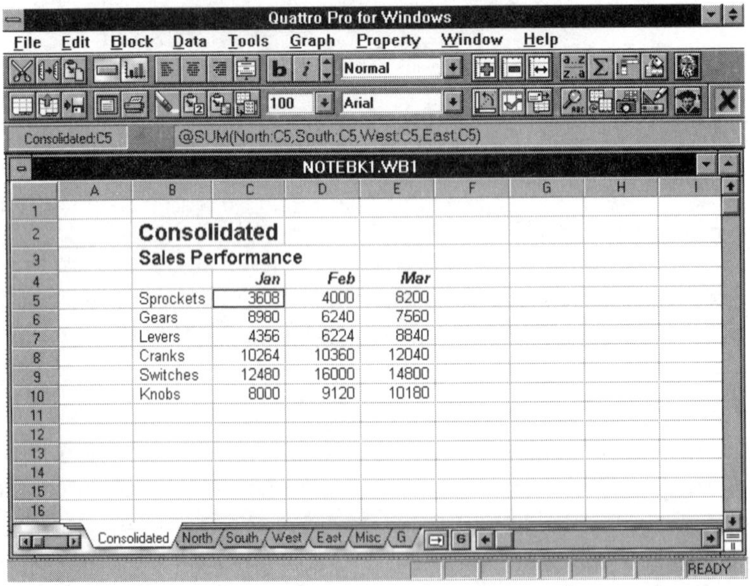

Figure 4.4 The page tab for page A changed to "Consolidated."

Naming pages makes it easier to remember which pages contain which information in your notebook applications. Any time you now refer to the page by name (as you will with linking formulas or the **Goto** command), you must use the new name you entered.

Change the Tab color

You can change the color of a page tab by using the **Tab Color** option in Active Page Properties. Just select a color from those provided, then click on **OK**. Each tab can be a different color if you like.

Inserting and Deleting Pages

Although the order in which your pages appear seldom really matters, you might decide you want to add a new page between two existing pages—rather than using a blank page at the end. You can insert new pages by using the **Block>Insert>Pages** command. To do this: Activate the page that is to follow the new page, select **Block>Insert>Pages**, enter a reference to indicate the number of pages you want to insert, and click on **OK**. For example, to insert three pages before page E, you would select page E, choose the **Block>Insert>Pages** command, enter the reference **E:A1..G:A1**, and click on **OK**. (Although you must include one, it does not matter what cell reference you use—only the page reference.) For more information about cell and block references and how to enter them, refer to Chapter 6.

To delete a page: activate it, select **Block>Delete>Pages**, enter a reference indicating the pages you want to delete, and click on **OK**.

Using Group Mode

Group mode lets you format and edit workbook pages in groups. The changes you make to one page affect all pages in the group. You can create a group out of any series of pages in a workbook—or out of several different series of pages. Just tell Quattro Pro which pages you are placing in the group; then make your changes to any page in the group. All other pages will then follow suit.

Group editing and formatting is effective for creating several pages that have the same basic design elements—including any elements added through the Object property inspector (fonts, borders, and so on), column headings, and even formulas. For example, if you have 12 pages for monthly sales data, plus one consolidated summary page, create the 12 monthly pages using Group mode. If you need to make changes to the 12 sheets later, place them into a group again before making the changes. To create a group, follow these simple steps.

1. Select **Tools>Define Group**. Doing so will produce the dialog box in Figure 4.5.

2. Enter a descriptive name in the Group Name edit box. This name applies to the group as a whole and can be used in formulas to identify a group.

3. Press **Tab**, or click in the First Page edit box; then enter the name of the first page in the group. This is the name on the page's tab.

4. Press **Tab** again to move to the Last Page edit box and type the name of the last page in the group. All pages between and including the first and the last will be placed in the group.

5. Click on **OK** to add the group to the list of defined groups.

6. Repeat these steps to add other groups to the notebook.

7. Activate group mode by clicking on the **Group** button:

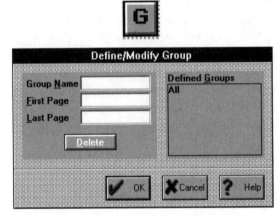

Figure 4.5 The Define/Modify Group dialog box.

Figure 4.6 shows how Quattro visually indicates that pages are grouped together and that Group mode is active.

Notice that all the groups are activated at the same time. You should not assume, however, that you can make changes to all these groups at the same time. The group affected by the entry or command is based on the page where the cell pointer is located. If you have a notebook with group1 defined as pages A through F, and group2 defined as H through M, making a change on page A will not affect any page in group2.

In other words, you cannot define a group that has noncontiguous ranges of pages. You must have an uninterrupted range of pages in each group.

Moreover, you cannot have two groups that share one or more pages. For example, if group1 is defined as pages E through J, group2 cannot be defined as pages G through M.

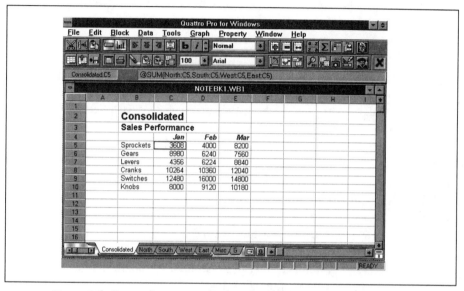

Figure 4.6 Grouped pages are displayed with a bracket under their tabs.

Remember that, while the Group mode is active, you can perform any of the commands and options in the Current Object property inspector (just right-click on any selected block). To quit Group mode and return to normal, single-page formatting, click on the **Group** button again.

You can return to the defined group at any time by clicking on the **Group** button. Note that you can modify the current group settings by returning to the Define/Modify Group dialog box and adding or deleting items from the group.

Creating a temporary group

You might want to define a group temporarily, without resetting the current group defined by the **Tools>Define Group** command. You can define a temporary group for one-time formatting activities without affecting the group you've set for the Group mode. To do this, click on the page tab of the last page in the group; then hold down the **Shift** key and click on the tab of the group's first page. The group will be defined, and you will automatically be in Group mode with the first page active. The page tabs will then be underlined—indicating that you're using a temporary group. To leave

Group mode and dissolve the group, click anywhere on the page. To make temporary groups work, you must position the cursor on the cell or block to be formatted and then establish the group. This is necessary because clicking any place on the page after the group has been activated will dissolve the group.

Entering Data into Grouped Pages

When you're in Group mode, Quattro Pro lets you enter data in the active page or in all the pages in the group. To enter data only in the active page, type the data in the usual way. To enter data in the same cell of each page in the group, type in the data and press **Ctrl-Enter**. This is particularly helpful when creating a group of pages with identical column headings and formulas.

Using the SpeedFill or Block>Fill command in group mode can create unexpected results

WARNING When you are in Group mode and select **SpeedFill**, maybe hoping to enter the same names of the months across several columns on each page, you will get a surprise. The first page will start off, say, with January, February, March, and April. The next page, instead of having the same column headings, will have May, June, July, and August. Quattro Pro treats the group as a single range—even though the range spans several pages.

Editing Data in Grouped Pages

Editing cells across pages in a group is as easy as entering data and is very similar in practice. To edit cell A7 in a group composed of pages A through D, follow these steps.

1. Move the cell pointer to cell A7 on one of the pages in the group. (If this is a temporary group, be sure to select cell A7 before setting the group.)

2. Turn Group mode on by clicking on the **Group** button—or set up a temporary group.

3. Press **F2** or click on the Input Line.

4. Make your editing changes and press **Ctrl-Enter** when finished. The changes will be made in cell A7 of each page in the group.

Copying Across Pages of a Group

Another task you can perform within grouped pages is copying data. You can copy data into all the pages in a group simultaneously. You can copy data from any worksheet into all the grouped worksheets at once by following these steps.

1. Turn off Group mode by clicking on the **Group** button.

2. Highlight the block that is to be copied; then click on the **Copy** button located on the Standard SpeedBar. You can copy data from any page.

3. Turn Group mode back on by clicking on the **Group** button once again.

4. Move the cell pointer to the desired destination on any page in the group and click on the **Paste** button. The data will be copied into the active page and all other pages in the group.

The **Cut**, **Copy**, **Paste**, **Clear**, and **Clear Contents** commands work on all pages in the active group simultaneously. To avoid this, just turn the Group mode off before using the command.

Splitting Windows

A notebook can contain 256 pages plus a Graph page. Each page contains 256 columns and 8192 rows. Quattro Pro provides a feature that lets you see data from different parts of the notebook at the same time. By splitting the Notebook window into two sections, you can see a portion of two different pages at the same time (see Figure 4.7) or two different areas of the same page. Windows can be split into horizontal or vertical panes. Figure 4.8 shows the same notebook as Figure 4.7 but in vertical panes. Panes can be created by using the mouse or the menu commands. As with most things, using the mouse is much quicker.

Splitting the window into panes is useful for viewing two different pages at the same time within a single window. This makes it easy to jump between the pages, copy information between pages, and perform other activities on two pages without having to use the page tabs continually in order to switch between them.

If you want to view two different portions of the same worksheet—or if you want to view two different pages in two different windows—you can add a new window view to the notebook using the **Window>New View** command. This command adds a new window to the screen, giving you two different windows for the same notebook. Each window can display a different page or portion of a page. Figure 4.9 shows a worksheet that displays two different windows.

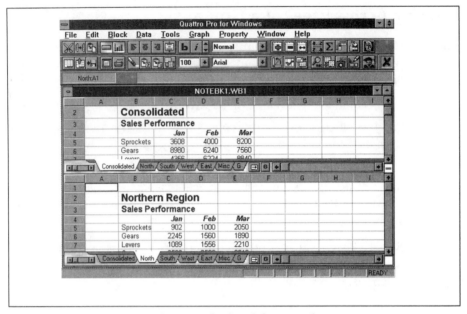

Figure 4.7 A notebook with horizontal panes.

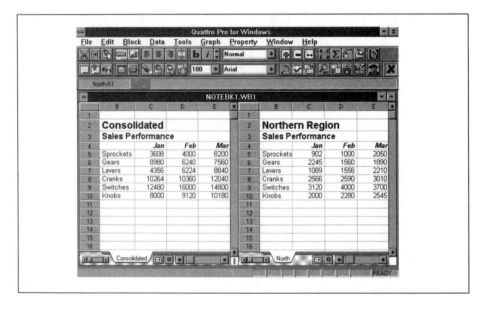

Figure 4.8 A notebook with vertical panes.

Quattro Pro lets you identify column headings at the top of the screen and lock them into place. With the column headings locked, you can scroll through the rest of the page without moving the headings out of place. This is useful for large tables of data that have a single heading at the top. As you scroll down to see more rows in the table, the locked column headings will remain in view.

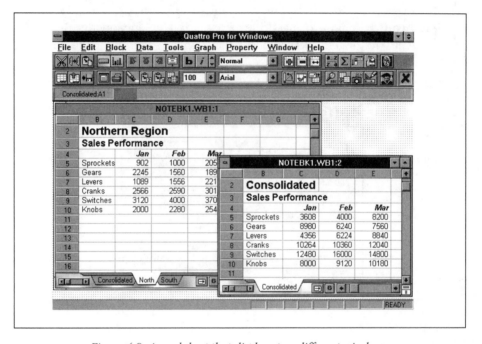

Figure 4.9 A worksheet that displays two different windows.

The following sections explain the various methods of creating and manipulating panes in your Quattro Pro Notebook windows. You'll also learn about splitting a worksheet into two or more window views and how to freeze column and row titles on the screen.

Creating Two Window Panes

There are two different ways to create window panes in Quattro Pro. First, you can use the **Window>Panes** command, described in these steps.

1. Position the cursor where you want the split to occur. For example, if you want to create vertical panes with the first one ending in column D, place the cursor somewhere in column E.

2. Select **Panes** from the Window menu to display the Panes dialog box, as shown in Figure 4.10.

3. Click on **Horizontal** or **Vertical** so that Quattro Pro knows which way to split the window.

4. Indicate whether you want the windows to scroll together (that is, to be synchronized) or independently. Remove the check mark from the **Synchronize** option to make the panes scroll independently. By default they will scroll together. This means that, as you scroll one pane, the other follows.

5. Click on **OK**. Quattro Pro will split the window as specified.

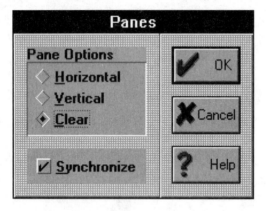

Figure 4.10 The Panes dialog box.

After a window is split, the two resulting panes cannot be split either vertically or horizontally again.

You can also use the mouse to create panes. In the lower-right corner of the Notebook window are the *pane splitters*:

To create a pane:

1. Drag either the horizontal or vertical splitter into the middle of the window.

2. Move the mouse pointer to the pane splitter. The mouse pointer will change to a double arrow joined by a vertical bar.

3. To create vertical panes, point to the vertical pane splitter and drag the splitter to the left until both panes are the desired size. A dotted line indicates
   where the first pane ends and the second one starts.

4. Release the mouse button. Quattro Pro will adjust the display accordingly.

By default, windows created with the pane splitter are synchronized. If you wish
to make the panes unsynchronized, use the **Window>Panes** command and
uncheck the **Synchronize** option. The windows will now scroll independently.

Resizing and Removing Panes

Regardless of how the windows panes were created, they are resized or cleared
in the same ways. When the window is split, one of the windows will contain a
pane splitter. This splitter can be used to resize or clear the window. To resize
the window:

1. Move the mouse pointer to the pane splitter.

2. Point to the pane splitter and drag the splitter horizontally (for vertical
   panes) or vertically (for horizontal panes), until the panes are the desired
   size. Then, release the button.

To resize the panes using the menus, you must first clear the existing pane and
then create new panes with the cell pointer in a different cell. To clear the
panes, select the **Window>Panes** command and click on the **Clear** option.

To clear the panes using the mouse, drag the pane splitter to the very bottom or right edge of the window; then release the mouse button. The window
will now show only one pane.

Locking Titles

Window panes are used primarily to show two different pages at the same
time—while switching between both pages frequently. However, you might find
the need to split a single page into two sections—one section at the top to hold
your column titles. As you scroll through the page, the column titles will stay in
place at the top of the screen. You might also want to show row titles along the
left side of the screen and leave them in place as you scroll across the sheet.
Whenever your worksheet spans two or more screens and contains titles along
the top and/or side, you can benefit from freezing the titles.

To lock titles, position the cell pointer just below the column titles (or to the right of the row titles) and choose the **Window>Locked Titles** command. Click to select horizontal titles (for column headings), vertical titles (for row headings), or both.

 Note that locked titles cannot be altered in any way until you clear them with the **Clear** option in the **Window>Locked Titles** command. You cannot even move the cell pointer into the title area.

Combining Titles with Panes

You can add locked titles as well as panes to a window if you like. Both commands work independently of each other. Because locked titles apply to the active page only, you can lock titles on one page and leave them unlocked on another.

Using Multiple Window Views

Another way to split the screen is to add new window views into the notebook using the **Window>New View** command. Each new window provides a new view to the notebook. For example, one window might be used to show page A whereas another shows page B.

How is using window views different from splitting a window into panes? Here are some differences.

- Windows can be sized, moved, and minimized. Each window you create can be moved and sized independently of other windows. Using two windows, you can show two different areas of a notebook, areas that have distinctly different proportions. For example, you might show a large square table in one window and a narrow column of options in another. (See Figure 4.11.) This would be difficult to do with panes.

- Windows cannot be synchronized. You cannot have two separate windows scroll in sync. Only panes offer this option.

- Windows can be arranged automatically. You can arrange windows with the **Window>Tile** and **Window>Cascade** commands for different purposes. Figures 4.12 and 4.13 each show three windows arranged differently.

- Each window can have two panes. You can add panes to each new window view if you want to.

- You can add multiple windows. You can have more than two different window views of the same notebook. In this way, you can view three or more pages at the same time. This is impossible to do with panes.

- Window views apply to one notebook only. Each new window you open to a notebook is just another way of viewing that same notebook. New windows do not open new files on the disk.

- Windows are saved with the notebook. The window views you add using the **Window>New View** command can be saved with the notebook. Just use the **File>Save** command with the windows in place. The next time you open the notebook file, the views will be active.

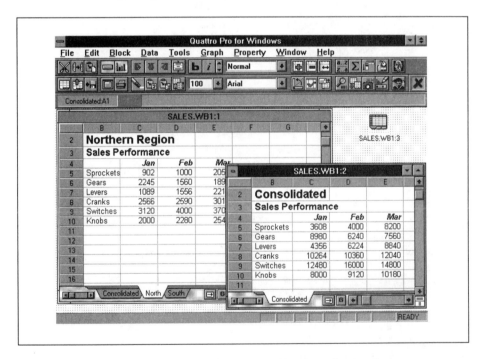

Figure 4.11 Windows arranged independently.

You can move or copy information among multiple windows by using the **Copy**, **Cut**, and **Paste** commands in the Edit menu. Just highlight the desired window before using the command.

Selecting a Window

In order to work with a window—to enter data, create a graph, or copy information, for example—you must activate the desired window. To activate a window, use one of these methods:

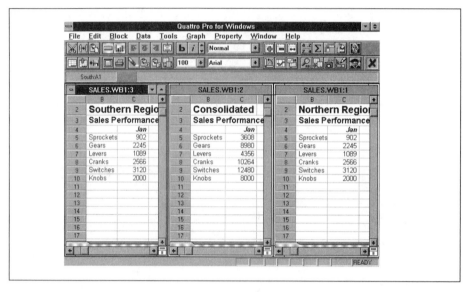

Figure 4.12 Windows arranged with the Window>Tile command.

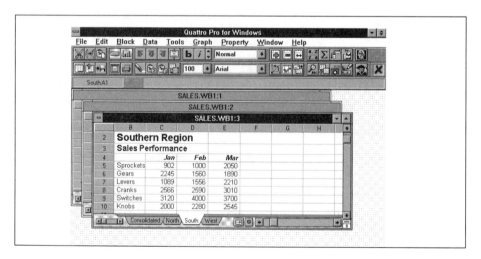

Figure 4.13 Windows arranged with the Window>Cascade command.

- Click on any part of the window. If the windows are cascaded, the Select window will come to the foreground. If they are tiled, the Title bar will change color.

- Display the Window menu and click on the name of the desired window. The window that is currently active will have a check mark to the left of its name.

- Press **Ctrl-F6** to move to the next window. **Ctrl-F6** will move through the windows on the work area in the order they were created.

Changing the Work Environment

The work environment involves the visual aspects of a notebook, such as the color of the background, the appearance of grid lines, and the size of data (the *magnification factor*)—topics to be covered in this section. You'll find that by changing the basic work environment for a notebook, you can build your applications more easily.

Removing Grid Lines

Grid lines are the row and column separation lines that appear automatically on each page of a notebook. You can remove the horizontal and/or vertical grid lines if you want to. If you are performing many formatting tasks to your notebook, you'll want to remove the grid lines to make your formatting changes easier to see. To suppress grid lines for any page, do the following:

1. Right-click on the desired the page tab.

2. When the Active Page property inspector appears, click on the **Grid Lines** option to reveal the screen shown in Figure 4.14.

3. Click to remove the check mark from the **Horizontal** and/or **Vertical** options. Removing the check mark removes the grid lines from the page.

4. Click on **OK**. Quattro Pro will apply the new setting to the page.

Repeat the process to add the grid lines again by checking the **Horizontal** and/or **Vertical** option. Remember that page grid lines appear on the screen only; they will not appear on your printouts.

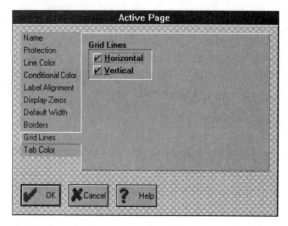

Figure 4.14 The Active Page dialog box showing the Grid Lines options.

Suppressing Zero Values

At one time or another, you will have a notebook page that contains formulas that equate to zero under certain conditions. If your worksheet has a lot of these formulas, you could end up with many zeros throughout your application. To make the worksheet easier to read, you might wish to display a blank cell rather than the zero. Quattro Pro lets you suppress zero values. Use the following procedure.

1. Right-click on the tab of the page on which the grids will be turned off.
2. When the Active Page dialog box is displayed, click on **Display Zeros**.
3. Check **No** to suppress zero values.
4. Click on **OK**. Quattro Pro will suppress all cells that contain the exact value of zero.

To redisplay zero values, follow the same steps, this time checking **Yes**. Note that the actual value in the cells is still zero—Quattro Pro is merely hiding that value.

Removing Display Elements

Quattro Pro gives you control over two elements of the notebook display: the page tabs and the scroll bars. Using the Notebook Properties dialog box, you can remove the scroll bars from the active notebook, making the page area larger. You can remove the page tabs to gain even more room. Figure 4.15 shows a notebook with these elements removed.

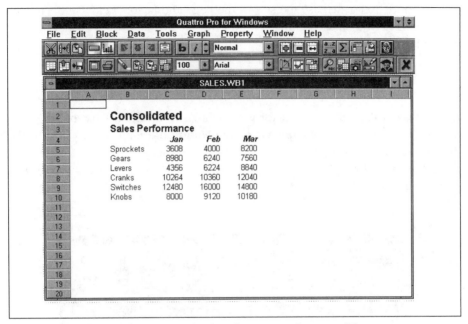

Figure 4.15 A notebook with no page tabs or scroll bars.

To remove these elements, right-click on the title bar of the active notebook or select the **Property>Active Notebook** command. Click the **Display** option to reveal the three display settings. Click to check or uncheck the desired settings; then press **Enter**.

Setting the Zoom Factor

Using multiple windows, splitting the screen into separate panes, and locking titles into place on a page are all good ways to view different parts of your application at one time. You might, however, just want to see more of it on one screen. Quattro Pro lets you reduce and enlarge the size of the notebook pages by using a *zoom factor*, a magnification setting. By reducing the zoom factor, or *zooming out*, you can see more of the page in one window; by increasing the zoom factor, or *zooming in*, you can enlarge the view and reduce the amount of data that appears on the screen.

You can select a zoom factor from the **Zoom List** tool on the Secondary SpeedBar. Just click on the down arrow beside the Zoom List to view the various factors available. Factors are available from 25% to 200% of normal size.

Factors above 100% increase the size of the page and factors below 100% reduce it. Experiment with these settings to find the factor that works best with your worksheet.

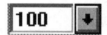

Another way to set the zoom factor is to right-click on the title bar of the active notebook (or choose the **Property>Active Notebook** command). Click on the **Zoom Factor** option to reveal a list of zoom percentages. Select a percentage using the drop-down list of percentage values and click on **OK**. Figure 4.16 shows the notebook reduced.

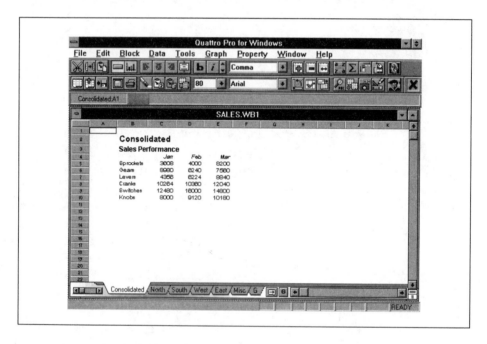

Figure 4.16 The notebook reduced with the Zoom Factor option.

Protecting Data in Cells

Cell protection ensures that your cell entries will not be changed accidentally. This is an especially helpful tool when creating notebooks and templates to be used by others. Data in a protected cell cannot be changed in any way. Just tell Quattro Pro which cells you want to protect on each page. Each page has an Enable/Disable switch that activates or deactivates the protection feature. When activated, protected cells cannot be changed. When deactivated, all cells can be changed. Use this *master switch* for pages that you want to modify without having to unprotect each cell or block that you've protected.

When you start a new notebook file, Quattro Pro automatically protects all cells in the notebook. The master switch starts out in the disabled position, so at this point, you can make changes to all the cells in a new notebook. If you have enabled the Protection feature, however, all cells would be protected. Therefore, your task is to go through a notebook and *unprotect* the cells and blocks that you don't want protected, areas that you want to modify, like data entry areas. Leave your valuable formulas and labels protected though.

In summary, there are two features that work together to protect the cells in your notebooks. Cell protection is used to unprotect the cells you don't want protected in each page of the notebook. Page protection is used to enable or disable Protect mode for each page. When enabled, Protect mode does not let you change protected cells.

To apply or remove protection from specific cells or blocks, use the Protection options in the Active Block properties as follows:

1. Highlight the block to be protected or unprotected.
2. Right-click on the block, or select **Property>Current Object**. The Active Block properties will appear.
3. Select **Protection**.
4. Click on **Protect** to apply protection and **Unprotect** to remove it.
5. Click on **OK**.

After you have set the desired cells, you're ready to activate page protection. To enable protection for an entire page:

1. Select **Property>Active Page**, or right-click on the page tab.
2. Click on **Protection**. The Active Page dialog box shows you two options: **Disable** and **Enable**.
3. Click on **Enable**.
4. Click on **OK**. The entire page is protected. Now if you try to enter anything into any protected cell, you will see the message box in Figure 4.17.

Applying protection to multiple pages at one time
You can apply page protection to several contiguous pages by creating a group (described earlier in the chapter). You can also unprotect cells across pages using a group.

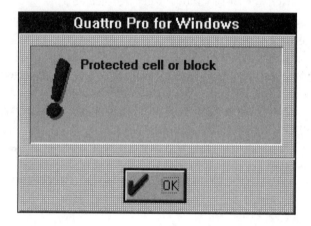

Figure 4.17 The protected cell error message.

Remember that cell protection applies to each cell individually and that you can protect any cell or block on a page by selecting it before using the Block properties with the **Protection** option. Also, remember that when you enable protection with the Active Page properties **Protection** option, protection is not enabled for other pages in the same notebook. You can protect several pages at once by first grouping them as described earlier in this chapter. Finally, you should note that cell protection does not prohibit a user from going into the Active Page properties and disabling **Protection**. In other words, anyone knowledgeable in Quattro Pro can remove the protection from individual cells.

Working with SpeedBars

You've probably become pretty familiar with the SpeedBar buttons at the top of the screen. The second row of buttons, called the Productivity Tools SpeedBar may not be as familiar yet. Actually, Quattro Pro offers several additional SpeedBars that you can add to the top of the screen. And you can remove any SpeedBar from the screen except the Standard SpeedBar at the top.

Quattro Pro's other SpeedBars are designed for specific purposes, such as the Spelling Checker SpeedBar and the Consolidation SpeedBar. Chances are, you would not want these SpeedBars on the screen when you are not using checking your spelling or consolidating data. However, you might want to add a custom SpeedBar to the screen.

To access secondary SpeedBars, just right-click in any blank area of the **Productivity Tools** SpeedBar (to the right of the font list is a good choice). Don't right-click on a button. This produces a pop-up menu containing the following commands:

Command	Description
Append	Add a SpeedBar below this one.
Insert	Add a SpeedBar above this one.
Replace	Replace this SpeedBar with a new one.
Remove	Remove this SpeedBar (you can also click the **Close** button at the far right of any SpeedBar to remove it.)

Select the **Append** command to add a SpeedBar to the screen, then choose one of the existing secondary SpeedBars listed in the menu—or click the **<Browse>** command to locate your custom SpeedBars (creating custom SpeedBars is described in the next section).

Creating Custom SpeedBars

You can create your own SpeedBars that combine various tools and buttons. Quattro Pro provides several sets of SpeedBar tools for this purpose and you can combine them in any way you like. The simple procedure for placing these tools onto your own SpeedBars follows. Chapter 16 goes even farther by showing you how to create your own, custom tools that you can then add to your custom SpeedBars. For now, lets explore the built-in tools.

1. Click on the **SpeedBar Designer** button:

A blank SpeedBar appears on the screen as well as the SpeedBar Designer tools. You will simply access the existing SpeedBar palettes, then copy tools from the palettes to the blank SpeedBar.

2. Click on the **Buttons** drop-down menu and choose any of the button palettes listed. Repeat this step to choose additional palettes. These are the built-in buttons available for your custom SpeedBar. Figure 4.18 shows the screen with a blank SpeedBar and two other palettes in view.

3. Click twice on the desired tool in one of the palettes (once to select the palette window and once to select the tool). You can select additional tools in the same palette by holding the **Shift** key down and clicking on other tools.

4. Click once on the blank SpeedBar to select it.

5. Click anywhere inside the blank SpeedBar to place the tool.

6. Repeat this process to add more tools.

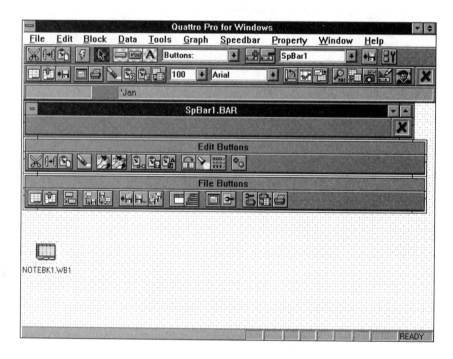

Fig. 4.18 The SpeedBar Designer in action.

Remember, you can access a brief description of each tool by moving the mouse over the tool's face and looking at the bottom-left corner of the screen.

You can reposition the tools by dragging them around the blank SpeedBar. When you are finished with your SpeedBar, choose the **SpeedBar>Save** command and name the new SpeedBar for future use.

To exit the SpeedBar Designer, just activate the notebook window that is minimized on the screen—or you can remove all SpeedBar palettes and blank SpeedBars from the screen. To access your new SpeedBar, refer to "Working With SpeedBars" previously in this chapter.

Saving the Workspace

You might find that you like to switch among different environment settings at different times while you work on a notebook. For example, you might like to display grid lines on the page and zoom the worksheet to 125% when you create an application but remove the grid lines and zoom out to 80% when you use the notebook on a daily basis. Or you might like different window arrangements at different times during your work—or even change the files that you have open at any given time. Quattro Pro for Windows lets you store sets of environment (or workspace) changes and switch among these sets at any time. Workspace settings can be named and saved on disk for use with any notebook you are using at the time. This way, you don't have to repeat settings that you use often—just save the settings and then apply them to any worksheet you use.

To save your workspace settings, first set up the workspace the way you want it. This includes the zoom factor, window arrangements, any open notebooks, and all settings in the Page and Notebook property inspectors. After you have established them, select the **File>Workspace>Save** command and enter a name for the workspace settings. For example, if you make certain workspace changes whenever you start a new notebook, you might save the set as **NEW-SHEET.WBS** for future use. Or you might save a workspace that includes your Sales Report notebook and your Budget notebook arranged on the screen with 80% magnification. If these files are not already open, restoring this workspace will also open the files. If the files are already open, they will quickly return to the environment settings you saved with the workspace.

Quattro Pro automatically saves the workspace settings into the QPW2 directory, unless you specify otherwise. Keep the WBS extension for these files, so you can easily identify them as workspace setting files.

To restore any previously saved settings, use the **File>Workspace>Restore** command and locate the **WBS** file you saved. When you select the **WBS** file, Quattro Pro immediately applies the settings to the current notebook.

Summary

Notebooks are an important concept in Quattro Pro. Each notebook contains a series of pages into which you enter data. You can use as many of these pages as you like and name the pages for easy identification. To switch pages, just click on the desired page tab to bring it to the front. You can also use the Tab Scroller to view more page tabs. The Active Page Properties dialog box provides many options for controlling each page. Some Active Page properties include changing the page name, protecting the page, suppressing zero values, and removing grid lines.

Even though you can alter the properties of individual notebook pages, you can also set some properties for the entire notebook. Use the Active Notebook properties to set the Notebook options. This includes reducing or enlarging the notebook (zooming) and removing elements from the notebook, such as scroll bars and page tabs.

When you become comfortable with notebook pages, you'll find it easy to create Quattro Pro applications that span several pages. For information about entering formulas that span several pages, refer to Chapter 3. The following chapter describes some formatting options you can apply to your notebooks to enhance their appearance.

Formatting Data and Worksheets

After you have entered the initial values, formulas, and labels in your worksheet, you might want to consider some ways of formatting the data for best readability. Using Quattro's formatting capabilities, you can create remarkably attractive and readable worksheets. Quattro Pro's formatting capabilities include:

- Changing the fonts and type styles in your worksheets
- Adding lines and borders to enhance your worksheets
- Changing the colors and shades used in the worksheet
- Setting reusable styles for worksheet data
- Formatting numbers and dates using various display styles

As you format your data and notebooks, you'll use one of the main concepts used throughout Windows programs: *Select then do.* First you select the data on which you want to perform formatting changes; then you make the change using the appropriate commands.

You will find many formatting options in the Object Properties dialog box shown in Figure 5.1 (also known as the *property inspector*). You can access the property inspector for any cell or selected block by right-clicking on the cell or block, then selecting **Block Properties** from the Shortcut menu that appears. Take a look at the properties along the left side of the dialog box. These are the attributes of the current block that you'll be able to change.

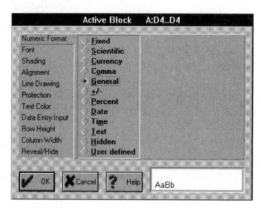

Figure 5.1 The properties of the Active Block include many formatting options.

As you can see, the property inspector provides access to many formatting features. We'll explore these options throughout this chapter. Other formatting features are available through the **Edit>Define Styles** command and some tools on the SpeedBar. This chapter describes the various commands and options available in Quattro Pro for formatting your data.

Selecting Fonts and Character Attributes

A font consists of a typeface, a type style, and a type size. A typeface is the graphical design of the letters and numbers; some faces are very businesslike, whereas others seem casual and friendly. You also have control over the type size and style used for your data. Type size is measured in *points;* a point is about one seventy-second of an inch. Type styles are the special enhancements you can apply to fonts, such as boldface, underline, and italics. By combining fonts, sizes, and styles, you can create a wide variety of type effects in your worksheets.

Quattro Pro behaves like any good Windows program when it comes to fonts. In Quattro Pro, you have access to all fonts installed in Windows. If you use Windows 3.1, this means you have access to all your TrueType fonts. And if you use a special font management program, such as Adobe Type Manager (ATM), you'll have access to PostScript Type 1 fonts as well. The nice thing about TrueType or ATM fonts is that you can use them in practically any size, and they print using the best quality your printer can provide.

In Quattro Pro, you can change the font, size, and style of each cell individually, or you can change a block of cells at the same time. However, you cannot apply different fonts to different parts of the data within one cell. In other words, each cell may have only one font applied to it. To change the font of a cell (or block of cells):

1. Select the cell or block that you want to change.

2. Choose the **Property>Current Object** command, or right-click on the selected block, then choose **Block Properties**.

3. Choose **Font** and select the typeface, point size, and style options you want by selecting from the options in the dialog box shown in Figure 5.2. You can include the styles **Bold, Italics, Underline**, and **Strikeout** for any font. As you make changes in the Active Block Font dialog box, you can see an example of the font you have selected in the Sample area in the bottom-right corner of the dialog box.

4. Choose **OK**. Quattro Pro will apply the changes you've made.

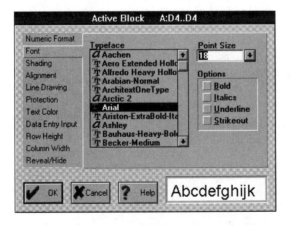

Figure 5.2 The Active Block dialog box showing the Font properties.

You can choose only one font and point size for the selected cell or block, but you can choose any combination of style options by checking the ones you want. Note that Quattro Pro applies the same point size to all the cells in the selected block. If you select a block of cells that have various point sizes, you'll be unable to change just the font and leave the existing sizes alone. This is an unfortunate limitation in Quattro Pro. Every time you change a font, you also must change the point size.

Font-formatting shortcuts from the SpeedBar

Quattro Pro provides some useful shortcuts for applying fonts, sizes, and styles to your cells. Two SpeedBar buttons quickly bold/unbold and italicize/unitalicize the selected cells, while the **Spin** button to the right lets you adjust the size of the font. Press the **Up Arrow** to increase the font size and the **Down Arrow** to decrease the font size. These tools look like this:

You can also create additional formatting tools using the SpeedBar Designer described in Chapters 4 and 16.

Changing Text Color

If you are using Quattro Pro with a color monitor, you have a choice of 16 colors in which to display your data. Data color can be changed cell by cell or one block at a time. When you print a color page on a black-and-white printer, the text will automatically print in black. However, if you want to see the colors you used on the screen, you must print the page using a color printer. (See Chapter 9 for more information about printing in color.) Follow these steps to change the color of your worksheet data.

1. Select the cell or range that you want to change.
2. Choose the **Property>Current Object** command, or right-click the mouse and choose **Block Properties**.
3. Select **Text Color**, and a color-selection palette like the one in Figure 5.3 is displayed in the dialog box.
4. Select the color (or shade, for monochrome monitors) for the selected text by clicking on the palette.
5. Choose **OK**. Quattro Pro will apply the changes you've made.

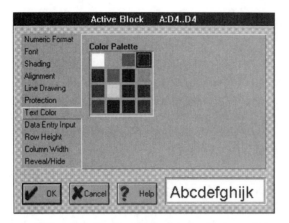

Figure 5.3 Quattro Pro's standard color palette.

For readability, not all 16 colors are practical choices

Some font colors will not be very effective. In particular, you should avoid choosing a font color that does not contrast well with the color in the cell. (You can change the cell's background color using the **Shading** option, discussed later in this chapter.) If the background color has been set to **Cyan**, selecting the same color for the text will make the cells appear blank. After a little bit of experimentation, you will also see that other color combinations are not as easy to read as are black on white or red on white, just to name two. Furthermore, when printed in black and white, different colors appear as shades of gray. The gray shades may contrast differently than their equivalent screen colors—hence, you might want to print your color choices to see if they are practical on the printer as well as on the screen.

Changing the color of your fonts can affect the printout—even on black-and-white printers. For more information on printing in color and shades of gray, refer to Chapter 9. Other ways of changing the color of data are covered later in this chapter.

Fonts and Colors Can Also Be Set for the Entire Notebook

To set a font color for the entire notebook, you must alter the style named Normal. See the discussion later in this chapter, "Applying Styles Globally: The Normal Style".

Getting More Font Colors

Quattro Pro gives you more color choices for the fonts used in your graphs than it does for fonts in your notebook data. Plus, you can fill text with special patterns and graduated fills for graph text. You can access these color features for labels and headings in your notebooks by inserting text graphs into the notebook. Refer to Chapter 10 for information about using graphs to insert text into the worksheet.

Applying Colors Conditionally

One of the best uses for color in your Quattro Pro notebooks is to show certain values in different colors—showing negative numbers in red, for example. Quattro Pro lets you set up conditions for applying color to your numeric values for just this purpose. You can set numeric limits and colors for these limits so that your numbers appear in the appropriate colors automatically. This is especially useful for formulas that might calculate different numbers depending on the data in the rest of the worksheet.

To apply colors conditionally, use the **Property>Active Page** command— or, for quick access, move the mouse pointer to the Page tab and click on the right mouse button. This displays the Active Page property inspector. Now follow these steps.

1. Select **Conditional Color**. When you do this, you will see the dialog box options depicted in Figure 5.4.

2. Indicate the smallest number you consider to be normal (normal numbers are displayed in the default color for the cell).

3. Indicate the largest number you consider to be normal. All values between the smallest and largest numbers will be displayed in the normal cell color.

4. Click on a numeric category; then choose a color for that category of values. Following are the categories:

    • **Below Normal Color** sets the color for values below the value set in Step 1. If you select zero as the smallest value, you might want this color to be **Red**, so negative numbers are displayed in red.

    • **Normal Color** sets the color for values greater than or equal to the smallest normal value entered—up to and including the greatest normal value entered in Step 2.

- **Above Normal Color** sets the color for all values greater than the greatest normal value entered.

- **ERR color** sets the color to be used when the result of a formula is ERR or NA. A good color for error values is **Yellow**.

5. Click on **Enable** to activate the color sets. Now select **OK** to see the changes.

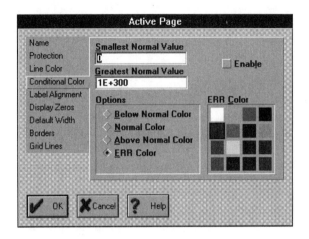

Figure 5.4 Active Page property inspector when Conditional Color has been selected.

You can now enter various values into the current page to test the color ranges. At any time, you can return to the Active Page properties and turn off the color selections by clicking on the **Enable** option to remove its check mark. This way, you don't have to reset each color range.

Suppose you are working on a budget application and you want to display all negative numbers in red, all values over 10,000 in blue, and all other values in black. You would set the Smallest Normal Value to 0 and the Greatest Normal Value to 10,000. Click on the **Below Normal Color** and choose **Red**. Click on the **Normal Color** and choose **Black**. Click on the **Above Normal Color** option and choose **Blue**.

When setting conditional colors, test them against the background color to be used

N O T E

Conditional colors are meant to set certain data apart from the rest of the entries on the page. When setting these colors, create a sample spreadsheet containing the text and background colors to be used. Then fill in the different types of data: normal, below and above normal, and ERR. Select your conditional colors and see whether they have the desired effect.

Changing Column Widths Manually

You can type up to 1024 characters in each cell, but the standard cell displays only 8 or 9 characters at a time. Text entries can spill into adjacent cells, but only if those cells do not contain data. Numeric entries simply revert to ******* when the entire number does not fit into the current cell width. Quattro Pro lets you change the width of each column on the worksheet. When you see ******* in a cell, it's a sign that you need to increase the column width. Similarly, if your printouts include ******* in some places, you should increase the column widths on the screen before printing again.

Besides displaying more data in each cell, you might want to change your worksheet's column widths to help make your data fit onto one page or on the screen. By reducing column widths (without chopping off data), you can reduce the overall space those columns take up on the page or screen. In this way, your columns more closely fit the data in them.

To change the width of a column using the mouse, follow these steps.

1. Move the mouse pointer to the column divider at the right edge of the column. This is the dividing line between the column headings. When you point directly at the column divider within the heading area, it changes again to the column-width changing pointer.

2. With the column-width changing pointer showing, click and hold the mouse button down and drag to change the column width (left to narrow, right to widen).

3. As you drag the mouse, you will see a gray line down the column indicating the proposed column width. Release the mouse button, and the column width will change.

To change the width of a column using the keyboard, follow these steps.

1. Select any range of cells for which you want the column width changed. Quattro Pro will change the entire column of the cells you specify, so you can actually select just one cell in each column you want to change.

2. Press the right mouse button and choose the **Block Properties** option, or select the **Property>Current Object** command.

3. Select **Column Width**.

4. Type a proposed column-width value in the Column Width entry box. (Use the number of characters you want to display in the column as a rough guide.) Note that the point size of the data affects the column-width setting.

5. Choose **OK**. The column width changes. (See Figure 5.5.)

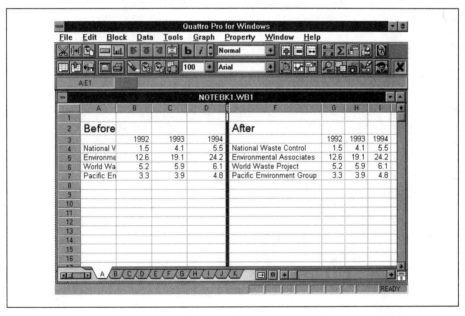

Figure 5.5 Making column widths fit the data more accurately—before and after.

You will probably find that you change column widths many times as you create and edit your worksheets. This is normal, since column widths do not automatically adjust when you change the data.

Uniformly Changing Column Widths and Row Heights

To change the widths of many columns to the same width, select the columns by dragging across the column header—or by pressing the **Ctrl** key as you click on each column heading. Now change the width of any of the selected columns. When you finish, Quattro Pro will change all selected columns to the new width.

Setting the Column
Width for an Entire Page in a Notebook

To change all columns on the active page at the same time or to set a new default column width for the page, select **Property>Active Page** (or right-click on the page tab); then click on **Default Width** and enter a width setting for the entire page. Note that all columns will change to the new default except those you've adjusted manually. You can set these columns back to the automatic width by selecting **Auto Width** from the Active Block properties.

Changing Column Widths Automatically

Although it's easy to change column widths throughout your notebook pages, you might find it difficult to determine the precise width for each column. You have to locate the largest entry in the column and fit the column to that entry. Since each column might be different, this could prove to be a lengthy proce- dure. Quattro Pro automates this process with its **Auto Width** option. The **Auto Width** option automatically fits the column to its largest data. To resize a col- umn to fit its widest entry, follow these steps:

1. Point at the column(s) to be adjusted, press the right mouse button, and then choose **Block Properties** from the Shortcut menu..

2. Select **Column Width** and click on **Auto Width**.

3. Click on **OK**. The column width will now be as wide as the longest label in the column.

If you use the Auto Width technique with multiple columns selected, Quattro Pro will resize each column separately, so they will likely end up with different widths—each one applied to its own data.

To apply the Auto Width feature using the Fit button, follow these steps:

1. Select a cell in each column you want to change.

2. Click on the **Fit** button found on the SpeedBar.

SHORTCUT

Using the Fit button to adjust all the columns on a page
A quick way to adjust all the columns on a page to the best width is to highlight an entire row by clicking on any row heading. Then click on the **Fit** button.

Changing Row Heights

You change row heights the same way you change column widths. When you use the mouse, you point at the row divider below the row you want to change (in the row heading area) and then drag the mouse up or down to change the height of the row.

You might not have to change row heights as often as you change column widths, because Quattro Pro automatically adjusts row heights to accommodate the point size of the data in the row. Quattro Pro adds a little extra space to the top of the row—to make the largest text fit comfortably into the row. If you change the size of the largest data in the row, Quattro Pro will automatically readjust the height. Nevertheless, you might find the need to adjust the heights of rows in your notebooks. From the keyboard, select a cell in the row you want to change; then press the right mouse button and select **Row Height** in the dialog box. (You can also select multiple cells to change many rows at once.) Quattro Pro measures the height of a row in points (or seventy-seconds of an inch). Quattro Pro uses the same measure for font size.

To make a worksheet easier to read, many people skip every other row on the worksheet, leaving a blank row between data rows. Unfortunately, the blank rows can cause problems when creating formulas or working with databases. You can accomplish this double-spacing effect by changing the heights of rows. Just select all the rows you want to expand; then expand all the rows at once. Leave the point size of the data about half the size of the row height to create the extra space. Figure 5.6 illustrates this technique.

This figure also shows how extra space between headings and data can make tables easier to read. You can use row heights to create space wherever needed in the worksheet—without having to insert cells.

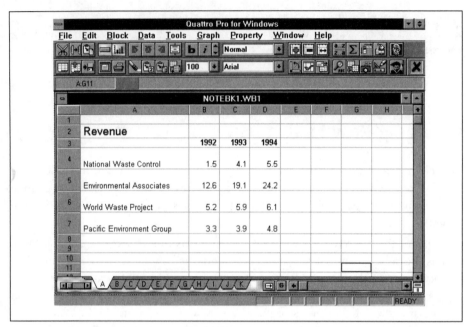

Figure 5.6 Using row heights to create extra space in a worksheet.

Changing Data Alignment

Quattro Pro lets you align data within the notebook's cells. This means that data can be pushed up against the right or left sides or be centered in the middle of the cell. Column width has a large impact on data alignment, of course, since an extra-wide column would exaggerate the differences in alignment and a column that closely fits the data might hide the data's alignment.

To change data alignment, you can use the alignment buttons on the SpeedBar or the **Alignment** option in the Active Block property inspector.

On the standard toolbar, you will find three tools dedicated to changing cell alignment: **Left**, **Center**, and **Right**. As with other formatting procedures in Quattro Pro, you first select the cell or range you want to align and click on the **Alignment** button; then Quattro Pro formats all the cells you selected.

Should you have a block of numbers and labels and wish to format them differently, another way to align a block is through the Active Block properties. Do this as follows:

1. Select the block of cells to be aligned.

2. Press **F12** or click the right mouse button, then choose **Block Properties**.

3. Select **Alignment**.

4. Choose the desired alignment option; then click on **OK**.

Quattro Pro will now apply the format selected. Note that the **General** option will format numbers to the right and labels to the left. This is the same format Quattro uses as the default when you first enter data. The **Center Across Block** option is covered in detail in the next section.

Typing in the Label Prefix as the Data is Entered Into the Cell

Another way to align data in a cell is to type in the desired label prefix as you are entering the data. Simply begin your entry with one of the following characters:

'   Left align

"   Right align

^   Center

These apply only to text labels. Using an alignment prefix with numbers converts the number to a text entry.

Setting Default Alignment for All Labels in the Active Page

You can also alter the alignment of labels for the active page. To do this, right-click on the page tab and select **Label Alignment**. Since you are setting only the alignment for labels and not numbers, **General** has been omitted.

Centering Headings Across Columns

Quattro Pro for Windows provides a quick and easy way to center headings across multiple columns on the worksheet. You can take a single heading and center it within any number of columns you like; Quattro Pro automatically centers it and keeps it centered even when you adjust the widths of the columns. This takes the guess work out of placing headings on your reports.

To center data across columns, highlight the cell containing the heading and all cells to the right of that cell into which the heading will be centered. For example, suppose you want to center a heading over columns B, C, and D. You would enter your heading into a cell in column B (let's say, cell B2), then highlight cells B2, C2, and D2. Figure 5.7 shows this example.

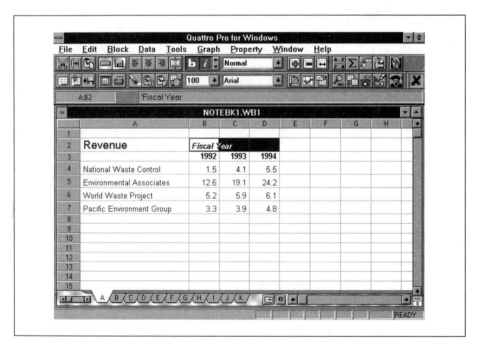

Figure 5.7 To center over columns, first highlight the heading and any adjacent cells.

Next, click on the **Block Center** button on the SpeedBar or right-click the highlighted range and choose **Center Across Block** from the Alignment options in the property inspector. Figure 5.8 shows the result from centering the data in Figure 5.7.

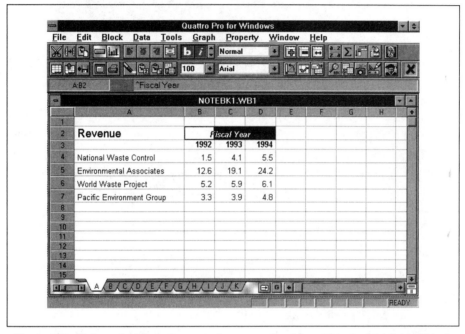

Figure 5.8 Click on the Block Center tool to center the data within the highlighted block.

Quattro Pro will center data only within blank cells. So if any cell within the highlighted block contains data (other than the leftmost cell), the heading will be centered between its existing cell and the cell containing data. In the previous example, if cell D3 contained data, the heading would be centered between cells B3 and C3. This can be useful for centering a group of headings that appear in every other cell of a row as shown in Figure 5.9.

Remember that you can change the widths of any column and Quattro Pro will recenter the headings to account for the changes. To return centered data to normal, simply choose any other alignment option for the cells. For example, you might switch the cells to left alignment by using the **Left Align** tool.

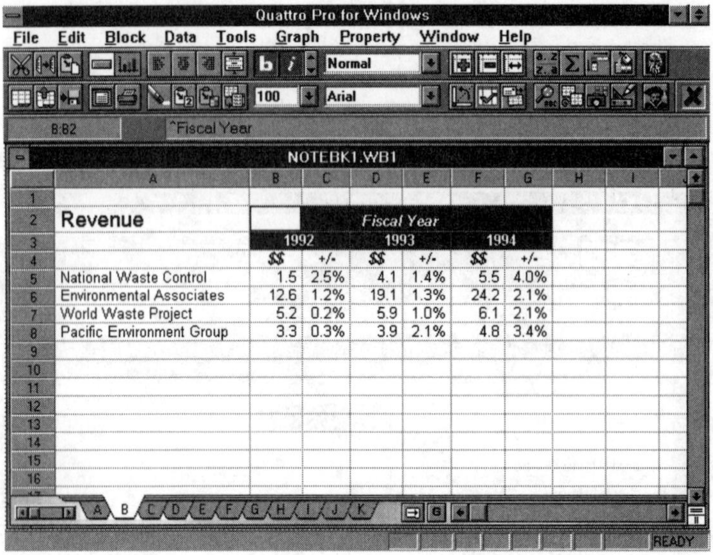

Figure 5.9 Centering multiple headings at once.

Using Columns of Text

Even though you normally think of each cell in Quattro Pro as a separate entry on the notebook page, you can combine several cells to appear as a column of text. This can be useful when you add small blocks of text to your printed reports.

Start by entering text into any cell or series of cells in a column. These entries should form the text of your column, but they don't have to adhere to any specific lengths. Enter as much information in each cell as you want (up to the maximum of 1024 characters). Now, to turn this entry (or entries) into a uniform column, follow these steps.

1. Select the cell(s) containing the initial entries.
2. Extend the block to include cells in adjacent columns. The width of your selection determines the width of the final column of text. Also extend the selection downward to indicate the approximate length of the finished column (see Figure 5.10).
3. Choose **Reformat** from the Block menu.
4. Choose **OK**.

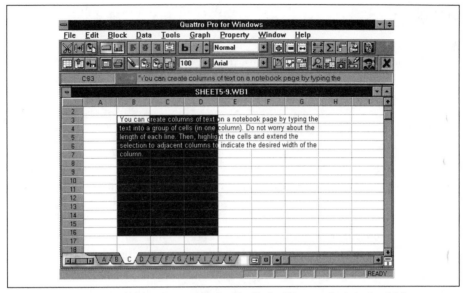

Figure 5.10 Highlight the text and a block of cells into which it should flow.

The text will now form a column the width and height of your selected cells. Figure 5.11 shows the completed example.

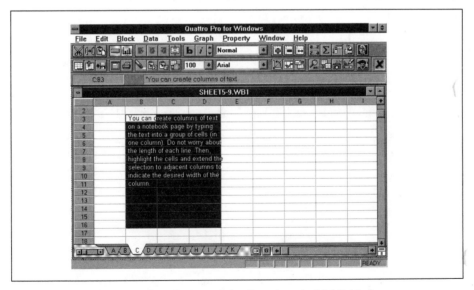

Figure 5.11 The reformatted text flows into the highlighted area.

NOTE

Note that you can perform this procedure in reverse—that is, you can make a narrow sequence of cells flow into a wider selection. Just highlight the entire block, plus the additional columns to the right, to indicate the desired width of the final block.

Formatting Numbers

When you create worksheets, you will use many different types of numbers: the current month's sales figures, the prime interest rate, the number of units sold, and so forth. Each of these numbers requires a different format for its expression. For example, the sales figures might require dollar signs and two decimal points, the interest rate is shown as a percentage with only one decimal place, and the units sold is shown as an integer without any decimal places.

Quattro Pro offers several ways of formatting numbers. By applying a number format, you can radically change the way a number looks in the cell. For instance, if you apply the Currency format to a cell containing the number **45678**, you would see $45,678.00 displayed in the cell. When you look in the Input Line, you will simply see 45678, since number formatting has no effect on the underlying value. To apply a number format, follow these simple steps:

1. Select the cell or block containing the numbers that you want to format.
2. Right-click on the highlighted block, then choose **Block Properties**, or select the **Property>Current Object** command. The Active Block property inspector is displayed, as shown in Figure 5.12. Because **Numeric Format** is the first item in the dialog box, the built-in number formats are already displayed.
3. Click on the desired number format to select it. When you select one of these formats, additional options might appear on the right side of the dialog box. Most formats let you enter the number of decimal places you want for the values.
4. Click on **OK**.

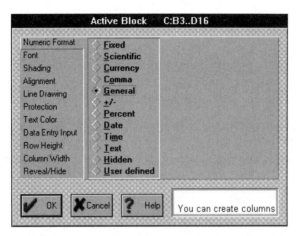

Figure 5.12 The Numeric Format choices allow you to change the appearance of numbers.

Before clicking on **OK**, you can set the number of decimal places for the values. This does not apply to the formats **General**, **Date**, **Time**, **Text**, **+/-**, and **Hidden**. For all other formats, simply enter the number of decimal places you would like applied to the values, then click on **OK** to complete the procedure. Generally two decimal places is the default.

Setting decimal places does not round the number

WARNING If you select a specific number of decimal places, such as two, Quattro Pro might appear to round the value to the specified number of places. This is for appearances only. The actual value stored in the cell is the original, unrounded value. This way, calculations that use the value will use the entire, precise value. If you want to change a value to its rounded format, use the @ROUND function described in Chapter 6.

If you choose a Date or Time format, you are given several variations from which to choose. These are simply different ways of displaying dates and times.

At the bottom of the dialog box, the Sample area tells you what the active cell will look like when you click on **OK**. Use this sample to examine each of the **Date** and **Time** options if you are formatting date or time values.

The Built-In Number Formats

Quattro Pro applies a number format to all cells in a worksheet. If you don't change a cell's number format, Quattro Pro uses its General format. The General format and all Quattro Pro's built-in number formats are as follows:

- **Fixed** Applies a fixed number of decimal places to the number. You determine how many decimal places are applied. Displays negative values with minus signs. Examples (using three decimal places): 12345.599 and 12345.599.

- **Scientific** Displays values in scientific notation. This is useful for long integers and other scientific values.

- **Currency** Displays values with a dollar sign and commas between each group of thousands. Defaults to 2 decimal places, but you can choose from 0 to 15 decimal places. Displays negatives in parentheses. Examples (using two decimal places): $12,345.60 and ($12,345.60).

- **Comma** Adds commas to the values. Displays negatives in parentheses. Use this format when you want to display columns of monetary values but don't want to apply dollar signs to all the values. (Too many dollar signs can make a financial report look amateurish.) Examples: 12,345.60 and (12,345.60).

- **General** Leaves the number as you enter it. Applies as many decimal places as required by the value. This will be the number of places you enter for the value or, in the case of values produced by formulas, the number of places to which the value calculates. Negative values are shown with minus signs. This is the default format used if you don't select a different number format.

- **Plus or Minus Sign** Displays the value as a quantity of + or - signs. The number of + or - signs displayed equals the value of the number. For example, the numbers **6** and **-6** produce +++++ and - - - - - -, respectively. Values of zero produce a single period (.), negative numbers produce minus signs, and positive numbers produce plus signs. Stacked on top of each other, these symbols create a simple text-based bar graph. Just expand the column containing the values. Chances are, you'll find Quattro Pro's graphing features make this number format obsolete.

It is important to protect hidden cells

Because the contents are hidden from view, it is easy to forget that anything is there. This makes it easy to overwrite the contents with something new. To keep this from happening, apply protection to the cell with **Property>Current Object**; then enable protection on the page with **Property>Active Page**.

- **Percent** Displays values as percentages. Note that values should be entered as decimals for proper percentage display. For example, to display 5.25%, you should enter the value **.0525** into the cell. You can also type **5.25%** into the cell, which Quattro Pro will automatically convert to **.0525**. Examples: 5.25% and -5.25%.

- **Date** Displays the value as a date. You can select from several different date formats. Generally, this command is used to change the format of a date—not to display a number as a date. You should first enter the date using **Ctrl-Shift-D**.

- **Time** Displays values as times. The values should already be entered as times by pressing **Ctrl-Shift-D** first, as described in Chapter 3. Use Time formats to choose among the different ways of displaying times.

- **Text** Displays the contents of a formula rather than the result. This is useful while you are creating complex notebook formulas and want to see each formulas on the screen as you work.

- **Hidden** Makes the selected data invisible. Although invisible, the data is still part of the worksheet and can be used in calculations. This is useful for preventing sensitive values from being seen or for hiding calculations that need not be displayed on the screen. This is an excellent alternative to hiding entire columns or rows in the notebook. To see the contents of a hidden cell, move the cell pointer to the cell and press **F2**. The contents of the cell will appear on the Input Line.

Built-in number formats appear in the Styles list as a shortcut

You can apply the built-in number formats by choosing them from the Styles list in the SpeedBar:

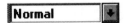

First, select the cell or block that you want to format; then choose the desired number format from the Styles list. Other formats that appear in the Style list, along with other uses for the Styles list are explained in detail under "Using Styles" later in this chapter.

Custom Number Formats

If Quattro Pro's built-in number formats don't provide the styles you need for your numbers, you can build your own. As with the built-in formats, your custom formats will be available through the Active Block property inspector for any cells in the notebook.

To create a custom number format, you need to combine formatting codes, which tell Quattro Pro how to display the number. First, right-click on the cell or block to which you want the custom format applied (you can apply the format to other cells later). The Numeric Format properties should already be showing in the property inspector. Now click on the **User Defined** format at the bottom of the list. A list of user-defined formats is displayed on the right side of the dialog box. Notice that several formats already exist. Following is a list of the existing user-defined formats.

- **N'Positive';N'Zero';N'Negative'** Displays the words *Positive*, *Negative*, and *Zero* for positive, negative, and zero values. If you enter **145**, this format displays the word `Positive` in the cell.

- **N9;N0;N"-"9** Displays positive values with no decimal places, zero values as 0, and negative values with a minus sign (-) and no decimal places. For example, if you enter **-2343.89**, this format displays `-2344`.

- **TMM' 'DD' 'YY' 'HH':'MM' 'AMPM** Displays the date and time in the format `12 23 93 12:45 PM`. Notice that the symbols MM, DD, and YY are separated by spaces enclosed in single quotation marks.

- **TMon** Displays the current month in a three-letter abbreviation. If you enter the date **12/24/93**, this format displays `Dec`.

- **TMonth' 'D', 'YYYY** Displays dates in the format `December 4, 1993`.

- **TWday** Displays dates with only the abbreviated weekday name of the date. For example, if you enter the date **12/4/93**, this format displays `Sat`.

- **TWeekday** Displays dates with the weekday name of the date. For example, if you enter the date **12/4/93**, this format displays Saturday.

- **TYYYY** Displays dates with only the year. If you enter the date **12/4/93**, this format displays 1993.

  If you don't like any of these user-defined formats, you can enter formatting codes to create your own. Just begin typing, and your codes will appear in the list box. When you enter formatting codes, remember the following rules:

  - Number formats can contain up to three parts, divided by semicolons. The first part determines the format for positive values, the second part determines the format for zero values, and the third part determines the format for negative values. Therefore, if you want to format each cell differently, based on whether its value is positive, negative, or zero, use all three parts. If you want to format positive and zero the same, use two parts—the first is for positive values and zero, and the second is for negative values. Here is an example:

    Positives and zero;Negatives

    Positives;Negatives;Zero

    Substitute your formatting codes for the words that appear in these examples. Note that date and time formats require only one part.

  - Begin each part with an **N** to create a number format or a **T** to create a date or time format.

  - The colons used to separate the codes do not appear in the format; they are merely the separators. However, anything you type in single quotation marks will appear as you type it. For example, entering **'dollars'** into a number format prints the word dollars into the cell.

Here are the number format codes:

- **0** Is a digit placeholder. Enter a zero to designate where digits appear. Use one zero to the left of the decimal point and any number of zeros to the right. The number of zeros used to the right of the decimal point indicates the number of places used. This format code will always display a zero if no value appears. For example, the format **N0.00** displays numbers with two decimal places. If you enter **.5** in a cell, the format displays 0.50.

- **9** Is a digit placeholder. This is similar to the 0 placeholder, but it does not add leading or trailing zeros. Hence, you need to enter only one 9 on each side of the decimal point. For example, the format **N9.9** displays numbers as you type them. If you enter **.5**, the format displays .5 in the cell. You can also combine this code with the previous one. For example, the format **N9.0** displays **.5** as .50.

- **, (comma)** Separates thousands with a comma. The format **0,000.00** displays the number **22334.5** as 22,334.50.

- **. (period)** Separates the integer from the decimal value. Use only one period in each portion of the number format. If you omit the period, no decimal values will appear.

- **%** Displays the number as a percentage value. For example, the format **0.0%** displays the value **.2** as 20.0%.

- ***** Repeats the character to the right until the cell is filled. For example, the format **N*.9.00** displays dot leaders: if you enter **25**, the format displays . . . . .25.00.

Here are the date and time format codes:

- **D, DD** Displays the day as a one-digit (D) or two-digit (DD) value. Single digits means that the numbers **1** through **9** do not include leading zeros. Double digits means the values **1** through **9** are displayed as 01 through 09.

- **Mo, MMo** Displays the month as a one-digit (Mo) or two-digit (MMo) value. Single digits means that the numbers **1** through **9** do not include leading zeros. Double digits means the values **1** through **9** are displayed as 01 through 09.

- **YY, YYYY** Displays the year as a two-digit (YY) or a four-digit (YYYY) value.

- **WDAY, WEEKDAY** Displays the weekday in an abbreviated (WDAY) or full (WEEKDAY) format.

- **MON, MONTH** Displays the month name in an abbreviated (MON) or full (MONTH) format.

- **H, HH** Displays the hour portion of a time value as a single digit (H) or two digits (HH). Single digits means that the numbers **1** through **9** do not include leading zeros. Double digits means the values **1** through **9** are displayed as 01 through 09.

- **Mi, MMi** Displays the minutes portion of a time value as a single digit (Mi) or two digits (MMi). Single digits means that the numbers **1** through **9** do not include leading zeros. Double digits means the values **1** through **9** are displayed as 01 through 09.

- **S, SS** Displays the seconds portion of a time value as either a single or double digit.

- **AMPM** Converts a time value to a 12-hour format and prints AM or PM when appropriate. Without this code, times are displayed in a 24-hour format.

Adding Borders and Lines to the Page

An important part of enhancing the appearance of your notebook pages is to separate blocks of information with borders and lines. Borders and lines make data easier to read. They can also add to the overall look and feel of your printed reports.

You can put a border on any or all sides of a cell. By combining borders across several cells, you can create many different effects, such as a long line under your headings, a box around a block of data, or lines separating the rows and columns in the notebook.

Besides placing borders along different sides of a cell, you can select from three distinct border styles: a single line, a thick line, and a double line. Figure 5.13 shows a worksheet with various borders applied.

To add borders to a cell or range of cells:

1. Select the cell or block to which you want borders attached. You might want to create a box around the block or add lines to all sides.

2. Right-click on the highlighted block and choose **Block Properties** to bring up the Active Block property inspector.

3. Click on the **Line Drawing** option from the Properties list. The screen should now look like Figure 5.14.

4. Click on one of the line types listed on the right side of the dialog box. To remove a line that has already been applied to the block, click on the **No Line** style; otherwise, select one of the three line styles.

5. Click on any of the four sides of the sample block in the middle of the dialog box—or click on the inside lines. As you click, Quattro Pro applies the line style you selected to that side. Continue to click on all sides to which you want this line style applied. Figure 5.15 shows what a box looks like after you've clicked on the double line style and then the top and bottom of the Line Segments sample.

6. Repeat Steps 4 and 5 to add other lines to the sides of the block. If you want to remove a line from a side, click on the **No Line** style and then click on the desired side.

7. Click on **OK** and Quattro Pro will add the borders to the cells you chose.

SHORTCUT

As a shortcut, Quattro Pro includes buttons for quickly applying the chosen line style to **All** sides, the **Outline**, or the **Inside** lines of the highlighted block. If you want to add lines in one of these three ways, just click on the appropriate button below the sample block (after selecting the line style).

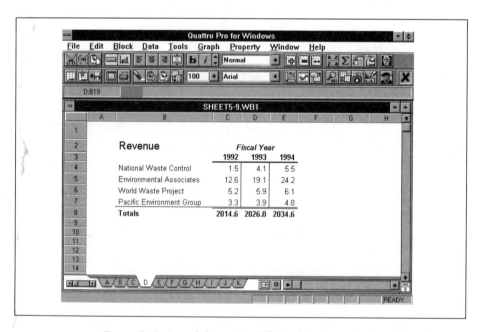

Figure 5.13 A worksheet with different borders applied.

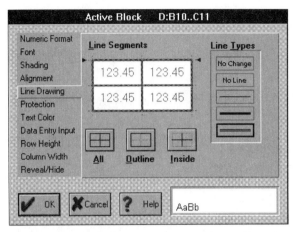

Figure 5.14 The Active Block property inspector's Line Drawing properties.

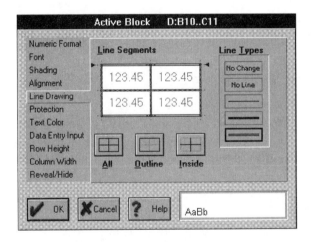

Figure 5.15 Click on the line style and then on the desired segment in the sample block.

Note that if you highlight only one cell—or a block of cells in a single row or column—the lines you apply to the inside of the sample block will not apply to the selection.

The **No Change** option allows you to leave a line segment exactly as it was before you started the procedure. This is useful when you are modifying a block that already contains some lines and want to leave certain segments as they currently appear while changing other segments.

Cell Borders vs. Grid Lines

Adding and removing the notebook grid lines (as described in Chapter 4) are quite different than adding lines to cells. Grid lines apply to the entire worksheet; you cannot change the color or style of the grid lines. Plus, grid lines do not appear on your printout, whereas borders and lines do.

Changing the Color of Lines and Borders

Quattro Pro lets you set the color of the border lines you apply to cells and blocks. However, you cannot change individual line segments; rather, you can change the color of all lines on the current page at once. Here's how:

1. Right-click on the page tab, or select the **Property>Active** Page command.
2. Click on the **Line Color** option.
3. Click on the desired color in the color palette. All lines on this page will appear in the color you select.
4. Click on **OK**.

The inability to change the color of individual line segments is not such a drawback when you consider that using several colors for lines on the same printout would probably be distracting anyway. Using a single color for the entire page makes the best design sense.

Changing the color palette
You can customize the colors in Quattro Pro's color palette using the **Property>Active Notebook** command with the **Palette** option. Use the **Edit Color** button to change any of the colors in the palette.

NOTE

Adding Background Colors to Cells

Quattro Pro can add a variety of colored backgrounds to your notebook pages. You can create blocks of colors on the page to highlight data. If you will be printing the worksheet in black and white, consider how the colors you apply will print on a black-and-white printer. Refer to Chapter 9 for more information.

Here's how to apply colors and shades to your cells:

1. Select the cell or block you want to color.

2. Right-click on the highlighted block and choose **Block Properties**. Quattro Pro will bring up the Active Block property inspector.

3. Click on **Shading** to display the shading color palettes.

4. Select a color from the Color 1 palette. Notice the change in the Blend palette.

5. Change the color in the Color 2 palette, if you so desire.

6. Select one of the blend combinations form the Blend palette.

7. Choose **OK**. Quattro Pro will apply the blend you selected to the selected cells.

The final shade or pattern applied to the selection will be a mixture of two colors. The shade or pattern finally placed in the cell(s) is determined by the selection made from the Blend palette. The bottom-right corner of the Properties dialog box shows you what the cell(s) will look like when you click on **OK**.

In applying shading to your notebook pages, remember to use moderation to enhance the readability of important data on the worksheet. If data appears inside the shaded block, consider changing the color of the text to contrast better with the cell shade. You might also consider using boldface to make the text more readable.

Using Styles

When you combine several formatting options to a cell or block, you might want to repeat those options again in another part of the notebook. For example, your worksheet might display important totals in the Currency number format using white text on a black cell shade. If your notebook has several totals to be formatted this way, you might find it tedious to set these formatting options over and over again.

To make this task easier, Quattro Pro lets you store combinations of formatting options so that you can use them over and over. These are known as *styles*. You can create as many styles as you like in each notebook and then use the style to format any cell or block in that notebook quickly. What's more, when you modify the style settings, all cells using that style will instantly change to reflect the new settings. In this way, you can easily make formatting changes throughout your notebook pages.

Each style you create contains information about seven different formatting categories: Alignment, Format, Protection, Line Drawing, Shading, Font, and Text Color. With any style, you can specify which formatting category or categories Quattro Pro will change—and which it will ignore. So one style might simply apply a font selection to your data, whereas another style applies a font choice, shading, and text color. Styles can be applied to an entire notebook, page, block, or an individual cell.

Applying a Style to a Cell or Block

On the standard SpeedBar, Quattro Pro for Windows supplies the drop-down menu seen in Figure 5.16. When you click on the arrow, you see a list of all the defined styles and number formats. Quattro Pro supplies several styles for you, and any custom styles you've created will also appear in this list (creating custom styles is described later in this chapter). To apply one of these styles to a cell or block:

1. Select the block of cells to be formatted.
2. Click on the arrow of the Style menu in the SpeedBar.
3. Click on the desired style.

The style you select will be applied to the highlighted cell or block; it's that easy. You'll probably find that using styles for formatting is so easy that you'll be anxious to create many styles of your own.

First, let's take a quick look at the built-in styles supplied by Quattro Pro. These include each number format (Comma, Currency, Date, Fixed, and so forth) plus the formats Heading 1, Heading 2, Total, and Normal. Figure 5.16 shows each of these styles applied to the notebook.

As you can see, the number format styles simply apply numeric formats to the cell—which has no effect on text entries. However, the Heading 1, Heading 2, and Total styles add text and cell-formatting options.

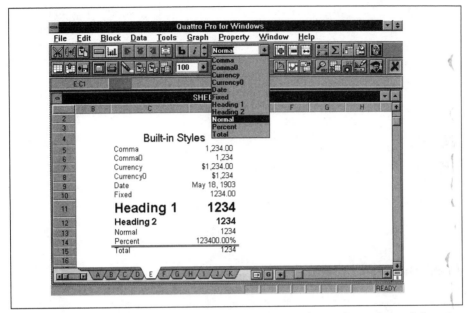

Figure 5.16 The Style menu on the SpeedBar along with samples on the worksheet.

Applying Styles Globally: The Normal Style

The Normal style is special: Quattro Pro automatically uses Normal on all cells in a notebook—unless you specifically change the cell to a different style. The Normal style, then, is the default for your cells. By changing the attributes of the Normal style, you can change the default used in the worksheet. That is, you can instantly change all cells in the worksheet that use the Normal style—which includes all cells that have not specifically been changed using another style or any formatting options, such as Boldface or a font selection. For example, if you change the Normal style on a brand new notebook, all cells will be affected by your changes. If you change the Normal style on an existing notebook that includes some formatted cells, only the unformatted cells will be affected by the change. Hence, if you want to change the default format for an entire notebook, it's best to change the Normal style before applying other formatting options. Some users choose to apply all formatting in the form of styles. That is, they do not apply individual formatting options to cells, but use styles only to format data. In this way, the worksheet formatting can be more uniform, and formatting changes can be made quickly and easily.

If you use the Normal style as is, it applies the General alignment and number format, protects the cell, sets the font to Arial 10, the text color to black, shading to white; the line drawing not applied. However, you can change the Normal style at any time, as described under "Creating and Editing Styles" below.

Returning a block to the default format
To return a block to the original format, select the block and then select **Normal** from the style drop-down menu. This will make the cell appear the way it did when the notebook was first created—or to the current Normal default if you have changed it.

N O T E

Creating and Editing Styles

The real power of the Styles list is that it stores your custom styles. You can combine any of the seven formatting options and store the setting under a special name in the Styles list. To create your own custom styles follow these steps.

1. Choose **Edit>Define** Style. The Styles dialog box seen in Figure 5.17 is displayed. The Define Style menu lists existing style names.

2. To create a new style, type a name into the entry box—replacing the current name in the box. You should be able to type the new name immediately after opening the dialog box. To edit an existing style, choose one of the names in the drop-down list.

3. Click on any of the seven buttons in the dialog box to establish the formatting for the style. A style need not contain all of the properties available; it can simply change the font or alignment of a cell without affecting the text color or other attributes. Each of the seven buttons produces formatting options from which to choose. More on this later.

4. After applying all the formatting you want for the style, click on **OK** from the Define/Modify Style dialog box. The new style now appears in the Styles list in the SpeedBar, or the existing style will be altered.

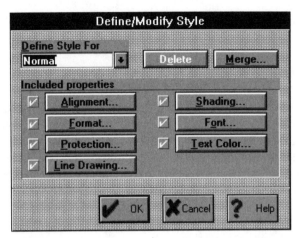

Figure 5.17 The Define/Modify Style dialog box.

When you enter a new style name into Define/Modify Style dialog box, Quattro Pro places a check mark beside each button in the dialog box. When a check mark appears beside a button, the style will include the settings in that category. If the check mark is removed, the style will not change those settings. For example, if you remove the check mark from the **Alignment** button, then your style will not affect a cell's alignment. Any existing alignment used in the cell will be retained, but all other styles will be applied to the cell. This is an excellent way to make modifications to cells that are already formatted—changing only the attributes you want to change.

As another option, you can also merge two different styles into one style. For example, if you want to add all the attributes in the Comma style to the Total style, choose the **Total** style in the Define/Modify Style dialog box, click on the **Merge** button, choose the **Comma** style from the Merge Style dialog box, and click on **OK**. The attributes of the merged style will be added to the style you are currently editing. If there are any conflicts between the two styles, the merged style will take precedence. You can also merge individual formatting from cells in the notebook by choosing the **Cell** option in the Merge Style dialog box and then identifying the cell in the Select Style entry box. All styles from that cell will be merged with the style you are currently editing. Merging is useful when you are not sure of the which attributes are being used in a particular style or cell and want to add them to another style. It can also be used to turn a combination of individual cell formatting into a style. Just format the cell as desired (using SpeedBar buttons and properties); then create a new style and merge the cell's formats with the new style. Instantly, you have turned the cell's formatting into a style.

NOTE

You cannot mix styles in the same cell
Although you can merge two styles into one, you cannot apply two or more styles to a cell at any given time. If you choose a second style for a particular cell, the second style will replace the first style, and all formatting will change to the second style's formatting. However, you can mix a style with manual formatting options. For example, you can format a cell with the **Right Align** button and then apply a style to the cell that does not change the alignment of that cell. The existing alignment will be added to the formatting of the style you applied.

When you redefine a style, all cells formatted with the style will change to the new definition—provided you have not added extra formatting to the cell using manual methods. For example, if you had a cell styled as Heading 1 and then used the SpeedBar's **Font Size** arrows to bump the point size up, the cell will not change at all when you change the definition of Heading 1. To ensure that the formatting of all applicable cells will change when you change style definitions, make sure you make all formatting changes through styles; don't just change something on the fly—without using a style.

Deleting Custom Styles from the List

Delete a style from the list by using the **Delete** button in the Define/Modify Style dialog box after choosing the style name from the list. When you delete a style, Quattro Pro goes out and finds all the cells formatted with that style and changes them to the Normal style.

When you choose the Normal style in the Define/Modify Style dialog box, the **Delete** button remains dimmed. Since Normal acts as the base style for every cell, Quattro Pro does not let you delete it. Although, if you want to, you can change its definition quite radically.

Formatting Tables with SpeedFormat

If your data appears in a standard table arrangement, you can use the **SpeedFormat** tool to quickly apply predesigned formatting combinations to the entire table. Speed formatting applies attractive layouts for tables that contain columns of data, column headings, and totals along the bottom and/or right edge. It can also be used to format lists of data containing column headings. To use the SpeedFormat tool, just highlight the table of data on the notebook page and then click on the **SpeedFormat** tool on the SpeedBar:

Quattro Pro displays a list of predesigned formats for your table with a sample of each, as shown in Figure 5.18.

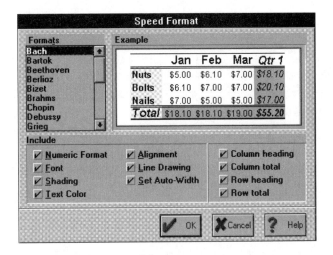

Figure 5.18 The SpeedFormat dialog box.

Click on the various formats along the left side of the dialog box; the formats are displayed under the names of famous composers. The dialog box displays an example of the chosen format so you can preview the style before applying it. When you see a format you like, click on **OK** to apply it to the selected table. You can use the **Include** options to modify the format you've chosen. For example, you might like the lines and colors used in Bartok, but you don't want to use the fonts. Remove the check mark from the **Fonts** option to eliminate the font settings from the format. The style will now not affect any existing fonts in the cells—so you can apply fonts individually.

If your table does not include all the elements listed along the right edge of the Include option, (Column Heading, Column Total, Row Heading, and Row Total), click on the check box to remove the check mark from the elements not present in your table. For example, your data might include totals along the bottom (column totals), but not along the right edge (row totals), so you would remove the check mark from **Row Totals**. If you remove the column and row totals, you can format database data or any other data that appear in a list. The Example window reflects the elements you choose in the **Include** options, so you'll always see exactly what you are getting.

Using Templates for Formatting

You can use the **File>Save As** command to save a copy of your active notebook under a different name or in a different subdirectory on the disk. This makes a second copy of the notebook, leaving the first copy intact. This is an excellent way of setting up a *template* notebook; templates can be used as the starting point for other notebooks—they might contain formatting and style settings that you want to use over and over in other notebooks. By starting with the master, or template, you don't have to set the styles in each new notebook—just save the notebook under a name different from the template.

In addition to saving formats and styles, you can save a skeleton of that budget or expense report you need to recreate once a month. What's included in a skeleton? We've already mentioned formats and styles, so now lets add formulas, print settings, graph settings, block names, and custom SpeedBars (see Chapter 16). Templates can include any data or formatting that you use over and over for new notebooks. Save different templates for different purposes if you like. For example, one template may contain only your custom styles and custom number formats as a starting point for any new application. You might have changed the Normal style to get a new default font, for example. Another template might be used to start new budget worksheets and will include column and row headings and even some formulas in place.

Use the same file extensions for all your template files
It is easy to open a template, enter your data, and then accidentally save the file without changing the file name, thus changing the template itself. To avoid this, try saving all your template files with the same file extension. A file name like **EXPENSE.TMP** might serve as a reminder

that you have been working in a template and need to give the file a new name. As a precaution, try saving the file under a new name (using **File>Save As**) immediately after opening the template itself. In this way, if you use the **File>Save** command without thinking, you will not destroy the template.

Summary

Formatting is an important part of creating notebooks. In fact, you'll probably find that you spend as much time formatting your notebook applications as you do creating formulas and entering data. The more you know about formatting, the more you can reduce this time investment.

This chapter described Quattro Pro's formatting capabilities. You can change the fonts and type styles of data, apply colors and shades to the data and the cell itself, add borders and boxes to the cells, and modify the widths of columns and the heights of rows. To use formatting over and over again throughout a notebook, use a custom style. In fact, if you apply all your formatting with styles, you'll have more control over the notebook for future changes. Finally, consider using templates to store "master" notebooks that can be used to start other worksheets. These templates might contain your custom styles, custom SpeedBars, and even some data and labels.

The next chapter takes you into the world of formulas and functions. Functions are the backbone of your notebooks. In the next chapter, you'll find all you need to know about using functions and creating more complex formulas. You'll also learn how to access all of Quattro Pro's functions—over 350 of them! But you don't need to learn them all; the next chapter provides details about some of the important functions for you to learn. The rest you can access from Quattro Pro's function help.

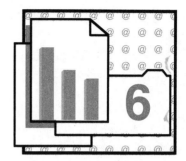

Formulas and Functions

Chapter 3 introduced the concept of formulas. You saw that you can calculate the data located in other parts of a page by using formulas that reference those values. Formulas lie at the heart of your notebooks and give you the power to calculate many different results from your data.

This chapter shows you how to get more from your formulas by using various forms of cell and range references. You'll learn how to

- Name your cells and blocks to make them easy to use in formulas
- Reference data from different pages of the notebook
- Keep cell and range references from changing when you copy them
- Use various functions to calculate specific values

Cell and Block References

The essence of notebook formulas is in the cell and block references they use. By entering these references, you can calculate the values in other cells of the page. References are simply the column and row labels for the cell. For example, cell C6 indicates the cell at column C and row 6.

A block reference identifies a group of cells. You can identify a block by typing the reference of any two corners of the block, separated by two dots. For example, the block of cells C5 through D10 is identified as C5..D10, D5..C10, D10..C5, or C10..D5.

The remaining sections will describe some special features associated with cell and range references.

Naming Cells and Blocks

By letting you name cells and blocks, Quattro Pro makes it easy to identify commonly used cells and blocks in your worksheets. A named cell or block can be identified by a name in a formula or function—rather than by its address. For instance, if you name the block C3..C7 as INCOME, then you use that name whenever you refer to that block:

@SUM(INCOME)

This function is identical to typing **@SUM(C3..C7)** and it's a lot easier to enter. Naming important cells in your notebooks makes it easier to decipher your formulas. For instance, the formula

+COST * QTY

might be used to calculate a total price for an item ordered. It's easy to see what is being calculated in this formula—as opposed to an equivalent one that uses cell addresses. To name a cell or block, follow these steps.

1. Highlight the desired cell or block using the techniques described in Chapter 3. The easiest way to highlight a block is to click and drag the mouse on the worksheet.

2. Select the **Block>Names Create** command. The dialog box shown in Figure 6.1 is displayed on the screen.

3. Type a name into the Name entry box. Make sure the Blocks box correctly identifies the block you've highlighted. (If you want to identify a different

block, just type the block reference into the space provided or cancel from this procedure and start again.)

4. Click on the **OK** button.

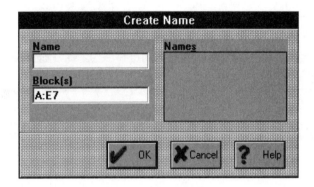

Figure 6.1 The Create Name dialog box.

Using Ctrl-F3 to create a new block name

The fastest way to create a new block name is to highlight the block and press **Ctrl-F3**. The Create Name dialog box will appear immediately, and the Block box will be filled in. The only thing left to do is enter the name of the block, and select **OK**.

Block names are limited to 15 characters. When specifying a block name, you can use any letter, number, or punctuation mark and some special characters. Avoid using characters that represent operators used in formulas, spaces, and names that look like cell addresses (such as A5). Do not create block names that contain only numbers (5678), as they cannot be used in a formula. You can enter names in upper- or lowercase letters—Quattro Pro does not distinguish between the two. When used in formulas, Quattro Pro always displays block names in upper-case letters.

In Quattro Pro it is possible to name more than one cell at a time, based on the contents of a column or row. This is accomplished with the **Block>Names>Auto Generate** command. Figure 6.2 shows a row of labels Jan through June—each labeling a column. In this example, you might want to name the columns Jan, Feb, Mar, and so on—so you can quickly refer to the values in each column (in column total formulas, for example). You might also want to name the rows using each company name, so you can refer to each row of values as well. In this case, you would have ten different block names if you named each row and column (not including the Totals). Rather than repeat the **Block>Names>Create** command ten times, you can perform the following task once.

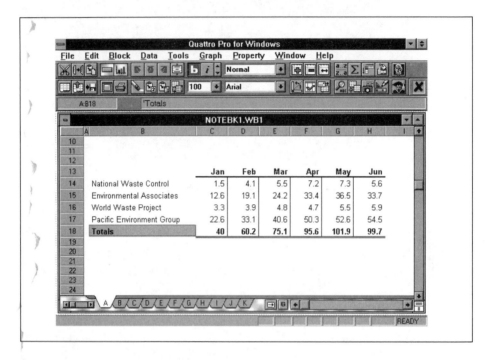

Figure 6.2 Use the Block>Names>Auto Generate command to create
several names at one time.

1. Highlight the entire block containing the data and the column and row headings. Note that you can select multiple blocks if desired.

2. Select **Block>Names>Auto Generate**.

3. Select the options that best describe the location of the blocks you want to name. **Under Top Row** uses the labels in the top row of the selected block to name the columns of data below them. **Right of Leftmost Column** uses the labels in the left column of the selected block to name the rows of data to the right. These are the two options we would use in the example in

Figure 6.2. Click on the desired options to place check marks beside them. Click again to remove the check marks. Check as many options as apply to the selection—the top two options are the most common.

4. If you want to name each cell that is at the intersection of a row and column, check the **Name Cells at Intersection** option. This gives names to individual cells by combining the row and column names. In the example, the name Jan_National Waste would apply to cell C14. Notice that the column label comes first, followed by an underscore and the row label.

5. Click on **OK** or press **Enter**.

Following are some guidelines for creating and using block names in Quattro Pro.

- Don't use names that look like cell addresses. Avoid using names that might be interpreted as cell addresses, such as A2 or EE1.

- Existing names appear in the **Block>Names>Create** dialog box. You can print a list of existing names in your worksheet by using the **Block>Names>Make Table** command.

- You can use two names for the same block. One block can be named two or more times if desired. Quattro Pro stores each unique name as well as the block reference to which it refers.

- You can use the same cell or block in two or more named ranges. A cell or block can appear as part of any number of other ranges.

- You can apply a name to a multiple-block reference. In Chapter 3 you learned how to select multiple blocks. You can apply a single name to one of these compound blocks to identify all the segments together.

- Use the **Block>Names>Delete** command to remove a block name. When the dialog box is displayed, select a block name to delete by clicking on it and then click on **OK**.

- Use the **Block>Names>Reset** command to delete all block names at once.

SHORTCUT

Jumping to named ranges
You can quickly move the cell pointer to the upper-left corner of a named block by using the Goto feature. Press **F5**, select the block name, and then select **OK**.

Entering formulas containing block names

While typing in the formula, press **F3** at the point where the block name would be entered. A Block Name list will appear on the screen, provided that at least one block name has been defined. You can select a block name to be entered into the formula by clicking on it and pressing **OK**. To view the coordinates of a block name, press the plus **+** (plus) key. To return to the original list view, press the **-** (minus) key. If you know the block name without having to use the **F3** command, you can simply type the name into the formula where it applies. However, if you type the name incorrectly, Quattro Pro will produce an ERR in the cell.

There are no rules restricting when block names can be created. Therefore, it is possible to create block names to define cell addresses that are already referenced in formulas on the page. When the block names are created, equivalent references in existing formulas will automatically change to display the block name rather than the cell address. For example, if you have the formula **+C5*2** and name cell C5 as VALUE, the formula will become **+VALUE*2**.

Referencing Blocks from Other Pages

In Quattro Pro, you can develop formulas that include references to cells or blocks on other pages in the notebook. Cell A5 on the first notebook page might add several cells from one of the other pages. To create a reference to other pages, just enter the cell or block name preceded by the page name. For example, to add cells C5 and C6 from page B of the notebook, you might enter this into any cell in page A:

+B:C5+B:C6

Notice that the page name precedes the cell address and is separated by a colon. Of course, you can combine different page references in the same formula:

+B:C5+C:C5

This example adds cell C5 from page A to cell C5 from page B. This is known as a *3-D formula*, because it uses the pages as a third dimension. In this case, you are adding cells *across* several pages.

Finally, remember that you can name the pages of your notebook. If you have already named the pages (see Chapter 4) use the name you applied to the page when you enter a notebook page reference. For example, if you named page B to be DEPT1, then the above formula would read

+DEPT1:C5+C:C5

3-D references are especially useful for block references. A *3-D block* is a group of cells selected across several notebook pages. You might have an application where page A is a summary of pages A through G. A formula on page A cell D7 might be the sum of the cells D7 on pages B through G. One possible formula is

+B:D7+C:D7+D:D7+E:D7+F:D7+G:D7

But a block reference is much easier to use:

@SUM(B..G:D7)

Here, the left side of the colon represents a range of pages: B through G, whereas the right side indicates that D7 is the cell address for each page. It is possible to expand the formula to include a block of cells for each page. The resulting formula might look like this:

@SUM(B..G:D7..H7)

Now we have indicated not only a range of pages, but also a block of cells from each page that should be included in the final value. In this case, the block D7..H7 will be summed across six pages.

Alternative syntax for 3-D formulas

The standard syntax for 3-D formulas, or formulas that reference other pages, is **STARTPAGE..ENDPAGE:RANGE**, where **STARTPAGE** is the first of a series of sequential pages and **ENDPAGE** is the last of the series; and where **RANGE** is any cell or range reference (or name) and applies to all the pages. Note that you can identify a single page if desired, as in **C:A1..C3**, or a single cell, as in **C..E:A1**, or both as in **C..E:A1..C3**. You can use page or range names anywhere in the syntax.

Another syntax for 3-D formulas is **STARTPAGE:STARTBLOCK..ENDPAGE: ENDBLOCK**, where **STARTPAGE** and **ENDPAGE** identify the page range and **STARTBLOCK** and **ENDBLOCK** identify the cells within those pages. Hence, you can identify a 3-D reference in either of these ways: **JAN..JUN:C5..G9** or **JAN:C5..JUN:C9**.

You can use block names from other pages too. For example, if you have named the block D7..H7 as SALES, to sum that range on a different page you can use the formula

@SUM(B:SALES)

This formula may appear on, say, page A. If you also named page B as SUMMARY, then the formula would be

@SUM(SUMMARY:SALES)

If you wanted a range of pages, you might get the following:

@SUM(JAN..JUN:SALES)

Referencing Blocks from Other Notebooks

Besides referencing blocks from other pages of your notebook, you can reference other cells or blocks in other notebooks. This may be useful if you use two or more notebooks in a single application, such as a complex accounting application. For example, suppose you have a sales-tracking application that uses several pages of a notebook called SALES. This tracks sales of your products for several regions of the United States. A Summary page in this notebook uses 3-D references to calculate grand totals across the entire product line. In addition to this application, you have a sales-forecasting notebook, called FORECAST, that projects sales for the year. At the end of each quarter, you want to compare the forecast with the actual sales figures and calculate differences and trends. This can be done by linking the two notebooks with *external references*, references to cells in other notebooks. For example, you might add a page to the FORECAST notebook that accessed information from the SALES notebook for your comparisons. Because the two notebooks are linked through external references, changes in the SALES notebook automatically update the linked formulas in the FORECAST notebook.

The syntax for creating external references is **+[FILE]PAGE:CELL**, where **[FILE]** is the name of the notebook, **PAGE** is the name of the page to which you are linking, and **CELL** is the cell address or cell name on the **PAGE**. For example, the formula **+[SALES]SUMMARY:F12** would pull the value from cell F12 in the SALES notebook's Summary page. This formula might appear in the FORECAST notebook.

Entering External References

One way to create external references is to type the linking formula directly into the cell of the receiving notebook. If the supporting notebook (the notebook specified in the link) is not open, you must include the entire path name to the file, as in **+[C:\DATA\SALES.WB1]SUMMARY:F12**. If the desired notebook is open, you can eliminate the directory path and enter only the notebook name, as in **+[SALES]SUMMARY:F12**.

Default path name for linked notebooks
Quattro Pro automatically assumes that the path of the linked notebook is the same as the notebook containing the linking reference.
For example, if the FORECAST notebook is contained in the **C:\DATA**
directory, then Quattro Pro assumes that the linked notebook is in the same directory. If this is so, then you can eliminate the path name from the linking formula. Otherwise, be sure to include the entire path name with the notebook name and extension.

You can also point to linked notebooks to enter them into linking formulas. Just open both notebooks (the one containing the link and the one to which you are linking); then start your formula in the receiving notebook with the plus sign or function name. For example, you might enter **@SUM** (to begin a summing formula, or just type a plus sign to begin a simple reference. Next, switch to the supporting notebook by using the Window menu or the **F6** function key. Finally, move the the desired page in the supporting notebook and click on the cell or range to which you are linking. Press **Enter** to complete the formula or type another operator to continue the formula; you will be returned to the receiving notebook. If you are entering a function that requires additional arguments, you can continue the formula by typing a comma; Quattro Pro returns you to the formula where you can complete the next argument. Press **Enter** when you are finished.

A final way to enter linking formulas is to copy the desired data from the supporting notebook and pasting it into the receiving notebook with the **Paste Link** option. Quattro Pro automatically creates linking references to the data you copied—so you don't have to type the references yourself. This is especially useful if you want to link to several cells in a block. Here's how to paste link.

1. Move to the supporting notebook (the notebook to which you are linking).

2. Highlight the data that you want to pull into the receiving notebook and use the **Edit>Copy** command or the **Copy** tool to copy the data.

3. Move to the receiving notebook and select the cell designating the upper-left corner of the linking references. The data from the linked notebook will appear in this area, along with all linking references.

4. Choose the **Edit>Paste Link** command.

The values in the copied cells appear automatically in the destination notebook along with all links in place.

Updating Links

After you have created linking references between notebooks, you can update the data at any time. If you open a notebook containing links, Quattro Pro gives you the option of updating the links. This can be done without the supporting notebook being open at all. Provided the links flow only from the supporting notebook to the receiving notebook, updating links will always give you up-to-date information. If, however, links flow both ways between the notebooks—or if the receiving notebook is a supporting notebook for other links, you should open all notebooks to keep the links up-to-date. If the supporting notebook is open when you open a receiving notebook, Quattro Pro will automatically update the links.

Using wildcards for quick linking
If you are linking to several notebooks within the same formula, you can use a wildcard instead of entering each notebook name. Just open the notebooks contained in the link and close any notebooks that are not included in the link. Next, enter the linking formula using the wildcard * as the notebook name, as in **[*]PAGE:Cell**. This automatically includes all open notebooks in the reference. This is useful in linking formulas that use functions, such as @SUM. For example, to sum cell A1 in all open notebooks, type **@SUM([*]A:A1)** and press **Enter**.

Copying Cell and Block References

Chapter 3 described how to copy data and duplicate it in another area of the notebook. You can use the drag-and-drop method or the **Copy** and **Paste** commands to copy data. When you copy a formula that contains a cell or block reference, Quattro Pro assumes that you want the resulting formula to adjust its reference relative to its location. Suppose you have the application shown in Figure 6.3. You want to copy the formula from cell C10 to cells D10, E10, and F10. When you copy the formula, Quattro Pro automatically adjusts the cell references to match the resulting cells. In this way, each copy of the formula will calculate the total of its own column—rather than getting four formulas that all calculate column C. Figure 6.4 shows the resulting page with the formula in cell D10 showing in the entry bar.

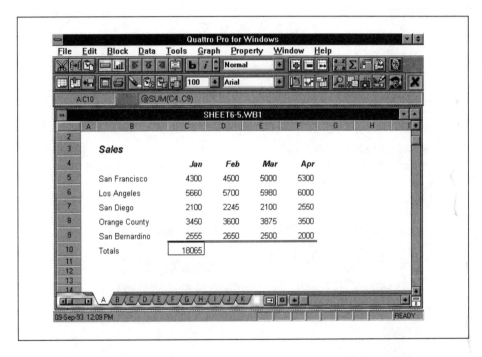

Figure 6.3 Ready to copy from cell C10 across to cells D10 through F10.

Normally this type of automatic adjustment, known as *relative referencing,* is desirable when copying formulas. But you might find occasions when you don't want cell references to adjust when you copy them. Instead, you want the reference to remain *absolute.*

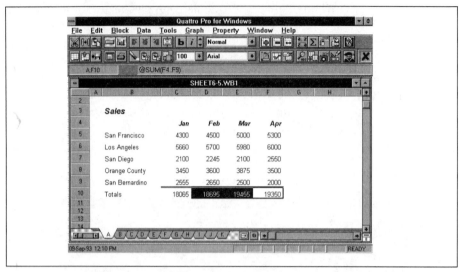

Figure 6.4 The result of copying the formula and range reference.

Suppose the previous worksheet example included a special adjustment as shown in Figure 6.5. In this case, the formula takes the overall adjustment into consideration when calculating the total.

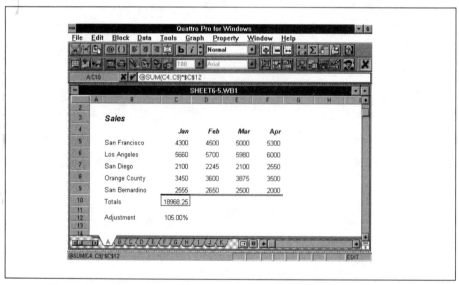

Figure 6.5 A new version of the notebook requiring an absolute reference.

If you were to copy this formula into the adjacent cells as before, you would end up with incorrect formulas in the resulting cells. Instead of using the same adjustment value from cell C12, each copy of the formula would reference a different cell. This is a case for using an absolute reference to cell C12, so that Quattro Pro does not adjust the reference when you copy the formula. Here are the details about each type of reference.

- **Absolute** An absolute cell address is one that refers to a particular cell and its contents. Absolute addresses are indicated by a dollar sign prior to the column and row indicator: **$D$5**, for example. Let's say that cell A6 contains the formulas **+$D$5**. If this formula is then copied to cell G7, the contents of G7 will be **+$D$5**.

- **Relative** A relative cell address is one that refers to a location containing a value to be used in the formula. This location has a relationship with the location of the cell containing the formula. When the formula is copied to a new cell, the cell address changes in relation to the new cell: the contents of cell B10 is **@SUM(B1..B9)**, for example. This formula is copied to cell E10. After the formula is copied, the contents of E10 are **@SUM(E1..E9)**. Unless you add the dollar signs to a reference, Quattro Pro assumes they are relative.

- **Mixed** A mixed cell address is one that contains both relative and absolute references. For example, the reference **$D7** uses an absolute column reference and relative row reference. The reverse is **D$7**. When copying a formula with a mixed cell address, the absolute portion of the address remains the same, whereas the relative portion changes. Lets say the cell B18 contains the formula **+25*$D7**. When we copy that formula to B12, it changes to **+25*$D1**.

SHORTCUT

Changing the reference of a cell address using the F4 key
Enter the desired cell address into the formula. Now press **F4.** The address will change from **D4** to **$A:$D$4**, indicating that the page and cell address are both absolute. Each time **F4** is pressed, the format of the cell address changes. Next is **$A:D$4**, then - **$A:$D4**, followed by - **$A:D4**, **$D$4**, **D$4**, and **$D4**.

Block names can be either relative or absolute. As with cell addresses, absolute block names are preceded by a dollar sign. The formula **+TOTAL** uses a relative block name, whereas **+$TOTAL** is an absolute block name. When copying a formula with an absolute block name, the block name will still be referenced in the formula's new location. For example, the formula in cell B15 is **+$TOTAL**, where **TOTAL** refers to the cell address A15. When the formula is copied to cell C15, it remains **+$TOTAL**. The same block name used as a relative reference, and copied to C15, changes to read **+B15**.

There are two ways to copy a total across several cells in a row (or down several cells in a column).

- Highlight the row or column that is to contain the totals. Now click on the **SpeedSum** button on the SpeedBar, and all the cells will be filled with their respective sums.

- Enter the desired sum formula into the first cell of the row and press **Enter** to complete the formula. Now use the **Edit>Copy** command to copy the first formula. Highlight the remaining cells in the row, and use the **Edit>Paste** command to duplicate the formula into those cells.

Using Functions

You can do many things by using formulas creatively. You can sum the values in a column or get an average of those values. But some things would be difficult to manage with standard formulas and worksheet logic. So Quattro Pro provides a set of special functions that help you calculate special values from your data. Some functions are simple and could be accomplished with formulas, such as the @SUM function, which simply totals the values in several cells, or the @PI function, which simply represents the value pi. Other functions are rather complex and cannot be duplicated easily with simple math. Quattro Pro offers many different types of functions from which to choose.

- **Financial** These functions perform financial calculations, such as determining parts of a loan (term, interest rate, payment amount, and so forth) and calculating annuities.

- **Date and Time** Date and Time functions help you perform date and time math. You can convert values into dates and times, produce the current date and time, and more.

- **Mathematical** These functions operate on numeric values and produce mathematical results. These include trigonometric and logarithmic calculations.

- **Statistical** These are functions that perform statistical analysis on your data. You can calculate trends and perform sample statistical operations on large amounts of data.

- **Miscellaneous** These are functions that help you locate values from tables and provide information about the notebook. You can search a table of values to locate information for your worksheets by using the lookup and reference functions.

- **Database** Database functions process information stored in a Quattro Pro database range. This includes database statistical analysis—such as counting certain entries in a database. Database functions are discussed in Chapter 12.

- **String** String functions manipulate text strings. They can convert numbers to text, display text in all uppercase letters, and more.

- **Logical** Logical functions make conditional tests and produce logical results based on the tests. Perhaps the most useful logical function is the @IF function.

- **Engineering** Engineering functions perform five different engineering tasks: number conversion, boolean math, complex number analysis, bessel calculations, and miscellaneous operations.

Parts of a Function

Functions contain three main parts: the @ symbol, the function name, and the arguments in parentheses. Functions can be entered by themselves, or as part of a larger formula:

@SUM(C5..C10)

+C1+@SUM(C5..C10)

@SUM(BUDGET)

Most functions perform operations on specific data, which you enter into the function's parentheses. These are called *arguments*. The arguments for the SUM examples above include the range C5..C10 and the range name BUDGET (which might be applied to the range C5..C10). Hence, the SUM function will produce the sum of those cells. Some functions require several arguments.

Generally, arguments must be entered in specific ways for the function to work properly. For example, the @VLOOKUP function, which searches a table for a specified value, requires that you first enter the value you want to find in the table, then the worksheet range containing the table itself, and then the column from the table that contains the result. This can be expressed like this:

@VLOOKUP(*x,block,column*)

The words *x, block,* and *column* are simply placeholders for the actual values you should enter. This form of expressing the function is called its *syntax*. All functions have a specific syntax that you must use to make the function work. Here are some tips to help make it easier to learn syntax.

- Arguments must be separated by commas. If a function requires more than one argument, use commas between them.

- Some arguments require that you enter a value. Arguments listed as *x, y, z,* or n indicate that you should enter a value. This can be a constant value or a reference to a cell containing a value—including a reference to another notebook page or even an external reference.

- Value arguments are not always listed with the word *value*. Some functions try to be more descriptive, with names like *NPer* and *Pmt*. These names help describe the purpose of the argument. You'll probably have to refer to the Quattro Pro *Building Spreadsheet Applications* manual or the function help screens for more details about these special values.

- Some arguments require that you enter a *block*. These are usually identified with the word block. When entering a block argument, you can enter any block reference (such as C3..C7) or block name (such as SALES).

Entering block references using the mouse or keyboard
You can type block references when you need them, or you can point to the desired block using the mouse or keyboard. When you are ready to enter the block, just use the mouse to highlight the desired block on the worksheet. Quattro Pro will automatically insert the reference of the highlighted block into the function. You also can highlight the desired block using the keyboard.

- String arguments can be entered as constants or references. If a function specifies the *string* argument, you can enter any text label in quotation marks or a reference to a cell containing the desired text. If you use a reference, then do not use quotation marks.

- You can enter function names in upper- or lowercase letters. Quattro Pro does not care whether you use upper- or lowercase letters for the function.

Quattro Pro has more than 300 worksheet functions from which to choose. You'll probably find that you use certain functions a lot, and you'll become familiar with those. (Some commonly used functions are covered later in this chapter.) But you might have to access a seldom-used function for a specific purpose. In this case, Quattro Pro's function listing will come in handy.

To view a list of worksheet functions, press **Alt-F3**. Select a function and press **F1** for a description. When you find the function you want to use, double-click on it in the function list. This inserts the function into the active cell (or into the formula bar at the location of the cursor). At the same time, the syntax of the complete function is displayed on the left side of the status bar. You can then replace the name placeholders with your actual data.

Some Essential Functions

Here are some of Quattro Pro's most commonly used functions, ones that will be useful in many of your notebooks. You can augment these with others from the function listing.

@AVG(List)

This function calculates the mean average of the values specified by *List*.

- **List** One or more items separated by commas. List can contain any combination of numeric values, cell addresses, block names, and formulas that contain values.

Caveat:

- If the list contains a blank cell, that cell is not included in the calculations. Cells containing labels or label prefixes are treated as though they contain a zero. If any of the cells in the list contain ERR or NA as a result of a formula calculation, the value returned by @AVG is ERR or NA, respectively.

Examples:

@AVG(A1..A5)

@AVG(BLOCK17)

@AVG(17,B5.B10,BLOCK8)

@SUM(List)

The @SUM function provides a simple way to total a block of values. Just enter the function and specify the desired block as the argument. You can enter cell or block references into the list. For example, to sum the block C5..C10, enter

@SUM(C5..C10)

You can point to the desired block using the mouse or keyboard. Just type **@SUM(** and then click and drag to highlight the desired block. Type in a close parentheses and press **Enter** when finished. The advantage to this method is that you can quickly sum any block of cells on the worksheet. Plus, you can specify a block name (assuming the desired block has been named) to make it easier to identify the block.

Using the SpeedSum tool to calculate totals
The fastest method of summing a column or row of values is to use the **SpeedSum** tool located on the SpeedBar:

SHORTCUT

When you click on the **SpeedSum** tool, Quattro Pro enters the @SUM function into the active cell and automatically enters the block above or to the right of the active cell as the argument in the @SUM function. Just click on an empty cell below a column of values (or to the right of a row of values), click on the **SpeedSum** tool, and then press **Enter**.

If your active cell contains data above *and* to the left, you can specify which block to use in the @SUM by highlighting the entire block plus the blank cell. Do this by clicking first on the blank cell; then drag to highlight the rest of the block. This leaves the blank cell as the active cell. Now click on the **SpeedSum** tool to place the @SUM function into the active cell. The highlighted block will be used as the argument of the @SUM function. Press **Enter** to complete the procedure.

@CELL (Attribute, Block)

This function returns information about the upper-left cell in a block depending on the attribute specified. It is used most often in macros and in conjunction with @IF.

- **Attribute** Attribute can be any of the items listed in the table below. They can be entered in either upper- or lowercase, but they must be surrounded by double quotation marks when entered directly into the formula. They can also be contained in a cell—in which case the attribute argument is a cell address or name containing the desired attribute.

- **Block** The cell address or block name of the block to be examined.

Here are the *Attribute* values you can use.

- **Address** The cell address of the first cell in the specified block.
- **Row** The row number of the first cell in the specified block.
- **Col** The column number of the first cell in the specified block.
- **Contents** The number, label, formula, and other material contained in the first cell in the specified block.
- **Type** The type of data contained in the first cell in the specified block.
- **Prefix** The label-prefix of the first cell in the specified block.
- **Protect** A designation determining whether the first cell in the specified block is protected.
- **Width** The width of the column in which the first cell in the specified block is located.
- **Format** The current format of the first cell in the specified block—for example, FN (Fixed), Cn (Currency), D6 (HH:MM:SS AM/PM), H (Hidden).

Caveat:

- @CELL does not recalculate automatically. To obtain the current value press **F9**.

Examples:

> **@CELL("prefix", A5)**
> **@CELL("row",TOTAL)**
> **@CELL("contents",A5.A10)**

@CELLPOINTER(Attribute)

@CELLPOINTER is similar to @CELL in that it returns the specified attribute of a cell. The difference is that with @CELL you can specify and cell or block, whereas @CELLPOINTER returns only the attributes for the cell currently containing the cell pointer.

- **Attribute** The values available are the same as those used with @CELL. They are entered in the same way.

Caveat:

- @CELLPOINTER does not recalculate automatically. To obtain the current value press **F9**.

Using @CELLPOINTER with a cell other than the current one
To specify a cell different from the current location, move the cell pointer to a different cell and press **F9**. The results of the @CELL-POINTER formula will reflect the attributes of this new cell.

Examples:

> **@CELLPOINTER("address")** Determines the current location of the cell pointer.
>
> **@CELLPOINTER("format")** Determines the format of the current cell.

@COUNT(List)

This function returns the number of nonblank cells in the specified *List*.

- **List** One or more items separated by commas. List can contain any combination of numeric values, cell addresses, block names, and formulas that contain values.

Caveat:

- Blank cells and text labels are treated as values of 0. However, if a blank cell appears in a block reference, Quattro Pro ignores the blank.

Examples:

@COUNT(JANUARY)
@COUNT(A7..A10)
@COUNT(A7,A5,JANUARY)

@HLOOKUP(Value, Block, Row)

This function allows you to access data in a table by searching for it horizontally (by row) based on an index located at the top of the table.

- **Value** Any value or reference to a cell containing a value. It can also be a formula that results in a value.
- **Block** The location of the table to be searched. Cell coordinates or a block name can be used. The table should have search values along the top row in ascending numerical order.
- **Row** A value indicating the row from which to return a value. If the value is 0, @HLOOKUP will return the value in the first row of the table. The value 1 will return a value from the first row below the index row, or row Z.

Caveats:

- If *Value* is a string, @HLOOKUP looks for an exact match, taking into account upper- and lowercase letters. If *Value* is a number and the exact number cannot be found, @HLOOKUP locates the closest number in the row that is lower than the specified *Value*. Index values must be in the first row of the table, and each cell of the index row must contain a value. If a referenced cell is blank, zero is returned by @HLOOKUP. If numbers are used in the index row, they must be in ascending order.

- These conditions produce an ERR value:

- *Row* is less than 0.

- *Row* is equal to or greater than the number of rows in *Block*.

- *Value* is less than the smallest value in the first row (index row) of *Block*.

- @HLOOKUP cannot find a match when *Value* is a string.

Examples:

@HLOOKUP("Jan",MONTHS,3)

@HLOOKUP(2000,AA1.AD15,10)

@HLOOKUP(D5,AA1.AD15,D6)

Figure 6.6 shows an example of an @HLOOKUP function.

@ISERR(X)

This function is used to determine whether a cell contains ERR. It is useful in conjunction with the @IF function for performing certain actions if an error occurs in a cell. It's also useful for determining whether incorrect entries are made, such as entries that would cause a "divide by zero" error.

- **X** A cell address, block name, formula, or numeric value. If ERR is found, a 1 (TRUE) is returned; otherwise, 0 (FALSE) is returned.

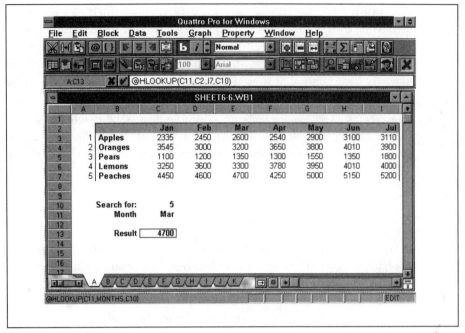

Figure 6.6 An @HLOOKUP example.

WARNING

ERR is not equivalent to the label ERR

ERR is a value returned by Quattro Pro when an error occurs. It can also be generated with @ERR.

Examples:

> **@ISERR(B3)**
> **@ISERR(C7/F6)**
> **@IF(@ISERR(C6),"An error occurred",500)**

@IF(Condition,Yes,No)

This function evaluates a condition and returns a value based on that evaluation. If the condition is true, Yes is returned. If the condition is false, No is returned.

- **Condition** The condition is any logical expression that can be evaluated to be true or false. Logical expressions can be created using one or more logical/relational operators. When #AND# is used to evaluate two logical expressions, both must be true for Yes to be returned. When #OR# is used, only one logical expression must be true for Yes to be returned. Refer to Chapter 3 for details about logical operators.

- **Yes, No** Yes and No are the values returned once the condition is evaluated. They can be numeric, text, formulas, or cell references where these values are stored. You can also enter another @IF test as a Yes or No value.

Caveat:

- If your condition looks for a label value, as in A1="January", and A1 contains a numeric value, the expression will evaluate to false. The same holds true if the condition is A1=0, and cell A1 contains a label. This is a change in functionality from the DOS version of Quattro Pro, where zero was treated as a match for a string or label.

Examples:

@IF(A1>5,D7*2,D7)

@IF(C3=10#OR#D5=10,25,@ERR)

@IF(B2=H17,100,75)

@LEFT(String,Num)

This function returns the number of characters indicated by *Num* from the *String*, reading from left to right. This is useful for manipulating text strings—splitting long text entries, for example.

- **String** A string value or cell or a cell name containing a string value.
- **Num** A numeric value greater than zero that represents the number of characters to be returned.

Caveats:

- If the *String* argument does not contain a string value but a numeric or date value, or if it is blank, @LEFT returns ERR.

- If the value specified for the *Num* argument is greater than the length of the string, the entire string will be returned.

NOTE

Using @LENGTH to determine Num based on the length of the string
@LEFT(D7,(@LENGTH(D7)-3)) *Num* is the length of *String* less 3. Regardless of the length of the string in cell D7, this formula will return all but the rightmost three characters.

Examples:

@LEFT(B3,5)

@LEFT(SALESMAN,7)

@MID(String, StartVal, Num)

This function returns the specified number of characters from the middle of a string.

- **String** Any text string enclosed in quotes or any cell reference containing a label or text formula.

- **StartVal** Any number greater than or equal to zero, representing the position of the first character in the string to be returned.

- **Num** The total number of characters to be returned. Any number greater than or equal to zero.

Caveat:

- When *StartVal* is greater than or equal to the length of *String,* or if *Num* = 0, an empty string or a blank is returned.

Examples:

> **@MID(D7,5,3)**
>
> **@MID(D7, D6, D5)**
>
> **@MID(D7,@LENGTH(D7)/2,4)**

@NOW

This function returns the serial number that corresponds to your computer's date and time settings. The value is updated each time you recalculate your notebook.

Using @NOW with other functions to display additional date and time information

To display only the date portion, use **@today** or **@int(@now)**. To display only the time portion, use **@mod(@now,1)**. **@int(@mod (@now,7))** returns the number of the day in the week. If the day is Thursday, the value returned is 5; Sunday = 1.

Displaying the serial number in a variety of Date and Time formats

Use **Property>Current Object>Numeric Format** to select the appropriate display format.

@RIGHT(String, Num)

This function returns a specified number of characters from the right side of the *String*.

- **String** A string value or a cell or a cell name containing a string value.
- **Num** A numeric value greater than zero representing the number of characters to be returned.

Caveats:

- If the string argument contains a numeric or date value and not a string value, or if it is blank, @RIGHT returns ERR.
- If the value specified for the Num argument is greater than the length of the string, the entire string will be returned.

Examples:

> **@RIGHT(A7,4)**

@STRING(Num, Decimals)

This function coverts a numeric value to a string, rounding it off to the number of decimal places specified.

- **Num** The numeric value to be converted. This can also be a cell referencing a numeric value or a formula resulting in a numeric value.
- **Decimals** The number of decimal places to which the numeric value should be rounded.

Caveat:

- Regardless of the display format of the original number, the converted string will be in the *General* format.

Examples:

> **@STRING(67.98,1)**
>
> **@STRING(A5,0)**
>
> **@STRING(15*A8,2)**

@TODAY

This function displays the system date. It is equivalent to `@INT(@NOW)`.

@VLOOKUP(Value, Block, Column)

This function locates data in a table by searching for it vertically (by column) based on an index located to the left of the table. It is very similar to the `@HLOOKUP` function.

- **Value** Value can be any string or number, a cell name or address referencing a cell containing a label or number, or a formula resulting in a string or numeric value.

- **Block** The location of the table to be searched. Cell coordinates or a block name may be used.

- **Column** A value, a cell address or name containing a value, or a formula that returns a value from 0 to 8191. If the value is 0, @VLOOKUP will return the value of the index. If *Value* and the index entry are string values and *Column* = 0, the return value is the column offset in which *Value* was found.

Caveats:

- If V*alue* is a string, @VLOOKUP looks for an exact match taking into account upper- and lowercase letters.

- If *Value* is a number and the exact number cannot be found, @VLOOKUP locates the closest number in the column without exceeding the specified *Value*.

- Index values must be in the first row of the table, and each cell of the index row must contain a value. If a referenced cell is blank, @VLOOKUP returns zero.

- If numbers are used in the index column, they must be in ascending order.

Examples:

@VLOOKUP("Jan",MONTHS,3)
@VLOOKUP(2000,AA1.AD15,10)
@VLOOKUP(D5,AA1.AD15,D6)

Summary

The real power of a spreadsheet application lies in the formulas and functions used. Quattro Pro offers some useful functions that help you get more from your data. When used with proper cell and range references, your applications can access and calculate data from anywhere in the notebook.

Remember that formulas always begin with an operator, value, or @ symbol. If you want to use a function in your formula, remember that you must adhere to the function's syntax requirements for the result to be accurate.

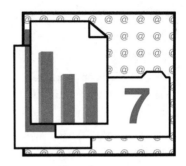

The Data Modeling Desktop

Spreadsheet programs work with some typical types of data and some typical problems. Analyzing sales and marketing information is a common spreadsheet task. When analyzing large amounts of information, you might want to employ the powers of the new Data Modeling Desktop (DMD), which lets you manipulate your data for different types of analysis. The Data Modeling Desktop is a tool for changing the way you interpret and view large amounts of information, such as sales and marketing data.

This chapter introduces and explains the Data Modeling Desktop. You'll learn how to create a data model and how to manipulate your data for various reports. Specifically, you will learn

- When to use the Data Modeling Desktop
- How to get data ready for the Data Modeling Desktop
- How to create a model from your data
- Ways to manipulate the model for various results
- How to use your data model inside Quattro Pro

What Is a Data Model?

A data model is also known as a *cross tabulation report*. Such a report summarizes large amounts of data into multidimensional models. The Data Modeling Desktop lets you manipulate and rearrange the model you create—providing numerous different "views" into your data.

Let's start with a basic, two-dimensional data model. A two-dimensional model simply displays two aspects of your data—or two pieces or data—in a readable form. Suppose your data consist of sales totals and products for the first half of 1994, two pieces of information for analysis. Figure 7.1 shows what this data might look like before and after you place it into a model.

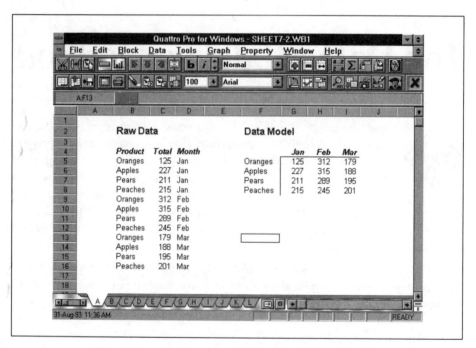

Figure 7.1 A simple two-dimensional model and its data.

As you can see from Figure 7.1, a data model is nothing more than a table-oriented presentation of raw data. Such a model gives you a better view of the data for analysis purposes. Plus, you can add totals and other calculations to the table, which would be difficult to add to the raw data. With simple, two-dimensional data, you might automatically place the data into a table-oriented format like this.

Now suppose you wanted to add a third element (or dimension) to the data. For example, suppose this data is divided into two regions: East and West. Figure 7.2 shows the raw data and a data model containing this added element.

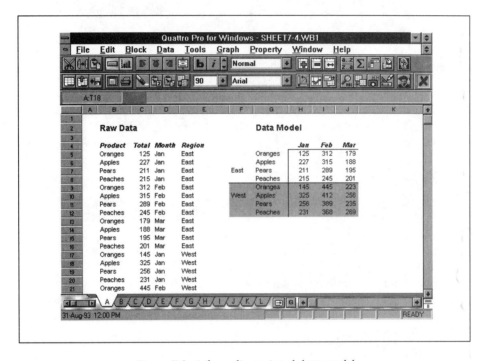

Figure 7.2 A three-dimensional data model.

Notice that the raw data is already getting difficult to see at one time. But the data model displays the added element easily. With this third piece of data, you can begin to see how the model might be manipulated in different ways. For example, the model in Figure 7.2 shows the data oriented by product and region. You could change the orientation of the model to emphasize the dates and regions—or in other ways as shown in Figure 7.3.

All these data models (tables) show the same data in different ways. And each one emphasizes a different aspect of the data. A regional manager would likely prefer the first data model in Figure 7.3, which emphasizes the regional split. A finance manager might prefer the second model, which is divided primarily by months, which helps her keep track of monthly income figures. A product manager might prefer the third style because it shows how each product performed.

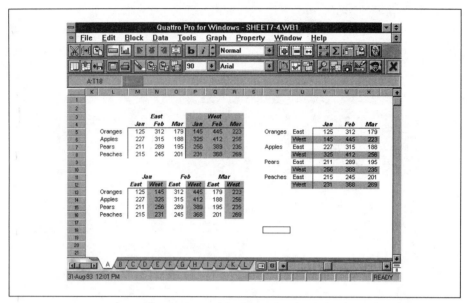

Figure 7.3 Different views of the three-dimensional data model.

With this simple, three-dimensional data, you can see how many ways you can present and analyze the data. Add different totals into this picture, such as monthly totals, product totals or regional sales totals, and the models become even more sophisticated.

The data models used in Figures 7.1 through 7.3 were all created inside Quattro Pro without the use of the Data Modeling Desktop. Hence, each data model was entered individually by referring to the raw data. This proved to be a lot of work entering and formatting the tables. With the Data Modeling Desktop, you can quickly and easily move from one model to the next without having to create all three models separately. By manipulating the main elements of a model (such as the month names or product names) you can change the orientation of the model—then quickly change it back again. The rest of this chapter shows you how to accomplish this type of modeling task using the Data Modeling Desktop.

The Data Modeling Data

Data modeling is used primarily for data consisting of three or more dimensions. Although we were able to create at least three separate models from the example data in Figure 7.3, this is actually a simple model, consisting of only three dimensions (or elements). Suppose your data consists of five or six elements? Such raw data might look like Figure 7.4.

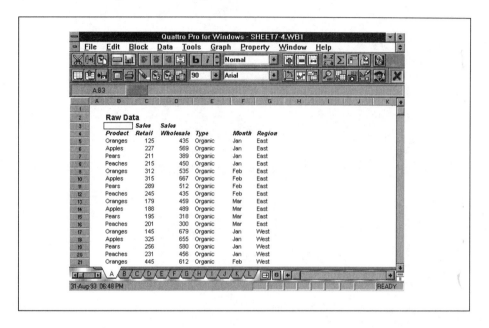

Figure 7.4 Multi-dimensional data.

Now the raw data is beginning to look more like a database of marketing or sales data. This might be data collected over time and stored either in the spreadsheet or in a database and then moved into Quattro Pro for analysis. Either way, it's important to begin your data modeling tasks with raw data as shown in the example. With this raw data, you can create any type of data model inside the Data Modeling Desktop.

Starting the DMD

After you have the appropriate data in place in a Quattro Pro notebook, you're ready to start the Data Modeling Desktop. The first step is to highlight the appropriate data in the notebook page. It can't hurt to highlight the entire database—whether you end up using all the data elements or not. After the data is selected, click on the Data Modeling Desktop tool in the SpeedBar:

The Send Data to Data Modeling Desktop dialog box appears as shown in Figure 7.5.

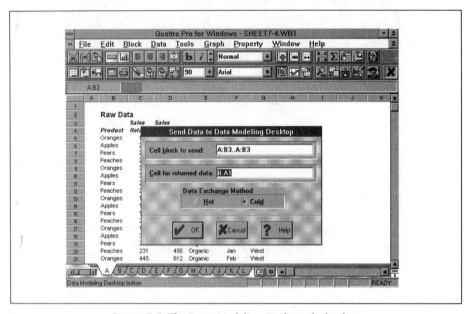

Figure 7.5 The Data Modeling Desktop dialog box.

This dialog box lets you specify the data being sent to the DMD and a location for the resulting model. When the model is complete, you can automatically place it into the notebook at a specified cell. Other options in this dialog box let you specify whether the data is sent to the DMD with live links or not. Following is a description of the options in this dialog box.

- Cell block to send Specifies the data block you are using for the model. The data inside this block will be used to create the model. If you highlight the block before clicking on the DMD tool in the SpeedBar, the block reference will already be in place. If you have not highlighted the block, or if you want to change the block you've selected, you can double-click in the entry area of this option and select the desired block. Press Enter after highlighting the block to return to the dialog box.

- Cell for returned data Specifies where the resulting data model will be sent when you complete the DMD procedure. In other words, the completed data model will appear in the notebook starting at this location. By default, Quattro Pro specifies cell A1 of the first blank page as the starting cell for the resulting data. You can specify any location you like, but indicate a cell that has plenty of blank cells to the right and below, so that the entire data model has enough room to fit into the location you specify. Using a blank page is a good idea.

- Data Exchange Method Specifies whether the DMD retains live links to the data being sent, such that changes to that data are reflected in the DMD data. The Hot option retains the links, and the Cold option copies the data into the DMD without links. Note that the Hot option requires more memory. If you don't plan to modify the data while you are working on the DMD model, choose the Cold option to conserve memory.

After you choose the options in this dialog box, press OK to send the data. The screen should now look like Figure 7.6. This is the Data Modeling Desktop screen with your data in place and ready to be used.

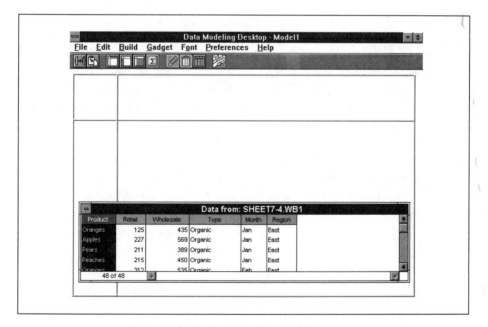

Figure 7.6 The Data Modeling Desktop screen.

The Data Modeling Desktop is a separate program
Note that the DMD is a separate program from Quattro Pro itself. Hence, you can switch between the DMD and Quattro Pro using **Alt-Tab** or the Task Switcher in Windows.

The Data From window shows the data you selected from the worksheet. You probably cannot see all the data inside the window, but all you really need to see are the headings. Behind this window is the Data Modeling Desktop page. The page is divided into three sections: The top row area (for column headings), the left column area (for row headings), and the center (for numerical amounts). By dragging the headings from the Data From window into these three areas, you can create a data model for the data. You can turn any of the headings used for the original data into either row or column headings in the model. The following section explains how to create the data model by dragging these headings into place.

Creating the Model

When you click on a column in the Data From window, you can then drag that column of data into any of the three areas in the DMD work area. This determines the basic orientation of the model. You can change this orientation at any time, so it's not critical that you figure out exactly how the model should look now. Just click on one of the headings in the Data From window and drag into one of the three areas on the DMD work area. As you drag into one of the three regions, an icon in the DMD SpeedBar confirms which region you have selected. Drop the data in that region to place the headings as row or column labels. Figures 7.7 and 7.8 show what it looks like to drag the Product column from the Data From window into the row heading area of the DMD work area. Notice in Figure 7.7 that the Row Heading indicator icon is highlighted. Figure 7.8 shows the result after dropping the data into that area.

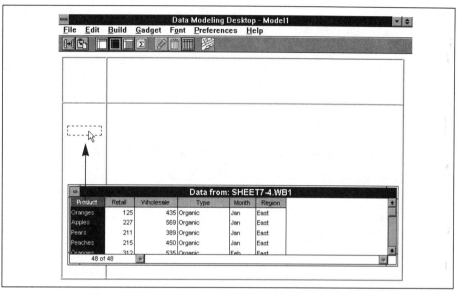

*Figure 7.7 Dragging a column from the Data From window
into the row heading area of the DMD work area.*

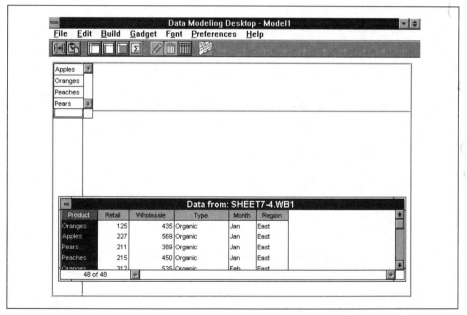

*Figure 7.8 The result after dropping the Products column into place
as row heading in the DMD work area.*

The result is a small table containing the headings for the data model. Notice that the data model takes up only as much space as is required by the data. As you add more headings and data to the model, you will see the model grow. This is unlike a normal spreadsheet, where you enter headings into existing rows and columns. The DMD creates rows and columns only as required by the data you insert into the model. Figures 7.9 and 7.10 show the process of adding the Month column to the column heading area and the resulting model at that point.

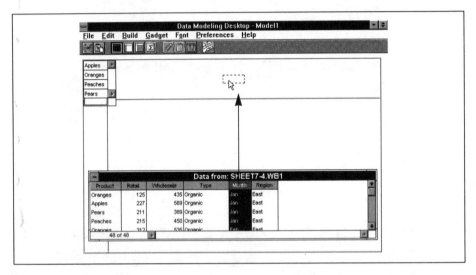

Figure 7.9 Adding the Month column as a column heading in the model.

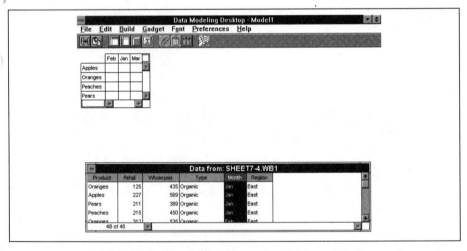

Figure 7.10 The resulting model with a row and column heading in place.

Now watch what happens when you add numerical data into the middle of the model. Figures 7.11 shows the process of dragging the Retail column into the middle of the model, and Figure 7.12 shows the resulting model.

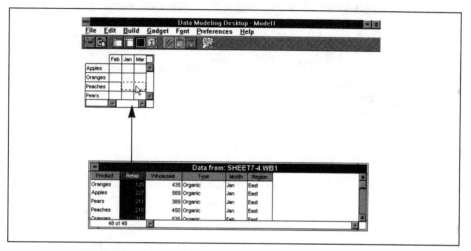

Figure 7.11 Adding numerical data to the middle of the model.

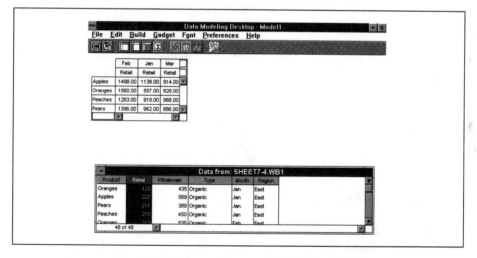

Figure 7.12 The resulting model with data added.

As you add more data to the columns, rows, and middle areas of the DMD, the model begins to take shape. Figure 7.13 shows the result after adding the Region column as a row heading in the model and the Type column as a column heading. Also, the Wholesale column was added to the middle.

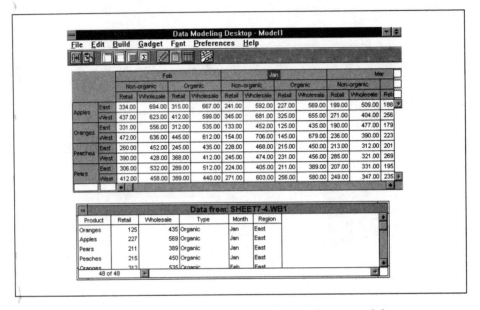

Figure 7.13 A complete data model with multidimensional data.

After the model is complete, you can close the Data From window to gain better access to the model. Do this by double-clicking on the Control menu of the Data From window. You can always redisplay the Data From window by clicking on the Source Data button in the DMD SpeedBar:

Creating the Model: Steps

Creating the data model is a simple procedure, once you get the hang of it. Following is a step-by-step guide to creating a model from your Quattro Pro data.

1. Highlight the desired data in the Quattro Pro notebook.

2. Click on the Data Modeling Desktop tool in the SpeedBar to get the Send Data to Data Modeling Desktop dialog box.

3. Confirm that the correct data block is entered into the dialog box as the Cell block to send. Also enter the desired location for the resulting data into the Cell for returned data entry area. This is where the resulting model will appear when you are finished. Choose a Hot or Cold data transfer depending on whether you require live links to the data (Hot) or not (Cold).

4. Click on OK to move the data into the DMD.

5. Drag the column headings from the Data From window into one of the three areas of the DMD work area. Dragging to the column heading area turns the source data into column headings. Dragging into the row heading area creates row headings from the data. Dragging into the middle of the model places numerical data into the middle of the model. Note that as you drag data into place, the indicator icons show which area you are highlighting.

6. Continue to drag column headings from the Data From window into the DMD work area until the model is complete.

7. Rearrange the model as desired.

Rearranging the Model

Notice in the example in Figure 7.13 that the months at the top of the model are in the wrong order. To fix this problem, we can move the February column to the right side of the January column. Do this by clicking directly on the February heading, and then dragging the label to the right side of the January column and releasing the mouse. The columns will trade places. Figure 7.14 shows the dragging procedure, and Figure 7.15 shows the result.

Data Modeling Desktop - Model1

File   Edit   Build   Gadget   Font   Preferences   Help

		Feb				Jan				Mar	
		Non-organic		Organic		Non-organic		Organic		Non-organic		
		Retail	Wholesale	Retail	Wholesale	Retail	Wholesale	Retail	Wholesale	Retail	Wholesale	Ret
Apples	East	334.00	694.00	315.00	667.00	241.00	592.00	227.00	569.00	199.00	509.00	188
	West	437.00	623.00	412.00	599.00	345.00	681.00	325.00	655.00	271.00	404.00	256
Oranges	East	331.00	556.00	312.00	535.00	133.00	452.00	125.00	435.00	190.00	477.00	179
	West	472.00	636.00	445.00	612.00	154.00	706.00	145.00	679.00	236.00	390.00	223
Peaches	East	260.00	452.00	245.00	435.00	228.00	468.00	215.00	450.00	213.00	312.00	201
	West	390.00	428.00	368.00	412.00	245.00	474.00	231.00	456.00	285.00	321.00	269
Pears	East	306.00	532.00	289.00	512.00	224.00	405.00	211.00	389.00	207.00	331.00	195
	West	412.00	458.00	389.00	440.00	271.00	603.00	256.00	580.00	249.00	347.00	235

Figure 7.14 Dragging to rearrange columns (or rows) in the model.

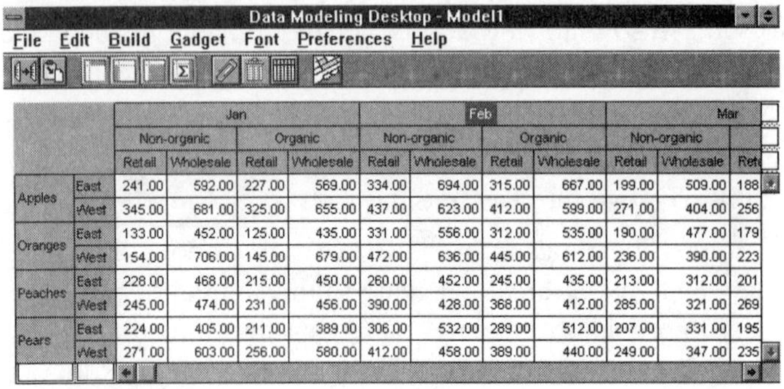

Figure 7.15 The result after rearranging the column headings.

Now lets make another change to the data. Suppose you want the East and West row headings to appear to the left of the product names—providing two sections of products and orienting the data to a regional view. You can change the order of the headings by dragging the "Tabs" that appear at the bottom of the headings. Figure 7.16 shows what it looks like to grab and drag a row heading tab, and Figure 7.17 shows the result after moving it to the left of another tab.

Figure 7.18 shows the result after moving the column heading tab for Type to the top position.

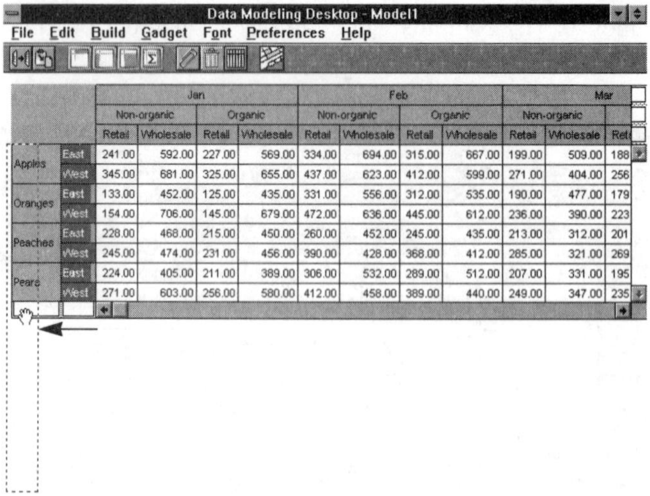

Figure 7.16 Dragging a column heading tab to rearrange the order of the column headings.

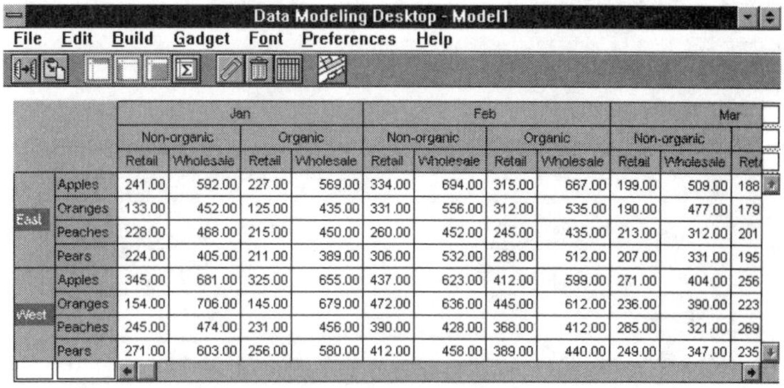

Figure 7.17 *The result after rearranging the column headings.*

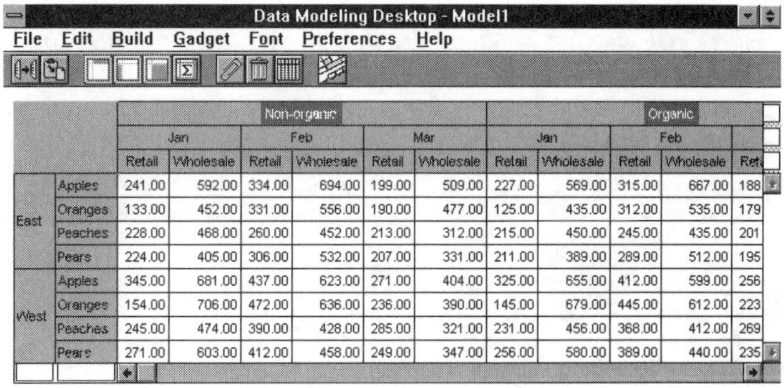

Figure 7.18 *Moving the Type column headings to the top of the*
column headings by dragging the tab.

Another way in which you can manipulate the data is to "pivot" the row and column headings. Using the pivoting feature, you can turn a row heading into a column heading and vice versa. Suppose you want the Type information in the example model to appear as a left-side (row) heading rather than as a column heading. You can make this change by clicking on the Type heading tab (which appears on the right edge of the screen) and dragging downward and leftward to "pivot" the block to the row heading area. Pivot the block all the way down to the vertical position before releasing the mouse. Figure 7.19 shows the pivoting motion, and Figure 7.20 shows the result. Modify the order of the new row headings as desired after the pivot is complete.

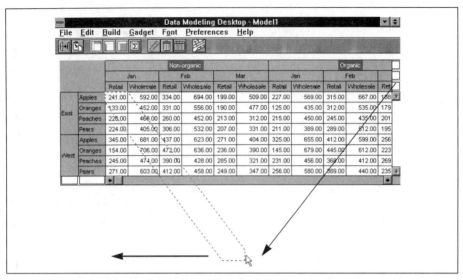

Figure 7.19 Pivoting a column heading into the row heading area.

			Jan		Feb		Mar	
			Retail	Wholesale	Retail	Wholesale	Retail	Wholesale
East	Non-organic	Apples	241.00	592.00	334.00	694.00	199.00	509.00
		Oranges	133.00	452.00	331.00	556.00	190.00	477.00
		Peaches	228.00	468.00	260.00	452.00	213.00	312.00
		Pears	224.00	405.00	306.00	532.00	207.00	331.00
	Organic	Apples	227.00	569.00	315.00	667.00	188.00	489.00
		Oranges	125.00	435.00	312.00	535.00	179.00	459.00
		Peaches	215.00	450.00	245.00	435.00	201.00	300.00
		Pears	211.00	389.00	289.00	512.00	195.00	318.00
West	Non-organic	Apples	345.00	681.00	437.00	623.00	271.00	404.00
		Oranges	154.00	706.00	472.00	636.00	236.00	390.00
		Peaches	245.00	474.00	390.00	428.00	285.00	321.00
		Pears	271.00	603.00	412.00	458.00	249.00	347.00
	Organic	Apples	325.00	655.00	412.00	599.00	256.00	388.00
		Oranges	145.00	679.00	445.00	612.00	223.00	375.00
		Peaches	231.00	456.00	368.00	412.00	269.00	309.00
		Pears	256.00	580.00	389.00	440.00	235.00	334.00

Figure 7.20 The result after pivoting.

A final way to manipulate the data is to remove column or row headings completely. You can do this simply by clicking once on the heading tab, and then on the Delete icon in the SpeedBar:

This removes the headings from the model and rearranges the data accordingly. You can reinsert the heading by displaying the Data From window again (click on the Source Data button) and then dragging from the Data From window back into the model.

Creating Totals

You can easily create column and row totals based on any of the headings in the model by highlighting the heading and clicking on the Sum button in the SpeedBar. Totals automatically use the SUM function to create simple sums of the data in the specified heading—and the DMD inserts the total into place in the model. For example, suppose you want to create totals of all products grouped by the Type (Organic or Non-organic). Simply click on the row heading tab for the type headings (at the bottom of the screen) and then click on the Sum button:

Figure 7.21 shows the resulting sum.

			Jan Retail	Jan Wholesale	Feb Retail	Feb Wholesale	Mar Retail	Mar Wholesale
East	Non-organic	Apples	241.00	592.00	334.00	694.00	199.00	509.00
		Oranges	133.00	452.00	331.00	556.00	190.00	477.00
		Peaches	228.00	468.00	260.00	452.00	213.00	312.00
		Pears	224.00	405.00	306.00	532.00	207.00	331.00
	Organic	Apples	227.00	569.00	315.00	667.00	188.00	489.00
		Oranges	125.00	435.00	312.00	535.00	179.00	459.00
		Peaches	215.00	450.00	245.00	435.00	201.00	300.00
		Pears	211.00	389.00	289.00	512.00	195.00	318.00
	TOTAL		1604.00	3760.00	2392.00	4383.00	1572.00	3195.00
West	Non-organic	Apples	345.00	681.00	437.00	623.00	271.00	404.00
		Oranges	154.00	706.00	472.00	636.00	236.00	390.00
		Peaches	245.00	474.00	390.00	428.00	285.00	321.00
		Pears	271.00	603.00	412.00	458.00	249.00	347.00
	Organic	Apples	325.00	655.00	412.00	599.00	256.00	388.00
		Oranges	145.00	679.00	445.00	612.00	223.00	375.00
		Peaches	231.00	456.00	368.00	412.00	269.00	309.00
		Pears	256.00	580.00	389.00	440.00	235.00	334.00
	TOTAL		1972.00	4834.00	3325.00	4208.00	2024.00	2668.00

Figure 7.21 Adding totals by product type.

Now suppose you wanted to total all rows to get Retail and Wholesale totals for all months. Simply click on the column heading tab for the Months headings and then click on the Sum button. Figure 7.22 shows the result.

Experiment with the Sum button to see how totals can be added to your model. To remove a total, click on the Total heading and click the Delete tool.

			Jan		Feb		Mar		TOTAL	
			Retail	Wholesale	Retail	Wholesale	Retail	Wholesale	Retail	Wholesale
East	Non-organic	Apples	241.00	592.00	334.00	694.00	199.00	509.00	774.00	1795.00
		Oranges	133.00	452.00	331.00	556.00	190.00	477.00	654.00	1485.00
		Peaches	228.00	468.00	260.00	452.00	213.00	312.00	701.00	1232.00
		Pears	224.00	405.00	306.00	532.00	207.00	331.00	737.00	1268.00
	Organic	Apples	227.00	569.00	315.00	667.00	188.00	489.00	730.00	1725.00
		Oranges	125.00	435.00	312.00	535.00	179.00	459.00	616.00	1429.00
		Peaches	215.00	450.00	245.00	435.00	201.00	300.00	661.00	1185.00
		Pears	211.00	389.00	289.00	512.00	195.00	318.00	695.00	1219.00
	TOTAL		1604.00	3760.00	2392.00	4383.00	1572.00	3195.00	5568.00	11338.00
West	Non-organic	Apples	345.00	681.00	437.00	623.00	271.00	404.00	1053.00	1708.00
		Oranges	154.00	706.00	472.00	636.00	236.00	390.00	862.00	1732.00
		Peaches	245.00	474.00	390.00	428.00	285.00	321.00	920.00	1223.00
		Pears	271.00	603.00	412.00	458.00	249.00	347.00	932.00	1408.00
	Organic	Apples	325.00	655.00	412.00	599.00	256.00	388.00	993.00	1642.00
		Oranges	145.00	679.00	445.00	612.00	223.00	375.00	813.00	1666.00
		Peaches	231.00	456.00	368.00	412.00	269.00	309.00	868.00	1177.00
		Pears	256.00	580.00	389.00	440.00	235.00	334.00	880.00	1354.00
	TOTAL		1972.00	4834.00	3325.00	4208.00	2024.00	2868.00	7321.00	11910.00

Figure 7.22 Totaling all rows.

Formatting Data and Using the Gadgets

You can format your data inside the Data Modeling Desktop if desired, or you can wait and format the data after you move it back into Quattro Pro. The options in the Gadgets menu let you format the data inside the DMD. Choose the Gadgets>Format command to select a numerical format for the internal data in the model; numeric formats are identical to those inside Quattro Pro. Just click inside the data model to highlight the desired item. You can highlight rows or columns of data by clicking on any cell inside the model. Move the mouse around inside the model to see the mouse pointer change between a horizontal and vertical arrow. When the arrow is vertical, clicking on the data will select columns; when the arrow is horizontal, clicking on the data will select rows. Press the Shift key while you click a second time to add more columns or rows to your selection. To format all the numbers at one time, choose the Edit>Select All command before choosing the Gadgets>Format command.

After selecting the desired rows or columns, choose the Gadgets>Format command and choose a number format from those provided. You may also double-click on any data to produce the Format dialog box. Click on the Apply button in the Format dialog box to apply the chosen format to the data.

The Gadget>Display command produces a dialog box that lets you change the lines and borders inside the model. The four buttons inside this dialog box let you remove all lines, add vertical lines, add horizontal lines, or add both vertical and horizontal lines to the model:

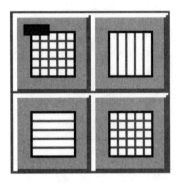

The Gadgets>Formula command lets you change the formula that is used to calculate totals in the model and is especially useful for totals you create with the Sum button. You can change the totals into averages by highlighting the totals column (by clicking on any cell in the column), choosing the Gadgets>Formula command, and then choosing the AVG function from the formulas list. Choose any of the formulas in the dialog box and then click on Apply to change the Totals column (or row).

The Gadgets>Name command lets you change the column and row headings in the model. Just select the desired column or row heading, choose the Gadgets>Name command, and then type a new name in the space provided.

The Gadgets>Limit command lets you choose data to display inside the model, based on numeric values or ranges—in other words, to "limit" the model to specific data. Here's how to use the Limit feature.

1. Click on the Source Data button to display the Data From dialog box.

2. Choose the Gadgets>Limit command to display the Limit dialog box.

3. Click on a column heading to choose a criterion field. For example, suppose you want to locate all Retail sales that are greater than 300. In this step, you click on the Retail column heading in the Data From window.

4. Click on the drop-down list in the Limit dialog box and choose a parameter for the field. For example, if you want to limit the model to all items with Retail amounts greater than 300, then choose the Greater Than option in the drop-down list

5. Click on the List button in the Limit dialog box:

Now choose the amount or value corresponding to your criteria. The list contains all values currently inside the model. If you want to select a value not inside the model (as in our example of "greater than 300"), then click on the Entry button:

then type the value into the space provided.

6. Whether you enter the value or locate it inside the list of existing values, click on the Check Mark button to add the value to the current list. Now repeat Steps 5 and 6 to add more items to the list if desired.

7. When you are finished with the criteria, click on the desired item in the list (in the example, you would click on the value 300 in the list at the bottom of the dialog box); then click on the Apply button. Figure 7.23 shows the result of limiting the model to Retail values greater than 300.

Returning to the full view

To return to the normal view of the data model, click on the Equals item in the Limit dialog box, display the list of existing values from the model, click on the Select All button, and click on Apply.

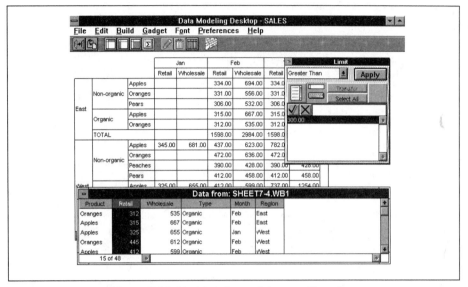

Figure 7.23 Limiting the model to specific values.

Inserting the Model into Quattro Pro

When you are completely finished with the data model and want to return the model to your Quattro Pro notebook for printing and further manipulation, just click on the Transfer to Quattro Pro button in the SpeedBar:

This quickly inserts the model into the notebook at the location you specified. You can copy the data into Quattro Pro with live links by choosing the Preferences>Copy to Quattro Pro Options command and choosing the Always Hot Link option. Do this before transferring the data.

Saving your data model

NOTE Remember that the Data Modeling Desktop is a separate program from Quattro Pro and it lets you save your data models as special documents with the DMD extension. You can then return to a data model without having to go through Quattro Pro by selecting the Data Modeling Desktop icon from the Windows Program Manager and using the File>Open command in the DMD to open the saved file.

Summary

The Data Modeling Desktop is a powerful analysis tool for large amounts of financial, sales, or marketing data. It produces cross tabulation reports and data tables from your data. Most important, you can manipulate and rearrange the data inside the model with the click of the mouse. Using the DMD, you can quickly and easily view your data models to emphasize different parts of the data for different purposes.

To use the DMD, you must begin with raw database data and then use the DMD tool to transfer that data to the DMD. You can then build the model from the column headings in the selected database data. After the data model is created, you can use mouse movements to move elements around the change the model.

When you are finished with the model, the Transfer to Quattro Pro button returns the finished model to your original notebook at the location you specify.

The next chapter explores two of the more advanced features in Quattro Pro for Windows: Notebook Consolidation and Scenario Management. With Scenario Management you can store sets of values in your notebooks and switch among the different sets to play "what if" scenarios. Notebook Consolidation lets you combine the values from several notebooks or pages and perform mathematical calculations on the combined data.

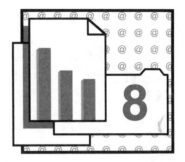

Special Spreadsheet Features

Quattro Pro includes some special features that warrant special attention. In particular, the Scenario Management and Consolidation features of Quattro Pro bring power and flexibility to your notebook applications. This chapter covers the basic steps in creating and managing scenarios and in consolidating blocks of data in your various notebooks. You will learn

- Uses for Scenarios
- Steps in the Scenario Management process
- How to switch among scenarios
- How to consolidate blocks of data
- How to store consolidation settings for future use

Creating and Managing Scenarios

When you create a spreadsheet model, such as a cost estimate worksheet or a budget, you most likely have some key values that are used in calculations throughout the worksheet. If you change the values in these cells, the calculations throughout the worksheet would change accordingly. You might find that you "play" with the values in some worksheets quite frequently—changing them to see how different values affect the results of the worksheet model.

Changing the values in your notebook applications is the essence of what-if testing. By changing the values in your budget notebook, for example, you might be saying "What if we spent $5,000 on advertising instead of $10,000?" Or "What if we had $50,000 net sales instead of $40,000?" What-if testing is a key strategy in using spreadsheets effectively. Any cell that is used in a formula can become a key cell in a what-if test.

If you change several key cells in a notebook application, you might say that you have created a new *scenario*—an entirely new set of values on which to apply the formulas and functions in your application. In fact, you might switch among several scenarios depending on the type of application. In a budget application, for example, you might have three different scenarios: one containing "worst case" values, another containing "average" values, and another containing "best case" values.

The Scenario Manager tool in Quattro Pro for Windows helps you create and manage various scenarios for your applications. Using the Scenario Manager, you can establish sets of values for a notebook (called scenarios) and name each set based on its purpose or emphasis. Then, you can store these named scenarios and access them at any time. When you access a named scenario, Quattro Pro automatically swaps the current values in the application with those in your scenario—giving you an instant what if test in your notebook.

Finally, the Scenario Manager can create a scenario summary report that compares the various scenarios side by side. This helps you see which values are changing when you change scenarios and how each change affects the formulas in the application.

Quattro Pro provides an Expert to help you create your scenarios. In the next few sections, you'll discover each step in the Scenario Expert procedure. First, lets begin with a sample application. Suppose you run an event-planning business and use Quattro Pro to produce your cost estimate worksheets for your clients. Because of the many changes and possibilities in the costs associated with an event, you must be able to provide several cost estimates to show the differences. The basic cost estimate worksheet might look like the one in Figure 8.1.

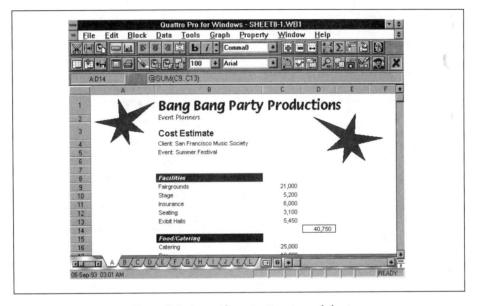

Figure 8.1 A sample cost estimate worksheet.

The goal is to create several scenarios based on changes in the costs: In each case, you might use a different caterer, band, and event location—changing the cost dramatically. With the basic worksheet model in place, your first step is to begin the Scenario Manager Expert by clicking the **Expert** tool in the SpeedBar and then clicking the **Scenario Expert**:

This brings up the first of four Scenario Expert screens. The next four sections discuss these steps.

Step 1: Choosing the Changing Cells

The first step in creating a scenario (shown in Figure 8.2) is to identify the cells within the application that will be changing with each different scenario. These are most likely cells that contain numeric values, but not formulas. Formulas in other parts of the worksheet may use these values to produce their results. In the example application, all cells in column C might be identified as changing cells.

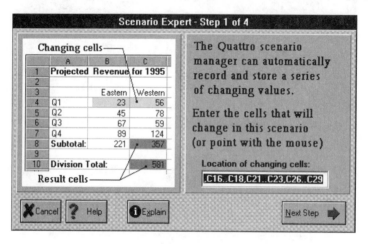

Figure 8.2 Step 1 of the Scenario Manager Expert.

To identify the cells, first move the Expert window aside by dragging its title bar. When you have access to the notebook page beneath the Expert window, click on the first changing cell. If you have more than one changing cell, drag the mouse to highlight them all or, if they are not adjacent, hold down the **Ctrl** key as you click on each cell. As you release the mouse button, you will see a reference to the cell or cells you selected appear in the Expert window. Remember that a multiple-block selection uses commas to separate each block.

When you have completed the selection and the entry inside the Expert window is correct, click on the **Next Step** button.

Step 2: Entering Scenario Values

Step 2 of the Scenario Manager Expert is to enter the values for each of the cells you identified as changing cells in the application. This step of the Expert is shown in Figure 8.3.

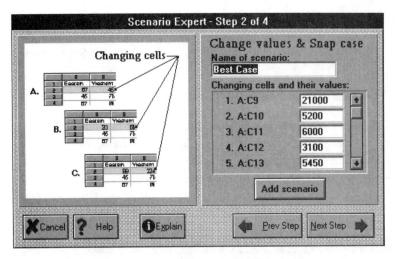

Figure 8.3 Step 2 of the Scenario Manager Expert.

If the cells you highlighted in step 1 already contained values, those values will appear in the Changing cells and their values list in this window. If these values are to be used as the first scenario, then half of your work is complete. All you need to do is enter a name for the current scenario—which contains the existing values. Type a name into the Name of Scenario entry box. When finished, click on the **Add Scenario** button to add this scenario to the list of defined scenarios for this application. Each scenario name will appear in a list, which you can use to access the values in that scenario.

If you want to add a second scenario, enter new values into the Changing cells and their values list. This list contains all the cells you highlighted in the first step of the Expert. Fill in values for any or all of these cells and provide a name for this set of values. Click on **Add Scenario** when you're finished. Repeat these steps to add as many scenarios as you like.

When you are finished adding scenarios, click on the **Next Step** button to continue with the Expert.

Step 3: Choosing a Scenario to Display

Step 3 of the Scenario Expert is simple; it merely determines which of the scenarios you defined will be displayed in the notebook at this time. You can always switch among the scenarios whenever you choose; this step just selects a scenario for now.

Click on any named scenario in the list provided and then click on the **Show Scenario** button. You can also remove scenarios in this step by using the **Delete Scenario** button. When you have finished, click on the **Next Step** button.

Step 4: Creating a Summary Report

In the final Scenario Expert step, you have the option of creating a summary report in a blank page of your notebook. The summary report contains a list of all changing cells in the application, and each set of values listed in columns. This lets you compare the different scenarios side by side in one place. In addition, all cells affected by these changing values are listed, showing how the different scenarios affect the values. Figure 8.4 shows this step.

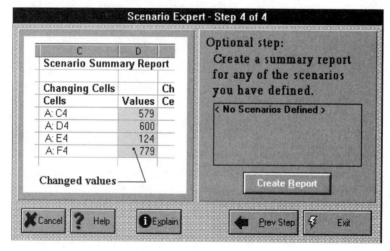

Figure 8.4 The last Scenario Expert step.

Highlight any or all scenarios listed; then click on the **Create Report** button. The report will contain values from all scenarios you selected and will appear in the first blank page of the notebook.

Using the Scenario Manager SpeedBar

You can access the Scenario Manager SpeedBar to choose a new scenario at any time. You can also use this SpeedBar to create new scenarios. Click on the **Scenario Manager** tool to produce this SpeedBar:

Your existing scenarios appear in the drop-down list, which contains the words **Base Scenario**. Click on this list box to switch among any of the scenarios you created in the Expert.

To add a new scenario to the list, just type any values you like into the changing cells of the application, then click on the **Add Scenario** button on the Scenario Manager SpeedBar:

Type a name for the new scenario; then click on **OK** to add it to the list.

You can create a scenario report by clicking on the **Report** button and then clicking on **OK** at the dialog box that appears. This creates a report containing all scenarios:

Consolidating Worksheets

Worksheet consolidation is a method of combining values into a single page to provide overall totals. The blocks that combine into the overall total might come from different pages within the same notebook—or even from different notebooks altogether. Generally, consolidation is used to create summary reports from multiple iterations of an application. For example, suppose you're a sales manager and you provide each salesperson on your staff with a Quattro Pro Sales Report application that you built. At the end of each month, the salespeople enter their sales totals into the application and send you copies of the completed notebook. At the end of each month, you get, say, four different copies of this application from your staff. Your job is to create a consolidated sales report that combines the totals from each of the four salespeople into a single summary report. You can do this using the Consolidation Expert.

Lets use the sales report example with the Consolidation Expert. Suppose you copy the four different sales notebooks into your personal Summary notebook—resulting in four pages of data, one for each of your salespeople's territory. Let's call the pages *North, South, East* and *West*. In addition, you have a fifth page that contains the consolidation of the other four pages. This page is called *Summary*. Figure 8.5 shows this application.

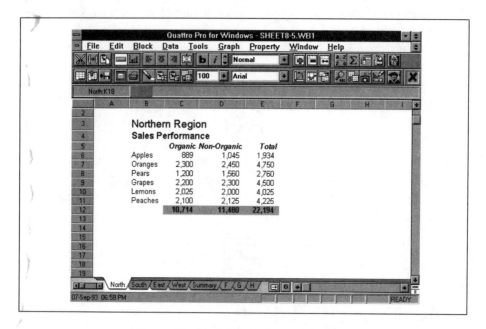

Figure 8.5 The sales summary application.

Begin by invoking the Consolidation Expert through the **Expert** button in the SpeedBar. Next, click on the **Consolidation Expert** button to start the first step of the Consolidation Expert procedure. The following sections discuss the various steps of the process.

Step 1: Choosing the Blocks to Consolidate

The first step in consolidating is to highlight the individual blocks that you want to consolidate. In this case, we have four separate blocks to consolidate—each on a different page. You can consolidate from different pages of the same notebook or from different notebooks if desired. To access a different notebook, click on the **Browse** button and open the desired notebook.

When you're ready to identify a block, double-click in the entry area of the Expert window to highlight the first block in the notebook. When highlighting a block, consider whether you want to include row and column totals or whether your consolidation page will contain its own totaling formulas. In the example, we've excluded the totals, but included the row and column headings as shown by the references in Figure 8.6.

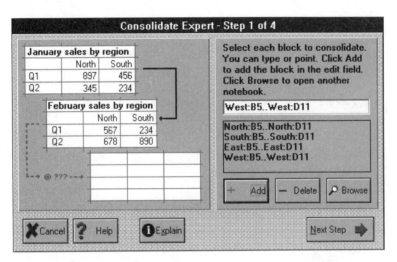

Figure 8.6 Specify the blocks to consolidate in Step 1.

When you are finished highlighting the first block, press **Enter** to return to the Expert window and then click on the **Add** button to add the block to the list of consolidation blocks. Now double-click in the entry box again to select the next block. Continue with this procedure until you've listed all blocks in this consolidation procedure. Figure 8.6 shows the resulting Expert window in the sample application.

When finished, press the **Next Step** button to continue.

Step 2: Choosing the Operation

The next step in consolidating is to specify the mathematical operation to perform on the blocks when they are combined. Normally, you'll want to sum the blocks, creating a numerical total of the values in all matching cells. However, you can average the blocks or perform a number of other functions. Choose the desired function from the drop-down list in Step 2 of the Consolidation Expert window. Then click on **Next Step** to continue. That's it for Step 2.

Step 3: Identifying the Destination Block

The next step is to specify the destination block for the consolidated data. Chances are, you'll want to specify a separate page for this operation. In this case, we already have a summary page in the notebook application. In the example, the consolidation is performed each month, so the summary page will already contain last month's data. We'll just replace that data with current data by specifying the same block for the destination. Figure 8.7 shows the example in Step 3.

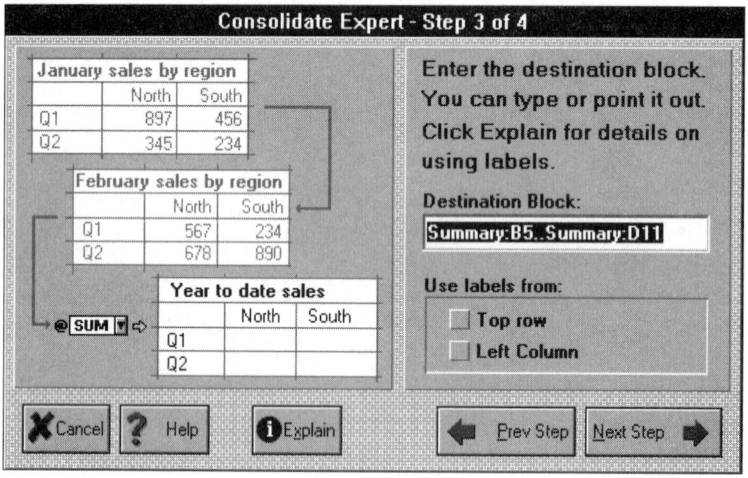

Figure 8.7 In Step 3 you specify a destination block for the report.

Click on the **Next Step** button when you are ready to continue.

Step 4: Naming the Consolidation

Each consolidation setup you create can be named and used again later. This way, you can return to the Consolidation Expert and create an entirely new consolidation model for the same notebook.

Type a name for the consolidation report and click on the **Consolidate** button to perform the consolidation. Figure 8.8 shows the result of the example application.

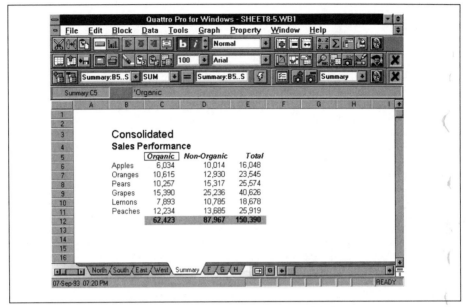

Figure 8.8 The final consolidation block.

Summary

This short chapter showed two important features of Quattro Pro for Windows: Scenario Management and Consolidation. With Scenario Management you can store sets of inputs for various cells in your application and then return to any of the sets at any time. This is useful for making what-if comparisons and for creating multiple versions of a report using different input amounts. Consolidation lets you combine the values in several blocks of a worksheet—or several different worksheets—into a single summary block. You can perform several types of mathematical operations on the values as you consolidate.

Both Scenario Management and Consolidation can be accomplished through Experts. Just click on the **Expert** button and choose either **Scenario Manager** or **Consolidation Experts**. This chapter has provided details on each step of these Expert procedures.

The following chapter provides detailed information about printing your notebooks from Quattro Pro. Several print options combine to provide a full array of possibilities for your printed reports. You'll find Quattro Pro's printing features are powerful, yet easy to use.

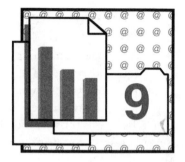

Printing

Quattro Pro gives you some of the best printing features of any Windows product. You can configure and set up your printer from within Quattro Pro, and you can enhance the basic printout by using page and printer setup options. In this chapter you'll learn about Quattro Pro's basic printing procedure, as well as many ways to fine-tune your printout, including

- Adding headers and footers
- Adjusting the margins
- Printing multiple blocks
- Scaling the printout
- Printing to a file on the disk
- Previewing the printout on-screen
- Storing page and printer setup options for future use

Selecting and Setting up the Printer

First of all, make sure your printer is properly configured and selected. When you select and configure a printer in one program in Windows, those settings are active in *all* your programs—until you change them again. This means that, if you are printing successfully from other Windows programs, you probably won't have any changes to make to your printer settings in Quattro Pro. Nevertheless, if you want to switch to a different printer or change the configuration of your selected printer, you can do so with the **File>Printer Setup** command as follows:

1. Choose **File>Printer Setup**.

2. Select the desired printer from the Printer list by clicking on its name. (To install new printers, refer to Chapter 1.)

3. Choose the **Setup** button to configure the printer, or choose **OK** to complete the printer-setup procedure.

Note that printer configuration options vary from printer to printer. Options include printer-specific settings—including the paper source, color choices, and resolution settings—and the selection of built-in or cartridge fonts.

Notice that the Printer Setup dialog box includes the **Redirect To File** option. This option lets you save the printout as a printer file, which you can either print later or copy onto a floppy disk and print from a different computer system. Note that the saved printer file can be printed only on the printer selected in the list. If you don't have a PostScript printer, you should therefore consider installing one onto your system using the Windows Control Panel. In this way, you can redirect your printouts to PostScript files that can be printed onto any PostScript device. (We'll discuss printing to files later in this chapter.)

Printing in shades of gray

N O T E If you have a black-and-white PostScript printer, you can still print your spreadsheets using a color PostScript printer. Printing on the black-and-white printer with a color printer selected converts the colors into shades of gray. You can experiment with various colors to see how they print in shades of gray. A good color PostScript printer to use for this procedure is the QMS ColorScript 100.

Setting Up the Page

Before you begin printing your report, you might want to change some basic page settings. Using the **File>Page Setup** command, you can control the following aspects of the printout:

- **Header and footer** Specify text that appears along the top (header) and bottom (footer) of all pages in the report. Headers are often used to identify the title of the report, whereas footers are useful for displaying page numbers, dates, and other credits.

- **Margins** Set the top, bottom, left, and right margins for the page. You can also set the amount of space taken up by the header and footer, if you've added a header and/or footer to the printout. Margin sizes, of course, affect the amount of data that the pages can hold.

- **Paper type** Select the type of paper you want from the sizes available for your printer. Different printers allow different choices of paper types.

- **Break Pages** You can tell Quattro Pro to ignore the margin settings, the headers, and the footers and print your report as a single, continuous page by removing the check mark from the Break Pages option. This option is useful for printing long tables or wide documents onto continuous-feed paper, but it can also be used on laser printers for piecing several pages together into one large sheet.

- **Print to fit** Print the entire selection onto a single page. With this option checked, Quattro Pro will attempt to print the selected data onto a single page. If this requires fonts that are too small to read, Quattro Pro will print the data onto as few pages as possible.

- **Center blocks** Center the data onto the page. This option makes the data fit evenly between the top, bottom, left, and right margins of the page.

- **Scaling** Enlarge or reduce the printout by a specified amount or print the report to fit onto as few pages as possible.

- **Orientation** Change the orientation of the pages from **Portrait** (upright) to **Landscape** (sideways).

The following sections discuss each of these settings in detail and offer useful tips for using them.

Adding Headers and Footers

A *header* is a block of text that appears at the top of each page in your printout. A header is often used to identify the document, the author, and convey other general information. A *footer* is a block of text that appears along the bottom of each page. A footer is useful for displaying page numbers, dates, and so on.

To add a header and/or footer to the report, just enter the desired text into the Header and Footer entry boxes in the **File>Page Setup** dialog box. If you type a single line of text for a header, it will appear as a single line above the worksheet data, beginning immediately to the right of the left margin and just below the top margin of the page. Similarly, a footer will begin at the left margin and just above the bottom margin of the page. The amount of space allowed for the header and footer (that is, between the header/footer text and the spreadsheet data) is determined by the Header and Footer margin settings. Refer to "Setting Page Margins and Page Breaks," later in this chapter, for more details.

Aligning the Header and Footer

Headers and footers can be divided into three main parts: the first part is aligned with the left margin, the second part is centered between the margins, and the third part is aligned with the right margin. You can type data into one, two, or all three parts of the header and/or footer.

To identify each part of the header and footer, enter one or two vertical bar characters (|)—it appears above the Backslash key on most keyboards—into the entry box. Text that follows one vertical bar will be centered on the page; text that follows two vertical bars will be right-aligned; text that precedes the vertical bars will be left-aligned. Here are some examples.

Example: July 22, 1993 | Financial Report | Balance Sheet

| 08/27/93 | Financial Report | Balance Sheet |

Example: July 22, 1993 | | Balance Sheet

| 08/27/93 | | Balance Sheet |

Example: | **Financial Report**

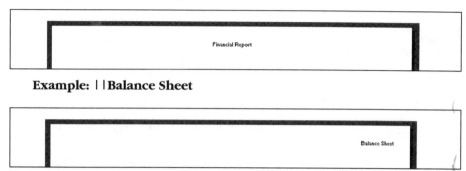

Example: | | **Balance Sheet**

Notice that you can include the vertical bars for separation without placing text in all the sections. This way, you can include just right-aligned data, or centered data, or any combination that is appropriate.

Printing Page Numbers, Dates, and Other Header and Footer Data

In addition to being able to enter any text into your headers and footers, you can add several pieces of data. Variable data are provided by Quattro Pro and include the current file name, page numbers, the current date, and so on. To get this variable information into your header/footer, just enter one of the codes listed below. (Enter the code into the desired section of the header/footer as described above.)

Table 9.1 Variable Data.

Code	Data
#d	Prints the current date in short form. This form can be controlled through the Windows Control Panel using the International settings.
#ds	Prints the current date in Quattro Pro's Short International Date format. This may or may not be different from the setting in the Windows Control Panel, since it is controlled from within Quattro Pro.
#D	Prints the current date in long format. This form can be controlled through the Windows Control Panel using the International settings.

Table 9.1 Variable Data (con't).

Code	Data
#Ds	Prints the current date in Quattro Pro's Long International Date format. This may or may not be different from the setting in the Windows Control Panel.
@	Enters your computer's current date. This code is provided for compatibility with Quattro Pro for DOS.
#t	Prints the short time as formatted in the Windows Control Panel.
#ts	Prints the current time in Quattro Pro's Short International Date format. This may or may not be different from the setting in the Windows Control Panel, since it is controlled from within Quattro Pro.
#T	Prints the current time in long format. This form can be controlled through the Windows Control Panel using the International settings.
#Ts	Prints the time in Quattro Pro's Long International Time format. This may or may not be different from the setting in the Windows Control Panel.
#p	Prints the page number.
#	Prints the page number. This version is included for compatibility with Quattro Pro for DOS.
#p+n	Prints the page number incremented by *n*. For example, entering **#p+5** starts printing at page 5.
#P	Prints the total number of pages printed. For example, entering **#p of #P** might print **1 of 5**.
#P+n	Prints the total number of pages printed incremented by *n*.
#f	Prints the file name of the notebook being printed. The file name will be displayed in the document window's title bar.
#F	Prints the full path and name of the notebook being printed.
#n	Begins a new line and prints all remaining information on that line. This enables a multiple-line header or footer. You can use up to three lines for both the header and the footer.

You should experiment with entering these codes and other text into your headers and footers. Here are some examples:

Example: #Ds | #f | John Smith

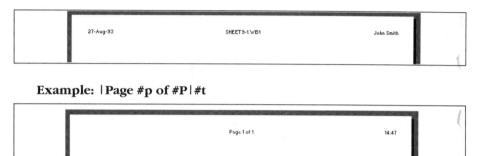

| 27-Aug-93 | SHEET9-1.WB1 | John Smith |

Example: | Page #p of #P | #t

Page 1 of 1   14:47

NOTE

Setting Header and Footer fonts

Use the **Header Font** button in the Page Setup dialog box to set the font for the header and footer text. If you don't set the font, Quattro Pro will automatically use the default page font, which normally is Arial 10.

Setting Page Margins and Page Breaks

If your printout is too large to fit onto a single page, Quattro Pro automatically splits the data between two or more pages. This is called *breaking* the pages. Quattro Pro will never create a page-break in the middle of a column; if an entire column of data will not fit onto the page, Quattro Pro moves it to the next page.

The margins you set will determine how much data can fit onto each page. Quattro Pro begins printing the data in the upper-left corner of the page, below the top margin and just inside the left margin. The bottom and right margin settings determine where the page breaks. The larger the margins, the less data will fit onto the page. The bottom and right margins will make little difference, of course, if the printout consists of one very small block.

There are six margins to be set: the top, bottom, left, right, header, and footer. The top, left, right, and bottom margins are measured from the edges of the paper you've selected. Depending on your printer's capabilities, you might have to set at least 0.25-inch margins on all sides. The header and footer margins are applicable if you add a header and/or footer to the printout. The header margin sets the distance between the end of the top margin and the beginning of the report, therefore also determining the amount of room available for the header text. If you have a multiple-line header, then you should increase the header margin. Otherwise, the default of 0.33 is usually appropriate. If you don't have a header, consider using a header margin of 0. Similarly, the footer margin sets the space for the page footer.

There are two ways to adjust margins for your printout: You can use the **File>Page Setup** command and enter margin settings into the Page Setup dialog box, or you can adjust the margins on the Print Preview screen by dragging margin-indicator lines around the page. Here we'll discuss the first method. (Using the Preview screen to adjust margins is discussed in "Previewing the Printout," later in this chapter.) To change the page margins:

1. Select **File>Page Setup**.

2. Press the **Tab** key to highlight the desired Margin entry box. Change a margin setting by highlighting the number you wish to change and typing a new one. Include the measurement either as **in** (for inches) or **cm** (for centimeters). For example, type **1in** for a 1-inch margin or **5cm** for a 5-centimeter margin. Use decimals to indicate partial inches or centimeters. For example, type **.25in** if you want a 0.25-inch margin.

3. When you're finished with all the margin settings, choose **OK**.

Although margin settings can be specified in inches or centimeters by using the **in** or **cm** additions to your entries, you can enter a value *without* specifying **in** or **cm** and Quattro Pro will automatically convert the entry to the default measurement system specified in the Windows Control Panel. If the default measurement system is inches, typing **3** will be interpreted as 3 inches. However, you can still type **3 cm**, to specify centimeters.

Don't use margin settings to center data on the page
Although you can adjust the left and top margins to center your report on the page, avoid using margins for this purpose—they will affect your headers and footers. Quattro Pro provides a **Center Blocks** option that automatically centers your printed data between the left and right margins. Select this option in the Page Setup dialog box.

Setting Manual Page Breaks

When printing data that will not fit on one page, Quattro Pro determines when to stop printing on one page and to continue on the next page. Quattro Pro inserts a page break for you—based on the page size, margins, and orientation you have selected. These are called *automatic* or *soft page breaks* because they change based on margins, column widths, and other settings you selected.

If you want less information on one page and would like to break the page sooner, you can insert your own manual page-break into the notebook. Manual page breaks are used primarily to break the page *before* Quattro Pro's automatic break occurs. You can insert manual page breaks horizontally (to break the bottom of the page) but not vertically, (to break the right edge). (See "Manual Page Breaks: Another Technique," later in this chapter, for information about breaking pages along the right edge.)

Fitting more data on each page

You might want to squeeze more data onto a page than Quattro Pro normally includes. To fit more data onto a page, you can decrease the margin settings, decrease the point sizes of the fonts used in the report, decrease row and column widths (if possible), or scale the entire report using the Scaling options. Scaling is covered later in this chapter.

To insert a manual page break, first check to see that you are inserting the breaks *before* Quattro Pro's automatic breaking locations. Otherwise, the automatic break will occur before your own. You can check the locations of the automatic page breaks by previewing the printout, a process described later in this chapter.

To set a page break along the bottom of the page, move to any cell in the first column of the print block; the cell you select will mark the beginning of the new page. In other words, the break will occur just before the cell you select. Now choose the **Block>Insert Break** command. Quattro Pro inserts a row into the notebook and places the marker **::** into the selected cell. The blank row and marker represent the page break; they will not print along with your report. Figure 9.1 shows a worksheet with a manual page break inserted in the first column of the print block.

Any information you enter onto the row containing a page break will not appear on the printout. The extra row just shows you where your pages begin and end. If you like, you can enter a special note onto this line, such as **End of page 1**. It will not appear in the report.

Remember that the page break must be added to the first column of the print block, as shown in Figure 9.1. When you print the report using the **File>Print** command, you will be asked to specify the exact block of data you want to print. Make sure that the block you specify matches the location of the page breaks you set. If a page break appears in the middle of a print block, it will not break the page, and the inserted row will appear in the printout. Figure 9.2 illustrates this problem.

N O T E

Entering the page break marker manually
Another way to insert a manual page break is simply to type the page break marker into a blank row of the print block. Just type the characters |:: into the desired cell. This cell must appear in the first column of the print block. Note that when you enter |::, only the characters : : appear in the cell. The entry will not print as part of the report, provided it appears in the first column of the print block.

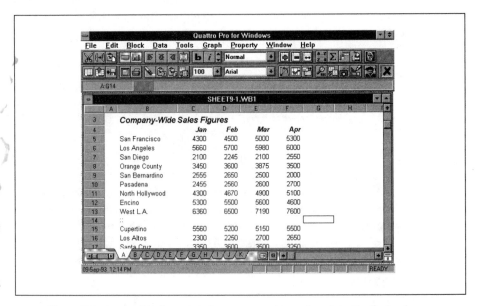

Figure 9.1 A print block containing a manual page break in the first column.

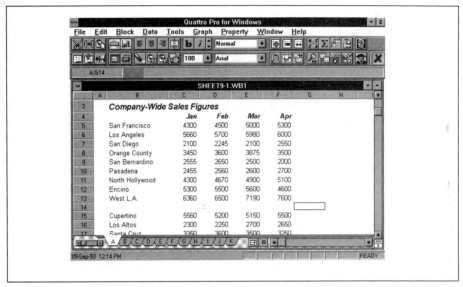

Figure 9.2 Inserting a manual page break into the middle of the print block does not break the page.

Manual page breaks can cause you some problems. If you don't get the page break marker into the correct column, the marker, as well as the blank row, will appear in the printout. You can solve this problem by moving the page break marker into the first column of the print block.

Another problem is that the inserted blank row appears across the entire notebook page, affecting all data adjacent to the print block. You might have to remove the page break if you want to print other areas of the notebook page. One solution for this problem is to avoid placing different print areas side-by-side in the notebook. Instead, place them corner-to-corner, so changes to rows and columns in one block have no effect on other blocks.

Also, because the manual page break does not affect the right edge of the page, you may want to set the right edge and the bottom edge manually—a technique described below.

Manual Page Breaks: Another Technique

Here's another technique for setting manual page breaks, one you might find easier. The idea consists of highlighting the print block in several distinct sections and then telling Quattro Pro to print each section on a different page.

Begin by selecting the data you want printed onto the first page; this may be a portion of the entire print block. Now hold the **Ctrl** key down as you select the data for the second page. Continue to highlight all the pages in the report this way. It's all right if two blocks appear adjacent to each other. Now name the composite range by using the **Block>Names>Create** command.

Now, use the **File>Print>Options** command to select the **Page Advance** option under the Print Between Blocks options. You are telling Quattro Pro to break the page between each print block. Click on **OK** and enter the name of the range you defined into the Print Block(s) entry box. Click on **Print** to begin printing.

By naming the ranges as a single block, you can easily return to the same print block again and again by using its name.

Choosing the Paper Size

Quattro Pro will display a selection of standard paper types from which you can choose. The size of the selection depends on your printer's capabilities. When you select a paper type from the list provided, all margin settings apply to the new paper size. For example, a 1-inch left margin begins at the left edge of the paper—regardless of the paper type.

Choose the appropriate paper type by clicking on its name in the Paper Type list box. Be sure that the printer is set up with the appropriate paper in place.

Printing Continuously and Other Options

 If you use a dot-matrix printer and continuous fan-fold paper, you can print long reports without any gaps between the pages—useful for printing wide reports sideways across several sheets, or long reports down several sheets. To eliminate the gaps between pages, remove the check mark from the **Break Pages** option in the Page Setup dialog box. Quattro Pro will then ignore your top and bottom margins settings and not print any header or footer text.

The **Print to Fit** option attempts to print your selected data onto a single page. It automatically reduces the data by the correct amount to fit the data onto one page. If the reduction required for this operation is too great, or if the fonts become too small to read, Quattro Pro will fit the data onto as few pages as possible. You can use this option instead of making several of your own attempts with the scaling option (discussed in the next section).

Another option available for your printouts is the **Center Blocks** option. This automatically centers your data onto the page between your margins. With this option checked, you don't have to use trial and error to find the correct left margin setting to make the report appear centered on the page.

Enlarging and Reducing the Page

There are two options provided for changing the size of your printed data. The **Print to Fit** option automatically reduces a large print block to fit onto as few pages as possible, while maintaining the legibility of your data. The **Scaling** option lets you select any reduction or enlargement size for the printout.

Print to Fit compresses large blocks of data so they will fit on fewer pages. This is particularly handy if your data are just over a page long. Checking the Print to Fit box, for example, can reduce your data enough so that your printout will take only one page. You can also use the option for long blocks of values so that your data fit across one page but down several.

Scaling allows you to increase or decrease the size of the data when they are printed. It will also reduce or enlarge the header and footer margins accordingly. The scaling factor is expressed as a percentage, where 100% indicates actual size. To increase the size of the data, increase the percentage beyond 100%. To reduce the size of the data, enter a percentage of less than 100%. Note that enlargement and reduction settings are also in the Page Setup dialog box.

Page Setup Scaling versus Printer Setup Scaling

When you access the File>Printer Setup>Setup dialog box for your printer, you might find a scaling option available there. You should *not* use this scaling setting in Quattro Pro, since Quattro Pro's scaling is much more powerful and flexible. The scaling option provided by Quattro Pro works with all printers, even those unsupported by the printer setup options.

Print to Fit and Scaling are Mutually Exclusive

If you change the scaling percentage to something other than 100 and also select the **Fit to Print** option, scaling will have no effect.

Page Orientation

The Page Orientation setting tells Quattro Pro which page dimension to use when printing your report. The two Orientation settings are **Portrait** and **Landscape**. As seen in Figures 9.3 and 9.4, Portrait orientation prints reports vertically on a page, and Landscape orientation prints reports vertically on a page.

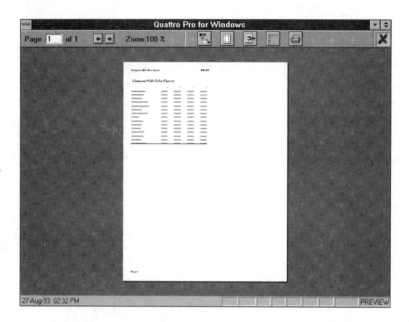

Figure 9.3 A report printed using Portrait orientation.

Your printer setup options can also include a **Page Orientation** setting. Use **File>Printer Setup** to set the default Print orientation for all your Windows programs. Select the Page Orientation setting you use the most. Then use **File>Page Setup** to set the orientation for Quattro Pro reports that require a different orientation than the one you set with the printer setup options.

The page orientation you select can depend on personal preference or on the amount of data you are printing. Reports containing very wide columns, or a large number of them, usually fit better when printed using Landscape orientation. Reports containing fewer columns but many rows of data are better suited to Portrait orientation.

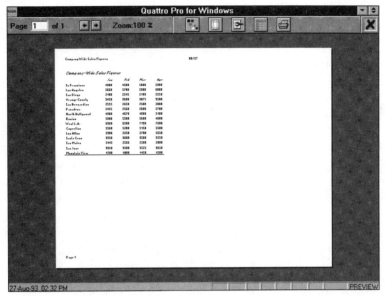

Figure 9.4 A report printed using Landscape orientation.

Printing the Report

After you have set the page and printer setup options, you're ready to start the printing procedure. This involves identifying the print block and setting any special print options. The **File>Print** command is the key to the printing process. When you choose the **File>Print** command, the dialog box in Figure 9.5 appears.

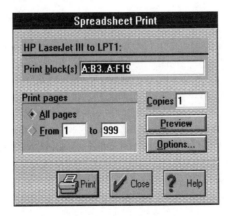

Figure 9.5 The Spreadsheet Print dialog box.

The Spreadsheet Print dialog box contains all the settings you'll need to print the report. Remember that your page and printer setup choices will also be active for this printout. Later, you'll learn how to store several different combinations of page setup and print settings.

Selecting the Print Block(s)

The first step to printing your data is to select the desired print blocks in the active notebook. Using the mouse or keyboard, highlight your desired print block(s). (Refer to Chapter 3 for details about selecting blocks.) Next, choose the **File>Print** command. This produces the dialog box shown in Figure 9.5. Notice that the dialog box already contains your selected print blocks. You can now modify the print blocks by typing a new reference into the Print block(s) entry box or by dragging on the notebook to select the blocks. You can select the blocks on the notebook while the Spreadsheet Print dialog box is in view. Quattro Pro will insert your selection into the dialog box.

Choosing File>Print before selecting the print block
You can enter the desired print block after choosing the **File>Print** command. There's an advantage to this: You can enter a block name instead of a block reference. For example, if you have named the block A1:G35 as REPORT1 using the **Block>Names>Create** command, you can simply type **REPORT1** into the Print block(s) entry box to print that block. This can save you time when identifying a print block that consists of several different blocks of cells.

Printing the entire page
If you want to print all information in the current page, *don't* click on the **Select All** button in the corner of the worksheet to set the print block. Instead, erase all information in the Print block(s) entry box and close the Spreadsheet Print dialog box using the **Close** button. Now select **File>Print** again. Quattro Pro automatically enters the active area of the worksheet as the current print block when nothing appears in the Print block(s) entry box. (Clicking on the **Select All** button in the upper-left corner of the page highlights every cell and causes blank cells to print with the data.)

Selecting the Page Range and Number of Copies

If you select a print block that spans two or more pages, you can choose whether you actually want to print *all* the pages in the block at this time. You might, for example, want to print a particular selection of pages, or just the first page.

You can select a range of pages to print within the print block by using the Print Pages options in the Spreadsheet Print dialog box. Normally, Quattro Pro is set to print all pages, but you can choose the **From/To** option to enter a page range. To print just page 1, type **1** into both the From and To entry boxes. To print from page 3 to the end of the report, enter **From 3 to 9999**.

It's easy to print multiple copies of the report. Simply enter the desired number of copies into the Copies entry box.

SHORTCUT

Speeding up multiple copies

If you print multiple copies of a report, Quattro Pro will send each copy of the page to the printer separately, causing each page to take the same amount of time to print. You can speed up multiple-copy printing by leaving the Copies setting on 1 and using the File>Printer Setup>Options screen to set the number of copies—if your printer supports this option. Remember to return to the printer setup options to set copies back to 1 when you're through.

Previewing the Printout

The Spreadsheet Print dialog box contains a **Preview** button that lets you view the report on-screen as it would appear on the printer. This is useful for checking your page and printer setup options before wasting paper. You can also preview the printout by using the **File>Print Preview** command. For details about the Preview options, refer to the "Previewing the Printout" section that appears later in this chapter.

Printing

When you are ready to print, choose the **Print** button at the bottom of the Spreadsheet Print dialog box. If your printer is connected and set up properly, the printing will begin. If you have activated background printing in Windows by using the Print Manager, Quattro Pro will first print the report to the Print

Manager, which will then send the report to the printer. The advantage of using the Print Manager is that you can return to your work more quickly and you can send multiple print jobs back to back. For more information on using the Print Manager in Windows, refer to the Windows User's Guide.

Additional Print Options

The **Options** button in the Spreadsheet Print dialog box provides some additional settings for your report. Using the options, you can add headings to the printout, print the notebook grid lines, or add the row and column headings to the report.

Adding Page Headings

Many reports will require more than one page. They will be either too wide or too long, even when reduced, to fit on one page. To make subsequent pages easier to read, you might want to print the column headings and/or row labels on each page.

Suppose you are printing a table that spans 10 pages. The top of the table contains column headings that explain what each column represents. You might want those column headings to appear at the top of all 10 pages instead of just the first page. You don't have to add the headings to each page in the printout manually, nor do you have to use the header entry area for this purpose. Quattro Pro provides a special print option that adds your headings to each page in the report. To specify headings for your printout, do the following:

1. Select **File>Print>Options**.

2. In the Top Heading entry box, enter the cell address of *any cell* in the row containing the column headings. For example, if the headings appear in row 4, enter cell **C4** or **B4** or **A4**. You can also click on the cell in the notebook to enter the cell's reference into the box. If you want to print two or more rows as a heading, enter a block reference consisting of a cell from each row. For example, if your headings are in rows 4, 5, and 6, you can enter the range **C4..C6** into the Top Heading entry box.

3. If desired, enter the cell address of any cell containing the row headings into the Left Heading entry box. These headings will appear along the left side of each page in the printout and are intended for extra-wide reports.

4. Click on **OK** and then proceed with the printing procedure.

If you specify headings for your printout, do *not* include those headings in the print block. Otherwise, they will print twice on the first page. For example, if your column headings are in row 4, and you have specified row 4 as the Top heading, do not include row 4 in the print block specification.

Printing Formulas

If you have constructed a complex notebook application and want to print the formulas that appear in the cells, you can do so by selecting the **Cell Formulas** option in the Spreadsheet Print Options dialog box. Instead of printing the results of your formulas, Quattro Pro will now print the formulas themselves. This is useful for checking errors in your worksheets.

Printing Grids, Column Borders, and Row Borders

Figure 9.6 shows a report that looks like the computer screen—along with the data, cell borders, column borders, and row borders were printed. You can add these elements to any printout by choosing the appropriate options in the Spreadsheet Print Options dialog box. The **Grid Lines** option adds the cell grid lines and the **Row/Column Borders** option adds the borders along the top and left side of the page. Normally, these options are left unchecked.

A	B	C	D	E	F
3	Company-Wide Sales Figures				
4		*Jan*	*Feb*	*Mar*	*Apr*
5	San Francisco	4300	4500	5000	5300
6	Los Angeles	5660	5700	5980	6000
7	San Diego	2100	2245	2100	2550
8	Orange County	3450	3600	3875	3500
9	San Bernardino	2555	2650	2500	2000
10	Pasadena	2455	2560	2600	2700
11	North Hollywood	4300	4670	4900	5100
12	Encino	5300	5500	5600	4600
13	West L.A.	6360	6500	7190	7600
14	Cupertino	5560	5200	5150	5500
15	Los Altos	2300	2250	2700	2650
16	Santa Cruz	3350	3600	3500	3250
17	San Mateo	1527	2083	2133	1550
18	San Jose	2340	1283	1308	425
19	Mountain View	6654	483	483	1234

Figure 9.6 A report that includes grid lines and row/column borders.

Printing Blocks That Contain Multiple or 3-D Selections

When you specify a print block that contains two or more blocks of cells from the notebook, Quattro Pro can automatically split each block onto a new page or add a specific amount of space between the blocks.

For example, if your print block is A1..G10, J1..P10 (a selection of two blocks), Quattro Pro normally prints both blocks together as a single unit. If a page break is needed, the break is inserted wherever necessary within the entire print range. However, if you wish, you can tell Quattro Pro to print the first block, A1..G10, onto page 1 and the second block, J1..P10, onto page 2. Just select the **Page Advance** option under the Print Between Blocks options in the Spreadsheet Print Options dialog box. You can also tell Quattro Pro to place a certain number of blank lines between the two blocks, which can be useful for adding space between main sections of a report when such space is not possible to add on the screen or for selecting extra rows in each block.

If you specify a print block that consists of a 3-D reference, such as A:A1..C:G10, you can choose similar options for controlling the various pages of the printout. You can tell Quattro Pro to place each worksheet page on a new page of the report by selecting the **Page Advance** option under the Print Between 3D Pages options. This would place the block A:A1..A:G10 onto the first page, the block B:A1..B:G10 onto the second page, and the block C:A1..C:G10 onto the third page.

Saving Page Setup and Print Settings

When you go to all the trouble to set up your report using the Page Setup and Print options, you certainly don't want to have to keep repeating these options each time you want to print this report. Even though the current Page Setup and Print options are saved when you save the notebook, you might want to save two or three different sets of options for different types of reports.

For example, you might create a report that prints the range A:A1..C:G10 using 0.5-inch margins, 50% scaling, and breaks between the 3-D pages. You might also want this report to print the grid lines on the page.

Using the same notebook application, you could set up a second report that includes the range A1..J100. This report might include print headings along the top of the pages, 0.25-inch margins, and a Print to Fit reduction setting. This report may also contain a header and footer.

Obviously, you can't have both sets of options active for the worksheet. And if you switch from one set of options to the other, you'll lose the first set; if you want to print the first report again, you would have to set each option again. Since Quattro Pro has a command that stores your Print and Page Setup settings under unique names, you can return to any settings by choosing the name under which they are stored. Save as many named settings as you like and switch between them at any time.

To store your Print and Page Setup settings under a unique name, follow these steps.

1. Use the **File>Page Setup** command to establish the desired Page Setup options for the report.

2. Use the **File>Print** command to establish the desired print settings for the report.

3. Choose **File>Named Settings** to see the dialog box in Figure 9.7.

4. Choose the **Create** button to start a new named set.

5. To name the currently active settings, press **Enter** or click on **OK** when finished.

6. Click on **OK** to return to the notebook and repeat Steps 1 through 6 to create another named setting.

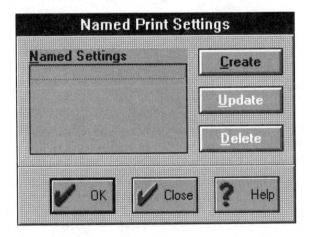

Figure 9.7 The Named Print Settings dialog box.

All the named settings you create appear in the Named Settings list when you select the **File>Named Settings** command. Select any one of these settings to print the report associated with that name. It's that easy.

Remember that named settings store Page Setup and Print options located in the Spreadsheet Page Setup, the Spreadsheet Print, and the Spreadsheet Print Options dialog boxes. Settings do not include printer setup options.

Printing to a File

You can send your printed report to a file on disk using the **Redirect to File** option in the Printer Setup dialog box. This creates a file that can be downloaded to your printer at any time. This option is useful for printing files on printers at other locations. You can copy the resulting file onto a floppy disk and move it to another computer for printing. You don't need Quattro Pro to print these files; just send them directly to your printer through a downloading utility.

Remember that the resulting file must be printed on the same printer selected when you saved the file. For example, if you select the HP LaserJet III and redirect the report to a file, then you must print the file on the same type of printer (or a compatible printer) later.

If you select a PostScript printer for storing the disk file, Quattro Pro saves a PostScript file, not an Encapsulated PostScript (EPS) file. This can determine how the file can be used later. To save an EPS file from Quattro Pro:

1. Choose the **File>Printer Setup** command from Quattro Pro.
2. Select the PostScript printer in your Printer list.
3. Choose **Setup**.
4. Choose **Options**.
5. Choose the **Encapsulated PostScript File** option and enter a file name into the space provided. This file name can include a directory path, if desired.
6. Click on **OK** three times to return to the notebook. Then print the report with the **File>Print** command. The result will be an EPS file on disk under the name you specified.

Remember that when you are finished printing you must return to the Printer Setup dialog box to cancel the **Encapsulated PostScript File** option and return printing to the printer. If you use these steps, do *not* select the **Redirect to File** option in the Printer Setup dialog box.

Printing Graphs and Objects to Disk Files

If your printout consists of graphs or graphic objects, you have several other options for printing the data to a disk file. For more information refer to Chapter 12.

Printing Graphs

Graphs can be printed by themselves or as part of a report containing data and graphs. A graph that is printed by itself can be printed from a Graph window. To print the graph:

1. Display the Graph window using the **Graph>Edit** command or any other method.

2. Select **File>Print**. The Graph Print dialog box shown in Figure 9.8 (an abbreviated version of the Spreadsheet Print dialog box) is displayed.

3. Indicate the number of copies to be printed. The default is 1.

4. If desired, preview the graph.

5. When everything is set, click on the **Print** button.

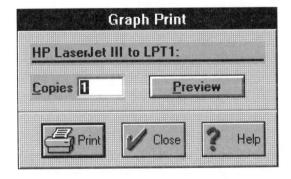

Figure 9.8 The Graph Print dialog box.

An alternative method is to go to the Graph page in the notebook, click on the desired graph icon, and then select **File>Print**. Using this technique, you can actually print several graphs back to back by selecting several graphs on the graph page. Quattro Pro will print the graphs in the order in which you select them. You can also print all the graphs in a slide show by clicking on the **Slide Show** icon and selecting the **File>Print** command.

Setting the Aspect Ratio of the Graph Before Printing

There are several aspect ratios for printing your graphs. Aspect ratios affect the width-to-height ratio of the graph on the printed page. Using the method described above for printing the graph, you might consider first selecting one of the aspect ratios in the Graph Properties dialog box. First display the graph in a window; then right-click the Graph window's title bar to display the Graph Window properties. Select from the aspect ratios provided. Details on these settings appear in Chapter 12.

Printing Graphs and Data Together

If your notebook page contains a graph, you can print that graph along with the worksheet data surrounding it—simply include the graph in the print block you specify. Just include all the cells on which the graph is resting, along with any other cells you want printed. For details about adding graphs to the notebook page (called *floating graphs*), refer to Chapter 10.

Floating graphs and page breaks
Be careful not to position a graph over a page break symbol. If you do, the printed graph will be split where the page break occurs.

Previewing the Printout

To preview a report prior to printing it, select **File>Print Preview**. Alternatively you can select **File>Print**, which will display the Spreadsheet Print dialog box. Then click on the **Preview** button. The preview workspace is shown in Figure 9.9.

Within the Preview screen you have several options. You can view each page of the printout, change the page margins, change the Page Setup options, and even print the report right from the Preview. The following list describes each option in the Preview SpeedBar.

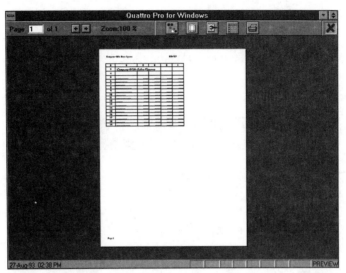

Figure 9.9 The Print Preview workspace.

 Previous and Next Displays other pages of the printout. When you preview a multipage document, by default you are show the first page of the printout. To see subsequent pages, use the **Next** button. To see pages prior to the current page, use the **Previous** button.

 Color Toggles the previewed image between color and black-and-white. This option allows you to see exactly what your printout will look like if you are using a black-and-white printer.

 Margin Displays the current margin settings using dashed lines. Figure 9.10 shows the current margins for a previewed document. To adjust the margins, use the mouse to drag the lines on the screen.

 Setup Displays the Page Setup dialog box and makes all functions available to you while you are previewing a document. This allows you to make necessary changes and see their effects immediately.

 Options Displays the Spreadsheet Print Options dialog box and makes all its functions available to you while you are previewing a document. This options allows you to make necessary changes and see their effects immediately. (This button does not appear in the SpeedBar when previewing a graph for printing.)

Close Exits the Preview screen, returning you to the Spreadsheet Print dialog box.

 Print Prints the report using the current settings.

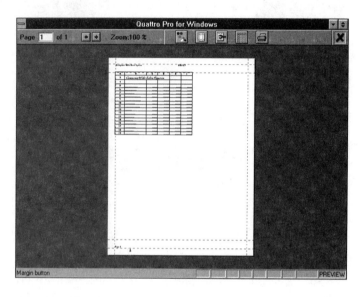

Figure 9.10 All margins are displayed and may be adjusted using the mouse.

In addition to the SpeedBar buttons and icons, you have a number of special commands available in the Preview screen. Here is a list of the commands.

Table 9.2 Commands available in Preview Screen.

Command	Description
Esc	Exits Preview, returning you to the Spreadsheet Print dialog box or your previous location.
F1	Displays the Help dialog box.
PgUp	Moves to the previous page.

Table 9.2 Commands available in Preview Screen (con't).

Command	Description
PgDn	Moves to the next page.
+ (plus)	Magnifies the screen by one level. You can press this command again to magnify the screen more.
- (minus)	Decreases magnification by one level.
Arrow Keys	Moves the screen in the direction of the arrow. This is useful when you have magnified the image.
Home	Moves to the top-left corner of a magnified page.
End	Moves to the bottom-right corner of a magnified page.

When in Preview, the mouse pointer will be in the shape of an arrow as it points to any area of the Preview window, with the exception of the document. When pointing directly at the document, the mouse pointer changes to one of two shapes: a double-headed arrow or a magnifying glass. When the pointer looks like a magnifying glass, clicking the left mouse button zooms the Preview one level up. Clicking the right mouse button zooms the preview one level down. The zoom factor is displayed on the SpeedBar preceding the **Color** button.

When the mouse pointer displays as a double-headed arrow, you are pointing to a margin. You can then click the left mouse button on the margin line and drag to move the margin around the page.

Summary

Quattro Pro's printing features let you get exactly what you want from your notebooks. You can change aspects of the page, such as margins and headers, using the **File>Page Setup** command. The **File>Print** command lets you establish the print block and several print options.

Before printing, make sure that the correct printer is selected and properly configured. You can do this from Quattro Pro by using the **File>Printer Setup** command.

In the next chapter, you'll learn about Quattro Pro's powerful graphing features, including how to use the new Graph Expert to create graphs almost automatically. You'll also learn how to modify graphs and choose from Quattro Pro's numerous graph types.

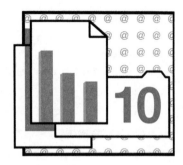

Creating Graphs

You can easily turn your raw numeric data into beautiful color graphs. Quattro Pro offers several different types of graphs from which to choose, including bar graphs, line graphs, and pie graphs. When you create a graph in Quattro Pro, the numeric data is linked to the graph; if you change the data, the graph automatically reflects the change.

This chapter introduces Quattro Pro's graphing powers. You'll learn some basic terminology involved in graphing, plus various ways you can create graphs from your numeric data. You'll see also how easy it is to modify graphs for your personal taste. In this chapter, you will learn about

- Creating a graph instantly with the **Graph** tool
- Creating a graph using the Graph Expert
- Creating a graph manually, for total control
- Editing the graph's data series
- Changing the graph's frame on the notebook page
- Adding titles to the graph
- Choosing an appropriate graph type
- Working with the notebook's Graphs page

Parts of a Graph

To fully understand the graphing procedure in Quattro Pro, you should be familiar with some basic graphing terminology. Each element on a graph has a unique name and special qualities. Figure 10.1 shows a graph and some of its basic elements.

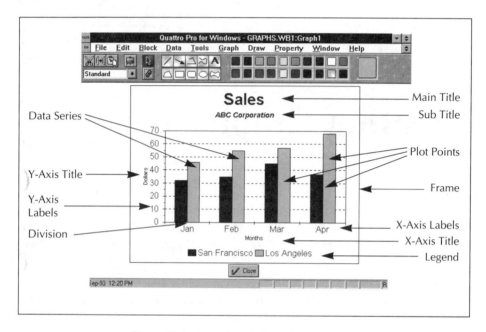

Figure 10.1 A graph and its various elements.

The following is a list of these graph elements.

- **Frame** The box in which the graph appears on the notebook page. Graphs appear in frames only when you insert them onto the worksheet. If a graph does not appear in a frame, you can view the graph using the **Graph>Edit** command.

- **Plot point** A single value in the graph. Each value in your graph data is plotted onto the graph as a plot point. Combinations of values representing a single product or item are called data series. The graph in Figure 10.1 has eight plot points.

- **Data series** A series of plot points that apply to the same item. Data series are values that appear in the same row or column, depending on the graph's data orientation. The graph in Figure 10.1 has two data series.

- **Division** A grouping of data series applying to a single X-axis label. Graphs can have one or more divisions, depending on the number of cells used in each data series. The more cells in each data series, the more divisions on the graph. The graph in Figure 10.1 shows four divisions, one for each month.

- **X-axis labels** The labels used along the X-axis that identify the divisions. Your graph should have as many X-axis labels as it has divisions.

- **Y-axis values** The values along the vertical axis of the graph. Y-axis values are automatically provided by Quattro Pro, but you can change them as described in Chapter 11.

- **Legend** The key to a graph's data series. Each data series can have a name that appears in the legend. When you select your graph data, you can include the legend entries in the first cell of each data series.

- **Main title** The title of the graph.

- **X-axis title** The title of the graph's X-axis. This title usually explains what the X-axis labels represent if it's not obvious.

- **Y-axis title** The title of the graph's Y-axis values. Often, you'll want to show that the graph values represent dollar amounts or some other unit. This can be done with the Y-axis title.

- **Subtitle** The graph's secondary title.

- **Secondary Y-axis** A Y-axis appearing along the right edge of the graph. This often applies to combination graphs. Adding a secondary Y-axis (also called a Y2-axis) is explained in Chapter 11.

- **Y2-axis title** If your graph includes a secondary Y-axis, you can give it a title.

Graphing Tools and Commands

Before we describe graphing and editing graphs, let's review Quattro Pro's graphing tools and commands. Quattro Pro offers tools for creating graphs and several commands in the Graph menu. Here is a brief description of each command and tool.

- **Graph Expert** Guides you through the process of creating a graph. Just highlight the desired graph data; then click the **Experts** button on the SpeedBar. Choose the **Graph Expert** and follow the steps presented on the screen. Details about the Graph Expert's steps appear later in this chapter.

- **Graph tool** Creates a new floating graph on the page. Highlight your graph data; then click on this tool and drag on the page to create the graph frame. The graph will appear inside the frame when you release the mouse button.

- **Graph>Type** Changes the graph type. Activate the graph window (by double-clicking on the graph frame or by using the **Graph>Edit** command); then select this command to change the graph type. Types include **Bar**, **Line**, **Variance**, **Stacked Bar**, **High Low**, **XY**, **Area**, **Column**, and **Pie**.

- **Graph>Series** Lets you change the data used for the graph. Activate the graph window; then choose this command to add a new data series to the graph or to modify the block used for other data series. You can also use this command to change the X-axis and legend labels.

- **Graph>Titles** Lets you add main titles to the graph. Activate the graph window; then choose this command to add up to five titles to the graph, including a main title, subtitle, X-axis title, Y-axis title, and secondary Y-axis title.

- **Graph>New** Lets you specify the data for a new graph. Use this command instead of the **Graph** tool to create a new graph when you don't want the graph to appear on the page or if you want to control the orientation of the data series. (You will learn more about this command later in the chapter.)

- **Graph>Edit** Activates a graph's window so you can edit the graph. Choosing **Graph>Edit** presents a list of all the graphs you've created in this notebook. You can select any graph from this list to display it in a window. After the graph is displayed, you can modify it by using commands in the Graph menu and many tools on the SpeedBar. (Refer to Chapter 11 and 12 for details about these tools.)

- **Graph>Insert** Inserts any existing graph onto a page of the notebook. Choosing this command presents a list of graphs available. Select a graph to insert it onto a page of the notebook.

- **Graph>Delete** Removes a graph from the notebook. Select any graph from the list provided.

- **Graph>Copy** Copies any graph or lets you format one graph with the styles used in another. (Details on this command appear later in this chapter.)

- **Graph>View** Displays any graph you've created on the screen in full size.

Besides these basic graphing commands, Quattro Pro gives you a host of graph-annotation tools. These tools appear in the SpeedBar when you activate a graph's window using the **Graph>Edit** command (or by double-clicking on a graph frame). These graph-annotation tools are discussed in Chapter 12.

When the graph window is active, you also have access to many graph properties. By right-clicking the mouse on an element in the graph window, you gain access to that element's properties. The various graph elements and their properties are described in Chapter 11.

Creating a Graph

Creating a graph consists of a few main steps. You must identify the data for the graph and then create the graph using one of two primary methods. After this, you might want to select a graph type from Quattro Pro's list of types and add any titles to the graph. After this, you can customize the graph in various ways; graph customization is described in Chapter 11. This chapter explains how to create graphs, edit them, and add graph titles. First, let's examine the three primary ways to create the graph: using the **Graph Expert**, instant graphing with the **Graph tool**, and manual graphing with the **Graph>New** command.

Using the Graph Expert

The easiest and most complete way to create graphs is to use the Graph Expert. The Graph Expert takes you through all the steps necessary to create and manipulate a graph. Using a series of steps, you select the desired graph data, choose data orientation and order, select a graph type, and enter titles for the graph. You can also decide whether the graph will appear on the page in a graph frame or in a separate window. Following are the details.

To begin using the Graph Expert, just click on the **Experts** tool in the SpeedBar and select the **Graph Expert** from the Expert options provided. This presents you with the first step in the graphing process: selecting your graph data. The following sections detail each step in the process.

Step 1: Selecting the Graph Data and Orientation

When you start the Graph Expert, you are presented with Step 1 of the graphing procedure: selecting the desired graph data. Figure 10.2 shows this step of the Graph Expert procedure.

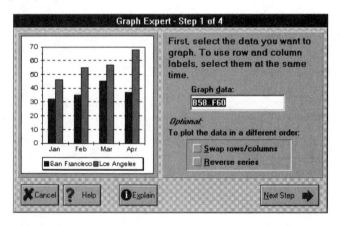

Figure 10.2 The first step of the Graph Expert is to select the graph data.

You can select the data first

You can highlight the desired graph data before starting the Graph Expert, and Quattro Pro will automatically use the highlighted block as the default data in this step of the Expert process. You can always change the selected block at this time or—if you didn't highlight a block to begin with—just choose it now.

To choose or modify the data block, simply type the desired block reference (a name or address) into the space marked Graph Data. You can also "point" to the block on the notebook page by double-clicking on the Graph Data entry box. This places you onto the notebook page where you can highlight the desired block. After you have highlighted the block, press **Enter** to return to the Expert dialog box.

Graph data can be any block of values and any column and/or row headings to help identify the values. Graph data can consist of a single row of values

Jan	Feb	Mar	Apr	May	Jun
123	231	231	332	334	242

a single column

Jan	123
Feb	231
Mar	231
Apr	332
May	334
Jun	242

or a block.

	Jan	Feb	Mar	Apr	May	Jun
Apples	123	231	231	332	334	242
Oranges	234	634	155	342	644	222
Pears	234	533	645	335	444	323
Peaches	654	442	334	434	342	144

Note that you can include labels with the values or not. If you don't include labels, you'll have the chance to add them later. For example, your row and column labels might not appear next to the data you want to graph. You'll see how you can change or add to the graph's data range later in this chapter in the "Editing the Graph" section.

The graph data can also consist of several noncontiguous blocks. By holding the **Ctrl** key as you select the blocks, you can create a graph from several different ranges on the worksheet. Figure 10.3 shows an example.

Notice that the various selections do not all contain the same number of cells. Although it's usually a good idea to highlight matching blocks, it's not a requirement.

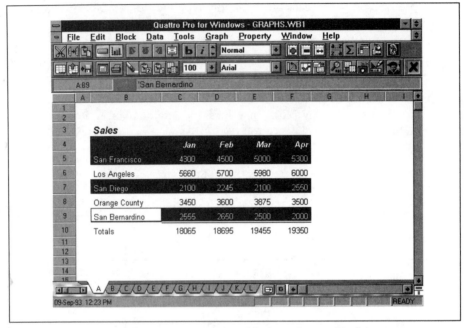

Figure 10.3 Selecting noncontiguous blocks as the graph's data range.

Here are some guidelines for selecting your graph data.

- Don't include column or row headings if they are noncontiguous. You should not include the column or row headings if they are separate from the data. To include the headings, make sure you highlight the row or column of values adjacent to the headings. For example, in Figure 10.3, you should not highlight the row 4 headings unless the row 5 data are part of the selection.

- Don't include totals in the graph data. If your graph data have totals at the bottom or side, don't include those totals with the rest of the data when selecting the graph data block. Totals will be misleading when displayed in a graph along with the values that comprise the totals. Instead, use a stacked graph type to show total values.

- Avoid graphing widely fluctuating values, unless appropriate to the graph. Graphs that display vast fluctuations in data can be difficult to read. Try grouping your data into value "ranges" and creating separate graphs for each range.

After you have highlighted the desired graph data and pressed **Enter** to return to the Expert screen, you will see a sample of your graph on the left side of the Expert dialog boxes. Using this sample, you can see exactly what your graph will look like at any given point in the process.

Another part of this step is the selection of the data order. You can change the order in which the data are plotted in the graph in two ways: you can swap rows and columns and reverse the data series. Swapping rows and columns affects the data orientation—or whether the rows or columns are used as the data series for the graph. Normally, if your graph data contain more rows that columns, the rows will become the data series and the row 3 headings will be used as the legend entries to identify those data series. If your graph data contain more columns than rows, the columns will be used as data series and column headings, as legend entries. This can make a big difference in your graph, as shown in Figures 10.4 and 10.5, which show two different orientations for the same graph data.

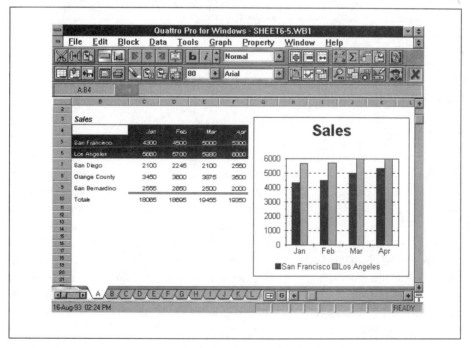

Figure 10.4 A graph showing rows as data series.

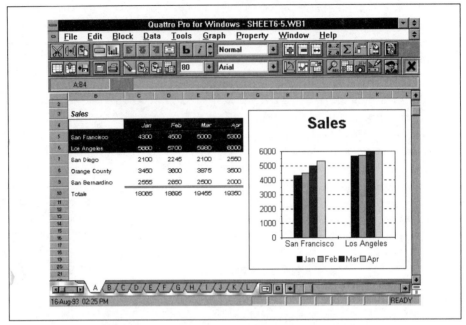

Figure 10.5 A graph showing columns as data series.

If you are not satisfied with the default orientation of your graph data, click on the **Swap Rows/Columns** option in the Expert Step 1 screen.

Reversing the data series is another method of controlling the data order on the graph. This option controls the order in which the data series are plotted in the graph and applies only if you have more than one data series. For example, the graph in Figure 10.4 shows two data series. Normally, the order in which series are displayed on the graph comes from the order in which the columns or rows appear in the graph data block. So, the first row becomes the first data series in each group or division. You can reverse this normal order by checking the **Reverse Series** option in the Expert Step 1 screen. This can be useful for 3-D graphs when larger data series obstruct the view of smaller ones. By reversing the order of the data series, you can often avoid such conflicts. Note that when you reverse the data series, Quattro Pro does not reverse the colors used for those series. In other words, the first data series will always be Blue, whether you swap the order of the values or not.

When you are completely finished with Step 1 of the Expert, click on the **Next Step** button to move to Step 2.

Step 2: Choosing a Main Graph Type

The next step of the graphing procedure is to choose a primary graph type. You have five primary types from which to choose, including Bar, Pie, Specialty, Rotated Bar, and Line or Area. This chapter provides complete details about each of these graph types under the heading "Selecting a Graph Type." For now, you can just click on the desired type and watch the sample graph reflect your selection. Additional versions of the type you select will be available in the next step.

When you are finished selecting a graph type, click on the **Next Step** button.

Step 3: Choosing a Specific Graph Type

In Step 3 of the Graph Expert procedure, you can choose from additional graph formats within the main graph type you chose in the previous step. For example, if you chose a bar graph in Step 2, you will be presented with numerous bar graph types in this step. Figure 10.6 shows this step.

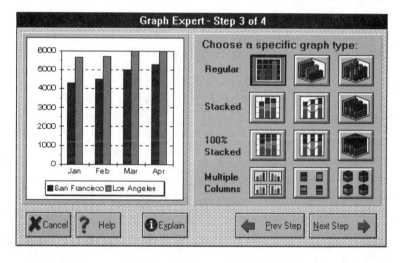

Figure 10.6 Step 3 of the Graph Expert lets you choose a specific graph type.

Just click on the button representing the graph type you want to use. If you are unsure of the type, just click on each one and watch the sample on the left side of the window. Details about graph types appear later in this chapter.

When you are finished, click on the **Next Step** button.

Step 4: Entering Graph Labels

This last step of the graphing procedure is fairly easy to understand. Here you can enter labels for your graph if desired. You can enter a main title, subtitle, X-axis heading, and Y-axis heading.

Press the **Tab** key to move among the spaces in this window and fill in the labels. Note that all these labels are not always necessary in a graph. You may not need a subtitle or axis labels for instance. When in doubt, it's best to keep the graph as simple and uncluttered as possible.

When you are finished typing the labels for the graph, you can determine the final destination of the graph itself. You have two choices.

- **Notebook Page** This option inserts the graph onto the notebook page at the location of the highlighted block. You can move or modify the graph frame that appears in the notebook as described later in this chapter.
- **Graph Window** This option does not insert the graph into the notebook at all, but rather presents it inside a graph window. The graph itself exists on the Graphs page of the notebook, which is described later in this chapter under "Storing Graphs in the Notebook." If you choose this option, you can always insert the graph into the notebook later.

When you are finished with these options, click on the **Create Graph** button to finish the procedure. You now have a completed graph in your notebook. You can edit the graph if you decide to change any of the selections you've made. Refer to "Editing the Graph" later in this chapter for more details.

Instant Graphing

Another way to create a graph is to quickly get a graph onto the page and then modify the graph after it appears. Using the **Graph** tool in the SpeedBar, you can quickly turn any data block into a graph that can be displayed on any notebook page. The resulting graph appears in a graph frame on the page, and you can manipulate the frame and edit the graph as you would any graph.

Selecting the Graph Data

To create a floating graph instantly with the **Graph** tool, you must first select the graph data. Refer to "Step 1: Selecting the Graph Data and Orientation" earlier in this chapter for information about choosing data blocks for graphs. Basically, you should highlight the desired graph data (a row, column, block, or combination or blocks) as the first step in this procedure.

Data orientation

If your graph data consists of more rows than columns, your graph will use rows as the data series. If the graph data contain more columns (or an equal number of rows and columns), the graph will use columns as the data series. You can change the data orientation after creating the graph, or you can force the desired orientation when you select the graph data. See "Changing the Graph's Data Orientation" later in this chapter for more information on data orientation.

Drawing the Graph Frame

After you have selected your graph data, click on the **Graph** tool in the SpeedBar and drag on the worksheet to create the *graph frame.* When you release the mouse, the graph will be displayed inside the frame. You can insert the frame anywhere in the notebook, including other pages. And you can determine the size of the graph by the size of the frame you draw onto the sheet. Figures 10.7 shows the procedure for drawing the graph frame onto the page.

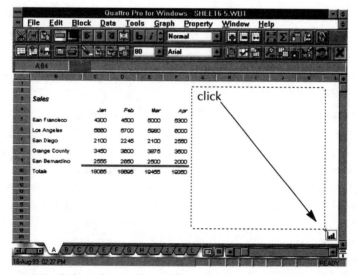

Figure 10.7 Click on the Graph tool, then drag on the page to create a frame.

Instantly, the graph appears inside the frame you created. By default, Quattro Pro provides a bar graph, but you can change the graph type as described later. Also, later in this chapter, you'll discover how to manipulate the graph frame in various ways. For now, remember that you can move the graph frame around the page by clicking on it and dragging the mouse.

Creating a Graph Manually

Although instant graphing is fast and easy, you might prefer to use the manual method of creating graphs. You'll find this comfortable if you've used Quattro Pro for DOS, Lotus 1-2-3, or other DOS spreadsheets. The manual method of creating graphs gives you more control over the selection of data. You can specify exactly which cells you want in each data series with no question about data orientation. Moreover, manual graphing lets you use combinations of rows and columns as data series. That is, within the same graph you can use a row of cells for one data series and a column of cells for another. When you graph data manually, your graph is not automatically displayed on the notebook page. If you want to insert the graph onto the page, you must do so manually. First we'll explain how to create the graph and then how to insert the graph onto the notebook page.

Identifying the Graph Data

The first step to creating a graph manually is to identify the data to be used. This is done with the **Graph>New** command. You can specify each element of the graph individually using these steps.

1. Select **Graph>New** to display the Graph New dialog box as shown in Figure 10.8.

2. Enter a name for the graph into the Graph Name entry box.

3. To move to the X-axis entry box press **Tab**; then enter a reference to the block containing the X-axis labels for the graph. Generally, these are column or row headings that appear along the bottom axis of most graphs. (You can also point to the range on the notebook page using the mouse. Just click on the word X-axis and Quattro Pro will move you to the Page where you can highlight a block. Quattro Pro will then enter the block reference for you.)

4. Click in the Legend entry box; enter a reference to the block containing legend entries for the graph. Again, these will probably be row or column labels for the data.

5. Click in the 1st entry box; then enter a reference to the first data series for the graph. Repeat this step to enter all desired data series for the graph. Do not include labels with these data blocks; use only numeric data.

6. Press **OK**.

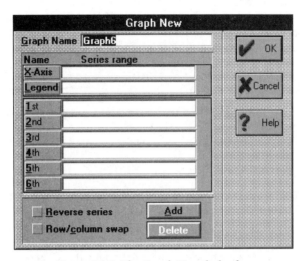

Figure 10.8 The Graph New dialog box.

Before you press **OK**, the Graph New dialog box may look something like Figure 10.9.

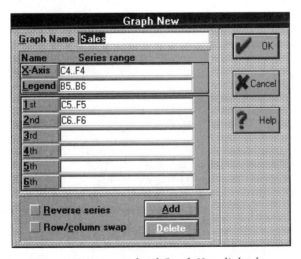

Figure 10.9 A completed Graph New dialog box.

When you choose **OK** after specifying all the graph data, Quattro Pro builds the graph and displays it in a graph window. The graph window is used primarily for editing the graph. Since creating the graph manually does not place the graph onto the notebook, however, the graph window is used to display the completed graph. The graph itself is stored with the notebook on the Graphs page (see "Storing Graphs in the Notebook"), and you can display the graph in a window at any time.

Inserting a Graph onto the Notebook

When you create a graph manually, the graph does not float on the worksheet in a frame. To insert the graph onto the sheet, use the **Graph>Insert** command, as follows:

1. Choose **Graph>Insert**.
2. Select the desired graph from the list provided and choose **OK**. This list displays all the graphs you've created in the notebook.
3. Click and drag on the page to draw a graph frame. When you release the mouse, the graph you chose will be displayed inside the frame.

You can draw the same graph over and over using these steps—or add to the notebook any graph that was created manually or instantly. In other words, all graphs you create will appear in this list, and you can add them to the notebook at any time. If you remove a graph frame from the notebook, it will still be available in this list. The graphs presented in this list also appear on the Graphs page of the notebook. For more information on this, see "Storing Graphs in the Notebook" later in this chapter.

Editing the Graph

Whichever method you use for creating a graph, you can always make changes to the graph at any time. The following sections describe ways in which you can edit the graph—including the data block, data orientation, titles, and graph type. If you use instant graphing or the manual method of creating the graph, you'll probably want to complete these procedures to get the graph exactly the way you want it.

Changing the Graph Data

If you're not happy with the graph's data, you can select a different block of cells for the graph. Quattro Pro lets you examine and edit the current data blocks used for each part of the graph. Use the following steps to edit the data used for your graph.

1. Choose **Graph>Edit** and select the graph's name from the list provided. This displays the graph inside a window. Alternatively, you can double-click on a floating graph to display it inside a window—or double-click on a graph icon that appears in the Graphs page.

2. Choose **Graph>Series**. Quattro Pro displays the data used for each element in the graph as shown in Figure 10.10.

3. Double-click in any of the entry boxes to redefine the block used for the corresponding part of the graph. For example, to change the X-axis labels, double-click in the X-axis entry box. After you double-click, Quattro Pro displays the notebook and highlights the current block identified in the entry box.

4. Select a new block and press **Enter**.

5. Repeat Steps 3 and 4 for other data in the Graph Series dialog box.

6. Click on **OK**.

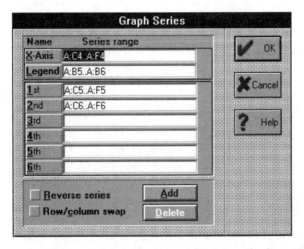

Figure 10.10 The Graph>Series command lets you edit the graph data.

You don't have to double-click in the desired entry box to change its block reference. You can click once on the name of the item in the Graph Series dialog box. For example, click on the name 1st to change the first data series. An alternative method is to click once in the box, backspace to remove the current reference and then type a new reference in its place. This way, you can enter range names used in the notebook.

You can also use these steps to add new data series to the graph using any empty slots in the Graph Series dialog box. If you want to remove an existing data series from the graph, click once in the entry box and press the **Backspace** key until the reference is erased.

Changing the Graph's Data Orientation

When you use the instant graphing technique to create a graph from a block of cells, Quattro Pro must make assumptions about the graph data you've identified. Do you want each row in the block to create a separate data series on the graph? Or should each column create a data series? To decide whether to use rows or columns, Quattro Pro follows a simple guideline: If the data range contains more columns than rows, rows are used for the data series. If the data block contains more rows than columns, or an equal number of columns and rows, columns are used for the data series.

If Quattro Pro's orientation guideline does not produce the desired orientation for the data you've selected—if, for example, your data block contains more rows, but you want each row to become a data series—you can manipulate the orientation in three different ways.

- Use the manual method for creating the graph. As described in the "Creating a Graph Manually" section earlier in this chapter, you can identify a separate row or column of cells for each data series individually. By indicating each data series individually, you also control the orientation of the data.

- Use the **Graph>Series>Row/Column Swap** option after creating the graph. If you've already created a graph and want to change the orientation, place a check beside the **Row/Column Swap** option in the Graph>Series dialog box. When you click on **OK**, the graph changes to reflect the new orientation.

- Select the graph data in two parts. As discussed earlier in this chapter, you can select two or more separate blocks as the graph data. The first block you select in a multiple-block selection (also called a *composite block*) sets the orientation for the graph. Hence, if the graph data contain more rows than columns (for example, if you want to use the block B4..F9), but if you want rows to form the graph's data series, highlight only the first row of data and the headings (for example, the range B4..F5), press the **Ctrl** key, and highlight the rest of the block (the range B6..F9). The graph data now consist of two blocks, the first block setting the orientation you want for the graph.

Use any of these methods to change or establish the orientation of a graph. You can always change your graph's orientation later by using the second method described above.

Reversing the Data Series

Another option in the Graph Series dialog box is **Reverse Series**. This option lets you swap the order in which the data series are plotted. For example, if your graph shows sales of three products over 4 months, one of the three products will appear first in the graph. That is, its bar will be placed to the left of the other bars in each division.

Quattro Pro plots data series in the order they appear in the data range— from top to bottom and left to right. If you check the **Reverse Series** option in the Graph Series dialog box, Quattro Pro reverses this order. You'll find this especially useful for combination graphs, to determine which data series is displayed by which type of graph.

Editing the Graph Frame

You can modify many aspects of the graph's frame on the worksheet. Of course, this applies to floating graphs only. Floating graphs are merely objects on the notebook page, and you can manipulate graph objects using a number of commands and options. Here is a list of modifications you can make to the graph frame.

- Delete the graph. You can remove any floating graph by clicking on the graph frame once (to select the object) and then pressing the **Delete** key. This activity merely removes the graph frame from the page; it does not eliminate the graph from the notebook itself. You can examine the graph using the **Graph>Edit** command or by turning to the Graphs page. Also, you can reinsert the graph using the **Graph>Insert** command. To remove a graph from the notebook permanently, turn to the Graphs page and remove the graph's icon that appears on that page— click on the icon and then press **Delete**. You can also use the **Graph>Delete** command.

• Move the graph. If the graph frame does not appear exactly where you want it, you can move it by dragging it with the mouse. Just click once on the graph frame and hold the left mouse button down. Drag the mouse (and the graph) to the desired location and release the mouse button. If you need to move the graph a great distance on the page, or between pages, delete the graph from its current location and reinsert the graph into the new location using the **Graph>Insert** command.

Copying a graph

You can insert two or more copies of the same graph into the note-book. Just use the **Graph>Insert** command to place the graph onto the page over and over again. Changes to the original graph will affect all copies that appear on the worksheet. You can also copy the graph inside the Graphs page as described later in this chapter.

• Change the size and shape of the frame. When you click on the graph frame, it becomes selected and small boxes will be displayed around its edges. Dragging on any of these boxes (called *size boxes*) lets you change the shape of the graph. Drag on a corner size box to change the overall size of the graph. Drag on a side size box to change that side.

• Change the color of the graph's border. The **Property>Current Object** command gives you access to several options for modifying the graph frame. You can change the color of the frame by right-clicking on the graph (or clicking once on the graph and choosing **Property>Current Object**) and choosing the **Border Color** option (see Figure 10.11). Quattro Pro presents a palette of border colors from which to choose.

• Change the border style or remove the border. You can change the type of box used around the graph. Right-click on the graph and choose the **Box Type** option to display the Box Type dialog box, as shown in Figure 10.12. Choose one of the box types and click on **OK**.

- Change the graph's name. Use the **Object Name** option in the Graph Properties window to change the name of the graph. Graphs drawn with the Graph tool are named automatically by Quattro Pro. You can give the graph a new name by using this option. The graph will then appear under this name when you use the **Graph>Edit** command or turn to the Graphs page of the notebook.

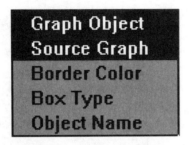

Figure 10.11 The object properties of the graph frame.

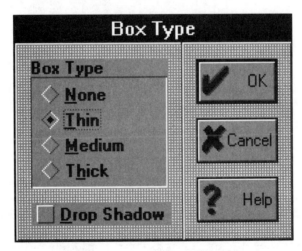

Figure 10.12 The Box Type dialog box.

Adding Graph Titles

It's easy to add titles to your graphs. Using the **Graph>Titles** command, you can instantly add up to five different titles to the graph. You can also return to the Graph Titles dialog box and edit or remove a title. Here are the steps.

1. Choose the **Graph>Edit** command to display the desired graph in a window. Alternatively, you can double-click on a graph's frame to display the graph inside a window.

2. Select the **Graph>Titles** command. Figure 10.13 shows the Graph Titles dialog box and the various titles you can add to the graph.

3. Enter any titles into the spaces provided; then click on **OK**.

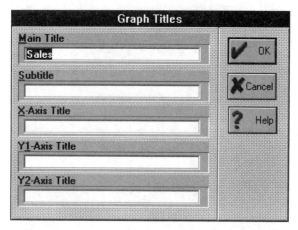

Figure 10.13 The Graph Titles dialog box.

When you use the **Graph>Titles** command to produce this dialog box, you can then enter any titles into the spaces provided. Press the **Tab** key to move from one entry box to the next. When you choose **OK**, Quattro Pro adds the titles to the graph. When a graph is displayed inside a graph window, you can select the **Graph>Titles** command to edit or remove existing titles.

Selecting a Graph Type

When you first create a graph, Quattro Pro automatically gives you the default bar graph. You may have other ideas in mind for your data. Selecting a graph type is an important decision—different graph types offer different information about the data and encourage their own comparisons and conclusions. Generally, you should know what type of graph you want to use before you begin the graphing procedure. Your data and the message you want to get across should dictate the type of graph you choose. To change the graph type after you've created the graph, simply double-click on the graph frame to get the graph into a window (if it's not already in a window). This produces the Graphing SpeedBar and menu options. Now choose the **Graph>Type** command and choose from the types available.

What follows are descriptions of each graph type in Quattro Pro. A brief idea of the graph's purpose and strengths is included. You'll also find tips on formatting and enhancing these graphs for maximum effectiveness.

2-D Graphs

Quattro Pro offers nine kinds of two-dimensional graphs from which to choose. These graphs are best for showing exact comparisons among data points. They are the simplest types of graphs and can often be the most effective. With proper use of color, shades, and fonts, 2-D graphs will be among the most powerful presentation tools you can use.

Line Graphs

Line graphs are used primarily for presenting fluctuations in data over time. Usually, the X-axis represents a progression of time in even increments, such as months or years. Line graphs connect individual plot points (called *data markers*) with lines. You can change the appearance of the data markers and the thickness and style of the lines. Figure 10.14 shows a typical line graph.

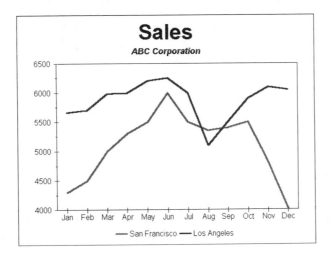

Figure 10.14 A line graph.

When creating line graphs, include as many divisions as you possibly can. Line graphs are more revealing when you plot a lot of data. Nothing is less exciting than a line graph that plots a series over only three or four divisions.

You should avoid plotting more than four data series on a single line graph. Too many lines can make the graph difficult to read. Instead, use the multiple-lines combination graph to plot the data.

Bar, Stacked Bar, Comparison, and Variance Graphs

Bar graphs are among the most common business graphs. They are best for showing how plot points compare to one another over time or over a group of divisions. You can plot a single data series over one or more divisions—or several data series over one or more divisions.

Like line graphs, bar graphs are more effective when you plot a maximum of four data series. You can use the multiple-bars combination graph to plot more than this. Figure 10.15 shows a typical bar graph.

Figure 10.15 A bar graph.

Stacked bar graphs require that you plot more than one data series. They stack the different data series on top of each other to produce a total. Each segment of the bar represents a portion of the total. In this way, you can compare totals across the bars and view how each segment changes from bar to bar. Figure 10.16 shows a stacked bar graph.

A variance graph is nothing more than a standard bar graph with a baseline other than zero. On a normal bar graph, only negative values will extend below the baseline. Using a variance graph, you can use any value as the baseline. Quattro Pro displays values less than the base as reversed bars—that is, bars extending below the baseline. Use the **Property>Y-Axis** command to set the baseline value for your variance graphs. Figure 10.17 shows an example.

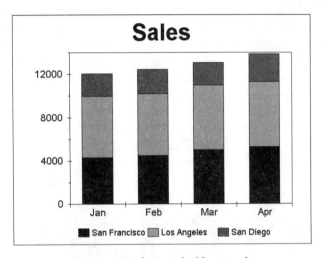

Figure 10.16 A stacked bar graph.

Figure 10.17 A variance graph showing a custom baseline value.

Comparison graphs are similar to bar and stacked bar graphs but include comparison lines between data series to highlight the comparison of values. This can be useful if you want to emphasize these differences.

Area Graphs

Area graphs are much like line graphs in that they show the progression of values over time. Because they are stacked, area graphs show how several items fluctuate over time. Each data series is stacked on top of the previous one to form a total. The top line of the graph shows how the total changes across the divisions. Each layer of the area graph represents the change in a single data series. Compare the thickness of each layer to the others. Figure 10.18 shows an example.

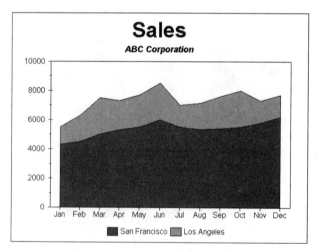

Figure 10.18 A typical area graph.

Like line graphs, area graphs are best when you have a lot of data to plot—the more divisions, the better.

Pie, Doughnut, and Column Graphs

Pie graphs show how several items make up an entire unit. Each slice of the pie is created from a different cell in a single data series. Pie graphs plot only one data series each. If you want to plot several series as different pies, use the multiple-pies combination graph. Figure 10.19 shows a pie graph.

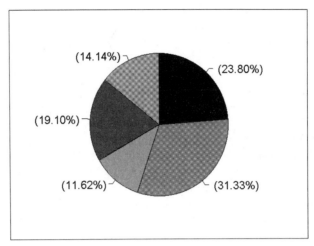

Figure 10.19 A pie graph.

You can customize the graph in various ways by using the Graph Properties window described in Chapter 11.

Doughnut and comparison graphs serve a similar purpose to pie graphs in that they show how parts make up a whole.

XY Graphs

XY graphs are useful for showing how two values can be plotted to form a single point on a graph. The patterns of individual points reveal trends in the data. To create an XY graph, you must have at least two data series. Each data series beyond the second one is used to form a new set of points on the graph. These points are plotted by combining each new data series with the first data series to create two values for each new point. Hence, all points align along the division markers, as shown in Figure 10.20.

To create an XY graph, you must use the manual method of identifying the data series. This lets you specify the correct cells for the X-axis data and the first data series: Identify the first data series, including a label in the first cell, as the X-axis series, and then also identify the second data series (the second column or row of data, including a label in the first cell) as the first data series. Hence, the first row or column of data is not really a data series, but rather the values used for the X-axis. Figure 10.21 shows the series used for the graph in Figure 10.20.

To complete the XY graph, you should remove the lines connecting the series markers. Do this by right-clicking on any marker, selecting the **Line Style** option, and choosing the first line style (**No Line**). This is described in more detail in Chapter 11.

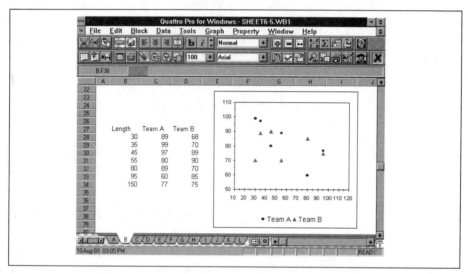

Figure 10.20 An XY graph plotting three data series

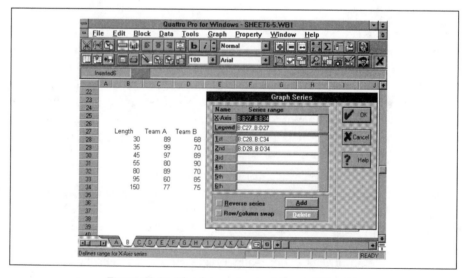

Figure 10.21 The data series used for an XY graph.

Adding a Regression Line to an XY Graph

XY graphs commonly include regression or trend lines. A regression line shows how the data progress along a linear trend and are calculated with the formula $y = mx + b$, where y represents the dependent value, x represents the independent value, m represents the coefficient, and b represents the constant.

To add a regression line to your XY graph, plot only one data series in the graph, as described above. Now follow these steps.

1. Select the command **Tools>Advanced Math>Regression**.

2. Reference the X-axis data block in the Independent entry box. This is the block identified in the Graph Series dialog box as the X-axis data.

3. Reference the first data series block in the Dependent entry box. This is the block identified in the Graph Series dialog box as the first data series.

4. Reference a cell in a remote corner of the worksheet in the Output entry box. Be sure that you have at least three blank columns to the right of the cell and ten blank rows below it. Quattro Pro will fill this range with the regression data.

5. Choose **OK**.

6. Add a new series of values to the graph data by multiplying each X-axis value by the X Coefficient in the regression data and adding the Constant value in the regression data. Figure 10.22 shows an example. Notice the formula displayed in the formula bar. This formula was copied to form a new block of cells.

7. Plot the new calculated values on the chart by using the **Graph>Series** command to add the block as a new data series on the graph.

8. Right-click on any marker in the new data series to format the line used for that series. Use the **Line Type** options for this.

High–Low Graphs

High–low graphs are used to show high and low values for each plot point. This is useful for plotting stock prices and other statistical data. You can also add an open and close value to a high–low graph to plot four separate values for each point. High–low graphs show the high and low values as the top and bottom of a line along the division marker; open and close values are plotted as left and right tick marks on the line. Figure 10.23 shows an example.

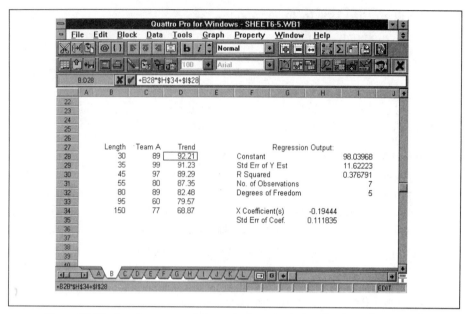

Figure 10.22 Creating a new data series by calculating the formula y=mx+b.

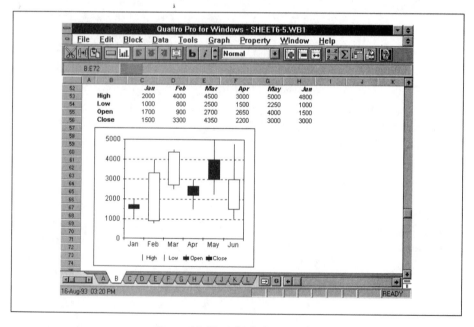

Figure 10.23 A high–low graph.

To create a high–low chart, highlight two, three, or four data series (rows or columns of data) with as many cells in each as you like. If you highlight three or four data series, you'll get open and close values for the graph.

You can select from four different ways of displaying the high, low, open, and close values on the graph. Just right-click on any plot point on the graph (with the graph window active); then select the **Hi–Lo Bar Style** option. Quattro Pro presents four different methods of showing the data. Experiment with these options.

Radar Graphs

A radar graph plots data along "spokes" of a wheel. Each data series creates a new spoke, and the data is plotted along the spoke—where the outside of the spoke is a higher value than the inside. This gives you a picture of how values compare to one another to comprise a complete set of data. For example, you might plot the scores achieved on tests with a radar graph to show which areas are stronger than others. Figure 10.24 shows an example.

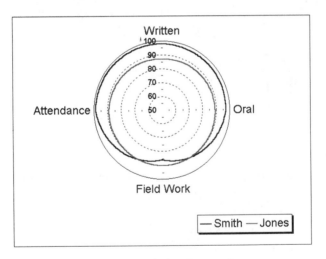

Figure 10.24 A radar graph.

3-D Graphs

Three-dimensional graphs are similar to their 2-D counterparts listed above. Quattro Pro gives you 3-D bar, line (called *ribbon*), area, column, and pie graphs. Even though it can be difficult to discern small differences in plot points on a 3-D graph, 3-D graphs are valuable for plotting several data series.

Quattro Pro includes a 2.5-D bar graph, which is the same as a 2-D bar graph but includes a depth effect on the bars. The 3-D bar graph actually plots the data series along a depth axis. Experiment with these graphs for best results.

After creating a 3-D graph, you can change the graph perspective by using the **3-D View** options in the Graph Setup and Background Properties dialog box (right-click on the graph background). Figure 10.25 shows the **3-D View** options.

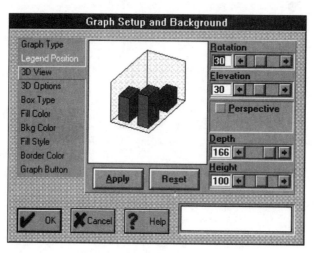

Figure 10.25 3-D View options in the Graph Setup and Background dialog box.

Rotated Graphs

Rotated graphs are two- and three-dimensional graphs turned sideways. These are useful for special types of presentations. Rotated bar graphs emphasize a competitive element among the bars. Figure 10.26 shows an example.

Combination Graphs

Quattro Pro's combination graphs come in two basic forms. One form combines two different types of graphs into a single image. The second form creates a separate graph from each data series in the graph data—giving you several graphs in the same frame.

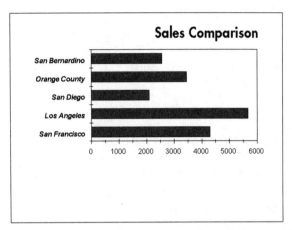

Figure 10.26 A rotated 2-D bar graph.

Combined graph types include bar/line, bar/area, and bar/high–low. However, these are merely combinations that Quattro Pro offers for you. They let you quickly format your graph using a combination of graph types. For more control, you can manually combine graph types—applying a different graph type for each data series. You can use any combination of bar, line, and area graphs in the same image.

To display a graph's data series in a different graph type, thus creating a combination graph, right-click on the data series; then choose the Override Type desired for that series. It's that simple. Figure 10.27 shows a combination graph.

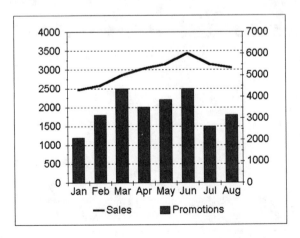

Figure 10.27 A combination graph using two different graph types.

If you create a combination graph consisting of multiple graphs, you can choose from multiple columns, pies, bars, 3-D columns, or 3-D pies. Each data series in the graph data produces a new graph. To display all the graphs, your graph frame should be quite large. Each individual graph in the frame can be manipulated as a separate graph.

Text Graphs

Text graphs are graphs that do not plot data in any way. They are simply blank graph windows (and frames) that you can use for drawing and annotating. They are used primarily for creating text slides for your slide shows. However, you can also use them for displaying graphic images on the screen or notebook page. For more information about text graphs, refer to Chapter 12.

Storing Graphs in the Notebook

Each and every graph you create in a notebook is stored on the Graphs page. The Graphs page is the last page in the notebook. You can view this page by clicking on the **Fast Forward** button at the bottom of the screen. This button appears to the left of the Group button containing the letter G and to the right of the page tabs. Figure 10.28 shows a sample Graphs page.

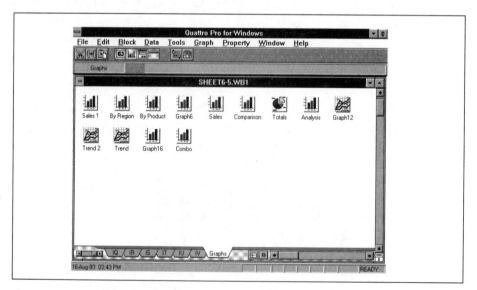

Figure 10.28 The Graphs page shows all your graphs as icons.

Notice that each graph is represented by an icon. The icon displays the graph's name and type. You can double-click on any of these icons to display the graph in its window. You can copy graphs by copying the icons. Moreover, you can move graphs from this page to the Graphs page of any other notebook: Open both notebooks and display the Graphs page in each; then drag the icons from the active notebook into the other notebook.

One of the primary uses for the Graphs page is to help you view your graphs for creating slide shows. Slide shows are discussed in detail in Chapter 13.

Summary

The graphing process can be quite simple when you use the Graph Expert. By selecting your graph data first and then using the Graph Expert, you can move through each step of the graphing process without having to complete it manually. Plus, you can always edit your graph later—changing the data block, graph type, and data orientation.

Some graph types—such as the XY type—must be created manually. By creating a graph manually with the **Graph>New** command, you can specify exactly which cells relate to each element of the graph.

The next chapter explains Quattro Pro's graph-customization options. Using these options, you can control every aspect of your graph and make graphs communicate more powerfully and efficiently.

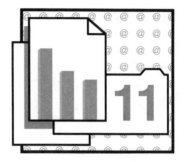

Customizing Graphs

The previous chapter introduced you to Quattro Pro's graphing powers. For many graphs, Quattro Pro's instant graphing features will meet your needs. However, you might need to add or delete data series or to change the overall "look" of a graph. Quattro Pro provides all the tools you'll require to create graphs that will meet your precise needs.

This chapter introduces Quattro Pro's graph-editing and customization powers. You'll learn how to control virtually every aspect of the data used to create your graphs, including their "look and feel." Some of the topics covered in this chapter include

- Adding and deleting data
- Changing graph text
- Changing graph colors and patterns
- Modifying axis values
- Changing the entire format, or "look," of a graph

Adding and Deleting Data

Let's start with a basic bar graph that we'll use throughout this chapter. Figure 11.1 shows a basic graph. In this section, you'll learn how to add and remove data from the graph by manipulating the graph's data series definitions.

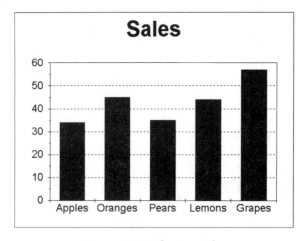

Figure 11.1 A basic graph.

Select the Graph Element First

Before applying a change to a particular graph element, you must first select that element on the graph by clicking on it with the mouse—use the right mouse button to select it and view its properties. You can also move certain graph elements around the graph window by dragging the element with the mouse. Use the **Edit>Select All** command to select the entire graph if you want to move all elements at once or click the **Select All** tool on the SpeedBar.

Adding a New Series

To add a new year of sales projections to the graph, we first return to the spreadsheet data and add a new row of data—in this case, for 1995. Select the graph by clicking on it with the mouse; then select **Graph>Series**, which displays the dialog box shown in Figure 11.2. You can also display this box by right-clicking anywhere on the graph, then choosing the **Graph Series** option from the Shortcut menu that appears.

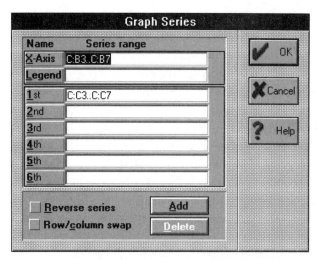

Figure 11.2 The Graph Series dialog box.

Click the button for the fourth series, which takes you back to the spreadsheet. (Quattro Pro allows you to plot up to six series in a graph.) Click and drag to select the new series; then press **Enter**. The series coordinates are automatically entered into the dialog box. Click on **OK** to accept the coordinates and plot the new series, or you can edit the series coordinates within the dialog box.

To include the new label as part of the graph legend, you'll need to edit the Legend series. You can manually edit the series coordinates in the Graph Series dialog box, or you can press the **Legend** button, click and drag to select the Legend series as you just did with the data series, and press **Enter**. Click on **OK** to accept the new Legend series.

Deleting a Series

To delete a series, select **Graph>Series** and the series to be deleted, press **Delete** to erase the series coordinates, and then click on **OK**.

When you delete the data series from the graph, the associated legend is no longer displayed, even though the reference to the legend is still included in the dialog box. Should you decide to add the data series back to the graph in the future, the legend will again be displayed.

Using Property Inspectors

Quattro Pro uses *property inspectors* to change the attributes (such as color, style, and size) of all graph elements. The rest of this chapter shows you how to change the attributes of each element (graph titles, axes, and data series), as well as overall graph attributes, using the property inspectors. In addition, you'll learn how to change the graph type and see how it affects the other graph elements. Some properties apply only to certain graph types. For example, Axis properties have no meaning in pie graphs, since pie graphs have no axes. Area, bar, column, line, and variance graphs do share similar properties, though.

 Right-clicking on an element in the graph window does not immediately bring up the property inspector, as you might expect. Instead, you will see a Shortcut menu containing four options: The first option takes you directly to the appropriate property inspector. The second option, Graph Type, presents the Graph Type dialog box where you can choose a new graph type. The third option, Graph Series, displays the Series dialog box where you can change attributes of the graph's data series. The fourth option, Graph Titles, displays the Titles dialog box where you can create or change the titles that appear on the graph. All of these options are available from the normal Graph menu, but you might find the Shortcut menu more convenient.

Graph Setup and Background

The "master" property inspector for graphs is the Graph Setup and Background inspector, which is activated by right-clicking anywhere in the margin of the graph window or by selecting the **Property>Graph Setup and Background** command when the graph window is active. This property inspector lets you change the graph type, and thus the overall look of your graph, with just a few mouse clicks. (Graph types were discussed in the previous chapter.) When you choose the Graph Setup and Background property inspector, the screen looks like Figure 11.3.

Chapter 10 briefly discussed each graph type. The important thing to remember is that the Graph Setup and Background property inspector gives you access to all graph types, and it intelligently displays just the properties that relate to the graph type you choose. What follows is additional information on the options available with this powerful tool.

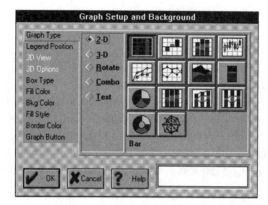

Figure 11.3 The Graph Setup and Background properties.

Graph Type Properties

These properties control the overall graph style (see Chapter 10 for details about each style). Select from **2-D**, **3-D**, **Rotate**, **Combo**, and **Text** slide styles by clicking on the associated radio button. For each category of graph style except **Text**, 5 to 12 graph buttons are displayed. Click on the button that represents the specific graph style you wish to use. The graph style is also displayed in words to confirm your choice. Refer to Chapter 10 for more information on these graph types.

Legend Position Properties

These properties control the legend position, for those graph styles that support legends. Three choices are available: **No Legend**, **Bottom Legend**, and **Right Legend**, each illustrated with a graphic icon. Click on the button corresponding to your selected legend position, or click on the **No Legend** button to delete the legend. (If you've selected a graph type that doesn't support a legend, this property inspector will be unavailable.)

3-D View Properties

These properties affect the rotation, elevation, depth, and height of all 3-D graphs (except 3-D pie and 3-D column graphs). All graph parameters can be entered from the keyboard or via sliders. Rotation and Elevation can be adjusted from 0 to 90 degrees, and Depth and Height can be adjusted from 8 to 200 "marks." The Height control actually changes the graph's height-to-width proportion. You can also choose to display the graph in Perspective, which displays each object's size directly proportional to how "close" the object is to you. If you turn Perspective on by clicking on its button, a Perspective slider is displayed. This slider can be adjusted from 0 to 100.

As you adjust the sliders, a 3-D graph window changes to reflect how your settings will look. This feature enables you to preview your graph without forcing you to switch repeatedly from the graph window to the property inspector and back again. After you've adjusted the settings to meet your needs, you can apply them to your graph by clicking on the **Apply** button. You can start over at any time by clicking on the **Reset** button, which will return all the slider values and selections to their original settings. Figure 11.4 shows an example of the 3-D View properties.

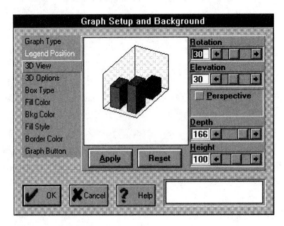

Figure 11.4 The 3-D View properties.

3-D Options Properties

In 3-D graphs (except for pie and column graphs), these options control whether the left wall, back wall, and base are displayed. They also allow you to choose between thick and thin walls. Each item can be individually turned on or off by clicking on its check mark button.

In 3-D graphs, the left wall corresponds to the Y-axis, the base corresponds to the X-axis, and the back wall corresponds to the grid lines. It's particularly difficult to figure out the values in 3-D graphs without these visual references, so be cautious in deleting them. The choice between thick and thin walls depends on how important it is to maintain the 3-D effect throughout the graph. Thin walls are "one line" thick and result in a two-dimensional look. Experiment with thick and thin walls to get the desired look. Figure 11.5 shows some examples.

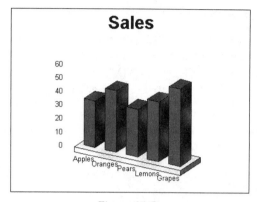

Figure 11.5a

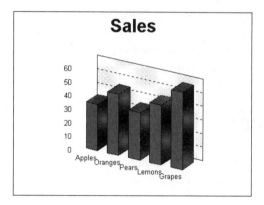

Figure 11.5b

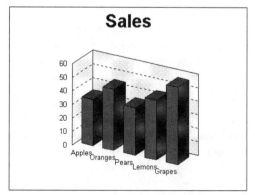

Figure 11.5c Use 3-D Options properties for various effects.

Box Type Properties

Box Type properties control the box that serves as the background for the entire graph. Twelve box styles are available, the first being No Box, or a borderless box. A variety of border styles and 3-D effects are available. Each style is selected by clicking on the button that represents the style.

Removing the box can be helpful for floating graphs, making the graph and notebook data appear closer together. Other borders can improve text graphs or data graphs used in slide shows.

Fill Color Properties

These options control the graph box's fill color, which helps determine the background area of the graph, the border of which can be changed with the Box Type options. Select a new color from the palette by clicking on the desired color, or create a custom color by selecting Hue, Saturation, and Brightness (**HSB**); Red/Green/Blue (**RGB**, or Additive colors); or Cyan/Magenta/Yellow (**CMY**, or Subtractive colors) values. The fill color won't be displayed unless an appropriate fill style is selected.

Bkg Color Properties

The background options set the background color for the graph box. The background color works along with the fill color to establish two colors for the background when you use the Pattern or Wash fill style. If your fill style is not a Pattern or Wash, the Bkg Color properties are not relevant.

Fill Style Properties

These properties control the graph box's fill style. The default setting is **None**, which leaves the background as a plain box (the appearance of the box border is controlled with the Box Type properties). Choosing **Solid** fills the background with the fill color selected in the Fill Color properties. Choosing **Pattern** provides a palette of 24 patterns from which you can choose (see Figure 11.6).

The patterns are made up of the fill color and the background color you selected previously. Choosing **Wash** provides a palette of six wash styles (see Figure 11.7). Again, the washes are based on the fill color and background color you've selected. The Wash palette shows you the direction of the colors as they wash across the background.

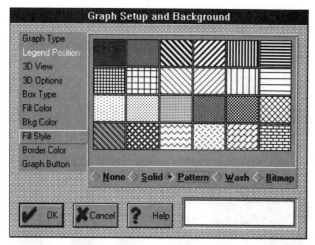

Figure 11.6 Quattro Pro's patterns for background properties.

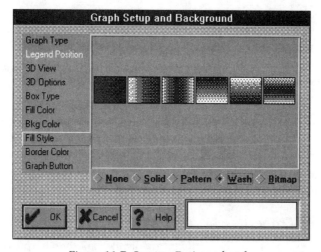

Figure 11.7 Quattro Pro's wash styles.

Remember, if you don't like the colors used for the wash, use the **Fill Color** and **Bkg Color** properties to change them.

Choosing **Bitmap** fills the graph box with a bitmap of your choice. You can either **Crop** or **Shrink** the bitmap to fit within the graph box. Click on the **Browse** button to search the directory for a bitmapped image. Bitmapped texture images are ideal for graph backgrounds. Several textures come with

Windows 3.1 and are usually stored in your WINDOWS directory. When using these Windows 3.1 textures, select the **Shrink to Fit** option in the Fill Style properties; this is helpful when bitmapped textures are too small to fill the entire background of the graph. When using textures that come with Quattro Pro, use the **Crop to Fit** option. Figure 11.8 shows texture applied to a background.

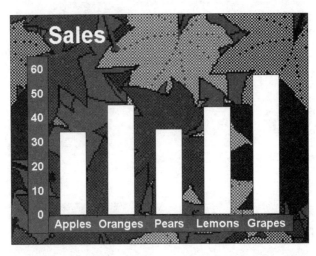

Figure 11.8 Using a bitmapped texture for the background fill style.

Border Color Properties

Border Color properties control the graph box's border color, using the color picker. A border will be displayed if you selected any of the 11 box types that include a border; if you selected the "empty" box type, no border will be displayed, and the color selection will be irrelevant.

Graph Button Properties

This option creates a text button that can display another graph or execute a macro. When you click on the graph, Quattro Pro can either display a different graph or run a specific macro. Graph Button properties are used primarily for slide shows. During a slide show you can branch to a different portion of the show, present a message, change values, or perform other operations when the viewer clicks on the graph. The graph itself becomes a "button" for the action you specify. Note that the button is active only when the graph is being viewed full-screen. You can view a graph full-screen in a slide show or with the

Graph>View command. For more information on slide shows and graph buttons, refer to Chapter 13.

Graph Titles

All graph types support Graph Titles. You can add a title, subtitle, and X- and Y-axis titles to a new or existing graph with the **Graph>Titles** command, described in the previous chapter. You can also right-click anywhere in the graph window, then choose the **Graph Titles** option from the Shortcut menu. After you add a title to the graph, you can change it by right-clicking on it. If you right-click in the text area of the title, you can change the text properties. If you right-click in the box portion of the title, you can change the text box properties. The following sections explain these properties.

Title properties apply to floating text, too

You'll find that the text and box properties for graph titles apply to any text that appears on the graph. Here we talk only about the five titles you can apply to a graph using the **Graph>Titles** command. In Chapter 12, you'll learn how to add floating text to a graph window and change its text and box properties.

Text Properties for Graph Titles

Text properties affect the color, background color, font, and style attributes of the actual text in your title. To view the text properties, you must right-click directly on the text itself then choose the first option that appears in the Shortcut menu. When you move the mouse pointer onto the text, the pointer shape changes to an *I-beam*, or vertical bar; this indicates that right-clicking the mouse will present the text properties. Properties include **Text Color**, **Text Bkg Color**, **Text Font**, and **Text Style**, which are explained in the following sections.

Text Color Properties

These properties change the color of the title text. Select a new color from the palette by clicking on the desired color, or create a custom color by selecting Hue, Saturation, and Brightness (**HSB**), Red/Green/Blue (**RGB**, or Additive colors); or Cyan/Magenta/Yellow (**CMY**, or Subtractive colors) values. Remember that the text color should contrast well with the color of the text box. Text box color is set with the Text Box properties, explained later under "Box Properties for Graph Titles".

Text Bkg Color Properties

These properties change the background color of the title text. The background color is meaningful if you use a Wash or Shadow text style (see "Text Style Properties" below). The background color you select is used for the shadow or the wash.

Text Font Properties

These properties change the typeface, point size, and other attributes (**Bold**, **Italics**, **Underline**, and **Strikeout**) of the text. Select a new typeface by clicking from the list provided. In addition to the typeface name, you can identify what kind of font the typeface represents by referring to an icon preceding the typeface name. A TT icon represents TrueType, a printer icon represents PostScript Type 1, and no icon represents a bitmapped font (usually for display use). Figure 11.9 shows the Fonts properties.

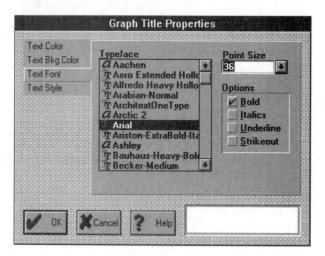

Figure 11.9 Change the title font using the Text Font properties.

Select the appropriate point size with the Point Size chooser by clicking on the **Down Arrow** button. Finally, select any combination of options by clicking on the Options check-boxes.

Text Style Properties

Text Style properties let you change the overall style of the text. The default is **Solid Colors**, which simply displays the text in the color you choose. Other style choices include **Wash**, which displays the text in a graduated color, and **Bitmap**, which fills the text with a bitmapped image—generally a texture. Selecting **Wash** displays a palette of six wash styles; the colors used in the wash are the text color and text background color selected above. If both colors are the same, the wash effect will not be visible. Clicking on **Shadow** adds a drop shadow (in the text background color you selected) to the text.

   Bitmap allows you to select a bitmapped image in BMP, GIF, PCX, or TIFF format with which to "fill" the title text. If the bitmap is bigger than the text, it must be cropped or shrunk to fit. **Crop to Fit** crops out portions of the bitmap that don't fit within the text size, whereas **Shrink to Fit** shrinks the bitmap to fit within the text size, discarding pixels wherever necessary. If the you know the name and path of the bitmapped file, you can enter it directly, or you can click on **Browse** and search for the file. Figure 11.10 shows some text effects using these Text Style properties.

NOTE

Using Text Style properties on graph subtitles

Subtitles are changed in exactly the same way, and with exactly the same options, as the main title. Right-click on the subtitle to display the GraphTitleBox dialog box, and you'll see that the options have changed from *Text* to *Subtitle* (that is Text Color becomes Subtitle Color, Text Bkg Color becomes Subtitle Bkg Color, and so forth).

NOTE

Using Text Style properties on axis titles

You can use text properties on axis titles, too. The only difference is that you get an extra option: You can change the title within the property inspector. That is, the property inspector for axis titles includes an option for changing the title text. Why other titles don't also have this option is a mystery.

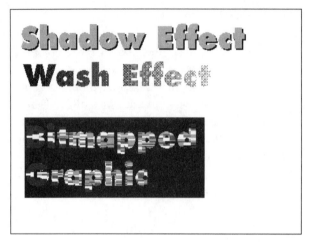

Figure 11.10 Use Text Style properties for various text effects.

Box Properties for Graph Titles

If you right-click in the box formed by the graph's text, but not directly on the text, you'll get a host of Box properties for the title. To produce this property inspector dialog box, the mouse pointer must appear as an arrow when you right-click in the text box. Then choose the first option that appears in the Shortcut menu.

This dialog box controls the box "behind" the graph title or subtitle (or any graph text for that matter). This box is normally invisible, but it can be displayed to highlight the graph titles. It is often used in text graphs (see Chapter 12 for details).

Box properties for graph text are shown in Figure 11.11. As you can see, these are identical to the properties used for the graph background described earlier in this chapter. The following sections will summarize these options; for more detailed descriptions, refer to "Graph Setup and Background" earlier in this chapter.

Box Type Properties

Box Type properties control the box appearance. Twelve box styles are available, including the default style (a box with no border). There are a variety of border styles and 3-D effects, each selected by clicking on the button that represents the style. Most of these styles are similar to the background style properties explained earlier in this chapter.

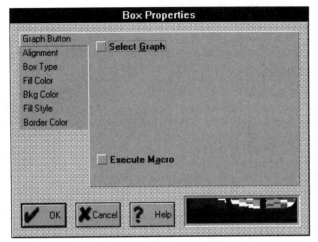

Figure 11. 11 Box properties for graph text.

Fill Color Properties

Fill Color properties control the box fill color, using the Quattro Pro color picker. Choose a color or use the numerical settings to specify a color for the graph box fill.

Bkg Color Properties

Bkg Color properties control the box background color. This color is used with the fill color above for patterned fills and washes. The background color won't be displayed unless a pattern or Wash fill style is selected.

Fill Style Properties

Fill Style properties control the box fill style. The default setting is **None**. If **Solid** is selected, the box will be filled with the fill color selected above. If **Pattern** is selected, you can choose from 24 styles by clicking on the desired pattern.

Border Color Properties

Border Color properties control the border color, using the color picker. A border will be displayed if you select any of the 11 box types that include a border; if you select the "empty" box type, no border or fill will be displayed.

Axis Properties

The X- and Y-axis properties can be changed independently. The Y-axis usually represents the dependent variable to be plotted, so Quattro Pro allows considerable control over the Y-axis scale, whereas the X-axis usually plots independent values, such as years, months, and so on, so Quattro Pro gives you more control over X-axis labels. These differences result in slightly different Property Inspector dialog boxes for the two axes. We'll examine the Y-axis controls in detail; most of the same controls apply to the X-axis, and we'll examine the controls unique to the X-axis.

The Y-Axis Property Inspector

To view the Y-axis properties for a graph, simply right-click on the Y-axis itself, then choose **Y-Axis Properties** from the options presented. If you find this a bit tricky, try clicking on the Y-axis values. The following sections discuss the properties available for the Y-axis.

Y-Axis Scale Properties

These options change the scale of the Y-axis. Either **Normal** (linear) or **Log** (logarithmic) scaling can be selected. The scaling you choose will depend on your specific application. If **Show Units** is selected, unit values will be shown along the Y-axis.

In general, the easiest way to control scaling is to click on the **Automatic** check mark button, which lets Quattro Pro calculate the scaling for you. However, you can manually control the scale by turning **Automatic** off and entering High, Low, and Increment values. You can also select the number of minor ticks between major ticks (the default is 1). Figure 11.12 shows these options.

Y-Axis Tick Options Properties

These options change the tick style and labels. Ticks can be displayed to the **Left** or **Right** of the axis or on both sides of the axis (**Across**), or they can be turned off altogether (**None**). If **Displayed Labels** is checked, axis label values will be displayed. (These labels aren't the same as the Y-axis label, which is controlled using the **Axis Label>Properties** command.)

If you choose to display labels, you can also choose to limit the length of labels anywhere from 0 to 255 characters. This option is useful when you have long labels that don't display well as part of the graph. For example, your spreadsheet might use full month names (January, February, March), but you might want to display only the first three letters (Jan, Feb, Mar). To do so, turn on **Display Labels**, click on **Length Limit**, and either type or scroll until you reach three characters. You can also turn the **Length Limit** off to permit labels of unlimited length. Figure 11.13 shows the tick properties.

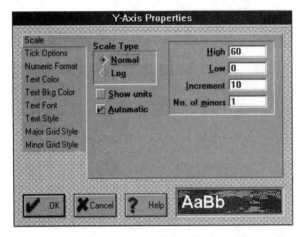

Figure 11. 12 The Y-Axis Scale options.

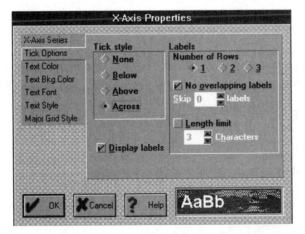

Figure 11. 13 The Y-Axis Tick Options properties.

Y-Axis Numeric Format Properties

These properties change the numeric format of the Y-axis labels. All Quattro Pro's format options are supported, except **Text** and **Hidden**, which aren't relevant.

Y-Axis Text Color Properties

These options change the color of the Y-axis labels, using the Quattro Pro color picker. Note that text color applies to the Y-axis values, not the Y-axis title.

Y-Axis Text Bkg Color Properties

These properties change the background color of the Y-axis labels, using the Quattro Pro color picker. Text Background Color defaults to black. Text Background Color is meaningful only with certain text style attributes or if shadowing is turned on.

Y-Axis Text Font Properties

These properties alter the Y-axis labels' typeface, point size, and options (**Bold**, **Italics**, **Underline**, and **Strikeout**). Select the desired font, size, and options. The graph is automatically redrawn and rescaled within the graph window to accommodate changes in the Y-axis labels.

Y-Axis Text Style Properties

These options change the Y-axis labels to solid letters, or they fill them with a wash effect or a bitmap. Six wash effects are available. The colors used in the wash are the text color and text background color selected above. (If the text color and text background color are the same, the Wash and Shadow settings have no effect. Solid and Wash labels can also have a drop shadow, selected with the **Shadow** button; the text background color is used as the shadow color.)

Y-Axis Major Grid Style Properties

These properties change the Y-axis major Grid line style. Major Y-axis grid lines are drawn left to right across the graph from the major tick marks. Eight grid line styles are available (four solid lines of varying thicknesses and four dotted/dashed lines), or the major grid lines can be turned off by selecting the "blank" style. The major grid's color can also be controlled with the color picker by choosing the **Color** option at the bottom of the dialog box. Figure 11.14 shows the grid-line styles available.

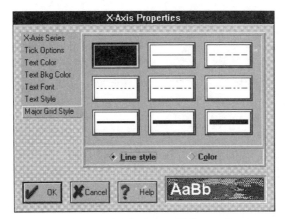

Figure 11.14   Axis grid line styles.

Y-Axis Minor Grid Style Properties

Changes the minor grid-line style. Minor Y-axis grid lines are drawn left to right across the graph, corresponding to the minor tick marks. As with the major grid lines, eight grid-line styles are available (four solid lines of varying thicknesses and four dotted/dashed lines), or the minor grid lines can be turned off by selecting the "blank" style. The minor grid's color can also be controlled with the color picker.

Minor grid lines tend to clutter the graph and make it more difficult to understand. If this occurs in your graph, decrease the number of minor tick marks (see "Y-axis Tick Options Properties," above) or turn the minor grid lines off. The default for both line and bar graphs is to turn minor grid lines off.

The X-Axis Property Inspector

To change the properties of the X-axis on a graph, right-click on the axis, then choose **X-Axis Properties** from the Shortcut menu to reveal the property inspector. Most of the properties for the X-axis are identical to those for the Y-axis, so we won't repeat them here. Here are the properties unique to the X-axis.

X-Axis Series Properties

These change the data series used to create the X-axis. Type the range coordinates into the *Select Range* box or move the cursor over the words Select Range and click; this will take you to the spreadsheet, where you can click and drag to select the X-axis series. Press **Enter** to enter the selected range in the dialog box.

X-Axis Tick Options Properties

Changes how X-axis tick marks and labels are displayed. Tick marks can be drawn **Above** or **Below** the X-axis or **Across** the axis line (both above and below). Select **None** for no tick marks.

If **Display Labels** is turned off, the X-Axis Series defined above is not used to create axis labels. (These labels aren't the same as the X-axis label, which is controlled using the Axis Label Properties property inspector.) If **Display Labels** is turned on, a Labels section is added to the dialog box. You can choose to have one, two, or three rows of labels. This option is especially useful when you have long labels that would otherwise overlap. Figure 11.15 shows these options in use.

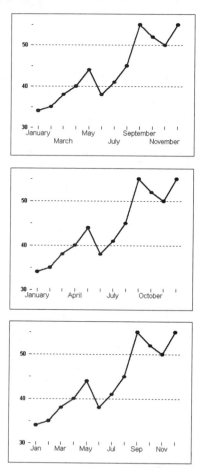

Figure 11.15 Use X-Axis Tick Options properties to cure crowded X-Axis labels.

If **No Overlapping Labels** is selected, labels are automatically skipped to avoid overlaps. If this option isn't selected, you can manually control the degree by which the labels overlap by skipping every *n*th label (from 0 to 255). You can also control the degree of overlap with the *Length Limit* button. When this option is selected, you can manually control the maximum label length, from 0 to 255 characters. When this option is turned off, each label will be displayed at its full length.

The combination of these controls enables you to handle a wide range of label sizes and conditions. Until you get the effect you're looking for, experiment with different combinations of the number of rows, label overlap, and length limits.

The Graph Pane

In bar, line, and area graphs, that part of the graph within the X- and Y-axis is called the *Graph Pane*. By right-clicking on the Graph Pane, but not directly on a bar series or axis, you activate the Graph Pane Properties property inspector. This property inspector controls the display, color, and style of borders, as well as the fill color, background color, and fill style. Quattro Pro's default is to turn all four pane borders on, but to turn off pane color fills. This usually results in the best-looking and least cluttered graphs. However, you have extensive control over the look of the Graph Pane. For example, some users only like axis lines, so they turn off the Top and Right borders. Others prefer dashed borders instead of solid-line borders, or they prefer thicker border lines.

You'll find the Graph Pane properties identical to those of many other elements in a graph, such as the graph background. This section will briefly describe each of these options.

- **Border Options** Controls the display of Graph Pane borders. The **Left**, **Top**, **Right**, and **Bottom** borders can each be toggled on or off with individual check mark buttons. Remember that the left border serves as the Y-axis line, whereas the bottom border serves as the X-axis line. In general, you should keep these two borders turned on at all times.

- **Fill Color** Controls the color of the Graph Pane. Select a new color from the palette by clicking on the desired color, or create a custom color by selecting Hue, Saturation, and Brightness (**HSB**),

Red/Green/Blue (**RGB**, or Additive colors), or Cyan/Magenta/Yellow (**CMY**, or Subtractive colors) values.

- **Bkg Color** Changes the background color of the Graph Pane. See above for details on how to select the new color. Graph Pane background color is meaningful *only* if you use a Pattern or Wash fill style (see below).

- **Fill Style** Controls the Graph Pane's fill style. The default setting is **None**. If **Solid** is selected, the Graph Pane will be filled with the fill color previously selected. If **Pattern** is selected, you can choose from 24 styles by clicking on the desired pattern.

  The patterns are made up of the fill and background colors previously selected. If **Wash** is selected, six wash styles are displayed, based on the fill and background colors you've selected. If **Bitmap** is selected, you can fill the Graph Pane with a bitmap of your choice. You can either crop or shrink the bitmap to fit within the available area. Click on the **Browse** button to search the directory for a bitmapped image.

  Be careful when using Graph Pane fills—especially washes, patterns, and bitmaps—which can make the graph hard to read and individual series data points hard to identify.

- **Border Color** Controls the Graph Pane's border color, using the color picker. A border will be displayed if you select any of the eight border styles.

- **Border Style** Changes the Graph Pane's border style. Eight border styles are available (four solid lines of varying thicknesses and four dotted/dashed lines), or the border can be turned off by selecting the "blank" style. Remember, if you turn the border off, the axis lines will also disappear, leaving you with just the axis tick marks. It's a good idea to leave the border on, select the appropriate border style, and control which border lines you wish to display with the Border Options property inspector.

Bar/Line/Area Series Properties

You can control the properties of each individual data series plotted in your graph, whether the series are plotted as a bar, line, or area graph. In fact, as you'll see, you can easily change one kind of series to another, and you can mix series types within one graph.

To view the property inspector for a series, just right-click on that data series on the graph, and then choose the first option in the Shortcut menu that appears, such as Bar Series Properties. If the series appears in a line graph, right-click on the line; in a bar graph, right-click on the desired bar; in an area graph, right-click on the desired layer. Here are the series properties you'll encounter for the various graph types.

Bar Properties

If you right-click on a bar that appears in a bar graph, Quattro Pro displays the Bar properties. These properties specify the coordinates of the data series, label series, and legend to be used to plot the bar series. You can also control the bar options, fill color, background color, fill style, border color, and style. Here is a list of these bar properties.

Series Options Properties

These change the Data Series and Label Series coordinates, the Legend label, and whether the series' Y-axis is to be plotted as the Primary or Secondary axis.

Figure 11.16 shows these properties.

Figure 11.16 The Series Options properties.

To change the Data Series coordinates, enter the new coordinates or click on the words **Data Series** to select a new series from the spreadsheet. Click and drag to select the range; then press **Enter** to set the new coordinates. You can specify a Label Series to correspond to the Data Series entries; your labels will be pasted into the graph, corresponding to the series' data points. You can also enter a Legend for the Data Series, which overrides any default legend specified when you created the graph. To delete the Label Series or Legend, simply delete any coordinates or text typed into the corresponding dialog box.

The series type can be changed by selecting Override Type. In this case, the default series type is **Bar**, but you can change it to **Line** or **Area**. For example, if you select **Line** and click on **OK**, the resulting graph becomes a combination Line/Bar graph.

Selecting **Default** changes the series type back to the default for the entire graph—in this case, to **Bar**. Finally, you can specify whether the Data Series is to be plotted on the primary or Secondary Y-axis. The primary Y-axis is the vertical axis at the left side of the graph, whereas the secondary Y-axis is on the right side of the graph. If you select **Secondary**, a series of secondary Y-axis labels will be displayed.

Analyze Options

Quattro Pro now has a selection of graph analysis options within the Series Properties dialog box. Click on the **Analyze** option to view these properties. Graph analysis options are too advanced for the scope of this book. For information about analytical graphing, refer to an advanced book about Quattro Pro for Windows.

Bar Options Properties

These change bar width and overlap. Quattro Pro automatically calculates bar width and the bar margin to achieve a good-looking bar graph, but you might want to change these parameters. (Keep in mind that this inspector changes the Bar Options for all the bars in the graph, not just the selected series.)

The first parameter is the Bar Width percentage, which is controlled with a slider and ranges from 5 to 100%. This specifies the percentage of graph width to be filled by bars. At 5%, the bars are thin; at 100%, the bars take up all the Graph Pane's horizontal space. Figure 11.17 shows a graph with 5% and 100% Bar Width settings.

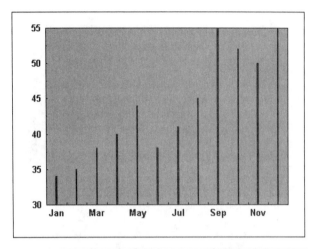

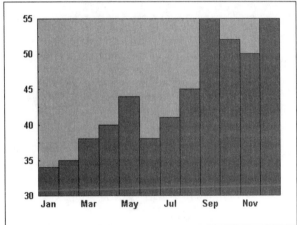

Figure 11.17 Examples of Bar Width settings.

The second parameter is Bar Margin percentage, which is the amount of "white space" between the bar series and the left and right sides of the Graph Pane. This percentage is also controlled by a slider and ranges from 0 to 100%. At 0% a narrow margin is established on either side of the bar series; at 100%, a wide margin is established, and the bars are "squashed" to fit between the margins. Figure 11.18 shows a graph with 0% and 100% bar margins.

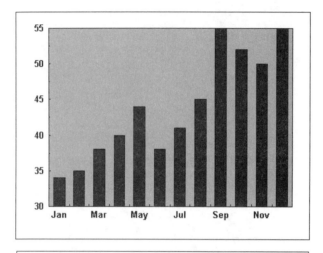

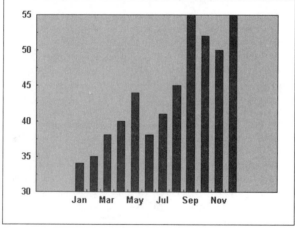

Figure 11.18   Examples of Bar Margin settings.

The final parameter is Bar Overlap. (This setting is meaningful only in graphs in which two or more bar series are plotted together.) Bars won't overlap at all, no matter what the settings for Bar Width and Bar Margin, if **No** is selected. If **Partial** is selected, bars will partially overlap. This setting can be useful when you need to plot series with many data points, which may cause you to run out of room in the Graph Pane. To completely overlap bars, select **Full**. **Full** is not suggested for use in 2-D bar graphs, because some bars may be partially or completely hidden by other series, but it is very useful in 3-D graphs, in which you can move the graph viewpoint to see multiple data series in perspective.

Fill Color Properties

These change the color of the selected bar series. Select a new color from the palette by clicking on the desired color or create a custom color by selecting Hue, Saturation, and Brightness (**HSB**); Red/Green/Blue (**RGB**, or Additive colors); or Cyan/Magenta/Yellow (**CMY**, or Subtractive colors) values.

Bkg Color Properties

These change the background color of the selected bar series. See above for details on how to select the new color. Bar background color is meaningful *only* if you use a Pattern or Wash fill style.

Fill Style Properties

These control the selected bar series' fill style. The default setting is **None**. If **Solid** is selected, the bar will be filled with the fill color previously selected. If **Pattern** is selected, you can choose from 24 styles by clicking on the desired pattern.

The patterns are made up of the fill and background colors previously selected. If **Wash** is selected, six wash styles are displayed, based on the fill and background colors you've selected. If **Bitmap** is selected, you can fill the bar with a bitmap of your choice. You can either crop or shrink the bitmap to fit within the bar. Click on the **Browse** button to search the directory for a bitmapped image. Figure 11.19 shows a graph using a bitmapped fill.

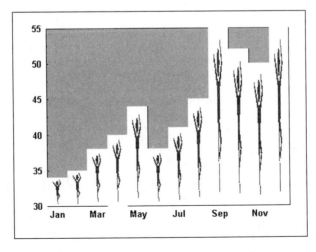

Figure 11.19 Using a bitmapped image to fill the bars in a graph.

Border Color Properties

These control the selected bar series' border color, using the color picker. A border will be displayed if you select any of the eight border styles.

Border Style Properties

These change the selected bar series' border style. Eight border styles are available (four solid lines of varying thicknesses and four dotted/dashed lines), or the border can be turned off by selecting the "blank" style.

Line Series Properties

Line series consist of individual data points, which are represented by *markers*, connected by line segments. You have complete control over the specification of the line series, as well as marker style and color and line style and color. All options in the Line Series properties are identical to those for Bar graphs, except Marker Style options. Refer to "Bar Properties" above for more information.

Marker Style Properties

Marker style properties change marker style and weight (size). Quattro Pro automatically assigns marker styles to each line series as it's created, but you can change and/or resize the marker styles with this property inspector. To choose a marker style, click on one of the 16 styles displayed. The Weight slider controls marker size; values run from 0 to 32. A 0 weight results in an invisible marker, whereas a weight of 32 creates a very large marker. Marker weight can be changed to emphasize a specific line series. For example, the critical series in a line graph with several series can have significantly larger markers than the other lines. To change the marker weight, click on the **AutoSize** check box to remove the check; then use the slider to set the desired size.

Area Series Properties

An area series can be thought of as a line series in which the line and the area under the line is filled. Area series are perhaps the simplest series, because there are no special scaling options and no markers. All properties for area graph series are identical to those for bar graphs. Refer to "Bar Properties" earlier in this chapter for more information.

Pie Graphs

Pie graphs are significantly different than the bar, line, and area graphs that we've examined. For example, there is no X-axis or Y-axis in a pie graph; a single data series is summed to determine the overall "size" of the pie. Also, a pie chart plots only one data series at a time. The result is that pie charts are simpler than other types, so they can be customized with fewer property inspectors than can line, bar, or area charts. Just right-click any slice of the pie, then choose **Pie Graph** Properties.

Explode Slice Properties

These change whether or not a pie slice is "exploded," or pulled away from the pie for emphasis, and determine the distance that an exploded slice is moved. The Explode distance is controlled by a slider, and ranges from 0% to 100% of the radius of the pie. As the Explode distance increases, the overall size of the graph increases, and the pie is automatically resized to fit the graph window. By turning the Explode check box button on, the selected slice will be exploded from the pie (see Figure 11.20).

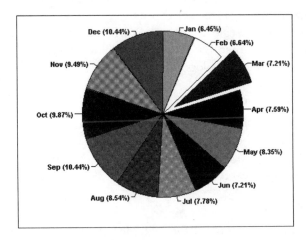

Figure 11.20 An exploded pie slice.

Label Options Properties

These options change the Label Series, set the format for the Data Labels, and turn tick marks on or off. These properties affect the entire pie graph, not individual slices. If no Label Series is specified for a pie graph, Quattro Pro defaults to displaying the percentage that each slice comprises of the whole pie as its Data label. You can specify a Label Series by typing the series coordinates into the dialog box or by right-clicking on the words *Label Series* to jump to the spreadsheet, where you can click and drag to select a label range. Press **Enter**, and the new range will be entered into the dialog box.

The Data Labels can be used in conjunction with—or in place of—the Label Series, or they can be deleted from the graph altogether. The Data Label buttons control the appearance of these labels. Select **Currency** to display the pie series values in currency (dollars and cents) format. Select **Percent** to display the pie series values as a percentage of the whole pie (default). Select **Value** to display the actual value of each pie series data point without formatting. Selecting **None** will turn the display of Data Labels off.

Quattro Pro's default is to display a small tick mark for each pie slice, which connects that slice with its label(s). You can display the ticks or remove them with the **Show Tick** check mark button.

Text Color Properties

If your pie graph contains labels for each slice, you can use these options to change the color of those labels. Select a new color from the palette by clicking on the desired color or create a custom color by selecting Hue, Saturation, and Brightness (**HSB**); Red/Green/Blue (**RGB**, or Additive colors); or Cyan/Magenta/Yellow (**CMY**, or Subtractive colors) values.

Text Bkg Color Properties

If your pie graph contains labels for each slice, you can use these options to change the background color of the pie slice labels. See above for details on how to select the new color. Text background color is meaningful *only* if you use a Wash or Shadow text style.

Text Font Properties

If your pie graph contains labels for each slice, you can use these options to change the typeface, point size, and other attributes (**Bold**, **Italics**, **Underline**, and **Strikeout**) of the pie slice labels. Select a new typeface by clicking on a style in the Typeface chooser. In addition to the typeface name, you can identify what kind of font the typeface represents with an icon preceding the typeface name; a TT icon represents TrueType, a "printer" icon represents PostScript Type 1, and no icon represents a bitmapped font (usually for display use). Select the appropriate point size with the Point Size chooser; by clicking on the **Down Arrow** button, all available point sizes will be displayed. Finally, select any combination of options by clicking on the Options check box buttons (these buttons toggle on and off by repeatedly clicking on them).

Text Style Properties

If your pie graph contains labels for each slice, you can use these options to change the text style of the pie slice labels. The default is **Solid**; other choices are **Wash** and **Bitmap**. You can add a drop shadow to Solid or Wash styles. Selecting **Wash** displays a palette of six wash styles; the colors used in the wash are the text color and text background color selected above. If both colors are the same, the wash effect will not be visible. Clicking on **Shadow** adds a drop shadow (in the text background color you selected) to the text.

Bitmap allows you to select a bitmapped image in BMP, GIF, PCX, or TIFF format with which to fill the label text. If the bitmap is bigger than the text, it must be cropped or shrunk to fit. **Crop to Fit** crops out portions of the bitmap that don't fit within the text size, whereas **Shrink to Fit** shrinks the bitmap to fit within the text size, discarding pixels wherever necessary. If the you know the name and path of the bitmapped file, you can enter it, or you can click on **Browse** and search for the file.

Fill Color Properties

These properties change the selected pie slice fill color using the Quattro Pro color picker. (See "Pie Graphs" for more information.)

Quickly changing the color of a slice

If all you want to do is change the color of a slice, a simple way to do so without using property inspectors is to click on the slice that you wish to change and then click on your desired color in the Graph SpeedBar palette.

Bkg Color Properties

These control the selected pie slice background color. This color is used with the fill color above for patterned fills and washes. The background color won't be displayed unless a Pattern or Wash fill style is selected.

Fill Style Properties

These control the selected pie slice fill style. The default setting is **None**. If **Solid** is selected, the selected pie slice will be filled with the fill color previously selected. If **Pattern** is selected, you can choose from 24 styles by clicking on the desired pattern.

The patterns are made up of the fill and background colors previously selected. If **Wash** is selected, six wash styles are displayed; again, the washes are based on the fill and background colors you've selected. If **Bitmap** is selected, you can fill the pie slice with a bitmap of your choice. You can crop or shrink the bitmap to fit within the selected pie slice. Click on the **Browse** button to search the directory for a bitmapped image.

The final two Border properties affect all the pie slice labels, not just the border of the selected pie slice. If the **Border** is turned off in the Border Style property inspector discussed below, tick marks will not be displayed, even if **Show Ticks** is turned on in the Label Options property inspector discussed above.

Border Color Properties

These control the border color for the entire pie, using the color picker. A border will be displayed if you select any of the eight border styles. The border will then be shown in the color you selected with this property.

Border Style Properties

These control the border style for the entire pie. Eight border styles are available (four solid lines of varying thicknesses and four dotted/dashed lines), or the border can be turned off by selecting the "blank" style.

Summary

Now that we've examined all the Graph property inspectors, you've seen the virtually infinite ways in which you can customize the look of your graphs with just a few mouse clicks. There's no reason to "make do" with the Quattro Pro defaults (even though they're very useful in most situations) when you can spice up your graphs with custom colors, patterns, layouts, and type styles.

The following chapter explains the drawing and annotation tools available in a graph window. Using these tools, you can spruce up your graphs even more or create useful text graphs for your slide shows.

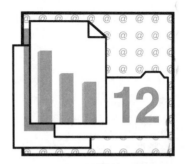

Annotating Graphs

You will sometimes find that the standard graphs and titles need something extra. Perhaps you need to add some text to call out an important point, or you need to create some special drawings or symbols in order to make a complex graph easier to understand. For these special situations, you can use Quattro Pro's drawing tools.

Drawing tools are also useful without graphs. You can use these tools to create simple illustrations, organization charts, logos, and so on. You can then insert these illustrations onto your notebook pages to spruce up your reports.

This chapter introduces these drawing tools. You'll learn how to add lines, shapes, and text to your graph. In addition, you'll learn how to import graphic objects, and how to link, group, and edit them. Topics covered in this chapter include

- Learning the annotation tools and commands
- Drawing and annotating
- Adding text to your graph
- Moving, resizing, and grouping objects
- Working with outside art, including bitmaps, backgrounds, and clip art

Before we continue, a word of caution: Quattro Pro offers so many annotation tools, and so many ways to enhance the look of your graphs, that you might be tempted to add lots of text, lines, and drawings. Remember that complex, cluttered graphs can be difficult for your audience to understand. Use annotations sparingly as a way to get your point across or to simplify complex data. You'll make your graphs easier to understand, and you'll save yourself time and effort.

Annotation Tools and Commands

The first step in annotating a graph is to open the graph window. To do so, you can either double-click on a floating graph on any page of your spreadsheet notebook, or you can flip to the Graph page of your notebook and double-click on the desired graph. Quattro Pro displays your graph, along with the Graph SpeedBar that was first introduced in Chapter 10. Figure 12.1 shows a graph window.

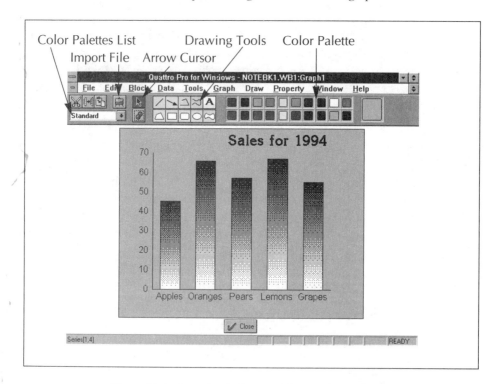

Figure 12.1 A graph window and the Graph SpeedBar.

The first three buttons on the SpeedBar are the Cut, Copy, and Paste functions, with which you're already familiar. Here are the new buttons and menus you'll be working with.

 Import Graphics File Displays a dialog box that enables an outside graphics file to be imported and manipulated as part of your graph. You can specify a file name by entering it into the dialog box directly—or by clicking to specify the target directory and drive and then double-clicking on the desired file. Eight graphic file types are supported: **BMP**, **CGM**, **CLP**, **EPS**, **GIF**, **PCX**, **PIC**, and **TIF**. Only file names with one of the eight graphic file type extensions listed above will be displayed as part of the list of available files. To import the selected file, click on **OK**.

 Color Palette List Selects the color palette for lines, fills, patterns, and washes. Quattro Pro comes with ten predefined color schemes: **Blends**, **Color Patterns**, **Draw**, **Fall**, **Monochrome**, **Spring**, **Standard**, **Summer**, **Washes**, and **Winter**. An additional choice, **Edit**, allows you to create, delete, edit, or rename palettes.

To select a color scheme, click on one of the names. The color palette will change into the selected color scheme.

 Arrow Cursor Tool Activates the arrow cursor for selecting, dragging, and resizing objects. Quattro Pro reverses the Tool button to white-on-black in order to indicate that the arrow cursor has been selected.

 Select All Tool Selects all objects in the Graph window. This is useful for making changes to the entire graph at one time or for moving the graph around the window.

 Color Palette Displays 20 fill colors, as selected from the color palette list (see above). The active fill color is displayed in the Selected Fill Color window in the SpeedBar. To select a fill color, click on the color in the palette. The Selected Fill Color window will change to your new color choice.

Here are the drawing tools, as shown in Figure 12.1:

 Line Tool Draws a straight line anywhere within the graph window. To select, click on the **Line** tool. The cursor will change to a reverse image of the Line Tool icon, with a crosshair in the upper left corner. To draw a line, move the center of the crosshair to where you want the line to begin, then click and drag the cursor to the line's ending point. Release the mouse button to draw the line.

Arrow Tool The Arrow tool works identically to the Line tool, except that it draws an arrowhead at the end of the line. The arrowhead can be filled with a solid color, pattern, wash, or bitmap.

Polyline Tool Draws a line that has more than one straight segment. To select, click on the **Polyline** tool. To draw a line, move the center of the crosshair to where you want the line to begin, then click and drag the cursor to where you want the line's first segment to end and the line's second segment to begin. Release the mouse button to draw the line. Repeat the process for each subsequent line segment. When you've drawn the last line segment, double-click the left mouse button or right-click to complete the line. Figure 12.2 illustrates this procedure.

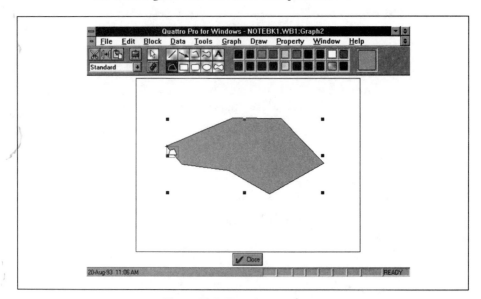

Figure 12.2 Drawing a polygon.

Closing a polygon

If you end any line segment at (or close to) the starting point of the initial line segment, Quattro Pro will assume that you wish to complete the polyline object and close the polygon. Unlike a polygon

NOTE

drawn with the Polygon tool, you cannot fill a polyline-based polygon; you can only change the line color and type.

 Freehand Line Tool Draws a freehand line anywhere in the graph pane. To select, click on the **Freehand Line** tool. The cursor will change to a reverse image of the Freehand Line Tool's icon, with a crosshair in the upper-left corner. To draw a line, move the center of the crosshair to where you want the line to begin; then click and drag the cursor to draw the line. Release the mouse button to complete the line. Figure 12.3 shows a freehand image.

 Polygon Tool Draws a polygon that can be filled with a solid color, pattern, wash, or bitmap. To draw a polygon, move the center of the crosshair to where you want the polygon to begin; then click and drag the cursor to where you want the polygon's first border to end and the polygon's second border to begin. Release the mouse button to draw the border line. Repeat the process for each subsequent border. When you've drawn the last border line, double-click the left mouse button or right-click to complete the polygon. Quattro Pro draws the border line from your last point to the starting point in order to complete the polygon when you double-click or right-click the mouse. After drawing the polygon, select a fill color from the color palette or use the current fill color.

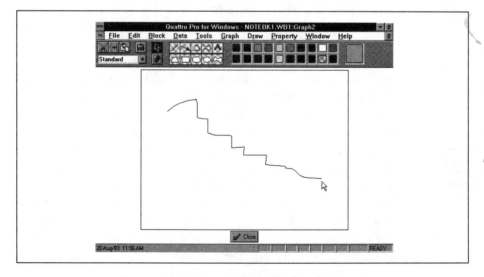

Figure 12.3 Drawing with the Freehand Line tool.

Rectangle Tool Draws a rectangle or square that can be filled with a solid color, pattern, wash, or bitmap. To select, click on the **Rectangle** tool. The cursor will change to a reverse image of the Rectangle Tool's icon, with a crosshair in the upper-left-hand corner. Select a fill color from the color palette or use the current fill color. To draw a rectangle, move the center of the crosshair to where you want the rectangle to begin, then click and drag the cursor until the rectangle is the correct shape and size.

Rounded Rectangle Tool Draws a rectangle with rounded corners. Rounded rectangles are drawn similarly to normal rectangles (see above).

Ellipse Tool Draws an ellipse or circle that can be filled with a solid color, pattern, wash, or bitmap. To select, click on the **Ellipse** tool. The cursor will change to a reverse image of the Ellipse Tool's icon, with a crosshair in the upper-left corner. Select a fill color from the color palette or use the current fill color. To draw an ellipse, move the center of the crosshair to where you want the ellipse to begin; then click and drag the cursor until the ellipse is the correct shape and size.

Freehand Shape Tool Draws a freehand shape that can be filled with a solid color, pattern, wash, or bitmap. To select, click on the **Freehand Shape** tool. The cursor will change to a reverse image of the Freehand Shape tool's icon, with a crosshair in the upper-left corner. Select a fill color from the color palette or use the current fill color. To draw a freehand shape, move the center of the crosshair to where you want the shape to begin; then click and drag the cursor to draw the perimeter of the shape. Release the mouse button to complete the shape automatically. Quattro Pro will draw a straight line from the point where you release the mouse button to the shape's starting point.

Text Tool Creates a text object that can be placed anywhere in the graph pane. To select, click on the **Text** tool. The cursor will change to a reverse image of the Text tool's icon, with a crosshair in the upper-left corner. Select a fill color from the color palette or use the current fill color. To draw a text box, move the center of the crosshair to where you want the shape to begin; then click and drag the cursor to draw the perimeter of the box. Release the mouse button, and Quattro Pro will draw the text box, fill the box with the active fill color, pattern, or wash; and place a flashing text cursor at the first character position within the box. The box automatically resizes as it fills with type. (See below for information on how to change type sizes, styles, and so on.)

Graph Window Properties

Before you start adding text and graphic objects to your graph, take a moment to understand the Graph Window properties. To activate the Graph Window property inspector, right-click outside the graph pane or in the title bar of the graph window. The Graph Window determines whether or not a grid is provided for aligning objects; it also controls your graph's *aspect ratio*. The aspect ratio is the ratio of your graph pane's height to its width. An example of aspect ratios is the difference between a sheet of 8.5 by 11-inch or A4 paper and your computer monitor screen. The paper is significantly longer than it is wide, whereas the screen is wider than it is long. Without adjustments in the aspect ratio, a circle printed on the piece of paper would be squashed into an ellipse on-screen. Quattro Pro allows you to adjust your graph to display or print correctly.

The grid settings allow you to display a grid for positioning your new text and graphic objects on the graph. The grid is especially useful when you're trying to align two or more objects along a common edge. You can also have Quattro Pro automatically move your objects to the closest grid coordinate; this is called *Snap to Grid*. When **Snap to Grid** is turned on, you can use the **Rectangle** tool to create a perfect square or the **Ellipse** tool to create a perfect circle. The grid is displayed only when the Graph SpeedBar is active; it is not displayed when using **Graph>View** or while viewing slide shows.

Aspect Ratio Properties

Aspect Ratio properties let you select the aspect ratio of the graph. Five choices are available: **Floating Graph**, **Screen Slide**, **35mm Slide**, **Printer Preview**, and **Full Extent**. These are shown in Figure 12.4. **Floating Graph** will change the aspect ratio to that of the associated floating graph (if any) on a page of the spreadsheet notebook. Do not select **Floating Graph** if you intend to incorporate the graph in a slide show—the graph could be grossly distorted in the show, although it'll look fine in the graph window. The Floating Graph aspect ratio should be used for graphs that appear in graph frames within the notebook pages.

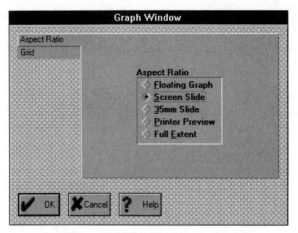

Figure 12.4 The Aspect Ratio properties.

Screen Slide selects the proper aspect ratio for displaying the graphs on screen; it is the preferred setting for on-screen slide shows. **35mm Slide** sets the correct aspect ratio for creating 35mm film slides from your slide show. This setting can also be used for on-screen slide shows—although the ratio is slightly different from the **Screen Slide** setting. **Printer Preview** sets the correct aspect ratio for printing on whatever printer you've selected—this is a sort of graph-preview mode, showing you what your graph will look like on the printer. **Full Extent** fills up the entire graph window with the graph image; it's useful for floating graphs.

If your graph floats on a notebook page, the aspect ratio setting you choose determines whether you can adjust the shape of the graph itself. Both the **Full Extent** and the **Floating Graph** settings change the shape of the graph based on the shape of the floating graph's frame. For example, if you stretch the graph frame to make it extra tall, the graph will also stretch to fill the frame, provided it uses the Full Extent or Floating Graph aspect ratio. If a different aspect ratio is used, the graph's proportions will not change when you elongate the graph frame. Figures 12.5 and 12.6 illustrate this feature. The graphs in Figure 12.6 are elongated versions of those in Figure 12.5. Notice that the Screen Slide graph does not change its proportions when you change the graph frame.

Set the aspect ratio before you annotate

Be sure to select the correct aspect ratio when you begin annotating your graph. If a graph is in one aspect ratio, and you add objects to the slide in another aspect ratio, you might have to edit or redraw some of the objects if the aspect ratio changes again.

NOTE

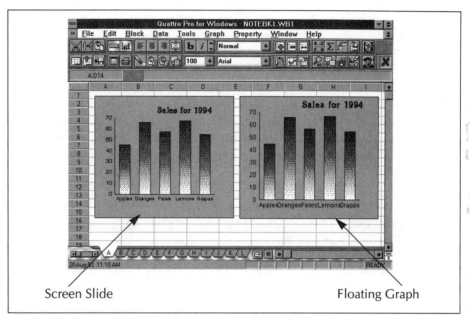

Figure 12.5 Floating graphs using various aspect ratios.

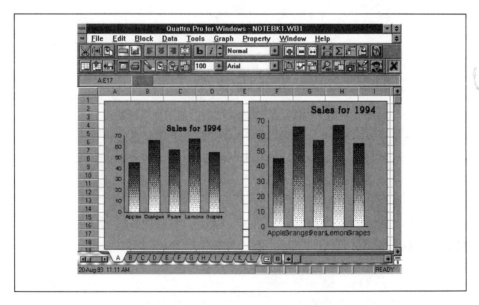

Figure 12.6 Changing the shapes of the graph frames.

Grid Properties

The Grid properties display the alignment grid and control the alignment of objects. The grid is a set of horizontal and vertical lines consisting of dots that overlay the entire graph pane. Normally the grid is invisible. To make the grid visible, select **Display Grid**. To control the fineness of the grid, use the Grid Size slider, which runs from 1% to 25% of the graph pane. The smaller the grid size, the finer the grid. To automatically align new objects to the grid as they're created, select **Snap to Grid**. Figure 12.7 shows a graph window with the grid made visible.

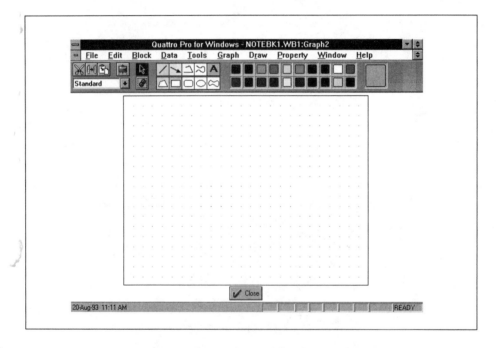

Figure 12.7 The window grid for aligning objects.

Selecting, Moving, and Sizing Objects

Now that we've examined all the drawing tools and learned how to draw each basic shape, let's look at moving and sizing these shapes.

Selecting Objects

To select a single object, such as a line or box, simply click on the object so that the object's handles (the small black squares at the ends or corners of the object) become visible. To select several objects at one time, click near (but outside) one of the objects and drag the cursor. A dotted box will be displayed. Stretch the box until it encloses all the objects that you wish to select; then release the mouse button. All the enclosed objects will display their handles. (If you accidentally select the wrong object or objects, simply move the cursor away from any objects and click again to deselect everything—then try again.) If you click on the **Select All** tool in the Graph SpeedBar, Quattro Pro will instantly select all objects in the Graph window. Figure 12.8 shows some selected objects.

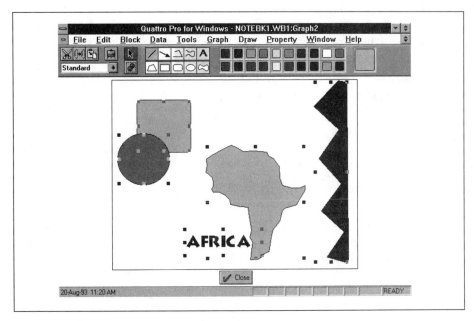

Figure 12.8 Selecting objects.

Moving Objects

Any object or group of selected objects can be moved anywhere within the graph pane. To do so, first select the desired object(s); then click anywhere on the selected shapes except on the handles. (If you click on a handle, you can resize the object; to move the object, click in the middle of a line or shape.) The selected objects will momentarily change into outlines. Hold down the mouse button and drag the outlines to the new location; then release the mouse button. The objects will be redrawn in their new positions.

Should you accidentally move the wrong object, or move the correct objects to the wrong place, you can correct your mistake by selecting **Edit>Undo Move**. As Quattro Pro has only one level of Undo, be sure to perform the **Undo Move** command before you perform any other operation on your graph; otherwise, you'll have to correct the mistake manually.

Sizing Objects

To resize an object or group of objects, make your selection (as described above); then move the arrow cursor over any one of the object handles. The cursor shape will change from an arrow to crosshairs when it is directly over a handle. Click and drag in any direction, and you'll see an outline of the object or group that stretches or shrinks as the mouse moves. Release the mouse button, and the object or group will be resized.

Sizing text boxes

When you resize a text box, the text itself is not resized—only the text box is. (To resize the text, you must use the property inspector described below.) If you have a multiline text box, however, and if word-wrap is on, the text may wrap differently when you change the size and shape of the box.

Managing Text

If you insert a text box in the manner described earlier in this chapter, you may find that the text is too big or small for your graph or that the typeface might be incorrect. You might want a different box fill color and border, or no border or fill at all. Text boxes have two property inspectors associated with them: one for the Text Box properties (the box itself) and another for the Text properties (the text itself). (These Text properties were described in Chapter 11 in our discussion of graph titles.) Graph titles and floating graph text have the same properties. The following sections provide a summary of the Text Properties; for further details refer to Chapter 9.

Text Properties

To customize the text inside a text box, right-click anywhere on the text, then choose the **Text Box Properties** option to display the Text Properties property inspector. When you right-click on the text, the mouse pointer should appear as an *I-beam* pointer shape, which looks like a vertical line. Here are the properties for text.

- **Text Color** Changes the color of the text. Select a new color from the palette by clicking on the desired color, or create a custom color by selecting Hue, Saturation and Brightness (**HSB**); Red/Green/Blue (**RGB**, or Additive colors); or Cyan/Magenta/Yellow (**CMY**, or Subtractive colors) values.

- **Text Bkg Color** Changes the background color of the text. See above for details on how to select the new color. Text background color is meaningful *only* if you use a Wash or Shadow text style.

- **Text Font** Changes the typeface, point size, and other attributes (Bold, Italics, Underline, and Strikeout) of the text. Select a new typeface by clicking on a style in the Typeface chooser. Select the appropriate point size with the Point Size chooser. By clicking on the **Down Arrow** button, you can scroll through a list of all the available point sizes. Finally, select any combination of options by clicking on the Options checkbox buttons.

- **Text Style** Changes the text style. The default is **Solid** colors; other choices are **Wash** and **Bitmap**. You can also add a drop shadow to Solid or Wash styles. Selecting **Wash** displays a palette of six wash styles; the colors used in the wash are the text color and text background color selected above. If both colors are the same, the wash effect will not be visible. Clicking on **Shadow** adds a drop shadow (in the Text Background Color you selected) to the text. **Bitmap** allows you to select a bitmapped image in BMP, GIF, PCX, or TIFF format with which to "fill" the title text. If the bitmap is bigger than the text, it must be cropped or shrunk to fit. **Crop to Fit** crops out portions of the bitmap that don't fit within the text size, whereas **Shrink to Fit** shrinks the bitmap to fit within the text size, discarding pixels wherever necessary. If the you know the name and path of the bitmapped file, you can enter it directly, or you can click on **Browse** and search for the file. Patterns and textures are the most effective graphics to use as text fills.

Text Box Properties

To change the Text Box properties, right-click anywhere in the text box, except directly on the text itself, and the Box Properties property inspector will be displayed. When you click the right mouse button, the mouse pointer should look like an arrow. Here's what each property does.

- **Graph Button** Converts the text box into a button that displays another graph or executes a macro. Graph Buttons are active only when a graph is displayed using the Graph>View menu item or when they are a part of a running slide show. (See Chapter 13 for more details.)

  When **Select Graph** is turned on, a dialog box containing a list of available graphs is displayed. Select the name of the graph you want to be displayed when the Graph button is clicked. Select the transition you want from the Effect list by clicking on the name of the desired effect. Choose a transition speed from the current to the new graph by clicking on **Slow**, **Med**, or **Fast**. Select **Overlap** if you want the new graph to overlap the existing graph transparently, instead of covering the existing graph. Specify the amount of time that the new graph should be displayed by entering a value into the Display Time box.

  The Graph button can also execute a macro. To do so, click on **Execute Macro** and enter a macro name.

- **Alignment** Controls text alignment and word processing properties within the text box. The Text Alignment property displays three icons: **Left Justified**, **Centered**, and **Right Justified**. Select the preferred alignment by clicking on the desired icon. Turn word-wrap on or off with the **Word-wrap** check-box button. If Word-wrap is on, the text will wrap around to best fit the width of the text box. If Word-wrap is off, the text will be centered in the text box, no matter how the box is resized. To set tab stops within the text box, enter an appropriate value in the Tab Stops Every__Inches box.

- **Box Type** Controls the box style. Twelve box styles are available, including the default style (a box with no border). A variety of border styles and 3-D effects are available. Each style is selected by clicking on the button that represents the style.

- **Fill Color** Controls the box fill color using the Quattro Pro color picker. The fill color won't be displayed unless a fill style is selected.

- **Bkg Color** Controls the box's background color. This color is used with the fill color for patterned fills and washes. The background color won't be displayed unless a Pattern or Wash fill style is selected.

- **Fill Style** Controls the box fill style. The default setting is **None**. If **Solid** is selected, the box will be filled with the fill color selected above. If **Pattern** is selected, you can choose from 24 styles by clicking on the desired pattern.

  If **Bitmap** is selected, you can fill the title box with a bitmap of your choice. You can either crop or shrink the bitmap to fit within the title box. Click on the **Browse** button to search the directory for a bitmapped image.

- **Border Color** Controls the border color, using the color picker. A border will be displayed if you selected any of the eleven box types that include a border; if you selected the "empty" box type, no border or fill will be displayed.

Overlapping Objects

Text and graphic objects can overlap each other in a graph. Each object lies on its own *plane*, above or below the other objects. Depending on how you've decided to overlap the objects, some may cover up others. Figures 12.9 and 12.10 show how objects can overlap differently.

Objects are layered according to the order in which they are drawn—unless placed otherwise. Objects drawn first appear on the bottom of the stack. To move an object to the top of the others, select the object and choose the **Draw>Bring to** Front command. Here is a summary of the **Object Overlap** commands in the Draw menu.

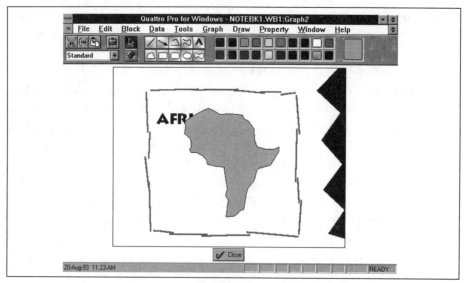

Figure 12.9 Overlapping objects.

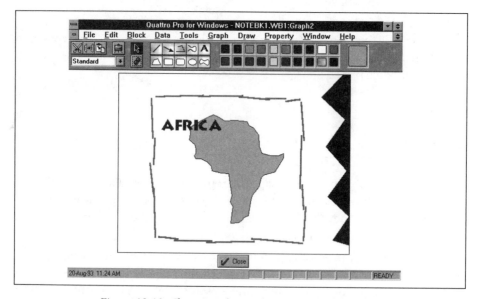

Figure 12.10 Changing the overlapping order of objects.

• **Draw>Bring to Front** Brings an object to the top of the stack, overlapping all other object and the graph.

- **Draw>Send to Back** Sends an object to the bottom of the stack and behind the graph.
- **Draw>Bring Forward** Brings an object to the next higher level.
- **Draw>Send Backward** Sends an object back one level.

Using these four commands you can control how objects cover each other. Remember that the graph itself is an object and can be manipulated with these commands. You can also access these commands by right-clicking a drawn object in the graph window, then choosing **Order** to see the four overlapping options.

Grouping

You can work with one object at a time or several objects at the same time, while keeping their relationship to each other the same. Suppose you want to enlarge three objects by the same amount without changing their relationship to each other. You could select and enlarge each object individually, but it would take a sharp eye and steady hand to keep all three objects aligned and in proportion to each other. Instead, select all three objects and enlarge the entire set, keeping alignment and proportions correct. Figure 12.11 illustrates how you can manipulate several objects at once by first selecting them all.

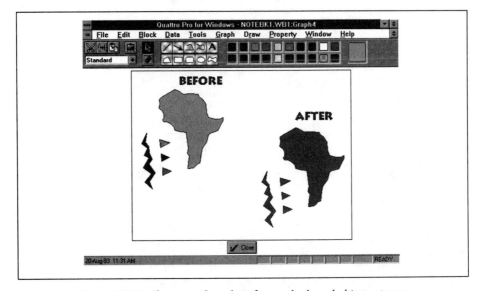

Figure 12.11 Changing the color of several selected objects at once.

What do you do if you want to make several changes to this set of objects? You don't have to click and drag to select them every time you want to make a change. Group the objects into a single object. To do so, select all the objects, then choose **Draw>Group** from the Menu bar. The individual objects now appear as a single object (see Figure 12.12).

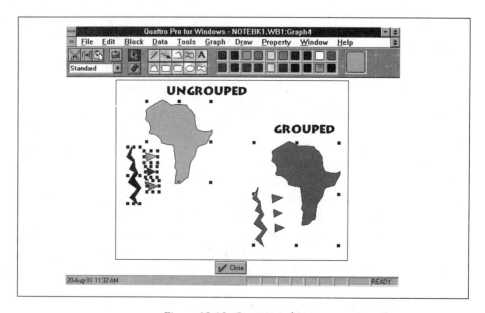

Figure 12.12 Grouping objects.

Notice that the separate sets of handles for each object are replaced with a single set of handles. Click on a handle and drag to resize the group; see how the group resizes.

If you group a text box with other objects, you cannot display the text cursor or edit the text. But what if you have to change one of the elements or edit the text? No problem—simply select the grouped object and choose **Draw>Ungroup** from the Menu bar. The handles reappear on all three objects, and you can make the changes.

WARNING

Groups within groups
You can include a grouped object inside other groups. The new group will treat your original group as a single part, rather than separating it into its original parts. Therefore, you must ungroup the objects in the same order as you grouped them.

Object Properties

We've already discussed Text Box Object properties. The following sections describe the properties of the graphic shapes. You'll find that object properties are somewhat repetitive; different types of objects may have similar properties. Actually, there are three basic sets of properties: those for lines, polylines, and freehand polylines; properties for arrows; and properties for all other shapes. The following sections describe these properties.

Properties for Lines, Polylines, and Freehand Polylines

These three shapes have the same properties. The following list refers to the Line property inspector, but you can substitute Polyline or Freehand Polyline for Line when you're modifying those objects. For example, the Line Color property changes to Polyline Color when you inspect a polyline object. Remember: To display the property inspector for an object, right-click on the object, then choose the first option that appears in the Shortcut menu, or select the object and choose the **Property>Current Object** command.

- **Line Color** Controls the color of the line/polyline/freehand polyline. Select a new color from the palette by clicking on the desired color, or create a custom color by selecting Hue, Saturation and Brightness (**HSB**); Red/Green/Blue (**RGB**, or Additive colors); or Cyan/ Magenta/Yellow (**CMY**, or Subtractive colors) values.

- **Line Style** Changes the style of the line/polyline/freehand polyline. Eight line styles are available (four solid lines of varying thicknesses and four dotted/dashed lines), or the line can be made invisible by selecting the "blank" style. The line can still be selected when it is blank, and its properties can still be inspected and changed.

Properties for Arrows

Arrow lines combine the attributes of lines with those of polygons, because the arrowhead is actually a special polygon that can be filled separately from the line color—in this case, the border color. Right-click on an arrow to display the following properties:

- **Fill Color** Controls the color of the arrowhead. Select a new color from the palette by clicking on the desired color, or create a custom color by selecting Hue, Saturation and Brightness (HSB); Red/Green/Blue (RGB, or Additive colors), or Cyan/Magenta/Yellow (CMY, or Subtractive colors) values.

- **Bkg Color** Changes the background color of the arrowhead. See above for details on how to select the new color. Arrow background color is meaningful *only* if you use a Pattern or Wash fill style.

- **Fill Style** Controls the arrowhead's fill style. The default setting is **None**. **Solid** fills the arrow with the current fill color. **Pattern** provides 24 patterns from which to choose. **Wash** provides six wash styles. **Bitmap** lets you fill the arrowhead with a bitmapped texture.

  Arrowheads are usually quite small, so patterns, washes, and bitmaps might not be visible. A solid fill color will usually give you the best results for small arrowheads.

- **Border Color** Controls the arrow line and arrowhead border color, using the color picker.

- **Border Style** Changes the arrow line and arrowhead border style. Eight border styles are available (four solid lines of varying thicknesses and four dotted/dashed lines). In addition, the border can be turned off by selecting the "blank" style. Remember, if you turn the border off, the arrow line will also disappear, leaving you with just the arrowhead fill area. This feature can be useful when you just want to display an arrowhead instead of a complete arrow.

Properties for Polygons, Rectangles, Rounded Rectangles, Ellipses, and Freehand Polygons

All five of these shapes have the same properties, even though they have their own property inspectors. When you right-click on one of these objects, the following properties appear:

- **Fill Color** Controls the fill color of the polygon. Select a new color from the palette by clicking on the desired color, or create a custom color by selecting Hue, Saturation and Brightness (**HSB**); Red/Green/Blue (**RGB**, or Additive colors); or Cyan/Magenta/Yellow (**CMY**, or Subtractive colors) values.

- **Bkg Color** Changes the background color of the polygon. Polygon background color is meaningful *only* if you use a Pattern or Wash fill style (see below).

- **Fill Style** Controls the polygon's fill style. The default setting is **None**. **Solid** fills the object with the current fill color. **Pattern** provides 24 patterns from which to choose. Wash provides six wash styles. **Bitmap** lets you fill the object with a bitmapped texture or graphic.

- **Border Color** Controls the polygon's border color, using the color picker.

- **Border Style** Changes the polygon's border style. Eight border styles are available (four solid lines of varying thicknesses and four dotted/dashed lines). The border can be turned off by selecting the "blank" style.

Changing the Color Palette

You can change the attributes of any color in the active color palette. This palette can then be saved under a new or existing name so that it can be used with other graphs. The palette colors have several attributes. Like the polygon and related shapes above, you can give these selections fill and background colors, patterns, washes, and bitmaps, and you can select their border color and style. Follow these steps to customize a color palette and save it for future use.

1. Choose the palette you would like to modify. Use the **Palette List** tool on the left side of the SpeedBar to choose the desired palette.

2. Right-click on any color in the palette to display the Edit Attributes property inspector. These properties let you control the color and border of the selected palette color and are similar to those for objects. When you are finished changing the properties of the selected color, click on **OK**.

3. Repeat these steps to change other colors.

4. On the Graph SpeedBar, pull down the palette list and click on **Edit**. Your modified palette is already called *new* in the Edit Palettes dialog box (see Figure 12.13).

5. Type a new name where *new* currently appears; then click the **New** button. To replace an existing palette with this new palette, use the scroll bar to locate the existing palette, click on its name, and then click on the **Replace** button. To delete an existing palette altogether, click on its name and then click on the **Delete** button. Be careful when replacing or deleting existing palettes—be sure that you don't need those colors together in the same palette again.

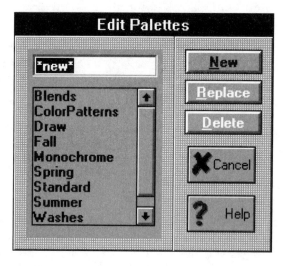

*Figure 12.13 Your modified palette appears as *new* in the palette list.*

You can create as many new palettes as you like to store your colors and patterns. Because only one palette is active within a notebook, changing the existing palette causes all object fills to change to the new palette settings. For example, if you change the color blue on the active palette to white, all objects using blue will change to white when you activate the new palette or modify the existing one. When you save a notebook file, the active palette is stored, too. In this way, each notebook can use a different palette.

Working With Outside Art

In previous discussions of fill styles, we've examined how to import bitmaps to fill a graphic object, but you can also use artwork created outside Quattro Pro for stylish, impressive backgrounds for your graphs. You can also import clip art and other graphic objects that would be difficult or impossible to create inside Quattro Pro.

The key tool for importing these graphic objects is the **Import Graphics** button on the Graph SpeedBar, or you can use **Draw>Import** from the Menu bar. Use the Import Graphics File dialog box to locate and identify the graphics file you need. In order to find a file, you must first specify the file type using the File Types list. Quattro Pro supports the following graphic file formats.

- **BMP** Windows Bitmap—the standard Windows 3.x bitmapped graphics format, used by a variety of paint programs. It's also the standard format for Windows wallpaper.

- **CGM** Computer Graphics Metafile—a vector-based file format used by many drawing and presentation programs. It is popular because it allows clip art to be distributed in a resolution-independent format.

- **CLP** A proprietary vector-based graphics format supported by Quattro Pro for DOS.

- **EPS** Encapsulated PostScript—a file that contains PostScript instructions and a low-resolution bitmapped equivalent of the PostScript image. Quattro Pro can display the bitmapped image but can't process the PostScript instructions.

- **GIF** Graphics Interchange Format—an eight-bit (256-color) bitmapped color image format originally developed by CompuServe but subsequently adopted by most on-line services and bulletin boards.

- **PCX** PC Paintbrush format—a bitmapped format supported by many DOS and Windows paint programs.

- **PIC** Lotus 1-2-3 graph format, used in DOS versions.

- **TIF** Tagged Image File Format—a bitmapped file format originally developed by Aldus and Microsoft, used primarily for scanned images and file interchange between PCs and Macintoshes.

After you select the file format, Quattro Pro displays the file as a rectangle overlaid upon your graph. You can resize the graphic to fit a particular space in your graph. Figure 12.14 shows a clip-art image imported into Quattro Pro's graph window.

Saving imported graphics under a different format

You can use Quattro Pro's powerful graphics formats to convert from one format to another. Simply export your graphic image under a different format after you have imported it. Do this with the **Draw>Export** command. Choose the desired format from the File Types list. All objects in the graph window will be exported when you use this command.

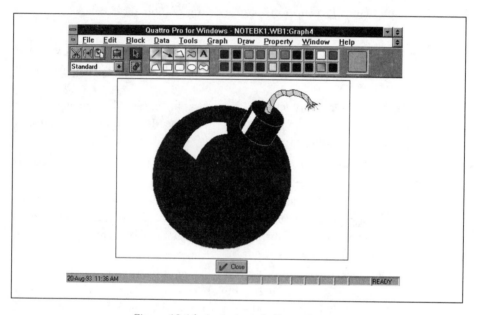

Figure 12.14 An imported clip-art image.

Importing and Resizing Bitmaps

Bitmapped graphics are altered with the Rect property inspector described in "Properties for Polygons, Rectangles, Rounded Rectangles, Ellipses, and Freehand Polygons." You can crop or shrink the bitmapped image to fit the rectangle by using the **Fill Style** inspector, which you can access by right-clicking anywhere on the bitmap, and then select Fill Style. Figure 12.15 shows the property inspector for bitmapped graphics.

Fill and Background color will have no effect on your bitmap unless you change the Bitmap fill style to **Solid**, **Pattern**, or **Wash**. When you do so, the bitmap will be overwritten with whatever color, pattern, or wash you choose.

Use an imported bitmap as a background

A bitmapped file can become your graph's background. Resize it to cover the entire graph pane area; then select **Draw>Send to Back** from the Menu bar. You might need to change other elements of your graph in order to avoid graphic conflicts with the background image.

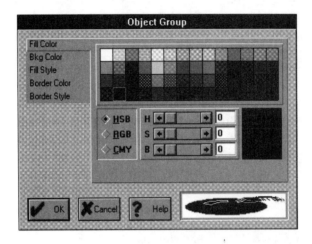

Figure 12.15 The properties available for bitmapped graphics.

Importing and Resizing Vector-Based Graphics

Vector-based graphics (CGM, CLP, and EPS), used primarily for clip art, are usually imported as a group of small objects that combine to form the entire image. Import the graphic exactly as described in "Importing and Resizing Bitmaps." Vector graphics can be resized the same way bitmaps are, except that they're automatically scaled when resized, so they don't need to be clipped or shrunk.

When you right-click on the vector-based graphic rectangle, the Object Group property inspector will be displayed; it has the same properties as those described for Polygons above. Be very careful when using the Object Group property inspector. Typically, vector-based objects are groups of smaller, individually colored and filled objects. If you select a new fill color, the entire grouped object will be filled with the color, pattern, or wash. You'll either have to ungroup the object and manually apply the color you want to every part, or cut the object, discard it, and start over. You can divide the grouped object into its individual elements using the **Draw>Ungroup** command.

To color a vector-based graphic:

1. Click anywhere on the graphic to select it.

2. Resize the graphic to make it as large as possible. (This will make it easier to grab individual objects.)

3. Choose **Draw>Ungroup** from the Menu bar to ungroup the graphic into individual vector-based components.

4. Click in the graph pane—not on the vector objects—to deselect them.

5. Carefully right-click on the object you wish to color/fill; then use the property inspector to make your changes.

Repeat Step 5 for each additional object. When you're done, select all the vector objects and use **Draw>Group** from the Menu bar to regroup them.

Linked Pictures and Objects

When you import a graphic file or object into Quattro Pro (using the **Draw>Import** command), that object is no longer linked to the application that created it. Subsequent changes in the original source file won't be reflected in your spreadsheet notebook. On the other hand, Windows' OLE (Object Linking and Embedding) technology lets you link a picture or other graphic object created in another Windows application to your Quattro Pro spreadsheet notebook. Object linking is useful whenever you wish to incorporate from another application a "live" graphic object—that is, an object that changes from time to time.

This process will work only if Quattro Pro has access to an OLE server that understands the picture or graphic object format. To insert a graphic object or picture, follow these steps.

1. Click on a the spreadsheet cell in which you want the graphic to be inserted. (This procedure is not performed in the graph window.)

2. Select **Edit>Insert Object** from the Menu bar. The Insert New Object dialog box is displayed (see Figure 12.16).

3. Scroll through the list of object types until you find one that most closely matches the picture or graphic type you want; then click on the graphic type to select it. For example, if you wanted to import an image from the Windows Paintbrush program, click on Paintbrush Picture. Quattro Pro launches the OLE server for PCX files, which is Windows' Paintbrush application.

4. In Paintbrush, select **File>Open** to open the desired bitmapped graphic—or you can simply create the graphic on the blank screen if one does not

already exist. If you open an existing graphic, you will be asked whether you want to update the linked image before opening the new image. Select **No**.

5. With the desired image on the screen, use the **Scissors** tool to highlight the desired portion of it, then select **Edit>Copy**. Figure 12.17 shows the screen at this point.

6. Select **File>Exit** to return to Quattro Pro.

7. Select **Edit>Paste Link** to paste the copied picture into the notebook. Figure 12.18 shows the result.

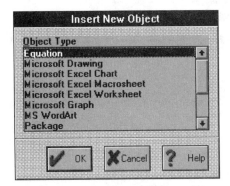

Figure 12.16 The Insert New Object dialog box.

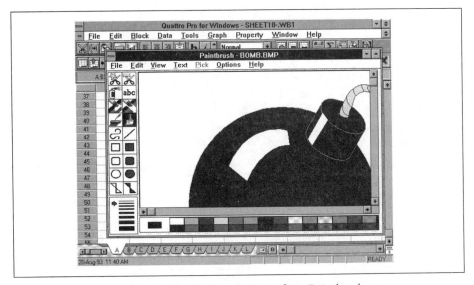

Figure 12.17 Copying an image from Paintbrush.

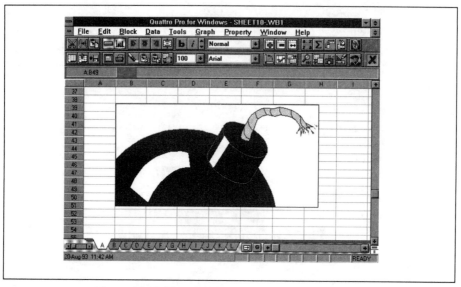

Figure 12.18 The pasted image linked to Paintbrush.

This is a brief overview of object linking. OLE offers many more powers. For more information on this powerful tool, refer to your Windows manual.

Summary

This chapter completed your education in the use of graphics in your Quattro Pro notebooks. You now know how to dress up your graphs with text and graphic shapes that you can place anywhere. You examined how to move, resize, and overlap these objects and how to change their properties. You saw how grouping allows you to tie several graphic objects together, as well as how to manipulate these grouped objects. In addition, you learned how to import and manage graphics in Quattro Pro. Finally, you saw how to link with files created by other applications to create spreadsheets with "live," changing information. With these tools, you'll be able to create an endless variety of customized Quattro Pro graphs.

In the next chapter, you'll learn about Quattro Pro's slide show production features. Using these features, you can create and run slide shows right from within Quattro Pro. Your data and text graphs combine to create slide sequences—plus you can add special effects. You'll find it easy to create and edit slide shows in Quattro Pro; the next chapter shows you how.

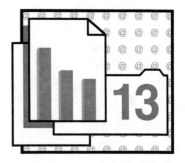

Creating Slide Shows

Chapters 10, 11, and 12 showed you how to create, customize, and annotate Quattro Pro graphs. Quattro Pro's graphing capabilities are so powerful, you'll probably want to use them to create sophisticated presentations. One key component of most presentations is *text graphs*—that is, graphs composed of words and numbers. This chapter will show you how to create interesting text graphs and display those graphs in a slide show. Slide shows are useful for on-screen viewing of your text and data graphs. You can combine a set of slides in a slide show and present the show without a projector—right on the screen.

In this chapter you'll learn about:

- Creating and editing text graphs
- Creating slide shows
- Editing slide shows
- Adding transition effects and duration
- Automatic vs. manual shows
- Interactivity with graph buttons and branching shows

Creating and Editing Text Graphs

A text graph is simply a Quattro Pro graph that uses text instead of bar charts, line charts, and so forth to make its point. You've seen text graphs many times before—in sales presentations, in training materials, on television, and in other places. A simple text graph consists of

- a title
- a subtitle (optional)
- one or more lines of text, or a paragraph
- one or more graphic elements (optional)

You learned in Chapter 12 all you need to know to create text graphs. You simply begin with a new graph, one containing no data. Choose the text graph type **Text** to get a blank graph window. Finally, you use the annotation tools (also known as the drawing tools) to add graphic elements and text to the graph. Text graphs can be made into title slides, bulleted lists, tables of values, flow charts, and so on. Figures 13.1 through 13.4 show some examples.

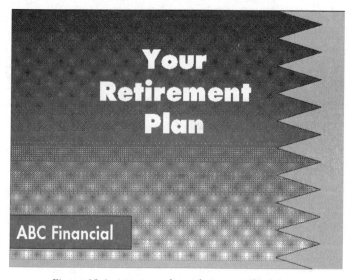

Figure 13.1 A text graph made into a title slide.

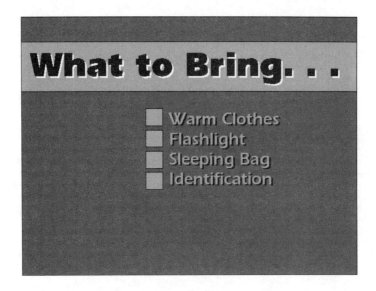

Figure 13.2 A text graph used as part of a sequence of items.

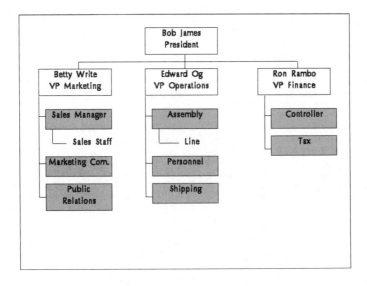

Figure 13.3 A flow chart.

Figure 13.4 A simple table.

Text graphs are not just for slides

The focus of this chapter is on using text graphs to create slides for a slide presentation, but you can use text graphs for other purposes. Any time you want to use the drawing and annotation tools in a blank window, you should use a text graph. You can insert your completed image into the notebook as a floating graphic. This lets you use Quattro Pro's drawing tools to insert images into your notebook pages and can be an alternative to object linking.

Here's an example to show you how easy it is to create a text graph. Start by moving to the Graph page; then select **Graph>New** from the menu bar. You can change the graph name to whatever you'd like, but don't enter any series ranges or other information. Simply click on **OK**, and an empty graph window will appear. Right-click in the Graph Pane to display the Graph Setup and Background property inspector. Under Graph Type, click on **Text**, and the dialog box will look like Figure 13.5.

Maximize the graph window

Maximizing the graph window while you work on text graphs can make it easier to complete your work. The proportions of the graph pane are not affected by the size and shape of the graph window.

Chapter 11 describes in detail how to use this property inspector. For now, let's keep it simple, using a light blue color as the background for the text slide. Select **Fill Color**; then click on a light blue shade.

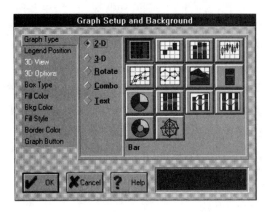

Figure 13.5 The Graph Setup and Background property inspector—
with 2-D Graph Type selected.

Click on **OK**, and the property inspector disappears, leaving you with the graph window and a light blue background. To add a title, click on the **Text** tool in the Graph SpeedBar. The cursor changes to the Text tool shape. Click and drag to draw a text box, then begin typing your title (see Figure 13.6).

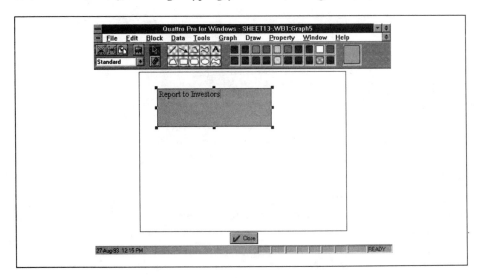

Figure 13.6 Text box with typed title.

The title should probably be bigger, so right-click anywhere on the text to open the Text Properties property inspector; then click on **Text Font**. Change the typeface, point size, and options to meet your needs; then click on **OK**. Remember that light text on a dark background works best for slides.

Next, click on the handle in the lower-right corner of the text box and drag to resize the box until it just fits your title. Figure 13.7 shows the title now.

Figure 13.7 Title with resized text box.

Use the same procedures again to add the body text to your graph. Draw a larger text box below the title; then start typing in the body copy. Simply enter each line the way you want it to look and press **Return** at the end of each line. You can use blank lines to separate items. The text box now looks like Figure 13.8.

You can right-click anywhere on this text to change its properties, just as you did with the title. When you're done, click outside the text box to complete the process. You might want to add bullet characters (special shapes) to the beginning of each line for emphasis. Quattro Pro supports nine special bullet characters, which you can access with bullet codes. The codes must be enclosed in backslash characters (\). Here are the nine bullets, along with the codes (including the backslashes) used to create them.

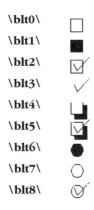

\blt0\
\blt1\
\blt2\
\blt3\
\blt4\
\blt5\
\blt6\
\blt7\
\blt8\

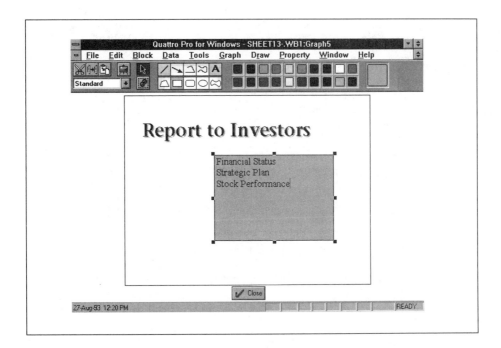

Figure 13.8 Text box with three lines of text.

To add the bullets to your existing text, click on the text box to select the char-acters you want; then insert the desired bullet code before each line of text. Your text box should look something like Figure 13.9.

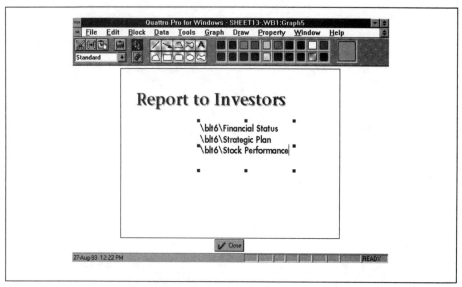

Figure 13.9 Text box, with bullet codes.

When you're done, click outside the text box, and you'll see that the bullet codes turn into bullet characters (see Figure 13.10).

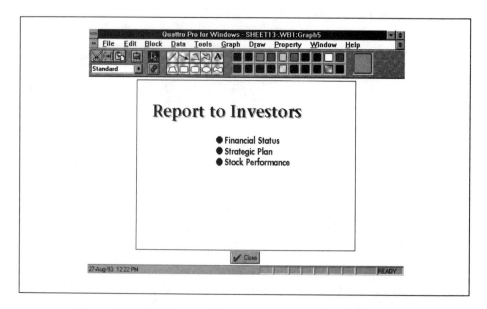

Figure 13.10 Text box, with bullet characters replacing bullet codes.

The bullet codes are hidden, but you can edit or delete them at any time by clicking on the text box and editing the text. Resize the text box to meet your needs.

You've created your first text graph! You can make your text graphs more interesting with graphic shapes, clip art, imported backgrounds, and more. Figure 13.11 shows an example. Refer to Chapter 12 for more information about annotating your text graphs.

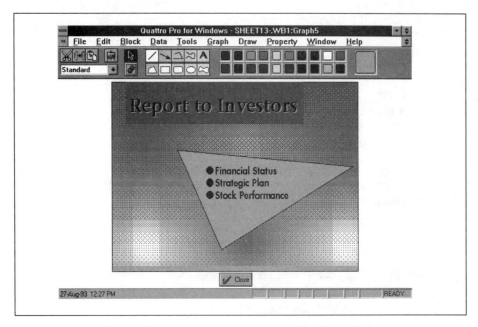

Figure 13.11 Annotating the text graph with graphics.

Creating Slide Shows

There are several terms that you need to know in order to understand Quattro Pro's slide shows.

- **Slide show** A group of one or more graphs, organized to be presented in a particular order. For each graph in a slide show, a Transition Effect, Transition Speed, and Display Time are specified. Also specified is whether or not that graph is to Overlay the previous one transparently.

Remember: Slides are just graphs

We use the term *slide* here when talking about slide shows. But slides are just text or data graphs. Any text or data graph you create in Quattro Pro can be used in a slide show.

- **Light Table** The dialog box used to edit the order and other properties of slides. The order in which graphs appear in a slide show is shown by *thumbnails*, or reduced images of the slides. To change the order, simply drag the thumbnail graphs into the proper sequence on the light table. The rest of the slide show will be reordered automatically.

- **Effect** Transition effect is a special visual effect used to display the graph. Quattro Pro offers 30 transition effects, which are similar to film and video effects. The simplest is **Cut**, which immediately replaces the previous graph with the new graph. A variety of fades, wipes, and digital effects are also available. Effects add interest to your slide show and can provide smooth transitions between slides.

- **Speed** Transition speed controls the amount of time that it takes to complete a transition effect. Quattro Pro offers three speeds: **Slow**, **Medium**, and **Fast**.

- **Overlay** Controls whether or not a graph will transparently overlay the preceding graph in a slide show. If **Overlay** is turned on, the selected graph will be displayed with a transparent background overlaid upon the preceding graph. This feature is especially useful when you wish to create slides that are built by several graphs or when you wish to annotate one graph with another.

- **Display Time** Controls the amount of time (in seconds) that a graph is displayed. Display time ranges from 0 to 3851 seconds. The graph will be displayed for as many seconds as specified in the Display Time setting, after which Quattro Pro will move on to the next graph. If a Display Time of 0 is selected, the graph will be displayed until the user clicks a mouse button or presses a key on the keyboard.

Quattro Pro presentations are given on-screen

Slide shows can be given with a slide projector or on the computer screen. If you plan to use a slide projector, you'll have to save each slide image as an EPS slide image file and send it to a slide imprint bureau to be transferred to 35mm film. If you use the computer screen as a projector, your transition effects can surpass those of a professional slide show given with projectors.

- **Automatic Show** A show that automatically moves from graph to graph. For a fully automatic show, all graphs must have a non zero Display Time.

- **Manual Show** A show in which the user manually moves from graph to graph by clicking the mouse. For a fully manual show, all graphs must have a Display Time of zero.

Adding a Show Icon

To create a slide show, you must first be on the Graphs page of your spreadsheet notebook. Slide the Tab Scroller or click on the **TurboTab** button to activate the Graphs page. Next, click on the **Create Slide Show** button in the Graphs page SpeedBar. This button is fourth from the left side of the SpeedBar. The dialog box shown in Figure 13.12 is displayed.

Figure 13.12 Create Slide Show dialog box.

Enter a slide show name (in this case, "My Show") and click on **OK**. A Show icon with the name you selected will be added to the Graphs page. To differentiate it from the graphs, the Show icon looks like a 35mm slide.

 You can add several slide shows to a single notebook
You can add as many slide shows as you like to the same Graphs page. Each show can display different graphs or some of the same graphs used in other shows—provided all the graphs appear on the Graphs page. Each new show you create will have its own icon and a unique name.

Placing Graphs into the Show

To add graphs to your new slide show, simply click and drag each Graph icon that you wish to add to the show over your Show icon. The Show icon reverses color to indicate that it has been selected (see Figure 13.13).

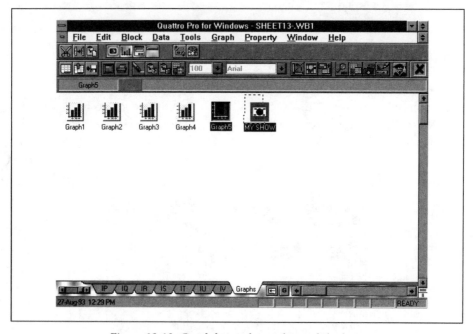

Figure 13.13 Graph being dropped into slide show.

The order in which you add the graphs to your slide show determines the order in which the slides are displayed (although you can change the order later if you like). A time-saving technique is to press the **Shift** key down and click on all the Graph icons you want in the show. Click on the icons in the order you want them displayed. Now drag the entire batch over to the Slide Show icon and release the mouse. All the highlighted graphs will be added to the show in the order they were selected.

Editing the Show with the Light Table

Editing your show involves arranging the slides in the desired order, adding transition effects, and setting duration for the slides. To edit your show, you can click on the **Slide Show** icon and then press the **Edit Slide Show** button in the Graphs SpeedBar. Alternatively, you can double-click on the **Show** icon. This displays the Light Table shown in Figure 13.14.

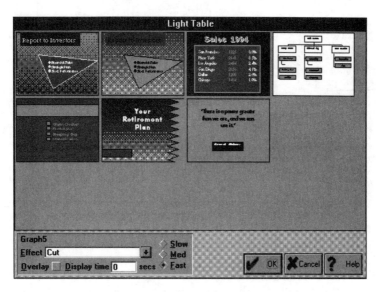

Figure 13.14 Light Table for "My Show" slide show.

Using this Light Table display, you can change various attributes of your show. The following sections explain these changes.

Changing the Order of Graphs

The order of graphs in the slide show runs from left to right, top to bottom, within the Light Table window. (If there are too many graphs to fit within the Light Table, a scroll bar gives you access to those not shown on the screen.) To change the graph order, click on the slide you wish to move. The arrow cursor changes to a hand. Drag the graph outline to where you want to move it. The graph already in that spot will reverse color to indicate that its position is where your selected graph will go (see Figure 13.15).

Release the mouse button, and the graph order will be changed.

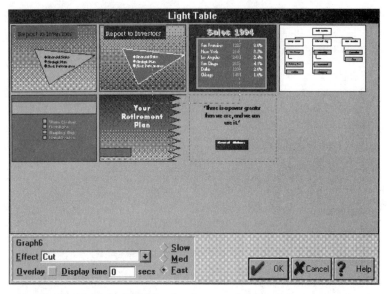

Figure 13.15 Light Table, showing graph order being changed.

Adding and Deleting Slides

You cannot add graphs to a slide show while the Light Table window is open. To add graphs to an existing slide show, close the Light Table window and click and drag the desired Graph icons to the **Show** icon, as described above.

To delete a graph from a slide show, open the Light Table window, click on the graph you wish to remove, and then press the **Delete** key. Adding and deleting graphs in a slide show does not affect the graphs themselves. The graphs will remain on the Graphs page and, if applicable, as floating graphs in the spreadsheet notebook.

You cannot edit a graph from the Light Table. To edit a graph, close the Light Table and double-click on the graph to open its Graph window. Edit the graph as described in Chapter 11.

Running a Slide Show

To run a slide show, click on its **Show** icon and then click on the **Run Slide Show** button in the Graphs SpeedBar (it's on the far right). Each graph in the slide show will fill the screen; no menu bar, SpeedBar, or window frame will be visible. While the show is running, the following controls are active:

Control	Effect
Left-click mouse	Display next slide
Right-click mouse	Display previous slide
Press **Backspace** key	Display previous slide
Press **Esc** key	End slide show
Click on graph button	Perform graph button's function (if any)
Press first letter of graph button	Perform graph button's function (if any)
Press any other key	Display next slide

Adding Transition Effects

Slide show transition effects have been briefly described earlier in this chapter. To examine or change the transition settings for the graphs in a slide show, double-click on the desired **Slide** icon on the Graphs page to open the Light Table. By clicking on any graph, its transition-effects settings will be displayed at the bottom of the Light Table. When a graph is first added to a slide show, its Transition Effect is set to **Cut**, the Transition Speed is **Fast**, and **Overlay** is turned off.

To select a different effect, click on the effect's **Down Arrow** button to open the list; then click on the desired effect. Twenty-four effects are available.

Cut	Tilt down
Fade out/fade in	Tilt up
Wipe right	Single vertical stripes
Wipe left	Double vertical stripes
Wipe down	Spiral
Wipe up	Dissolve: 1-by-1 pixels to 64-by-64 pixels
Sides to center	Curtain down
Center to sides	Curtain up
Double edge vertical in	Diamond in
Double edge vertical out	Diamond out
Square edges in	Square corners in
Square edges out	Square corners out

These effects determine how one graph replaces another on the screen. A cut immediately replaces whatever was on-screen with the new graph, whereas a dissolve causes the old graph to be overwritten by the new graph, a few pixels at a time. Remember that the effect takes place as the graph is displayed on the screen—not as it leaves the screen. Hence, if you want an effect applied to the graph as it leaves, add the effect to the next graph. Figure 13.16 shows the center effect in progress.

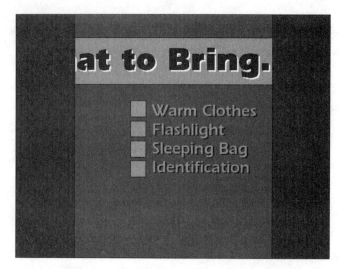

Figure 13.16 A Sides-to-center effect in progress.

The Speed control determines how quickly the transition effect runs. For a short presentation, you can use **Slow** to make the presentation run longer; for presentations with a lot of slides, use **Medium** or **Fast** speeds. Keep in mind that some effects take much longer than others to complete. A 4-by-4 pixel dissolve, for example, will take much longer than a Wipe, no matter what the Speed setting.

With all these effects, it's easy to become confused about which effects to use and when to use them. For most presentations, you will never need to use anything other than the cut, fade, and wipe effects. The fancier effects are impressive, but they can wear on the audience after a few graphs. For most shows, stick with the simple effects; reserve the fancy ones for long presentations, when you sometimes have to grab an audience's faltering attention. Remember: It's the information on your graphs that's important, not the transitions between graphs.

Overlap Effects

A useful tool for drawing attention to key points of your presentation is *overlapping*, which allows you to paste one graph over another while letting the audience see through the new graph to the original. When you create overlap effects, you should start with a data or text graph as the first slide. Since it will overlay the first one, the next slide should contain just those elements you want to add. These elements should be in the proper positions on the slide, so that they align when the two slides are overlapped.

Here's an example of how to use Overlaps. First, take a normal bar graph, as shown in Figure 13.17. Make a copy of this graph using **Graph>Copy**. (Select the Bar graph in the list; then enter a new name on the right side of the dialog box. We'll call this WORKGRAPH.) Now, edit WORKGRAPH, adding an annotation to call attention to an important feature of the chart. Figure 13.18 shows an example.

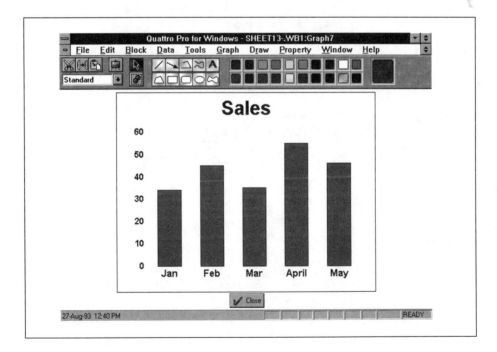

Figure 13.17 A normal bar graph.

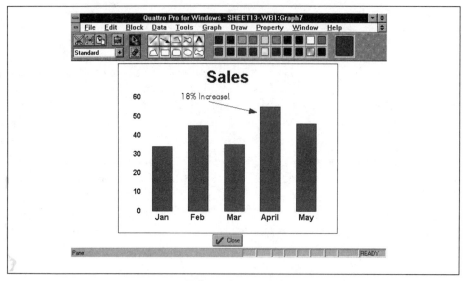

Figure 13.18 Bar graph with annotation.

Make a copy of this annotated chart, using **Graph>Copy**. But this time, turn off **Copy Data** in the Graph>Copy dialog box. When you edit the new graph, you'll see that everything except the graph itself is copied (see Figure 13.19).

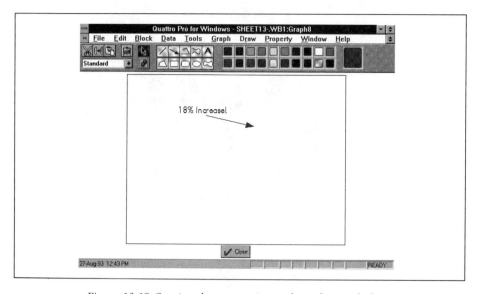

Figure 13.19 Copying the annotation without the graph data.

Now add the original graph and the annotation to your slide show. Double-click on the **Show** icon to display the Light Table and arrange the charts so that the original chart comes first, immediately followed by the annotation-only chart. Select the annotation-only chart and turn **Overlay** on, pick the **Fade out/fade in** effect, select **Fast** for the transition speed, and then run the slide show. You'll see the annotations magically fade into place on the original slide.

N O T E

Start with the final image

When creating overlapping effects, you can start with the final image containing all overlapped elements. Then copy the graph and remove elements from the copy. Do this as many times as needed for the overlay slides. This helps keep elements in position as you prepare the slides.

Setting Duration

In addition to the transitions between graphs in a slide show, you can also control how long each graph is displayed. There are two ways to control display duration: manually, with the mouse, or automatically, with the Light Table's Display Time control. When viewing a slide show, you can always step ahead from one graph to the next by clicking the mouse button, or you can go backward one graph at a time by right-clicking the mouse. However, you can let Quattro Pro do the driving by specifying the Display Time for one, some, or all of your graphs.

Control over the display time is especially useful when:

- The show is being run in a fully automatic mode.
- The show is semiautomatic, and you want to give your audience enough time to read the graphs without getting bored.
- The show uses interactive Graph buttons and includes test questions with a time limit for answers.

To specify Display Time, open a slide show by double-clicking on its **Show** icon; then click on a graph. The selected graph's Display Time, in seconds, will be displayed in the dialog box. Quattro Pro accepts display times of 0 to 3851 seconds (a little over an hour). (You can enter a number larger than 3851, but Quattro Pro will set the actual value to 3851.) A Display Time of 0 seconds will cause Quattro Pro to display the graph continuously until the mouse is clicked. Whenever a new graph is added to a slide show, the default setting is 0 seconds.

Skipping slides while a show is running

A mouse click will always cause the show to advance to the next slide, no matter what that slide's Display Time setting is. This feature is useful when you need to override unusually long display times or when you need to skip through some slides to get to a specific graph.

Setting Global Show Properties

Quattro Pro slide shows have their own set of properties that establish global settings for the show. If you right-click on a **Slide Show** icon on the Graphs page, then choose **Slide Show Properties**, you'll see the Slide show properties, including Name, Default Effect, and Show Pointer. Here are the details about these properties.

- **Name** Establishes the name of the show. Use this option to change the slide show's name.

- **Default Effect** Sets a transition effect and display time for all the graphs in the slide show at once. Use this option to set a global effect and a display time; then change individual slides if desired.

- **Show Pointer** Determines whether the mouse pointer is active (displayed) during a slide show. When your slide show is fully automatic and contains no graph buttons, you might want to remove the mouse pointer from the screen so that the audience is not distracted by it.

Automatic and Manual Shows

Slide shows can be Automatic, Manual, or a combination of the two. Automatic shows have Display Time settings of more than 0 seconds for every graph, whereas manual shows have Display Time settings of 0 for all graphs, meaning that the viewer must click the mouse to step from graph to graph.

Automatic shows are useful for "self-running" demonstrations—that is, presentations in which you want the audience to observe but not participate. Manual shows are useful for a broad range of presentations and applications. However, they can be used *only* when a presenter or the viewer has access to a working mouse or keyboard, because a manual slide show will not move past the first graph without a click of the mouse or the press of a key.

A combination of Automatic and Manual graphs is often the best choice for presentations. By setting a reasonable display time, you can ensure that a graph will stay on-screen long enough for your audience to read and understand it, whereas a viewer who wants to step through the presentation faster can simply click the mouse to move to the next graph.

There are no absolute rules for when you should use automatic or manual graphs in your slide shows. Experiment with different combinations to see what works best for you and your presentation style.

Graph Buttons and Branching Shows

In Chapter 12 you saw how to turn a text box into a Graph button. Now we'll explore how to use Graph buttons to make your slide shows interactive. First, remember that slide shows are normally linear: Click on a graph to move to the next one, until you reach the end of the show. However, it's often useful to be able to skip around within a slide show; this way the audience can find the information it needs without having to sit through information it doesn't need.

Consider a sales presentation for an automobile. Let's say you were primarily interested in performance and price features—but you had to watch presentations on the automobile's interior, safety features, climate control, and so on, before you got to the "good parts"? You'd be bored, and you might even walk away. If you were presented with your choice of information about the car, however, and could immediately choose those points of primary interest, you'd get your critical information faster, with less boredom, and you might even be more likely to purchase the car.

That's the kind of control that Graph buttons give you. With them you can create slide shows that viewers can tailor to their own needs. You can create instructional shows capable of training, testing, and evaluating students. There are endless other possibilities.

Suppose you wanted to create four choices for your automobile presentation. Your opening screen might contain four buttons, as shown in Figure 13.20.

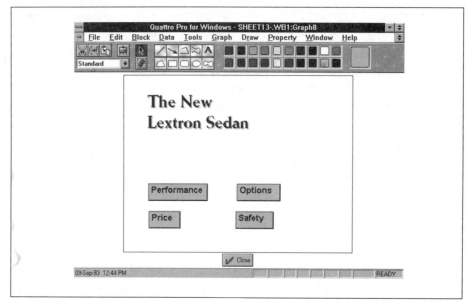

Figure 13.20 The starting screen for an auto demonstration.

The buttons at the bottom of the screen are created from text boxes. Just right-click the desired text box and the Box Properties property inspector will be displayed. Select the **Graph Button** properties and choose **Select Graph**. Finally, indicate the graph to which this one will branch when the button is clicked. Figure 13.21 shows the completed properties.

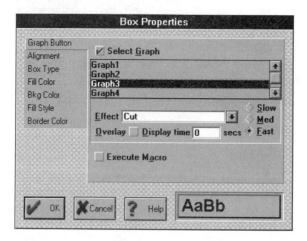

Figure 13.21 Properties for a Graph button.

Each of the text boxes on the start-up screen can be turned into a button, and each button can branch to a different slide in the show.

You can also turn the graph's background into a button. Often this is used to present a message—like "Please click on one of the buttons below." Another useful technique is to have the Background button branch back to the graph currently being displayed. If the user clicks on the graph's background, the slide will simply display itself again. In this way, the entire Graph Pane has been turned into a Graph button, and the button has been linked back to itself. Remember that slide shows automatically advance to the next graph when the mouse is left-clicked—*except* when you're clicking on a Graph button, in which case you go wherever the Graph button says to go. This feature gives you complete control over how the user interacts with your slide show.

This is just an introduction to the power of Graph buttons and branching slide shows. By using these features, along with Quattro Pro's sophisticated macro capabilities, you can develop a limitless range of interactive presentations, educational and training materials, and even games.

Summary

In this chapter, you learned how to create text graphs. You were introduced to Quattro Pro's slide shows, and you learned how to create and organize your slide show presentations. You saw how to control the visual transition effects and display time of every graph and how to create automatic and manual shows. Finally, you were given a taste of the power of interactive slide shows by using Graph buttons to control the flow of your presentation. With the graphing tools introduced in the last four chapters, you can now use Quattro Pro to create anything from a simple line chart to a sophisticated interactive presentation.

The following chapter shows you how to use Quattro Pro to manage database information. Many spreadsheet applications require that you store and manage records, such as financial records, employee information, stock transaction data, and so on. These data management tasks can be accomplished with Quattro Pro's powerful database tools. The next chapter introduces these tools and provides an overview of database management in Quattro Pro.

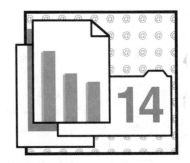

Using Database Features

While building a spreadsheet application, you might find you need to store and access certain pieces of data frequently. Applications that involve transactions, such as billing, inventory, purchasing, and payroll, are likely candidates for Quattro Pro's database features. Using database features, you can enter your business or personal records for permanent storage. If you need to access those records, a host of database management tools do the trick. This chapter covers Quattro Pro's database features and gets you up and running with database management tasks. At the end of this chapter, you'll be able to add a database to any of your Quattro Pro applications and manipulate the data you've stored. Specifically, you'll learn about

- Building a database range
- Using field names
- Using the data form to enter records
- Creating a criteria range
- Creating an extract range
- Entering records into a database
- Performing database queries
- Extracting records from the database
- Sorting data
- Using database statistical functions

Database Basics

A *database* is a system of storing and retrieving information. By using Quattro Pro's database features you can store your records right inside your notebooks. And you can retrieve information from those databases quickly and easily. Examples of some useful databases include a customer name and address file, a transaction file for accounting and record-keeping, a purchase order file, and a checkbook transaction file. Each of these databases consists of individual records. A *record* is a single unit of a database, such as a single transaction in the transaction file or a purchase order in the purchase order file.

Each record consists of a series of entries called *fields*. Within a database, each record contains the same types of fields. For example, in the customer address file, each record would contain the following fields:

- First Name
- Last Name
- Company
- Address
- City
- State
- Zip

All these fields appear on each and every record, giving the records a uniform appearance.

In Quattro Pro, your database data can be integrated with your normal spreadsheet data. You simply enter records across the rows of a particular block of cells. Each new row constitutes a new record. The cells in a row are used to contain the fields for that record. Hence, the columns identify the fields, and the rows identify the records. Figure 14.1 illustrates this database structure.

The fields are identified at the top of the columns with unique headings, called *field names*. Field names are an important part of your database; they determine exactly what information will be included in your records.

After you have a database full of records, you can perform various database management tasks. These include adding, deleting, and editing records; sorting the database in alphabetical or numerical order; and a host of database query procedures. In short, database management is simply the process of manipulating the records in your database. The rest of this chapter shows you how to create and manage your Quattro Pro databases.

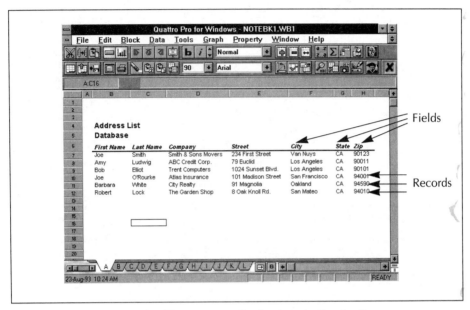

Figure 14.1 The structure of a database in Quattro Pro.

Setting Up the Database and Entering Data

Database management consists of a few simple procedures, including entering new data into a database, searching for existing records, extracting data from a database, and editing information currently inside the database. These tasks can all be accomplished in a Quattro Pro database. First, we'll describe how to set up a database and type records into the database block. You'll learn how to use the data form to enter and view records or just enter them directly on the notebook page. Next, you'll learn how to search for records within a database— either using the data form or a criteria range. Finally, you'll discover how to extract information from a database and place that extracted information anywhere on the notebook page—or even onto another page.

Databases consist of three basic components: the database block, the criteria block, and the extract block. The *database block* is the notebook area that contains your database data and field names. You will enter new records into this area frequently and generally manage your database records here. The *criteria block* is used to select subsets of the database (records that have common elements) for query procedures. Query procedures include locating, extracting, and deleting records. The *extract block* is used along with the extract procedure; it holds data extracted from the database range.

You'll find it easy to set up your database components. The main requirement is that you enter a set of field names for your database data. These field names will be used in all three blocks of your database setup.

Entering New Data

The database block is simply an area on the notebook page that contains the database data and column headings above the data, called field names. To create your database block, you need to type only the field names into a row of cells and then to enter data beneath these headings. As you saw in Figure 14.1, each row of data below the field names constitutes a new record in the database. The following sections explain how to create field names and enter database data.

Field Names

The first row of your database block should contain the database field names. Field *names* are simply words that identify the data in each column. Unlike column headings for other notebook data, database field names must meet these requirements.

- Field names must be unique. Each field name you enter into the first row of the database block must be unique, that is, you should not use the same field name for two columns. Doing so will disrupt your database searches and other procedures. Note that upper- and lowercase letters are not considered unique; the field name Zip Code is identical to ZIP CODE. Field names should also be text labels and not formulas or values.

- Limit field names to 16 characters. Your field names can be a maximum of 16 characters, including any spaces or special symbols. If you use more than 16 characters in a field name, Quattro Pro will ignore characters past the sixteenth.

- Field names must not begin or end with a space. Leading or trailing spaces in your field names can cause confusion and errors in searching and extracting procedures. For the best results, use spaces only in the middle of your field names. Or better yet, use underscore characters instead of spaces, as in First_Name and Product_Code.

- Use a maximum of 256 field names in your database. You can have up to 256 fields in your Quattro Pro database. (It's unlikely that you will use 256 unique fields in a single database.)

Within these requirements, you can use any words or codes that help you remember what the column contains. Examples of good field names include:

First_Name

Company

Address

Zip Code

ID_Num

Entering Records Directly on the Page

One way to enter new records into your database is to simply begin filling in the rows beneath the field names you created. You need not complete every cell in each row, but you should avoid leaving a row completely blank.

To make your data entry easier, try using the **Restrict Entry** option to keep the cell pointer within the database range. This way, you don't have to keep moving the cell pointer to the first cell in each new record.

1. Highlight several blank rows at the bottom of the database block as shown in Figure 14.2.

2. Choose the **Property>Current Object** command or right-click on the highlighted range.

3. Select the **Protection** option from the Properties dialog box.

4. Choose **Unprotect** to remove protection from the highlighted cells. Click on **OK** when finished.

5. Select **Data>Restrict Input**. Confirm that the correct range is identified, then click on **OK**.

6. Use the arrow keys to move from cell to cell within the specified range. When you reach the end of one row, pressing the **Right Arrow** key will automatically wrap to the beginning of the next row.

7. Press the **Escape** key to cancel the restricted entry mode.

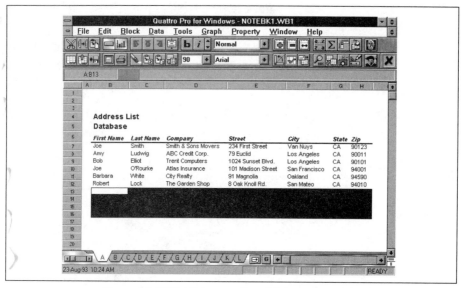

Figure 14.2 Highlight rows for adding new records.

When entering records into a database block, remember the following points:

- Quattro Pro will hold a maximum of 8181 records. If you need to hold more than 8181 records, you should look into using a database product, like Paradox.

- Avoid leaving rows (records) completely blank. Remember to fill at least one piece of data in each row. Although you don't have to complete each record, you should not leave a record completely blank.

- Name the database block. Using the **Block>Names>Create** command to name the database block is a good practice. You can then refer to the database by its name when you perform queries and other tasks.

Making Entries into an Expanding Database Block

When you perform query procedures within your database, you must identify the database block. You can do this by providing the block reference or by naming the block and providing the block's name. You can also name blocks using the **Block>Names>Create** command, described in Chapter 6.

When you add records to a named or referenced database block, you will probably be entering records outside the named block. For example, if you start with the database from Figure 14.2, your original database block would be B6..H12. Now suppose you name that block AddressList using the **Block>Names>Create** command. When you add new records beneath this range, the named block does not automatically include the new entries. You will have to use the **Block>Names>Create** command again to include the new records if you want the name AddressList to apply to the entire database. This will be important if you've identified the block for the query procedures.

One way around this problem is to include numerous blank rows in the block name. For example, you might refer to the block B6..H100 as the AddressList block. Then, you need not update the block name until you enter more than 99 records.

Another technique is to make the block reference expand as you enter new records. In Quattro Pro, you can make any range reference or range name expand if you insert new rows into the middle of the range rather than at the bottom. Using the previous example as a guide, you might insert new rows starting at row 11, leaving row 12 beneath the inserted records. To insert five rows, you would highlight the block B11..H15 and then use the **Block>Insert> Rows>Partial** command. Figure 14.3 shows the result of this operation. The named range will now include the extra rows.

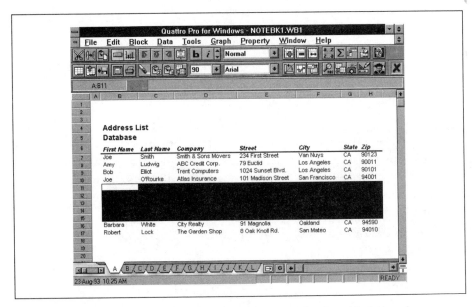

Figure 14.3 Inserting records into an existing database block to make its reference expand.

By using this technique, you never have to reapply a name to the block or reidentify the range when using database query procedures.

Add one blank row to your database block

NOTE A common practice is to add a blank row at the bottom of your named database block. This blank row helps ensure that you insert new rows into the middle of the block. If you insert your new rows at the bottom of the existing data, the blank row will actually still be under your inserted rows, allowing the database range to expand. If you frequently sort your database records, you might want to fill this extra row with **ZZZZZZZ** in each field. This keeps it at the bottom of the database when you sort the records. Alternatively, you can sort all records except the last one.

Entering Records Using the Data Form

Perhaps the easiest way to enter new records into a database block is to use the new data form. The data form displays your database data and field names in a special window. You can use the form to type new records into the database, search for database records, or edit existing records. The data form will be discussed throughout this chapter; the following steps explain how to view the form and use it to enter new records.

1. Highlight your database block—which includes the field names and any records beneath them. If you don't have any records entered, just highlight the field names and one blank row beneath them.

2. If the database block currently contains protected cells, unprotect them by right-clicking the mouse, choosing the **Protection** option, and clicking on **Unprotect** and then the **OK** button. Remember that notebook cells are normally protected, so if you have not specifically unprotected the data, do so at this point. (For more information about protecting cells, refer to Chapter 3.)

3. Choose **Data>Form** and confirm that the database block is properly identified.

4. Click on **OK**, and the data form appears for the database you specified. Figure 14.4 shows the data form for the example database.

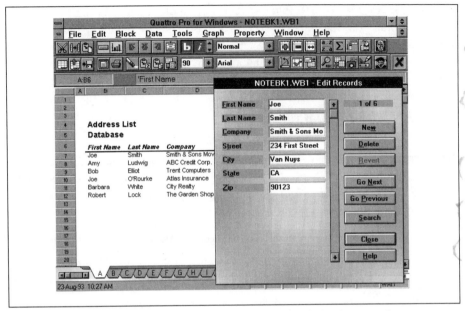

Figure 14.4 Use the Data>Form command to view the data in a form.

You can now use the data form to view your existing database records or enter new ones. The data form displays one record in the database at a time. You can flip forward through the records by clicking on the **Go Next** button and flip backward through the records using the **Go Previous** button. You can also flip through the records by manipulating the scroll bar that appears in the data form: Click on the down arrow or move the scroll box down the scroll bar to move forward through the database.

To enter new records into the database using the data form, just click on the **New** button. Quattro Pro gives you a blank form to fill out. Begin typing the first field; then press the **Tab** key to move to the next field. When you have completed the form, click on the **New** button to add another record or click **Close** to return to the notebook page. The data form automatically adds the record to the end of your database block.

Searching for Records

You can locate records in your database using either the data form or the database Query procedure. The data form will locate records based on information you enter. If you type **Smith** into the Last Name field, for example, the form can display all Smiths in the database. You can also use the database Query procedure, which involves using a criteria block. This technique provides additional flexibility and control over your database searches. The following sections provide the details.

Searching with the Data Form

To locate any record or group of records in your database, you can use the data form's **Search** option. First, access the data form for your database records. Do this by highlighting the database fields and data (i.e., the data block), selecting the **Data>Form** command, and choosing **OK**. With the data form in view, follow these steps to locate a record:

1. Click on the **Search** button. You will see a blank record appear in the form.
2. Press **Tab** to move the cursor into the desired field of the database.
3. Enter the criteria information into this field and any other fields in the data form.
4. Click on **OK**.

Quattro Pro will locate records that match the criteria you enter into the data form. Criteria tells Quattro Pro what you are looking for. For example, you can locate all records with Smith in the Last Name field by typing **Smith** into the Last Name field of the search form. Figure 14.5 shows a search form with two entries in place. The more entries you make into the blank search form, the more you narrow the search down to specific records. If you are specific enough, you may get only one record to match your criteria.

Click on the **Go Next** button to view the first record that matches your criteria entries. Continue to click **Go Next** to view other records that match your criteria. Use **Go Previous** to review previous records. To exit the search procedure, click on the **Edit** button in the data form. This returns to the normal data form display.

If you are searching for numeric data, you can include conditional operators in your search entries. For example, if you enter **100** into the Amount field and click on the **Go Next** button, you'll get the first record with 100 in the Amount field. However, if you enter **>100** into the Amount field, you'll get the first record with an amount greater than 100 in this field. Refer to Chapter 6 for more information about conditional operators.

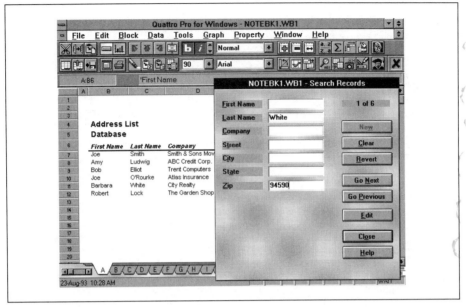

Figure 14.5 Enter criteria into the blank search form.

Searching with the Criteria Block and Query Command

A second way to search for data in your database is to use a criteria block. This is a block of cells used to specify conditions for searches, or queries. When you include a criteria block, you can use Quattro Pro's **Data>Query** options to search the database block for groups of records that have common elements— all records with a Last Name field containing Smith, for example—or all transactions made on a certain date. You can use general search criteria to find many records, or you can get very specific with your criteria to find only one record that matches your criteria. The more records you have in the database, the more important these query options become, since it will be difficult to glance down the columns to locate the desired information.

Query options let you do more than just locate specific records or groups of records; these options can be used for deleting records and extracting records from the database into another area of the sheet.

The criteria block is frequently added above the database block. It consists of a row containing the field names from the database block (you can copy these headings for the criteria block) and another row beneath the headings. Figure 14.6 shows a typical criteria block.

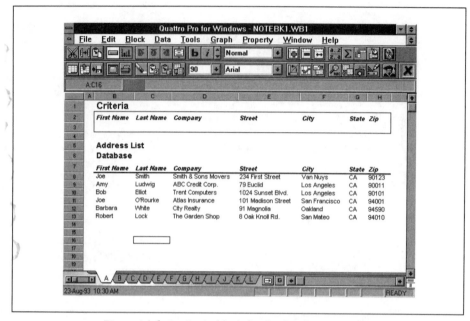

Figure 14.6 A criteria block for the database example.

In this example, we've added an outline to make the range easier to see. Notice that the field names match those in the database block exactly. This is important: Any differences between the criteria field names and the database field names will destroy your ability to search that field. For the best results, you should copy the field names from the database block into the criteria block.

Simple Criteria Entries

The first row under the criteria headings is for your criteria entries. This is where you tell Quattro Pro what information to find in the database. If you want to find all records that contain Smith in the Last Name field, simply enter **Smith** under the Last Name field in the criteria range, as shown in Figure 14.7.

Notice that you don't need to fill in each of the fields—only those for which you have specific search requirements. In fact, if you never use certain fields for criteria entries, you need not include them in the criteria range at all. However, it doesn't hurt to include them. Use the **Data>Query>Locate** command to locate the records you've identified (see "Database Queries" later in this chapter for details).

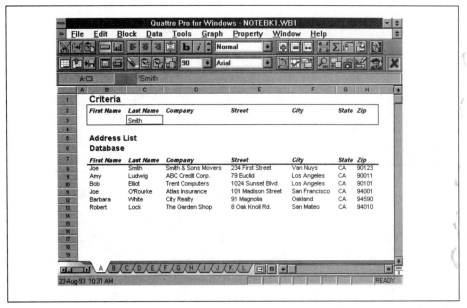

Figure 14.7 Entering a simple criteria entry to locate records with a Last Name of Smith.

You can fill in as many fields as you like to narrow the search. The more fields you use in the criteria range, the more specific the requirements. To be located, a record must match all the data you enter. For example, if you enter **Smith** in the Last Name field and **92123** in the Zip field, a record must meet both criteria. A record that contains Smith but a different ZIP Code will not be included in this query. Using multiple fields for your criteria entries is called using *AND logic*; the last name must be Smith AND the ZIP must be 92123.

Using Wildcards

You can use wildcards in your criteria entries to find groups of records that have similar entries. Using wildcards, you can find all records with a Last Name entry that begins with *S*. Or you can locate records with a State other than CA. Wildcards can be included in any text criteria entry, but not in numeric entries. Quattro Pro offers three different wildcards for these operations.

* The asterisk (*) takes the place of any single character or multiple characters in an entry. For example, typing **S*** specifies entries beginning with *S*. Typing **S*r** specifies entries beginning with *S* and ending with *r*, and typing ***s*** specifies entries containing *s*.

?   The question mark (?) takes the place of any single character. For example, typing **T?p** specifies entries such as Tip, Tap, and Top.

~   The tilde (~) reverses the logic of the criteria, specifying all information *except* what you specify. For example, typing **~Smith** specifies all records except those containing Smith. Typing **~S*** specifies all records except those beginning with *S*.

Use these wildcards inside your criteria entries to extend the range of possible matches in the database. Figure 14.8 shows an example.

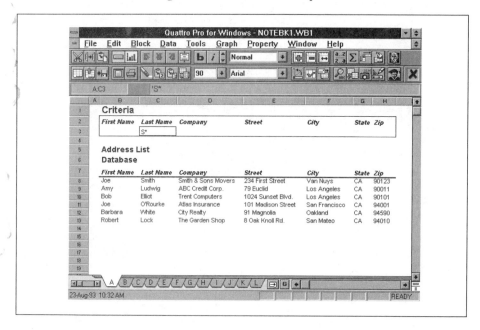

Figure 14.8 Using a wildcard in your criteria entries.

Using Conditional Criteria

Wildcards are useful for extending the possible matching records when your criteria is text. When you enter numeric criteria, however, you can include conditional operators in the criteria entry. Using conditional operators, you can specify records whose ZIP is greater than 90000 or whose PO_Number is greater than 12480 and less than 13000.

Before you can use conditional criteria, you must identify the field names in your database range by using the following procedure:

1. Highlight the cells in the database block that contain the field names for the data. This should be the first row in the database block.
2. Select the **Data>Query>Field Names** command.
3. Choose **Close**.

This procedure names each cell in the row with its own field name. You can achieve the same result using the **Block>Name>Create** command. You can now refer to these field names in your conditional criteria entries.

After the field names are established, you can create formulas in your criteria entries that specify values for the various fields. These formulas should specify the field name you want to use and a logical operation. For example, you can enter **+ZIP>90000** to specify that the ZIP Code should be greater than 90000. Figure 14.9 shows an example.

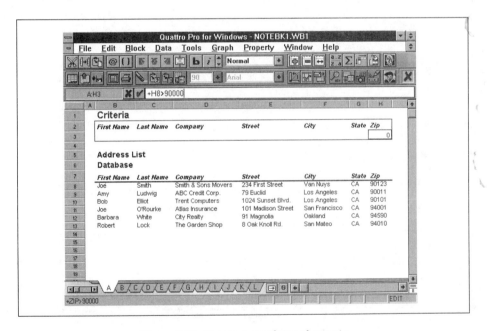

Figure 14.9 Entering conditional criteria.

Notice that the entry begins with a plus sign—this makes it a formula. The result of the calculation is not important; what's important is that you have specified a condition for the criteria and any query operation you perform.

You can also specify a range of values for a single field by using a formula such as

+PO_NUMBER>12480 #AND# PO_NUMBER<13000

For more information on conditional operations and formulas, refer to Chapter 5.

Using OR Logic in Criteria Entries

A final variation you can make in your criteria entries is the use of *OR logic*. OR logic states that either one criteria entry or another can be true. For example, the Last Name field contains Smith OR the Zip field contains 92123. Either one or both of the conditions can be met for a record to match the criteria. Using OR logic, you actually increase the potential for finding matching records than you would using AND logic.

To use OR logic for your criteria, simply enter each separate condition on a new row under the criteria block's field names. Figure 14.10 shows an example.

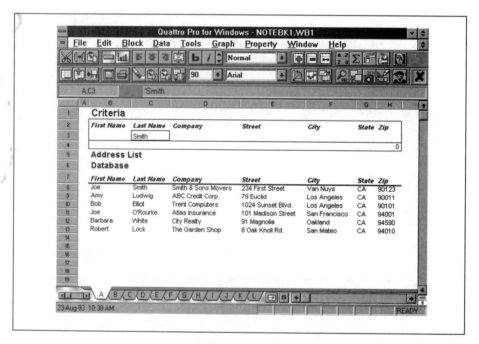

Figure 14.10 Using OR logic in your criteria range.

Note that you can combine AND logic and OR logic in the same criteria range by placing AND conditions on the same row and OR conditions on different rows. Figure 14.11 shows an example.

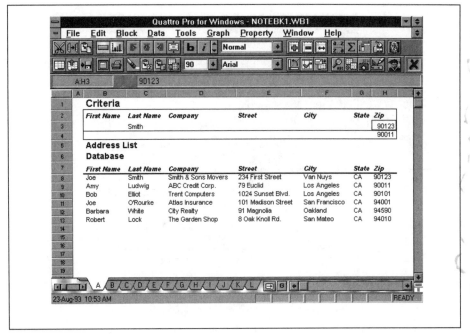

Figure 14.11 Combining AND and OR logic in your criteria range.

Database Queries

Your criteria block is the main ingredient for a database query procedure. By entering criteria into the criteria block, you can specify individual records or groups of records for searching and extracting procedures. Any time you view or manipulate a subset of the entire database, you must use a query procedure to specify the desired records.

Query procedures are available from the **Data>Query** command. Selecting this command produces the dialog box in Figure 14.12. In the three entry boxes in this dialog box, you should identify the database, criteria, and extract blocks for your database. If you have named these blocks, you can simply enter their names into the appropriate spaces. Otherwise, you can highlight each block on the worksheet to enter the block reference into the dialog box automatically. As soon as you click on the worksheet, the dialog box disappears. When you release the mouse button, the dialog box reappears so you can enter the next reference.

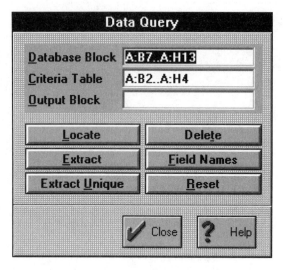

Figure 14.12 The Data Query dialog box.

When specifying the criteria block, remember to include only one row under the field names —unless you have used OR logic in your criteria entries. If you've used OR logic, highlight all rows used for the entries. Be sure that all rows in the criteria range contain criteria entries, or Quattro Pro will assume you want to find all database records.

Clear out the criteria entries
If you have trouble finding the records you've specified in your criteria range, clear out the criteria entries by highlighting the row and pressing the **Delete** key. Sometimes blank spaces appear in these cells and destroy the integrity of your query.

When entering the extract block reference, include only the one row containing the field names. Including more than one row will limit the extraction to as many rows as you've highlighted. For example, if you highlight the extract field names plus four blank rows, Quattro Pro will extract only the first four records. If you highlight only the extract field names, all records matching the criteria will be extracted.

After you have specified the three blocks in your database setup, you're ready to perform the queries. The query procedures available through this dialog box are as follows:

- **Locate** Displays specified records on the screen within the database block. Records matching the criteria will be highlighted as you press the **Down Arrow** and **Up Arrow** keys. Press the **Left Arrow** and **Right Arrow** keys to move among the fields of the currently highlighted record. Edit records by typing new data or using the **F2** key to edit the existing data. Press the **Escape** key to return to normal operation.

- **Extract** Duplicates the specified records into the extract range. Only records that match your criteria will be extracted. Original records remain in the database block.

- **Extract Unique** Same as **Extract**, but it does not extract more than one copy of the same data. If two records contain the same information in the fields you've included in the extract range, only one will be extracted. This is useful when your database contains historical records, such as customer orders or transactions. When printing a mailing list from a customer transaction database, you want only one instance of each customer—even if the database contains numerous records for that customer.

- **Delete** Removes specified records from the database.

- **Field Names** Identifies the field names in the database block and names each field in the notebook. This is useful for complex criteria formulas, when you want to refer to fields by name.

- **Reset** Clears the dialog box settings.

After you have entered the database blocks into the **Data>Query** command, you need not enter them again. The dialog box will remember your most recent specifications. Simply change your criteria, choose **Data>Query**, and select the desired procedure. However, if you use the **Data>Query** command with a high-lighted block of cells, Quattro Pro will replace the previous settings with a reference to the highlighted block. Make sure that only one cell is highlighted before using the **Data>Query** command; this eliminates the need to enter the database, criteria, and extract block references over and over.

Extracting Data

The *extract block* is an optional third component of your database setup. You need an extract block only if you perform data extraction using the **Data>Query>Extract** command. The purpose for extracting data from the database block is to view a subset of the database in one convenient columnar report. When you use the extract procedure, Quattro Pro copies the specified records from the database block and places them into a separate block, the extract block, so you can view all the records in one convenient list. The extract block, then, contains a subset of the database block—a subset determined by your criteria entries.

An extract block is simply an area where records can be placed when extracted from the database block. A good location for the extract block is directly under the database block. This gives you plenty of room for extracted records. Simply type the names of the fields you want to include in the list; you need not duplicate every field name or even match the order of fields in the database block. You should, however, make sure that the field names in the extract block are typed exactly as they are in the database block. For best results, copy the desired field names from the database block. Figure 14.13 shows an extract block for the database example.

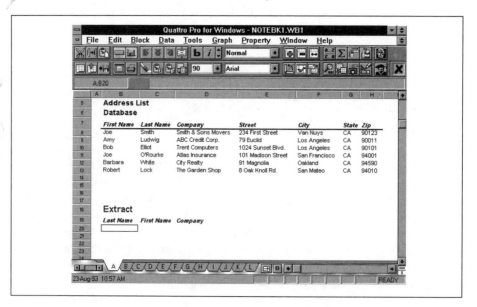

Figure 14.13 Adding an extract block to the database setup.

Notice that the field names in the extract block are ordered differently than they are in the database block—and not all the fields are included. To extract records into this area, enter your desired criteria into the criteria block, then use the **Data>Query>Extract** command.

Database Statistics

Quattro Pro provides a number of statistical functions for analyzing database data. These functions let you calculate values from specific records in a database range. The database function uses your criteria entries to select certain records from the database and makes its calculation. For example, suppose you have a database of financial transactions; each transaction shows an income or expense item, its date, and its amount (see Figure 14.14). You might want to get the sum of all expenses for a certain period, such as the first quarter. This would be the sum of all cells in the Expense column for records that fall in the specified date range.

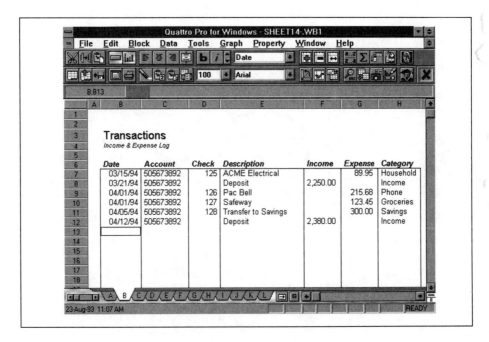

Figure 14.14 A transaction database.

You can do this by extracting the appropriate data from the database block using the **Data>Query>Extract** command and then calculating the sum of the extracted data. However, Quattro Pro's @DSUM function provides a much easier way. You simply identify the database and criteria blocks and then enter the column in the database that you want to sum. The following is the syntax for the database functions @DSUM(block,column,criteria).

Enter the reference of the database block into the *block argument.* This can be a block reference or a block name if you've named the database block. Enter the number of the field that you want to calculate—such as sum—into the *column argument.* Fields are numbered from left to right, beginning with zero (0); so, the fourth column is identified as 3 for database statistical functions. In the worksheet in Figure 14.14, you would identify column 5 for the @DSUM function, since you want to sum the Expense column. Finally, enter the desired criteria range as the *criteria argument.* Note that you can have several different criteria ranges for different database functions if you like. You need not specify the same criteria range used for query procedures.

The following is a list of database statistical functions:

Table 14.1 Database statistical functions.

Function	Description
@DSUM	Totals the values in the column you specify for all records that match the criteria.
@DMAX	Finds the maximum value in the column you specify for all records that match the criteria.
@DMIN	Finds the minimum value in the column you specify for all records that match the criteria.
@DSTD	Calculates the standard deviation among the subset of records identified by the criteria.
@DSTDS	Calculates the standard deviation among the subset of records identified by the criteria. This function uses sample statistics and assumes that the records are a sample of the entire population.
@DVAR	Calculates the variance among the subset of records identified by the criteria.
@DVARS	Calculates the variance among the subset of records identified by the criteria. This function uses sample statistics and assumes that the records are a sample of the entire population.

Sorting Records

A common database procedure is to sort the records into alphabetical, chronological, or numerical order. Sorting rearranges the database records into order based on a particular field in the database, called a key field. The *key field* is the one that determines which information is sorted. For example, you might want to sort an address list by the Last Name field, making Last Name the key field. You may want to rearrange that database into ZIP Code order by making the Zip field the key field. You can sort and resort the data whenever you like.

Quattro Pro offers a simple sorting mechanism, known as the *TurboSort tool*. To sort your database records (or any data on the notebook page, for that matter), follow these steps.

1. Select the database block without the field names. Remember not to include the field names in the sort block.

2. Press and hold the **Ctrl** and **Shift** keys; then click on the field by which you want to sort (that is, the key field). You can click anywhere in the column to identify the key field.

3. Click on the **TurboSort** button on the SpeedBar. Clicking on the top half of the button sorts the data in ascending order (from A to Z) and clicking on the bottom half sorts the data in descending order (from Z to A).

Summary

Your spreadsheet applications will likely include some data to be stored and retrieved as database data. In this chapter you learned how to set up and manage a database in Quattro Pro. Database setup includes three blocks: a database block, a criteria block, and an extract block. With all three blocks in place, you can perform database queries with the **Data>Query** command.

Remember that the database statistical functions @DSUM, @DAVG, @DMIN, and so on, provide useful calculations for subsets of your data. The **TurboSort** button helps organize your data in a more orderly fashion.

In the next chapter, we'll explore the world of macros. Using macros, you can automate complex or repetitious tasks. With the touch of a button or key combination, your macro will perform any actions you specify. Macros can be simple or complex, depending on your needs. In the next chapter, you'll learn the basics of Quattro Pro's macro features.

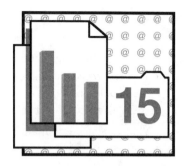

Creating Macros

You may think that macros are a complicated affair. This is not true. With Quattro Pro it's easy to create and use macros. This chapter will show you how to add the power of macros to your worksheets so you can automate those tasks that you perform over and over again. You'll find that macros are time-saving tools that can be as simple or as complex as you like. In this chapter, you'll learn

- What macro commands are and how they work
- How to record simple macros
- Several ways to play back your macros
- How to build custom menus

393

What Is a Macro?

A *macro* is a list of instructions for Quattro Pro to carry out. This list consists of *macro commands* that tell Quattro Pro exactly what you want it to do. You simply enter commands down a column of cells, and Quattro Pro reads them when instructed. Each command is carried out in order.

What types of commands appear in a macro? The same types of commands that you can perform through Quattro Pro's menus and options. For example, you can instruct Quattro Pro to print a certain area of the notebook, or you can tell Quattro Pro to change the values in certain cells. Anything you can do using the mouse or keyboard, you can place in a macro for Quattro Pro to do automatically.

Why use a macro when you can perform the commands yourself? Because Quattro Pro executes a macro much faster than you can perform the commands manually. Plus, macros are ideal for repetitious or complex tasks—tasks that would take much time to complete manually.

An easy way to create a macro is to record your actions and play the recording back again later. Quattro Pro offers a special macro recording tool that translates your every action into macro commands—building a macro as you go. Later, you can "play back" this macro recording to repeat everything you did. In this way, you complete a procedure only once, and Quattro Pro can repeat it thousands of times.

Macros are ideal for printing tasks, moving around the notebook, formatting, and any task that you perform repeatedly. You can even use macros to customize the notebook.

Recording Simple Macros

The easiest way to create a macro is to let Quattro Pro do the work. Quattro Pro's special macro recorder can automatically convert your keystrokes and mouse movements into a macro—and store that macro anywhere in your notebook. The macro recorder literally records everything you do so you can play it back later.

To record a macro, begin with the desired notebook in view and the cell pointer in the desired location. Remember that your movements will be recorded relative to your starting point. If you start recording your macro with page B of your notebook active, you should have page B active when you replay the macro, too. Here are the steps for recording a macro.

1. Select the **Tools>Macro>Record** command.

2. Enter the page and cell address where you want Quattro Pro to store the completed macro. For best results, enter the address of a single cell (not a block) on a blank page of the notebook. For example, you might enter **D:A1** to store the macro on page D, starting at cell A1. You can click on the desired cell and page to enter its reference into this dialog box automatically, or you can enter a block name if you have named the desired cell. (If you select a block, Quattro Pro will not exceed the size of the block when listing macro commands. Hence, your macro might be cut short.)

3. Choose **OK**. Quattro Pro is now recording your every move and storing the recording in the location you specified.

4. Perform the desired actions, commands, and procedures. As an example, try turning the notebook grid lines off by selecting the following commands:

   Properties>Active Page

   Grid lines

   Vertical (remove check mark)

   Horizontal (remove check mark)

   OK

   When you are finished, choose **Tools>Macro>Stop Record**.

5. Move the cell pointer to the first cell in the macro. This is probably the cell you specified in Step 2, above. The macro should look something like Figure 15.1.

6. With the cell pointer on the first cell of the macro, choose **Block>Name>Create** and enter a name for the macro, as shown in Figure 15.2. Choose **OK** when finished.

After you have completed the macro recording, you can run the macro to repeat the actions you recorded. As mentioned earlier, these actions will be repeated much more quickly than you originally performed them. To run the macro, choose **Tools>Macro>Execute** and select the macro's name from the list provided. If the macro does not appear in this list, you may not have performed Step 6 of the previous list.

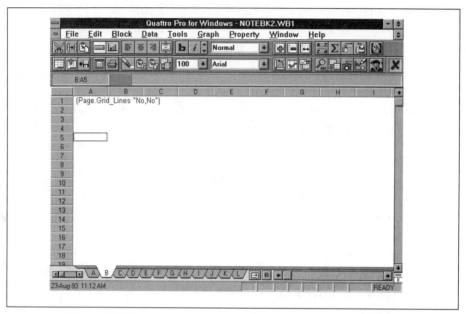

Figure 15.1   A sample macro recorded onto page B of the notebook.

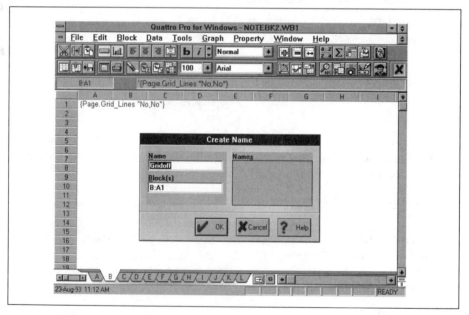

Figure 15.2   Remember to name your macros after you record them.

Use a common starting point

Remember that your starting point might have changed since you recorded the macro—and this could affect the macro when you run it later. For example, if you recorded a macro that turns off the current notebook page's grid lines, you should run the macro only when the current page has grid lines. If the grid lines are already off when you run the macro, nothing will happen. A macro that makes changes to data on the page or uses relative record references (see "Relative Recording," later in this chapter) could cause problems if run from the wrong starting point.

Here are some guidelines for recording your macros.

- Enter the macro onto a blank page. You can specify any cell as the starting point for the recorded macro, but storing the macro onto a blank notebook page is a good practice. If you record several macros for the same notebook, they can all appear on the same page—perhaps spaced two columns apart. This makes them easier to manage and edit.

- Name the macro. After recording the macro, remember to move to the macro page, place the cell pointer in the first cell of the recorded commands, and use the **Block>Name>Create** command to name the macro. If you fail to name the macro, you can't use the **Tools>Macro>Execute** command to run it.

- Start the macro with your worksheet in the desired state. The macro will duplicate your recorded commands and actions exactly as you recorded them. You might have to start the macro with the notebook set up as it was when you recorded it.

- Enter a single cell for the macro location. Unless you have a reason to limit the number of commands the macro will record, enter only one cell when specifying the location for the macro. As Quattro Pro records you actions, it enters commands down the column, starting at the cell you specified.

Relative Recording

If you move the cell pointer or select blocks of cells while recording a macro, you could notice that the macro repeats exactly what you recorded—it selects the same blocks you selected. For example, suppose you highlight the block A:B1..M1 and select the **Boldface** tool; you record these actions in a macro. No matter where you move the cell pointer within the notebook, when you run this macro, it will highlight the same block, A:B1..M1, and invoke the boldface format.

Suppose, however, that you want the macro to boldface the range B1..M1 on whichever page you happen to be using at the time. If you have page C active, running the macro adds boldface to the range C:B1..M1. If you have page D active, the range D:B1..M1 gets boldface applied to it. In this way, the macro is applied relative to your current position. If you start on cell B1, you get the range B1..M1. If you start on cell G5, you get the range G5..S5. Using this type of relative macro, you can record commands that can later be applied to any block of cells on any page.

Here's how you record a macro that applies commands relative to your current position. Select the **Tools>Macro>Options>Relative** command before performing the actions you want to be made relative. You can switch back to Absolute references at any time during the recording if you want to record normally. Try this experiment.

1. On a new, blank notebook page, move the cell pointer to cell B1.

2. Choose **Tools>Macro>Record**.

3. Choose **Tools>Macro>Options>Relative** and press **OK** when finished.

4. Enter the reference **B:A1** as the location for the macro and choose **OK** to start the recording.

5. Type **January** into cell B1 and press **Enter**.

6. Hold the **Shift** key as you press the **Right Arrow** key five times. This highlights the range B1..G1.

7. Click on the **Fill** button on the SpeedBar (it's the second button from the right edge). This enters the month names into the highlighted block.

8. Select **Tools>Macro>Stop Record**.

9. Move to B:A1 and name the macro with the **Block>Names>Create** command.

Now move the cell pointer to cell G5 on page B and run the macro using the command **Tools>Macro>Execute**. The macro will automatically enter the month names, starting at cell G5 on page B. This is a relative macro. Now repeat the procedure without Step 3 and run the macro again. You'll notice a big difference. This time, Quattro Pro will add the month names to the range A:B1..G1.

Creating a Macro Manually

You can create a macro by entering macro commands manually, typing them into the worksheet. The main advantage to this method is that you can use commands that are unavailable through the macro recorder. Not all macro commands are equivalent to a menu command or mouse movement, those available for advanced macros, for example. These commands let you create custom menus, control the flow of the macro, pause for user input, and perform different tasks based on values entered. You can even use macros to display messages on the screen when certain actions are performed.

If you enter macro commands by hand, you must place them in a column in the order you want them executed. When finished, you must name the macro by moving to the first command in the column and choosing the **Block>Names>Create** command. Be careful not to stack two macros on top of each other without a blank cell between them.

The disadvantages of manually creating macros are somewhat obvious. You must find and correctly enter each and every macro command into the worksheet in the proper order. This means you should have a complete listing of macro commands handy for your reference. Such a listing is available in the Quattro Pro for Windows *Building a Spreadsheet Application* manual that comes with your Quattro Pro product. Remember that any errors in entry can render the macro useless.

Running Your Macro

Running macros (also known as *executing*) is a way of replaying them when you need them. After recording or typing a macro, you can run it at any time. You've already seen one method of running your completed macros: By choosing the **Tools>Macro>Execute** command, you can run any macro stored in the active notebook. But Quattro Pro gives you several other ways to run macros. You can attach them to buttons if you want to run the macro at the click of the button. You can create custom menu commands to run your macros, and you can run macros automatically when you open a notebook.

Using the Execute Command

One common way to run macros is to use the **Tools>Macro>Execute** command. This command presents a list of macros currently available on the active notebook. These are macros that you have properly named. Just choose the desired macro from the list and click on **OK**—or double-click on the macro's name to execute it.

Using a Macro Shortcut Key

Quattro Pro lets you assign special shortcut keys to as many as 26 different macros in the same notebook. By pressing the **Ctrl** key along with the shortcut key, you can quickly execute the macro. Shortcut keys can be any letter of the alphabet. Assigning the **A** key to a macro lets you run the macro by pressing **Ctrl-A**.

 Use upper- or lowercase letters

You can use either upper- or lowercase letters for your shortcut keys. Quattro Pro will run the macro whether you press **Ctrl-A** or **Ctrl-a**.

To assign a shortcut key to a macro, simply enter the desired key, preceded by a backslash (\), as the macro's name using the **Block>Name>Create** command. For example, to assign the **A** key to a macro, move to the first command in the macro and choose the **Block>Name>Create** command. Now enter **\A** as the macro name and press **Enter**. After you have done this, you can run the macro by pressing **Ctrl-A**. By using the **Block>Names>Create** command twice, you can assign a normal name to the macro—in addition to \A.

Buttons and Tools

Another way to run a macro is to attach it to a button on the notebook. Unlike SpeedBar tools, notebook buttons are part of the notebook page on which you place them. Clicking on the button runs the macro attached to it. Notebook buttons are useful for macros that apply to specific notebook pages—or specific areas of a notebook page. For example, you might add a button next to a table of values that prints the table. This button might simply display the words Print Table to indicate its purpose. This button remains beside the table at all times, and you can click on the button only when the table is in view. Hence, notebook buttons are useful for performing actions specific to an area of the notebook. Some other ideas include:

- Displaying or altering a graph
- Altering values in a table to show other scenarios
- Printing an area of the notebook
- Displaying notes about an area
- Displaying a custom dialog box that relates to the area

Drawing the Button

To add a button to the notebook, you must draw it onto the page using the **Button** tool in the SpeedBar. Click on the tool—the fourth from the left edge of the toolbar—then click and drag on the page to draw the button. When you release the mouse, the button appears (see Figure 15.3).

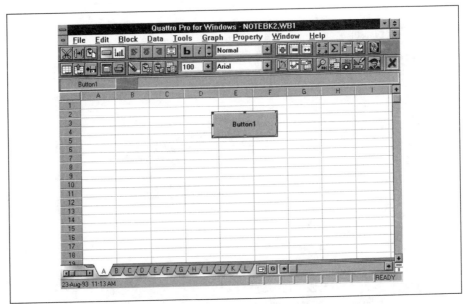

Figure 15.3 A notebook button drawn onto the page.

Before you assign a macro to the button, you can move and resize the button using the mouse. Move the button by dragging it to a new location. Resize the button by dragging one of the selection boxes (also known as *handles*) that appear around the edges when you click on the button. The mouse pointer will change to a plus sign when positioned over one of these handles. Now you may click and drag on the handle to change the size and shape of the button.

After you assign a macro to the button, you can move or size it by right-clicking directly on the button. This selects the button and displays the handles around its edges.

Changing the Button's Appearance

The next step in creating your notebook button is to customize its appearance. You can change the text inside the button or even display a picture in it. Other enhancements include changing the button's border style and color.

By right-clicking on the button, you can inspect the various properties associated with the object. Figure 15.4 shows the property inspector for button objects. These properties are explained below.

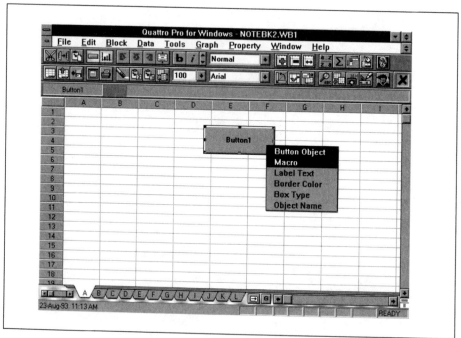

Figure 15.4 Right-click the button to display its properties.

Table 15.1 Properties Table.

Properties	Description
Macro Text	Use this option to attach a macro or to assign a few simple macro commands to the button. This option is described in "Attaching the Macro," later in this chapter.
Label Text	This option lets you change the text inside the button.
Border Color	Choose this option to change the color of the button's border. To remove the border, use the **Box Type None** option.
Box Type	This option affects the button box. You can use a thick or thin line, add a drop-shadow, or remove the box completely.
Object Name	An object's name can be used in macros to manipulate that object. If you will be manipulating the button from a macro, use this command to establish a unique name for the button.

Using these commands, you can create buttons with a variety of shapes, sizes, and styles. You can even create invisible buttons, which can be useful for covering up parts of your notebook. When you select a cell underneath the button, you click on the button, and you can retrieve it.

Another way to enhance your buttons is to fill them with graphic images. You can paste any bitmapped graphic image into a button, as shown in Figure 15.5. You can copy the graphics from any graphics program, then switch to Quattro Pro, select the button object, and choose **Edit>Paste**.

Using Quattro Pro's powerful graphics-importation capabilities, you can also perform the entire procedure right within Quattro Pro. Follow these steps.

1. Select **Graph>New**.

2. Click on **OK**.

3. Using the **Rectangle** tool, draw a rectangle in the graph window. Draw the rectangle the exact size and shape you want for the final button (see Figure 15.6).

4. Right-click on the rectangle and choose the **Fill Style** option.

5. Click on the **Bitmap** option at the bottom of the window. Then, choose the **Browse** button to locate and select the desired graphics file. This should be a file with the BMP, GIF, PCX, or TIF extension. The path name of the file you choose will appear in the dialog box.

6. After selecting the file, choose **Crop to Fit** or **Shrink to Fit**, depending on the type of image you selected and the outcome you want. (Refer to Chapter 12 for more information on these options.)

7. Click on **OK**. The rectangle should now contain the bitmap shown in Figure 15.7.

8. Select **Edit>Copy** to copy the object and its graphic fill.

9. Activate the worksheet and select the button. If the button has a macro attached, you must right-click to select it.

10. Choose **Edit>Paste**. The button will now appear like the rectangle but will retain its button qualities. Figure 15.8 shows the completed example.

For more details on using graphics, see Chapter 12.

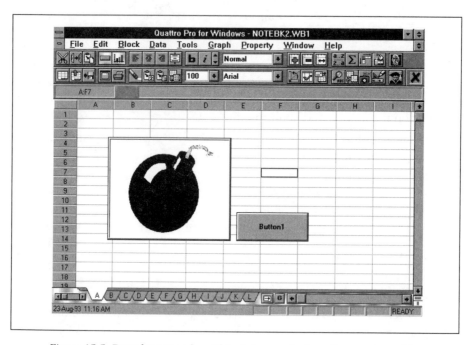

Figure 15.5 Paste bitmapped graphics into your buttons for a unique effect.

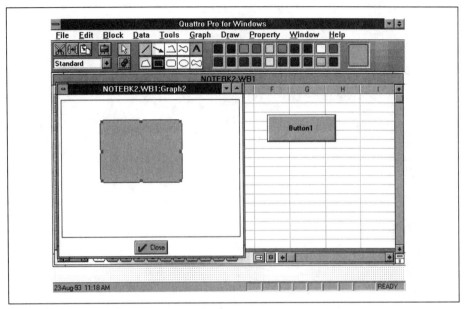

Figure 15.6 Drawing a rectangle for the graphic image.

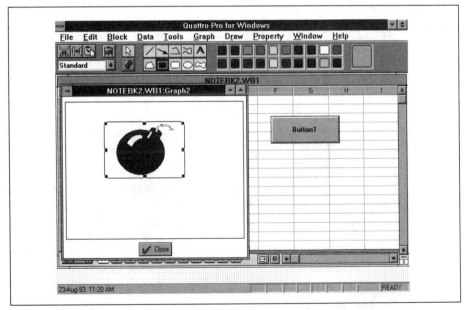

Figure 15.7 Fill the rectangle with the desired bitmapped graphic.

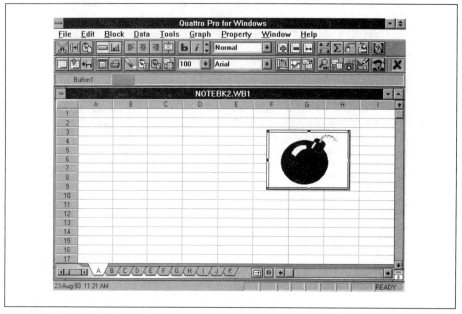

Figure 15.8 Paste the rectangle into the button object.

Attaching the Macro

When you are ready to attach a macro to the button, simply right-click on the button and choose the **Macro** option. The dialog box in Figure 15.9 will be displayed.

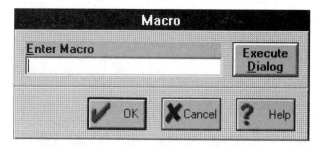

Figure 15.9 The Macro dialog box.

In the space provided, you can enter either a series of macro commands or a reference to a macro stored in the notebook. If you enter a series of commands, you will be limited to 200 characters. Entering commands directly into the space is useful for simple procedures, such as displaying graphs or printing. Figure 15.10 shows an example. For more complex procedures that exceed the 200-character limit, you should refer to a macro located in the notebook.

Figure 15.10 Enter the macro command directly into the Macro dialog box.

To refer to a macro, enter the command **{BRANCH *name*}**, where *name* is the name of the macro you want to run. For example, to run a macro named Months, which is contained on page B of the current notebook, you would enter **{BRANCH B:Months}** into the dialog box, as Figure 15.11 shows.

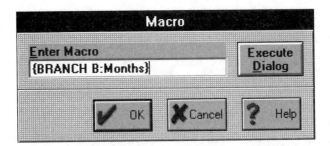

Figure 15.11 Branching to a macro contained in the notebook.

Executing a dialog box from a notebook button

The **Execute Dialog** button in the Macro Text dialog box lets you display a custom dialog box by clicking on the notebook button. Click on **Execute Dialog** to display a list of custom dialog boxes in the active notebook, choose the dialog box you want to display, and then click on **OK**. Whenever you click on the notebook button, the dialog box will be displayed. For information on creating custom dialog boxes, refer to Chapter 16.

Custom Menus

You can conveniently run your macros through a custom menu. You can add a new menu to Quattro Pro's menu bar—each command within the menu can be the name of a different macro. This way, you don't have to remember shortcut commands or use the **Execute** command to run your macros. Adding custom menus is a useful technique when your notebooks and macros will be used by other operators—who might not be familiar with your macros or with Quattro Pro. By adding a custom menu, all your automation macros can be accessed as if they were part of Quattro Pro. Figure 15.12 shows a custom menu with several commands in it.

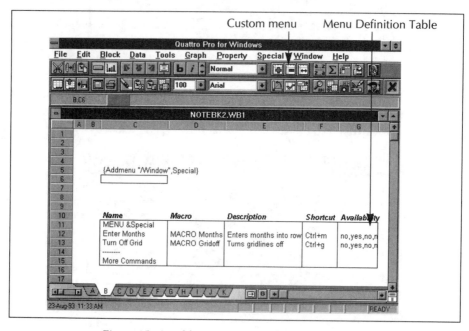

Figure 15.12 Adding a custom menu to Quattro Pro.

Each command in the menu runs a different macro stored in the notebook. To create a custom menu, you must first create the macros to run for each menu command; then you need to add a table to the page containing the macros. This table defines the menu and its commands; it should contain five columns. Finally, add a simple macro to invoke the menu into action. This macro needs only one command—although it can contain more—called **ADDMENU**. In summary, custom menus require three components:

- A macro, consisting of the **ADDMENU** command, to activate the menu
- A menu-definition table
- Macros to run when the menu's commands are selected

You already know about the third item in this list; these are the individual macros that you want to invoke from a menu. The next two sections will explain the menu-definition table and the command used to activate the menu.

The Menu-Definition Table

The menu-definition table contains five columns that describe the menu and its items. Figure 15.13 shows a typical menu-definition table, with headings to describe each of the five columns. Note that the headings are not technically part of the table itself; they are added to make the table easier to read.

Name	Macro	Description	Shortcut	Availability
MENU &Special				
Enter Months	MACRO Months	Enters months into row	Ctrl+m	no,yes,no,n
Turn Off Grid	MACRO Gridoff	Turns gridlines off	Ctrl+g	no,yes,no,n
--------				
More Commands				

Figure 15.13 A typical menu-definition table.

Column One: The Menu Name and Commands

Column one of the table contains the names of the menu and its commands. The first cell in the column should begin with the command **MENU *name***, where *name* is the name of the menu you want to add. For example, enter **MENU Special** to give the name Special to the menu. Place an ampersand (&) before any character in the name that you want used as the action key. For example, enter **MENU &Special** to establish *S* as the action key for the menu; enter **MENU Spe&cial** to establish *c* as the action key. In this way, you can invoke the menu by pressing **Alt-S** or **Alt-c**. Be sure to specify an action key that is not already used for another menu.

Under the menu name, enter the names of the commands you want inside the menu. These do not have to match your macro names; you can use any name you like, including two or more words. Use the ampersand (&) to specify the action keys in these names. You can specify an action key for a command name even if it was used for a menu, since only the action keys within the same menu will conflict. To create a line between commands, type eight dashes, beginning with the apostrophe, as in '--------.

Column Two: The Macro To Run

Beside each command name, enter the command **MACRO** *name*, where *name* is the name of the macro you want to run when the command is selected. In the example, the command **Enter Months** is followed by **MACRO B:Months**. The command you specify can be on any page of the active notebook or on any other notebook page—provided you enter the entire macro reference. If you leave this column blank, the command (or dividing line) will have no effect.

Column Three: Status Line Text

In column three of the table, enter any text you want displayed on the status line when the command is highlighted. When you use the mouse to highlight the command, the text in column three appears on the status line. All Quattro Pro menu commands display these status-line messages.

Column Four: Shortcut Key

If the macro referenced in column two is named with a shortcut key (such as \m), you can include that information in the menu. Just type **Ctrl-m** into column four of the definition table. This will appear beside the command name to remind the operator that the shortcut **Ctrl-m** will also invoke the macro. This column is added for convenience, to help you link the shortcut key (if used) to the menu command.

Column Five: Availability

In column five you can specify when the menu command is available. There are six areas of availability for your command:

- When no notebook is active
- When a notebook is active
- When a graph window is active
- When a dialog box is active
- When you are editing the Input Line
- When the graphs page is active

As you can see, most macros are created to operate on the active notebook and should not be allowed when a dialog box or graph is active. To specify under which of these conditions the command is available, enter **yes** (available) or **no** (unavailable) for each of these six areas in a text string (surrounded by quotation marks). Enter these in the order shown above. For example, you might enter **no, yes, no, no, no, no, no** into column five to indicate that the command should be available only when a notebook is active. If you omit this column, the command will be available at all times.

Adding Submenus

You can make a menu command display more menu commands if you like. Just leave column two blank for the desired command and place the next level of commands one cell below and to the right of the command. Then enter all five columns for the commands in the submenu. Figure 15.14 shows an example.

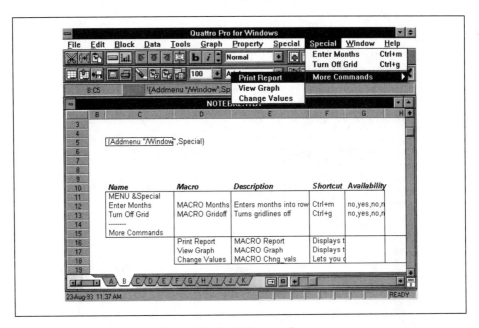

Figure 15.14 Adding a submenu.

Just remember that each submenu level extends the definition table by one column. Later, when you identify the definition table, you must include all rows and columns that contain the menu and submenus.

Activating the Menu

When you have completed the definition table, you are ready for the final step: creating the macro that activates the menu. This macro is very simple and requires only one command:

{ADDMENU *"menu_path",definition_table*}

This command requires two arguments. The *menu_path* argument identifies where the menu should appear. Enter the name, preceded by a slash, of any existing menu on the Quattro Pro menu bar. This places the new menu onto the menu bar just before the menu you specify. For example, to place your custom menu between the Property and Window menus, enter **"/Window"** as the menu_path argument. Be sure to include the quotation marks.

You can add your menu as an item within an existing menu by including a command within the menu_path. For example, to add your menu above the Tile command in the Window menu, enter **"/Window/Tile"** as the menu_path.

The *definition_table* argument identifies the menu definition table you built. It should be a block name or a reference to the block containing the table. If your definition table includes submenus, be sure to include the entire submenu into the block. Figure 15.15 shows the completed macro.

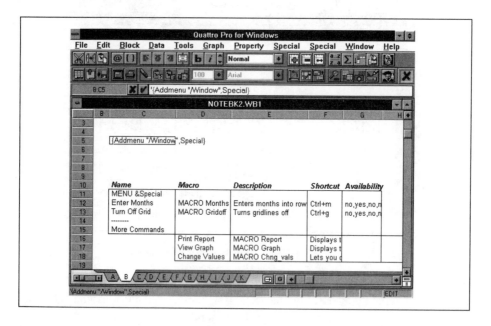

Figure 15.15 The finished menu activation macro.

When you are finished with the macro, be sure to name it using the **Block>Names>Create** command. You can assign the macro a shortcut key if you like; this lets you bring up the custom menu when you press the shortcut key. Attach the macro to a notebook button to activate the menu when you click on the button. You can also make the macro an autoexec macro if you want the menu displayed as soon as you open the notebook. (Autoexec macros are discussed below.)

Remove Your Custom Menus When Finished

Use the **DELETEMENUITEM** command to remove your custom menu from the menu bar. This command can be added to a separate button on the notebook, or it can be placed in a command in the custom menu itself (for example, as a Remove this menu command).

Custom Dialogs

Custom dialog boxes can be used to run macros. Chapter 16 explains how to create custom dialog boxes and SpeedBars in Quattro Pro. Generally, custom dialog boxes are activated by a notebook button or a custom menu.

Autoexec Macros

A final way to run a macro is as an *autoexec macro*. An autoexec macro runs each time you open the notebook and is useful for adding custom menus or performing tasks that apply each time you use the notebook.

You can make any macro an autoexec macro by naming it **\0** (backslash zero). Do this with the **Block>Names>Create** command. Now save the notebook. When you next open the notebook, the macro specified as \0 will automatically run. As always, you can apply a second, more descriptive name to the macro.

An Overview of Macro Commands

Chances are, most of your macros will be simple, recorded ones. If you simply want to automate a procedure using a macro, you can probably avoid having to type macro commands manually. Just record and name the macro, and you're done. But you might run into tasks that require additional macro power. In this case, an overview of Quattro Pro's macro commands will come in handy. The following sections explain most of Quattro Pro's macro commands.

Command-Equivalent Commands

Many macro commands are simply equivalent to menu and dialog box commands. These commands are all recordable using the macro recorder. If you want to know the macro command that duplicates the **File>Open** procedure, for example, simply turn on the macro recorder, use the **File>Open** command, stop the recorder, and then look at the macro to see what command was used. You'll always be able to determine command-equivalent macro commands this way. Hence, we will not list them all here.

Mouse and Keystroke Commands

Like command-equivalent macro commands, mouse and keystroke commands duplicate actions you can take with the mouse or keyboard. You can duplicate each and every keystroke or mouse movement in a macro using these commands. Since these are all recordable, we won't list the commands here. To determine the command required for a mouse or keyboard activity, simply record the activity and examine the results. You'll find the resulting commands quite easy to decipher. They will remind you of their purpose. For example, pressing the **Home** key will result in the macro command {**HOME**}.

Macro Programming Commands

Macro programming commands are useful for controlling your macros. You can use these commands to control the flow of a macro, to activate windows in which a macro should run, and more. Following is a summary of these commands.

- {**ACTIVATE** *WindowName*} Activates the window specified by *WindowName*.
- {**BREAKON**} {**BREAKOFF**} Enables or disables the **Ctrl-Break** command, which cancels a macro midstream. Using {**BREAKOFF**} prohibits a user from interrupting the macro.
- {**WINDOWSOFF**} {**WINDOWSON**} Enables or disables screen updating during a macro. Use {**WINDOWSOFF**} to eliminate the screen movement during long macros.
- * {**PAUSEMACRO**} Pauses a macro. This is useful after invoking a dialog box.

- **{WAIT *DateTimeNumber*}** Pauses a macro for a specified time indicated by *DateTimeNumber*.

- **{BRANCH *Location*}** Branches macro flow to another location specified by *Location*. This is useful in buttons and dialog boxes to run long macros when the button is pressed. It is also useful in graph button macros.

- **{IF *Condition*}** Tests for a condition and, if met, continues macro flow. If the condition is not met, the macro stops.

- **{*Subroutine*}** Branches to a macro subroutine or another macro. Simply enter the name of the macro or subroutine in braces.

User Interface and Interaction Commands

These commands are useful for building a custom user interface in Quattro Pro. Some of these commands were explored in this chapter; others appear in Chapter 16. Following is an overview of the interaction commands.

- **{?}** Pauses the macro and accepts input from the keyboard. When the user presses **Enter**, the macro continues.

- **{ADDMENU *MenuPath,MenuData*}** Adds a menu, specified by *MenuData* to the menu location specified by *MenuPath*. Refer to examples earlier in this chapter for details.

- **{ADDMENUITEM *MenuPath,Command*}** Adds a menu item to an existing menu specified by *MenuPath*. The menu item is specified by *Command*.

- **{BEEP <*Number*>}** Plays a "beep" for the specified number of seconds.

- **{*CHOOSE*}** Displays a list of windows from which you can choose. This is useful for menu commands or dialog box buttons.

- **{DELETEMENU *MenuPath*}** Removes a menu specified by *MenuPath*.

- **{DELETEMENUITEM *MenuPath*}** Deletes a menu item specified by *MenuPath*.

- **{DODIALOG *DialogName,OKExit?,Arguments,MacUse?*}** Activates the dialog box specified by *DialogName*. This is required for displaying custom dialog boxes.

- **{GET *Location*}** Pauses the macro and accepts keystrokes from the operator. Keystrokes are stored in the location specified by *Location*.

- **{GETLABEL *Prompt,Location*}** Pauses the macro, displays the message indicated by the *Prompt* string and accepts keystrokes from the operator. Keystrokes are stored as text in the location specified by *Location*.

- **{GETNUMBER *Prompt,Location*}** Pauses the macro, displays the message indicated by the *Prompt* string and accepts keystrokes from the operator. Keystrokes are stored as values in the location specified by *Location*.

- **{GRAPHCHAR *Location*}** Stores a keystroke used to exit a message or on-screen graph. The character is stored in *Location* and can be used to perform specific actions depending on which key is pressed. This command allows you to create messages the include instructions like "Press Y to continue."

- **{MENUBRANCH *Location*}** Branches to a custom menu table stored at *Location*.

- **{MESSAGE *Block,Left,Top,Time*}** Presents a message located at *Block* for a specified *Time*. The arguments *Left* and *Top* determine where the top-left corner of the message box appears on the screen.

Summary

Macros are not as complicated or advanced as you may have thought. This chapter gave you a complete introduction to Quattro Pro's macro capabilities and showed you how to create your own macros quickly and easily using the macro recorder. You also learned how to identify and enter macro commands into a notebook.

Remember that macros should be recorded or typed onto a blank page of the notebook for best results. After you have entered your macros, you can run them in many different ways: from custom menus, from notebook buttons, using the **Tools>Macro>Execute** command, or as autoexec macros.

Now that you have an understanding of Quattro Pro's macro features, you're ready to build your own dialog boxes and SpeedBars. You can invoke your macros through the buttons and controls in your custom dialog boxes and SpeedBars. The next chapter shows you how to uses these elements to build a custom user interface for your notebook applications.

Building a Custom User Interface

A user interface is a combination of elements with which a user interacts. Quattro Pro's user interface includes three primary elements: menus (appearing on the Menu bar at the top of the screen), dialog boxes (which are usually presented after choosing a Menu command), and SpeedBars (which contain buttons and tools to make tasks easier). Creating a custom user interface is simply a matter of creating your own menus, dialog boxes, and SpeedBars. In the previous chapter, you saw how to create custom menus. This chapter describes how to create your own dialog boxes and SpeedBars and how to present these elements when you want to use them. Specifically, you will learn about

- Placing tools onto a dialog box or SpeedBar
- Making your tools perform actions with macros
- Making tools control the values in your notebooks
- Connecting dialog boxes and SpeedBars to menu commands
- Connecting dialog boxes and SpeedBars to buttons

This chapter provides a solid grounding in custom user interfaces, a topic that can involve many advanced techniques and procedures. For more information, refer to an advanced book about Quattro Pro for Windows.

Why Build a Custom User Interface?

A custom user interface is useful when your notebook application will be used by people other than yourself. You can make it easy for others to enter data, print reports, and generally get around in your application, by including custom menus, dialog boxes, and SpeedBars. The more you customize the user interface, the less a user needs to know about Quattro Pro for Windows. Your custom commands and tools will take care of everything.

For example, suppose you create an income-and-expense log to record all monetary transactions for your business. At the end of each month, you can use database query procedures to summarize these transactions under specific categories. This report shows how much you've spent in each expense category. Rather than teach your assistant how to perform a database query in Quattro Pro, you can create a custom menu command—such as Create Summary Report—that performs the procedure automatically. All your assistant has to do is choose the menu command.

With custom user-interface elements, you can create custom data-entry forms; secondary SpeedBars that combine tools used for specific tasks; report-printing commands, buttons, or menu commands for moving among various pages or sections of an application; and dialog boxes that manipulate values on the page.

When creating custom interface elements, imagine the easiest and best way to accomplish a task in your application—then decide whether you can accomplish that through a custom interface.

Building Dialog Boxes and SpeedBars

You've already seen how to build custom menus in Quattro Pro for Windows. You've also seen how to build your own SpeedBars using the built-in tools available in the SpeedBar Designer. This chapter concentrates on creating dialog boxes and SpeedBars that contain custom-built tools; you'll learn the major techniques for making your dialog boxes and SpeedBars perform actions that you determine. The basic procedure involves creating the dialog box or SpeedBar in the UI Builder; adding custom tools; defining the activities that each tool performs; attaching macros to these tools; and linking the dialog box or SpeedBar to a menu command, notebook button, autoexec macro, or other tool—so that it can be accessed in a natural way. The following sections provide an overview of the process.

The Basic Process

Quattro Pro offers dozens of options for your dialog boxes and SpeedBars. Just looking at them all can be intimidating. When you cut through the extraneous options, however, the basic procedure is quite simple. There are five basic steps:

1. Create a dialog box or SpeedBar using the **Tools>UI Builder** command or by moving to the Graph page and clicking on the **SpeedBar** or **Dialog Box** tools. You can also enter the UI Builder through the SpeedBar Designer, which is useful for adding custom tools to your existing SpeedBar.

2. Add controls and set properties for those controls. Add controls using the UI Builder SpeedBar that appears at the top of the screen after you complete Step 1. After you add a control, right-clicking on the control presents a list of its properties.

3. Establish links and connections. Each control can be *linked* to a macro to perform specific actions. Alternatively, a control can be *connected* to a cell in the notebook. When the cell changes, the control changes, and vice versa.

4. Test the controls. Run the dialog box or SpeedBar in test mode to see whether your links and connections are working.

5. Link the dialog box to a {DODIALOG} macro somewhere in your notebook.

The following sections explain these steps and provide hints for keeping your custom dialog boxes and SpeedBars simple and effective.

Starting a New Dialog Box or SpeedBar

Each new dialog box you create is added as an icon to the notebook's Graphs page. In this way, you can create numerous dialog boxes and work on each of them by double-clicking on the icon. These icons can be manipulated similarly to the graph icons that are displayed on this page. Figure 16.1 shows a Graphs page with these icons present.

Choosing the **Tools>UI Builder** command automatically starts a new dialog box and adds it to the Graphs page of the notebook. You can also move to the Graphs page and click on the **Dialog Box** tool:

Figure 16.2 shows a new dialog box on the screen.

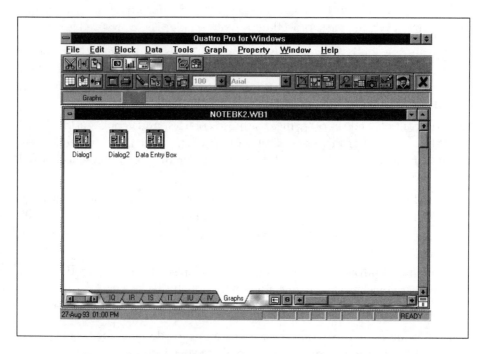

Figure 16.1 Dialog Box icons on the Graphs page of a notebook.

Notice that the **OK** and **Cancel** buttons have already been added to the box. These are standard buttons for exiting the box. The **OK** button invokes the options you choose in the dialog box, and the **Cancel** button aborts them. Although you can remove these two buttons from the dialog box, you'll probably want to keep them.

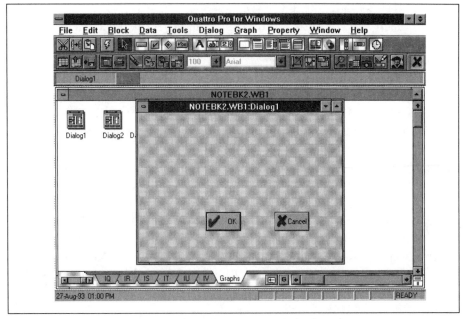

Figure 16.2 Starting a new dialog box.

To start a new SpeedBar, move to the Graphs page and click on the **SpeedBar** tool:

This gives you a brand new SpeedBar inside the UI Builder. You can also bring existing SpeedBars into the UI Builder to add custom tools to the built-in tools already on the SpeedBar. To bring an existing SpeedBar into the UI Builder for further development, enter the SpeedBar Designer and create or open the desired SpeedBar as described in Chapter 4. When you are ready to add custom tools to your SpeedBar, click on the **UI Builder** icon inside the SpeedBar Designer:

This takes you directly into the UI Builder with your SpeedBar in view. You can now add custom interface tools to the SpeedBar.

SpeedBars are not added to the Graphs page; they're saved as special files on disk, called *SpeedBar files*. SpeedBar files are given the BAR extension when saved. Since custom SpeedBars are saved on disk, they can be opened in any notebook application. Dialog boxes, on the other hand, reside in the notebook in which they were created and can be used only with that notebook. Although SpeedBars can be used with many different notebooks, you can still create them for use with specific notebooks. Generally, however, custom SpeedBars are generic to notebooks and contain controls that apply to any notebook.

SpeedBars are stored in the QPW directory

NOTE

Quattro Pro's secondary SpeedBars can be found in the QPW directory. Others may appear in the QPW\SAMPLES directory. You might want to save your custom SpeedBar files in this same directory to keep them all together. SpeedBar files can be opened by using the **Property>Application>SpeedBar>Browse** command or by right-clicking in the blank area of a secondary SpeedBar and using the **Append>Browse** command from the properties menu that appears. Refer to Chapter 4 for more details about accessing secondary SpeedBars.

Dialog Box and SpeedBar Properties

Once you add a custom dialog box or SpeedBar to the Graphs page, you can access special properties for the item. With the dialog box or SpeedBar on the screen, right-click on the background to access the properties shown in Figure 16.3.

Figure 16.3 Dialog box and SpeedBar properties.

Here is a summary of these properties.

- **Dimension** Using an X and Y coordinate, sets the dimensions of the dialog box or SpeedBar. The Width and Height settings control how large the box is. An easier way to set dimensions is to change the window position and size using standard windowing procedures.

- **Title** Determines the title displayed in the dialog box's title bar.

- **Position Adjust** Specifies the resulting movement of a dialog box control when a parent control is moved.

- **Grid Options** Enables or disables the window grid for aligning controls within the dialog box. Also lets you control the window grid size. This is useful when you are first adding controls to the dialog box or SpeedBar.

- **Name** Sets the name of the dialog box or SpeedBar. This name is useful for macro commands, such as {DODIALOG}, that refer to the dialog box.

- **Disabled** Determines whether the dialog box is enabled or disabled. A disabled dialog box cannot be used.

Exiting the UI Builder

While you are working in the UI Builder on your dialog box or SpeedBar, you will have access only to the UI Builder commands and tools. To exit the UI Builder section of Quattro Pro, simply activate the notebook window. You can do this by clicking on the window if it appears behind the dialog box or SpeedBar window you are currently using—or you can minimize the dialog box or SpeedBar window to gain access to the notebook window. The notebook window may appear as a minimized icon within the workspace. As soon as you activate the notebook window, all normal commands and options return to the screen. You can return to the UI Builder by activating the dialog box or SpeedBar windows again.

If you are finished with your custom SpeedBar, be sure to save it to disk before leaving the UI Builder.

Adding Controls

Controls are the primary element in dialog boxes and SpeedBars. When you create a new dialog box or SpeedBar, Quattro Pro displays the UI Builder SpeedBar at the top of the screen. Using the tools in this SpeedBar, you can add numerous controls to your custom dialog box or SpeedBar. Figure 16.4 shows the UI Builder SpeedBar.

Figure 16.4 The UI Builder SpeedBar.

The following sections describe most of the tools in this SpeedBar (some of the tools are too advanced for this book). With this information, you'll know how to add controls, set the controls' properties, and move and resize controls. Each control has specific properties that you can access by right-clicking on the control after you add it to the dialog box. A summary of each control's important properties follows each description.

Some controls are not effective in SpeedBars

N O T E

Not all UI Builder controls are useful in your custom SpeedBars because of the SpeedBar's limitation in size and shape. For example, large list boxes will not be useful in your SpeedBars. If you attempt to use (dock) a SpeedBar that is too big, Quattro Pro will give you the message "SpeedBar height cannot exceed 56 pixels." You can control the height of a SpeedBar by right-clicking on the SpeedBar window in the UI Builder and choosing the Dimension properties.

Creating Buttons

You can add five different types of buttons to your custom dialog boxes and SpeedBars: push buttons, radio buttons, check-boxes, OK buttons, and Cancel buttons:

To add a button, click on the desired tool; then click once in the dialog box. Quattro Pro will add the button control to the dialog box. To create a **Cancel** button, create an **OK** button; then right-click the button and choose **Button Type>Cancel Exit Button**.

Radio buttons are always used in groups, because they present either/or options. Only one radio button in a group can be selected at a time. To create a group of radio buttons, refer to "Combining Controls into Groups" later in this chapter. Check-boxes are also often used in groups; since they present and/or options, however, they can be used individually as well.

Note that the **OK** and **Cancel** buttons that are automatically displayed in a new dialog box always exit the dialog box when pressed. The **OK** button accepts the changes made in the dialog box, and the **Cancel** button aborts the dialog box changes. Additional **OK** buttons can be turned into *picture buttons* (buttons that display various pictures). These buttons do not automatically exit the dialog box when pressed. To select a picture for the new **OK** button, right-click the button and choose **Bitmap**; then choose from the bitmaps provided for your buttons. As you click on the bitmaps in the list, a sample is provided in the Preview box (see Figure 16.5).

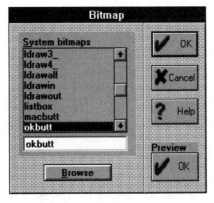

Figure 16.5 Selecting a bitmap for your extra OK buttons.

These are the button bitmaps (pictures) that Quattro Pro provides for you. They come from existing images in Quattro Pro. In this list, you can find an image to match any button or tool in Quattro Pro—including all tools in the primary and secondary SpeedBars and all tools within Quattro Pro's dialog boxes. Note that using one of these images for your button does not make the button perform any particular action—these are merely pictures that you can attach to your custom button. The action performed by the button is established through the macro you attach to it. Refer to "Attaching Macros to Controls" later in this chapter for more details.

Buttons are your primary controls in SpeedBars

N O T E

SpeedBars consist primarily of button controls; besides the built-in controls you can add using the SpeedBar Designer, you can use OK buttons that display special pictures. These button can perform any action you determine with a macro. Since you cannot exit a SpeedBar with an OK or Cancel button, as you would exit a dialog box, all OK and Cancel buttons you add to a custom SpeedBar are simply picture buttons. Select from the numerous pictures available for these buttons. For information about setting actions to these buttons, see "Attaching Macros to Controls" later in this chapter.

Some controls are missing from the SpeedBar Designer

N O T E

The SpeedBar Designer you used in Chapter 4 contains built-in controls (tools) for many functions within Quattro Pro. These built-in tools are available in the Buttons list inside the SpeedBar Designer screen. These buttons not only provide appropriate pictures, they also automatically perform related actions. However, you might have noticed that some procedures are not represented in the SpeedBar Designer's built-in tools.

You can build custom SpeedBar buttons to accomplish these procedures. Just add a new picture button (**OK** button) to your SpeedBar in the UI Builder; then attach an appropriate bitmap to the button as described above. Finally, create a macro that performs the desired action and attach it to the macro.

After you have added a button to your dialog box or SpeedBar, right-click the button to set its properties. Here is a summary of the key properties for button controls.

- **Bitmap** Lets you select a bitmap image to use as the button's face. This is available for buttons added with the **OK Button** tool only.

- **Label Text** Sets the text used for the button.
- **Default Button** Makes the selected button the default button in the dialog box. When the user presses **Enter**, this button will be selected. Only one button can be the default in a dialog box, and it's usually the **OK** button.
- **Help Line** Determines what text will be displayed at the bottom of the screen when the mouse pointer moves over the button face.

Adding Descriptive Text

You can add text to your custom dialog box or SpeedBar by using the **Text** tool. Just click on the tool and then click once in the dialog box. Right-click the tool and choose the **Label Text** property to set the entire text line. You can make your label text run a macro or perform specific actions when clicked, but label text is usually used for descriptions only. Here are the key properties available for label text.

- **Label Text** Sets the text used in the label.
- **Label Font** Sets the font of the label text.
- **Help Line** Determines what text will be displayed at the bottom of the screen when the mouse pointer moves over the tool.

Creating Edit Fields

Edit fields are boxes into which you can type information. The can be single-line boxes or larger boxes for multiple lines:

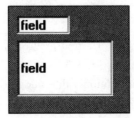

To create an edit field, click on the **Edit Field** tool, then drag onto the dialog box to create the box. Here are the important properties used with edit fields.

- **Field Type** Sets the type of information that can be entered into the Edit field. Types include **Integer** (a numeric integer), **String** (any text or numbers), **Real** (any real number), **Block** (a cell or block reference), and **Hidden** (any text). The Hidden type does not display its data in the field and is useful for requesting secret codes.

- **Minimum** Sets the minimum value allowed in an Integer field. This property appears only when you've selected the **Integer** field type.

- **Maximum** Sets the maximum value allowed in an Integer field. This property appears only when you've selected the **Integer** field type.

- **Default** Sets the default value allowed in an Integer field. This property appears only when you've selected the **Integer** field type.

- **Allow Point Mode** Lets you enter a cell or block reference into the field by pointing to the notebook.

- **Terminate Dialog** Deactivates the **Default** button, so pressing **Enter** inside the Edit field does not invoke the **Default** button. This is useful for Edit fields that require multiple lines of text.

- **Help Line** Determines what text will be displayed at the bottom of the screen when the mouse pointer moves over the tool.

Creating a Spin Control

A *spin control* (also called a *number wheel*) displays numbers between a certain value range. Add a spin control by clicking on the **Spin** tool and then once in the dialog box.

The following properties help determine the attributes of the spin control.

- **Minimum** Sets the minimum value allowed in the control.
- **Maximum** Sets the maximum value allowed in the control.
- **Default** Sets the starting value for the control. (You can also link the starting value to the value in a cell—see "Connecting Controls to Cells" later in this chapter.)

- **Help Line** Determines what text will be displayed at the bottom of the screen when the mouse pointer moves over the tool.

Drawing Rectangles in the Dialog Box

You can draw boxes inside your dialog box or SpeedBar using the **Rectangle** tool. Just click on the tool and drag in the dialog box. This is similar to drawing rectangles in a graph window as described in Chapter 12.

Combining Controls into Groups

Controls can be grouped together to make them easier to understand and use. Radio buttons should always be used in groups. To form a group, click on the **Group** tool and then drag in the dialog box. While the Group box is selected, click on any tool to add controls inside the group. Be sure to draw the control inside the selected Group box. Test whether the control is actually part of the group by moving the Group box; the control should move with the box. Figure 16.6 shows a typical group of controls.

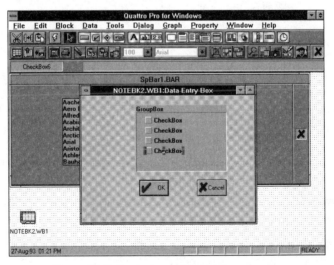

Figure 16.6 Controls combined into a group.

Use the Group Text property for the Group box to change the title of the group.

Creating List Boxes

A list box displays a list of items from which you can choose. The chosen item is then entered into a cell in the notebook. Use list boxes to present a finite set of items from which to choose—such as the names of states, product code numbers, and employee names.

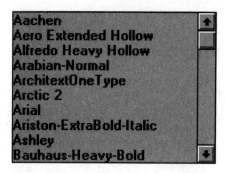

To create a list box, click on the **List Box** tool; then drag in the dialog box. The following properties are important to your list box.

- **List** Determines what list will be displayed in the list box. Type your list of items into a block in the notebook; then enter the block reference after selecting this property (see Figure 16.7). Alternatively, you can simply copy the block of items from the notebook; then return to the custom dialog box, select the list box, and choose the **Paste** button. The list you copied will be entered into the list box. For more advanced dialog boxes, you can choose from the existing lists provided, including a Fonts list, Drive list, and Bitmapped Graphics list. (Using these built-in lists is beyond the scope of this book.)

- **Ordered** Determines whether the list is displayed in alphabetical order.

- **Number of Columns** Sets the number of columns for the list.

- **Selection Text** Lets you change any item in the list. Just click on the item; then choose this property.

- **Help Line** Sets the line of text that is displayed at the bottom of the screen when you move the mouse pointer over the list box.

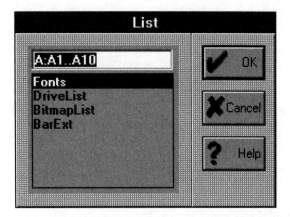

Figure 16.7 Enter the block containing the list.

To determine where the selected item is inserted into the notebook, refer to "Connecting Controls to Cells" later in this chapter.

Creating Combo Boxes

Combo boxes are like list boxes, but they allow you to add items to the list. You can then store these items for the next use. Combo boxes contain their lists in a *drop-down* fashion. This means you must click on the **Right Arrow** button beside the list box to display the items. Click on any item to select it, or enter a new item into the list box.

Here are the important properties used with combo boxes.

- **List** Determines what list will be displayed in the list box. Type your list of items into a block in the notebook; then enter the block reference after selecting this property. Alternatively, you can simply copy the block of items from the notebook; then return to the custom dialog box, select the list box, and choose the **Paste** button. The list you copied will be entered into the combo box.

- **Allow Point Mode** Lets you enter a cell or block reference into the combo box by pointing to the notebook. You must first click the mouse pointer in the combo box to position the cursor.

- **Add Down Button** Adds or removes the **Down Arrow** button beside the combo box.

- **History List** Stores entered list items and displays them the next time you use the dialog box. Set this option to **Yes** to activate this feature or **No** to deactivate it.
- **List Length** Sets the number of items in the list.
- **Ordered** Determines whether the list is displayed in alphabetical order.
- **Help Line** Sets the line of text that appears at the bottom of the screen when you move the mouse pointer over the list box.

Creating Pick Lists

Pick lists are similar to combo boxes, but they do not let you add items to the list. When you click on a pick list, the list appears. A pick list is like a standard list box, but in a drop-down style control. Refer to the two previous controls for details on using pick lists.

Creating Scroll Bars

Scroll bars are useful in dialog boxes as numeric *sliders*. A slider lets you select a value by sliding the box along the scroll bar. The top of a vertical scroll bar represents the highest value; the bottom represents the lowest. (Scroll bars can also be horizontal.)

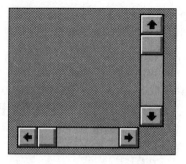

The most important property for scroll bars is Parameters, which sets five different parameters for the scroll bar.

- **Min** The minimum value of the scroll bar.
- **Max** The maximum value of the scroll bar.

- **Line** The unit of movement when you click on a scroll arrow.
- **Page** The unit of movement when you click in the scroll bar.
- **Time** The amount of time Quattro Pro waits before moving the scroll box in response to your clicks.

Using the Time Tool

The **Time** tool is useful for displaying the current date and time in your dialog boxes or SpeedBars. It can also be used to set an alarm. Use the following properties with your Time control.

- **Show Time** Displays or hides the time within the timer.
- **Current Time** Lets you set the current time.
- **Timer On** Determines whether the timer is active or inactive.
- **Alarm Time** Sets the time of the alarm.
- **Alarm On** Determines whether the alarm is on or off.

Cutting, Copying, and Pasting Controls

You can use these three tools (which also appear on the standard SpeedBar) to remove, copy, or move controls. After you create a control, just click on the control to select it (see "Selecting, Moving, and Sizing Controls," below), then use the **Cut** tool to remove the control and place it onto the clipboard, or use the **Copy** tools to copy the control onto the Clipboard. After the control is on the Clipboard, the **Paste** tool will place it back into the custom dialog box. You can also remove controls by selecting them and pressing the **Delete** key.

Testing the Dialog Box

When you have finished adding controls and determining their actions with macros and links, you can test the dialog box by selecting the **Test** tool. In Test mode, the dialog box and controls are active. Each control will perform its designated task. Test mode is useful for finding errors in your controls and macros, but you can also use it to run dialog boxes at any time.

If you are testing a dialog box, press the **OK** or **Cancel** button to return to the UI Builder. If you are testing a custom SpeedBar, press the **Escape** key while the SpeedBar is active to return to the UI Builder.

Selecting, Moving, and Resizing Controls

When you want to select, move, or resize a control, you should click on this tool first. After clicking on this tool, the mouse pointer becomes an arrow. You can click the arrow on any tool to select it, or hold the **Shift** key down and click on several tools. Drag any selected control or group of controls to move them around the dialog box. Dragging on the size boxes around a selected control changes the size and shape of that control. These activities are similar to using the drawing tools described in Chapter 12.

Connecting Controls to Cells

After you create your controls, you're ready to connect them to cells in your notebook. Connecting a control to a cell means that the value or data selected with the control will automatically be displayed in the cell when you click on the **OK** button in the dialog box. In this way, a dialog box can become a data entry form for your notebook pages. Plus, you can set specific values from which to choose, using the minimum and maximum values for certain controls. List boxes let you select from specific items.

To connect a control to a particular cell, select the control, choose **Dialog>Connect**, and then enter the desired cell into the dialog box that is displayed (see Figure 16.8).

Connection
<u>S</u>ource [SpBar1.BAR]
<u>T</u>arget [ ]
✔ <u>D</u>ynamic Connection
✔ OK   ✗ Cancel   ? Help

Figure 16.8 Connecting a control to a cell.

Check the Dynamic Connection box to make the cell and the control influence each other. When the dialog box is opened, the cell's value will be displayed in the control. When the dialog box is closed with the **OK** button, the control's value is placed back into the cell. A dynamic connection overrides any defaults you have established for a control.

Suppose you connect cell A1 to a scroll bar. When you move the scroll bar, the value in cell A1 changes to reflect your setting. If you choose an item from a list box, that information will be displayed in the connected cell. Connect all your controls to cells in the notebook.

When it comes to using your buttons, you'll want to attach macros to make them perform specific actions. Attaching macros to buttons is the subject of the next section.

Attaching Macros to Controls

Your customized SpeedBars will probably contain buttons. To make these buttons perform actions, you can attach macros to them. Here are the steps for attaching a macro to a button control.

1. Select the button control.

2. Choose **Dialog>Links**.

3. Click on **Add**. The dialog box will look like Figure 16.9.

4. Click on **RECEIVE** and hold the mouse button down. Now move to the **DOMACRO** option and release the button. The dialog box should look like Figure 16.10.

5. Type the macro commands you want to perform into the space provided. You can use the {BRANCH} macro command to branch to a macro in your notebook, or just enter all the macro commands in the space provided.

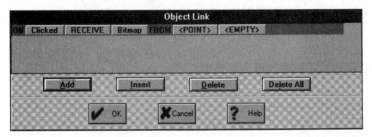

Figure 16.9 Adding a new link to the button control.

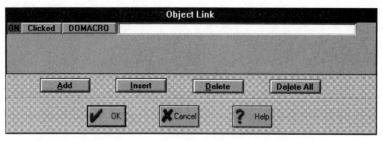

Figure 16.10 Performing a DOMACRO function.

For SpeedBar buttons, you will want to enter command equivalent macro commands into the DOMACRO space. When you click on the button, the macro will perform the command you specify. Many buttons are designed with specific macro commands in mind. Here is a suggested list.

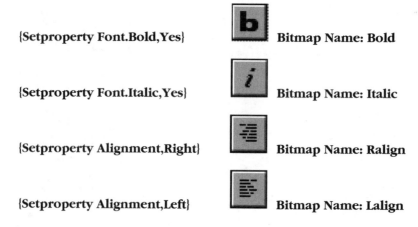

{Setproperty Font.Bold,Yes}   Bitmap Name: Bold

{Setproperty Font.Italic,Yes}   Bitmap Name: Italic

{Setproperty Alignment,Right}   Bitmap Name: Ralign

{Setproperty Alignment,Left}   Bitmap Name: Lalign

Record Your Keystrokes to Find Macro Commands

You can record any command or keystroke to determine the macro equivalent. Refer to Chapter 15 for more information on this technique.

Invoking Dialog Boxes

You can invoke your dialog box by using the DODIALOG macro command in a macro. You can enter this command as part of a custom menu or attach it to a notebook button. You can also make the macro an autoexec macro so that it opens the dialog box as soon as the notebook is opened. Where you use the DODIALOG macro command determines how and when the dialog box is made available.

The DODIALOG command uses the following syntax:

```
{DODIALOG DialogName,OKExit?,Arguments,MacUse?}
```

The *DialogName* argument is the name of the dialog box you created. This is determined by the dialog box property *Dialog Name*, as described earlier in this chapter. Enter a cell address as the *OKExit?* argument. This cell will contain a value of 1 or 0 to show how the dialog box was exited. A value of 1 indicates that the **OK** button was pushed; 0 means the **Cancel** button was pushed. You can test for a 1 in this cell to continue with the dialog box procedures.

The *Arguments* argument determines the defaults values for the dialog box. If your dialog box controls are dynamically connected to cells in the notebook, omit this argument. Otherwise, enter a block of cells containing values for your dialog box controls. Enter the values in the order in which you created the controls.

The *MacUse?* argument determines whether the dialog box is controlled by the user or by a macro. Keep this value set to 1 unless you have a reason for changing it.

Summary

This chapter took you a short way into the world of custom applications. Quattro Pro has many powerful tools for building custom applications. You can create applications that don't even resemble a spreadsheet. Use the UI Builder to create your own dialog boxes and SpeedBars containing custom-designed controls. Generally you will add buttons to SpeedBars and attach simple macros to those buttons. The attached macros will duplicate menu commands and options.

Dialog box controls can be connected to notebook cells. This way, the controls can actually set the values in those cells. Several different controls are available for your needs.

You now have a thorough understanding of Quattro Pro for Windows and its most important features. Spend some time experimenting with these commands and options, then check out Appendix B for a summary of advanced options available in Quattro Pro.

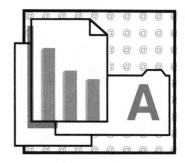

SpeedBar Tools and Menu Commands

This appendix contains a summary of the tools in Quattro Pro's various SpeedBars and in the tool sets inside the SpeedBar Designer. You will also find a summary of Quattro Pro's menu structure.

SpeedBar Tools

Quattro Pro for Windows has several built-in SpeedBars, as well as many tools available for your own custom SpeedBars. The following is a summary of these SpeedBars and tools.

Standard SpeedBar

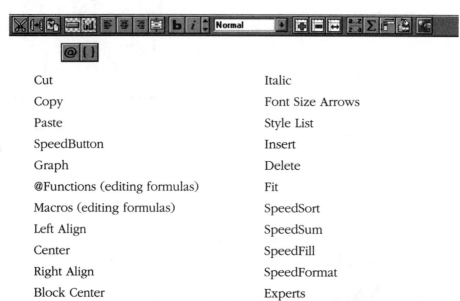

Cut	Italic
Copy	Font Size Arrows
Paste	Style List
SpeedButton	Insert
Graph	Delete
@Functions (editing formulas)	Fit
Macros (editing formulas)	SpeedSort
Left Align	SpeedSum
Center	SpeedFill
Right Align	SpeedFormat
Block Center	Experts
Bold	

Productivity Tools SpeedBar

New Notebook	Font List
Open Notebook	Data Modeling Desktop
Save Notebook	Database Desktop
Print Preview	Workgroup Desktop
Print	Spell Check
Undo	Consolidator
Paste Values	Scenario Manager
Paste Properties	SpeedBar Designer
Auto Generate Names	Interactive Tutors
Zoom List	

Spell Check SpeedBar

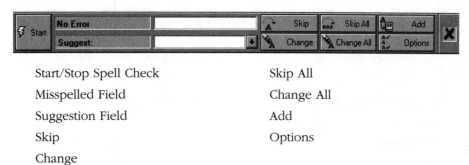

Start/Stop Spell Check

Misspelled Field

Suggestion Field

Skip

Change

Skip All

Change All

Add

Options

Scenario Manager SpeedBar

Capture Scenario

Delete Scenario

Scenario Names List

Find Scenario Cells

Add Scenario Cells

Remove Scenario Cells

Toggle Highlights

Report Button

Group Button

Group Names List

Scenario Manager Expert

Consolidator SpeedBar

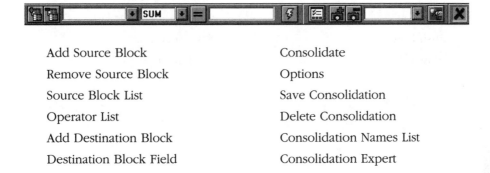

Add Source Block

Remove Source Block

Source Block List

Operator List

Add Destination Block

Destination Block Field

Consolidate

Options

Save Consolidation

Delete Consolidation

Consolidation Names List

Consolidation Expert

Analysis Tools SpeedBar

Amortization Schedule	Correlation
Mortgage Refinancing	Covariance
Exponential Smoothing	Descriptive Statistics
Fourier	F-Test
Histogram	Rank and Percentile
Moving Average	Advanced Regression
Random Number	Sampling
Anova: One Way	t-Test
Anova: Two Way with Replication	z-Test
Anova: Three Way without Replication	Experts

SpeedBar Designer SpeedBar

Cut	Label
Copy	Button Palette List
Paste	New SpeedBar
Test	Remove SpeedBar
Selection	Custom SpeedBar List
Push Button	Save SpeedBar
Bitmap Button	UI Builder

UI Builder SpeedBar

Cut	Spin Control
Copy	Rectangle
Paste	Group Box
Test	List Box
Selection	Combo Box
Push Button	Pick List
Bitmap Button	File Control
Radio Button	Color Control
Ok/Cancel Button	Vertical Scroll Bar
Label	Horizontal Scroll Bar
Edit Field	Time Control

Menu Structure

File

New	Start a new notebook
Open	Open an existing notebook
Close	Close the active notebook
Save	Save the active notebook
Save As	Save the active notebook under a new name
Retrieve	Open an existing file
Save All	Save all open notebooks
Close All	Close all open notebooks
Print Preview	Preview the printout on screen
Page Setup	Set the page options for printing
Print	Begin printing
Printer Setup	Set up the printer options

Named Settings	Select and store the print settings
Workspace	
Save	Save the workspace
Restore	Open existing workspaces
Exit	Exit Quattro Pro

Edit

Undo	Reverse the last action
Cut	Erase the selection
Copy	Copy a selection
Paste	Paste data from the clipboard
Clear	Clear a selection
Clear Contents	Clear a selection and leave the formatting
Paste Link	Paste from the Clipboard with links
Paste Special	Paste with options
Paste Format	Paste the format only
Select All	Select all elements
Goto	Jump to a specified location
Search and Replace	Change instances of data
Define Style	Select or change a format style
Insert Object	Insert a linked object

Block

Move	Change the location of a data block
Copy	Copy a data block
Insert	
Row	Insert selected rows
Columns	Insert selected columns
Pages	Insert pages
File	Insert a file
Delete	

	Rows	Delete selected rows
	Columns	Delete selected columns
	Pages	Delete pages
Fill		Fill a block of cells
Names		
	Create	Establish block names
	Delete	Remove block names
	Labels	Use labels for block names automatically
	Reset	Revert names to normal
	Make Table	Insert a block name table
Transpose		Transpose a block of data
Values		Convert formulas to values
Reformat		Reformat a block
Move Pages		Change order of pages
Insert Break		Insert a page break
Object Order		Change order of notebook objects

Data

Sort	Arrange the data in alphabetical order
Restrict Input	Establish the data entry form
Form	Automatic data entry form
Query	Find the data in a database
Table Query	Create a data table
Parse	Dissect the data
What If	Establish the scenarios for data entry
Frequency	Create the frequency distribution
Database Desktop	Create the SQL links to database applications
Data Modeling Desktop	Transfer data to the Data Modeling Desktop
Workgroup Desktop	Share, publish, and subscribe

Tools

Macro

	Execute	Run a macro
	Record	Record a macro
	Options	Set the macro options for recording
	Debugger	Find errors in a macro
Spell Check		Activate the spelling checker
Scenario Manager		Activate the Scenario manager
Consolidator		Activate the Consolidator
Define Group		Establish a page group
Combine		Merge pages
Extract		Pull data from a database
Import		Import a graphic object or data
Update Links		Correct or change link references
	Open Links	Open linked documents
	Refresh Links	Start new links
	Delete Links	Remove the link references
	Change Links	Change the link references
Analysis Tools		Advanced numerical, financial, and statistical tools
Optimizer		Find optimum values
Solve For		Solve an equation in reverse
Advanced Math		
	Regression	Perform a regression analysis
	Invert	Invert a data block
	Multiply	Multiply data blocks
SpeedBar Designer		Activate the SpeedBar Designer
UI Builder		Activate the User Interface Builder

Graph

Type	Set the graph type
Series	Set the data series values
Titles	Enter or change graph titles
New	Start a new graph
Edit	Edit the existing graph
Insert	Insert a graph onto a page
Delete	Delete a graph
Copy	Copy a graph
View	View a graph full-screen
Slide Show	Create a slide show from graphs

Property

Current Object	View properties for a selected object
Application	View properties for Quattro Pro
Active Notebook	View properties for the active notebook
Active Page	View properties for the active page

Window

New View	Establish a window view by name
Tile	Arrange window in the tiled fashion
Cascade	Arrange windows in a cascaded fashion
Arrange Icons	Organize icons in the program workspace
Hide	Hide a notebook window
Show	Show a hidden notebook window
Panes	Split the window into panes
Locked Titles	Lock title in place in the notebook

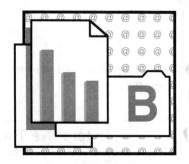

Additional Topics

This book provides a start to learning about Quattro Pro for Windows. As a beginning book, it cannot possibly cover all the advanced options of the program and remain easy to understand for first-time users. Following is a brief overview of some features beyond the scope of this book—or that were otherwise not appropriate for detailed discussion in this book. For more information about these features, look for a more advanced book about Quattro Pro for Windows from your local bookstore.

Interactive Tutors

Quattro Pro comes with a built-in training system that gives you a basic understanding of the spreadsheet. Using the Interactive Tutors, you can learn about simple procedures, such as entering data, changing columns widths, and moving around in the notebook. To activate the Interactive Tutors, click on the **Interactive Tutor** tool in the Second SpeedBar:

Clicking on this tool brings up the Interactive Tutor Catalog as shown in Figure B.1.

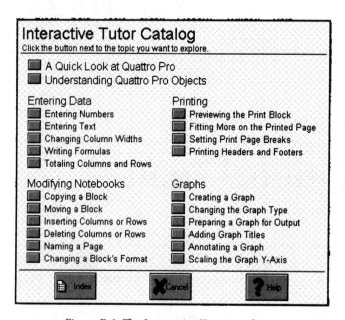

Figure B.1 The Interactive Tutor catalog.

Click on any of the buttons to complete the lesson of that title. You can click on the Index button to search for a topic, if you cannot find what you want in the titles. Each tutorial lesson gives you the chance to perform the indicated action right on the worksheet using your own data—or using a sample worksheet and data. If you use your own data, you can actually get your work done as you learn how to use Quattro Pro for Windows.

When you complete a tutorial lesson, the Catalog screen places a check mark into the box (or button) beside the lesson's title. You can then see which lessons you still need to complete.

Analysis Tools and Advanced Math

Quattro Pro's analysis tools are accessible from the **Tools>Analysis Tools** menu command. This command brings up a SpeedBar full of advanced math operations for special purposes. Each button on the SpeedBar presents a dialog box that asks for inputs for the function being performed. Values are then returned to the active cell or a specified cell. Analysis tools are provided for specialized financial, analytical, and statistical purposes. You may also find some advanced analysis capabilities in Quattro Pro's specialized @functions.

Other advanced math tools appear in the **Tools>Advanced Math** command. Within this command, you can perform regression analysis and matrix operations, such as transposing two matrices. You can use regression analysis to add simple trend lines to your XY graphs as described in Chapter 11.

Solve For and Optimize

Quattro Pro's **Solve For** command lets you solve an equation backward. You provide the desired goal for the equation and the value of a variable and Quattro Pro finds the correct value for a second variable to match your goal. A more powerful version of Solve For is accomplished with the **Optimize** command.

The **Optimize** command lets you establish a business model for calculating optimum values. Using Optimize, you can determine the best amounts of materials to purchase based on their individual costs and markup amounts. Optimization can tell you how to achieve a particular sales revenue based on your model of costs and expenses. Use **Optimize** for purchasing, shipping, sales goals, budgeting, and other business models.

When you select the **Tools>Optimizer** command, you can specify the cell containing the goal you want to reach. For instance, if you want to know how to purchase inventory to achieve one million dollars in net sales, you can establish a target value of 1,000,000. Quattro Pro also lets you find maximum and minimum values from your models. For example, you can determine the maximum profit from a particular inventory/purchasing model.

Constraints let you find target values under specific conditions. For instance, you can determine what inventory to purchase to best reach one million dollars in net sales, but with the constraint that you must purchase at least $2,000 of each item.

Database Desktop

Borland's family of database products is legendary. Using Quattro Pro's Database Desktop features, you can easily link Quattro Pro to your Paradox, dBASE, or other database server through SQL links and Dynamic Data Exchange (DDE). Database Desktop features let you use Quattro Pro as a front and back end to your database data. Through the Database Desktop, you can even link to mainframe computers through your networked PCs. If you have large database applications that you want to downsize or use in spreadsheet analysis, look into the Database Desktop features of Quattro Pro.

Workgroup Desktop

Quattro Pro's Workgroup Desktop lets you share your individual notebooks and notebook pages with other users on a network. You can share data as a client or server—provided your network is properly installed for such transactions—and transfer your Quattro Pro data across the network so that you and your coworkers have access to the same data at the same time. The Workgroup Desktop requires that you have a network fully running and installed.

Index